1 GROUP BOMBER COMMAND

An Operational Record

1 GROUP BOMBER COMMAND

An Operational Record

Chris Ward
with
Greg Harrison and Grzegorz Korcz

Pen & Sword
AVIATION

First published in Great Britain in 2014 by
Pen & Sword Aviation
an imprint of
Pen & Sword Books Ltd
47 Church Street
Barnsley
South Yorkshire

S70 2AS

Copyright © Chris Ward, 2014

ISBN 978 1 47382 108 8

The right of Chris Ward to be identified as Author of this Work has been asserted by him in accordance with the Copyright, Designs and Patents Act 1988.

A CIP catalogue record for this book is available from the British Library.

Printed and bound by CPI Group (UK) Ltd, Croydon, CR0 4YY

Pen & Sword Books Ltd incorporates the Imprints of Pen & Sword Aviation, Pen & Sword Maritime, Pen & Sword Military, Wharncliffe Local History, Pen and Sword Select, Pen and Sword Military Classics and Leo Cooper.
For a complete list of Pen & Sword titles please contact:
PEN & SWORD BOOKS LIMITED
47 Church Street, Barnsley, South Yorkshire, S70 2AS, England
E-mail: enquiries@pen-and-sword.co.uk
Website: www.pen-and-sword.co.uk

Foreword and Acknowledgements

As always in my books I have attempted to provide as much detail as possible in the narrative section. There is enough information to produce a full book on each individual squadron, so there is clearly insufficient space in a group setting to make mention of every detail and every loss. Therefore, as in the other books in the series, I have featured particular squadrons as representative of the fortunes of all within the group operating the same aircraft type at the same time.

I would like to register my gratitude to those who have contributed information and or photographs for this book, first and foremost among them the usual suspects, Andreas Wachtel and Steve Smith. I am also indebted to new collaborators, Grzegorz (Greg) Korcz and Greg Harrison. Greg K is a customs officer in Gdansk, in Poland, and is a leading authority on the Polish bomber squadrons. I look forward to further collaborations with him as we work together on the histories of the four Polish bomber units for Pen & Sword. Greg H is a 1 Group researcher of long standing, and the "go-to" expert on 100 Squadron and the Special Duties Flight.

I also wish to extend my thanks for the help received from Dave Briggs and Martin Nichols of the Fiskerton Airfield Association, Peter Coulter and his colleagues at the 550 Squadron Association, Anne Laws at Wickenby and David Fell, who is always a mine of information on 103 Squadron and Elsham Wolds.

Finally, it is always sad to hear of the passing of one of the unsung heroes who keep the associations going, or look after squadron archives to ensure that we remember the gallant generation of men and women who brought us through the Second World War. Roger Audis of Bardney, a veritable encyclopaedia on 9 Squadron, recently passed away suddenly and unexpectedly. I will miss our telephone conversations, and I offer my condolences to his family.

Chris Ward. Lutterworth. September 2013.

Contents

VIII   *1 GROUP BOMBER COMMAND*

CHAPTER ONE

In the Beginning

1 Group was born at Abingdon in Oxfordshire on the 1st of May 1936, and replaced the Central Area of the Air Defence of Great Britain. Initially it inherited three stations and ten squadrons, four of the latter, XV, 40, 98 and 104 based at Abingdon, while 18, 21, 34 and 39 Squadrons resided at Bircham Newton and 57 and 218 at Upper Heyford. At the time of its formation 1 Group was equipped with the Hawker Hind, but with expansion to eight stations and seventeen squadrons by late 1938 came Bristol Blenheims and Fairey Battles. As the world headed inexorably towards war in 1939 the Group was reduced to five stations, Abingdon, Harwell, Benson, Bicester and Boscombe Down, each of which housed two of the Group's reduced cadre of ten squadrons equipped exclusively now with their cumbersome Fairey Battles. On the 24th of August, and in accordance with a pre-arranged plan, the group was mobilized in preparation for its departure to France as an advanced air striking force. The move to airfields in the Reims region of France took place on the 2nd of September, at which time Headquarters 1 Group became Headquarters Advanced Air Striking Force.

A new 1 Group was formed on the 12th of September with its headquarters at Benson. The intention was that it would assume command of the Fairey Battle element, now designated 71,72,74,75 and 76 Wings, once the second echelon of formerly 2 Group squadrons had arrived in France to join it. Headquarters Advanced Air Striking Force would then be placed in overall command. At the end of September, however, it was decided to postpone the dispatch of the second echelon, of which Headquarters 1 Group was a part, and the group was subsequently disbanded on the 22nd of December. Strictly speaking, the activities of the former 1 Group squadrons during the Battle for France fall outside of the scope of this work, but the intense experiences of the surviving aircrew prepared them uniquely for what lay ahead, and provided the new 1 Group with a steely core of battle-hardened recruits. For this reason we will look briefly at the experiences of the units destined to be founder members of the newly constituted 1 Group. The experiences of 12 Squadron will stand as representative of all of the Fairey Battle squadrons for the eight-month period dubbed by the Americans as the "Phoney War, and the few weeks of insanity that preceded the fall of France and the withdrawal of the shattered remnant to the UK.

Sixteen 12 Squadron aircraft departed Bicester on the 2nd September under the command of S/L Lywood, and took up residence at Berry-au-Bac. Having settled in the squadron mounted its first sorties on the 17th, when F/L Gillman led a three aircraft formation on an afternoon reconnaissance of the frontier and returned without incident. Gillman was one of a number of officers who would survive their time in France, and then enjoy distinguished careers in Bomber Command. Sadly, he would lose his life on operations in May 1943 while in command of the Pathfinder's 83 Squadron. W/C Thackray succeeded S/L Lywood as commanding officer on the 28th, and the latter would take command of XV Squadron in December. Thackray had previously commanded 35 Squadron for two years to September 1938. For the remainder of the year activity was restricted to training, army cooperation exercises and occasional leafleting operations. A move was made to Amifontaine on the 8th of December in the midst of what was becoming one of the harshest winters in living memory.

1940

The winter actually seemed to deepen as the new year progressed, and flying was a rare treat as the conditions froze the aircraft to the ground. The first operations for 12 Squadron only took place on the 24th of March, when F/L Simpson and F/O Clancy carried out leafleting and reconnaissance over Germany, and noted some flak activity. A number of night operations followed, but it was not until the German advance on the Low Countries on the 10th of May that the gloves came off and the war began in earnest. Proceedings opened with the Luftwaffe bombing many of the AASF airfields at first light, although Amifontaine was subjected to a strafing rather than bombing attack. It was late afternoon before 12 Squadron's first four sorties were launched, and not one of the Battles survived to fight another day. F/L Simpson was sent to attack troop columns advancing through Luxembourg, and L4949 was shot down by murderous ground fire in the target area. Although the crew survived, F/L Simpson sustained severe burns that would keep him in a French hospital for an extended period. P/O Matthews and crew also came down in the target area in L5190 and were captured, and P/O Hulse dragged his badly damaged L5249 back to base, where it was ultimately abandoned. F/L Hunt force-landed P2243 before making it back to base on foot with his crew.

Two days later, on Whit Sunday, six volunteer crews were briefed for an attack on the Vroenhoven and Feldwezelt bridges over the Albert Canal at Maastricht. The three aircraft assigned to each target were attempting to slow the flow of German mechanized units now streaming across. Typical of the indecisiveness of the period, it was only after the Germans had established themselves around the bridges and set up formidable defences that the operation was given the go-ahead. In the event only five aircraft took off from Amifontaine, F/O Thomas in P2332 leading P/O Davey in L5241 to the target at Vroenhoven for a medium level attack. The former was brought down by a combination of ground fire and fighters, and the crew was captured. Davey suffered a similar fate before ordering his crew to abandon ship and crash-landing. One of his crew sustained an injured foot and was taken prisoner, but Davey and the other man made it back to the squadron. The attack on the Feldwezelt bridge was led by F/O Garland, who favoured a low-level approach, but the outcome was the same, and P2204 crashed near the target killing all on board. Garland and his observer, Sgt Gray, were each awarded a posthumous Victoria Cross, but the third member of the crew, LAC Reynolds, was, for some reason, not deemed worthy of a decoration. Sgt Marland and his crew also lost their lives when L5227 crashed close the their objective, while P/O Mcintosh and his crew were captured after force-landing L5439 in Belgium.

On the 14th the targets were pontoon bridges at Sedan, over which the Germans were pouring more armour and troops. Between 15.00 and 16.00 everything available was thrown into the fray, 12 Squadron providing five Battles to attack troop columns on the road leading from the town. L4950 went down killing F/O Vaughan and his observer, and F/L Clancey alone of his crew survived the loss of L4952 south-east of the target. The crew of Sgt Winkler in L5188 fell into enemy hands, as did the gunner in P5229, but his pilot, Sgt Johnson and the observer were killed. This was the AASF's darkest hour, and the moment that it was effectively knocked out of the war. Of the seventy-one Battles committed to the fray on this day, forty-four were lost. Despite that, most of the Battle squadrons would have to endure a further month of attrition before the hopelessness of their situation forced a withdrawal.

Orders were received on the 15th for 12 Squadron to begin pulling back to Echemines, and this was carried out over the next two days. However, six aircraft were flown to 226 Squadron's new base at Faux Villecerf that night to carry out an attack on enemy columns on the north bank of the Meuse. Six further 12 Squadron Battles were airborne from Echemines on the morning of the 19th to attack targets in the Hannogne area led by S/L Lowe. Set upon by a pack of BF109s two Battles, L5538 and N2178 were shot down. P/O McElligott in the former sustained wounds to which he later succumbed, and his gunner was also wounded, but he and the observer regained the squadron. In the latter, the observer was killed during the engagement, while F/O Barr and his gunner also picked up wounds from which they recovered in hospital. The above-mentioned S/L Lowe would survive his time in France and go on to command 103 Squadron in 1941 as we shall see. Five 12 Squadron Battles took part in a night operation on the 20th, and four more bombed roads and tanks in the late afternoon of the 23rd, as a result of which F/L Drinkwater had to force-land. As attention shifted to the Dunkerque area, two 12 Squadron aircraft bombed tanks on the Hesdin road on the 25th, and on the 26th, when the evacuation began, carried out a night operation, again without loss. Night operations were also conducted on the 28th, when airfields and a railway were the objectives, and then atrocious weather conditions thwarted attempts to destroy parked aircraft on an airfield at Laon on the 31st.

The crew of P/O Mcintyre was lost in P2269 on the 3rd of June, and on the 7th P2162 was shot down in flames while attacking Panzers around Poix. On the 8th a further withdrawal was made to Souge, the day on which L5546 was lost while operating in support of the land battle raging below, and F/O Brereton was captured as the sole survivor of his crew. On the 13th the few remaining serviceable Battles now operating out of Souge were once more thrust into the fray against Panzers in the Foret de Gault, and three were promptly shot down. The observer in L5324 was the only fatality among the three crews, his pilot, P/O Shorthouse, and gunner regaining the squadron. Not so fortunate were P/O McPhie and crew in L5531 and P/O Parkhouse and crew in L5580, all of whom became PoWs. The annihilation of the AASF was now all but complete, and the final nails were driven into the coffin over the next few days. On the 14th Sgt Wilcox and crew were killed attacking targets at Evreux in L5383, and P/O Blowfield and his observer, Sgt Batty, survived the demise of L5396, only for Blowfeld to be shot and killed on the ground while attempting to evade capture, a feat that Batty successfully accomplished.

103 Squadron flew most of its surviving aircraft directly to Abingdon on the 15th, while the commanding officer, W/C Dickens, who had succeeded W/C Gemmel on the 12th of March, took an unserviceable Battle to Nantes with leaking fuel tanks and structural damage, plus two passengers in the form of S/L Tait and F/O Max. Max flew a reserve aircraft from there, while Dickens and Tait continued in the wreck, stopping off at Jersey to top up the tanks. The aircraft and crews moved into Honington

on the 16th, where they would remain until the 3rd of July. Having lost most of its aircraft, 12 Squadron began withdrawing to the UK on the 16th, abandoning unserviceable aircraft in France. Finningley was the first destination, and it was during the brief stay here that W/C Blackden would be appointed as the new commanding officer on the 28th. He had previously commanded 107 Squadron for twenty months up to June 1939. For much of their time in France 12 and 103 Squadrons had not been part of Bomber Command, but now they were to be founder members of a new, reconstituted 1 Group, which officially came into being on the 22nd, with headquarters at Hucknall in Nottinghamshire. The other founder units were 142 and 150 Squadrons, which would be joined soon by two Polish units, 300 and 301 Squadrons.

Five days after the group's reformation Air Commodore J J Breen was installed as the Air-Officer-Commanding. Curiously, the recording of the group's activities in an operations record book would not begin until the 1st of August. By now 12 Squadron had acquired a dubious reputation as a "chop" squadron, and this it took with it to Binbrook on the 3rd of July. Like 103 Squadron, 142 Squadron returned to the UK on the 15th and took up temporary residence at Waddington under the command of W/C Falconer, who had been in post since March 1939. 150 Squadron was another to arrive back on English soil on the 15th, and moved initially into Abingdon. Following a brief stay at Stradishall the squadron arrived at Newton on the 3rd of July, which it was to share with 103 Squadron.

For the time being at least the group would retain its Battles for operations against the invasion barge concentrations gathering in the Channel ports of France, Belgium and Holland. The first official operation by 1 Group took place on the last night of July and involved six aircraft drawn from 12 and 142 Squadrons at Binbrook. The intended target was the aerodrome at Rotterdam, which only three reached, and in the conditions of low cloud even they were unable to carry out an attack, so they jettisoned their bombs into the sea in accordance with instructions. 12 Squadron's L5568 was intercepted and shot down off Skegness by a friendly fighter, and there were no survivors from the crew of F/O Moss. To make it easier to conduct these operations the two squadrons moved south onto Coastal Command stations, 12 Squadron to Thorney Island on the 7th of August and then to Eastchurch on the 12th, the day on which 142 Squadron also arrived. While away from Binbrook the two squadrons were neither fully 1 Group nor Coastal Command, which left 1 Group effectively with just two squadrons on its books, 103 and 150, and both of these were engaged in training. 12 Squadron's P6597 failed to return from

Boulogne on the night of the 19/20th, and it was learned later that the crew of P/O Cook was safe but in enemy hands.

Following the defeat of Poland in the September campaign of 1939, many of its airmen escaped via the neighbouring countries of Hungary, Romania, Lithuania and Latvia, and ultimately made their way to France. Here they were gathered on a station at Lyon-Bron, where they were organised into mainly fighter training groups. The bomber crews eventually found themselves in Africa, mostly at Blida in Algeria, and it was from there that they arrived at Eastchurch in December 1939. This was to be the start of a strong association between 1 Group and Polish airmen, which would continue to the end of the war. The contribution by Poles to Bomber Command's war can not be overstated, for not only did they serve in front line bomber units, their work in support of the Special Operations Executive and Special Intelligence Service with 3 Group's 138 Squadron at the highly secret Gibraltar Farm, otherwise known as Tempsford, was vital in maintaining communications with resistance organisations in eastern Europe.

The 22nd of August brought the arrival of 300 Squadron and its Fairey Battles to Swinderby. The squadron had been formed on the 1st of July at Bramcote in Warwickshire, a new station opened on the 4th of June. W/C Makowski had been installed as its first commanding officer, and W/C Lewis was appointed as his British adviser and intermediary between Polish airmen and British officialdom. Makowski was born in Russia in 1897, and graduated from primary flying training in 1919. Thereafter he was involved in a number of aviation roles, including test pilot, and from 1930, until being called up once more for military duty, he served as the head of the Polish airline LOT. He arrived in the UK in December 1939 and initially organised a training school at Upavon in Wiltshire. Over the 28th and 29th of August the second Polish unit, 301 Squadron, began its move from Bramcote to Swinderby with sixteen Battles. Formed on the 24th of July, the squadron was commanded by W/C Rudkowski with S/L Skinner as his adviser. Rudkowski was born in 1898 and saw service with the Polish Legions during the Great war. He graduated from flying training school in 1923 and served in a variety of units, mostly fighter, and was involved in the September campaign of 1939. With the defeat of Poland he made his way to Romania and eventually France, before reaching England after the French capitulation. By the end of August the 1 Group summary showed no operations, and details not yet to hand with regard to 12 and 142 Squadrons away on the south coast.

142 and 12 Squadrons returned to Binbrook on the 6th and 7th of September respectively, the month which would see the climax of the

Battle of Britain. On the evening of the 7th six aircraft each from 103 and 150 Squadrons were dispatched from Newton to Calais to attack invasion barges, and although all returned safely, searchlights and conditions generally had impeded the accuracy and assessment of the bombing. A further six Battles from Newton carried out a repeat operation on the evening of the 9th, and one from 103 Squadron failed to return and was lost without trace. Calais had been the intended target for a further assault on the late evening of the 10th, but it was changed during the day to Boulogne, and all six participants returned safely from what was another indeterminate operation.

The Polish squadrons were eager to begin operations, and were given their chance on the night of the 14/15th, when invasion barges at Boulogne were the target. All aircraft returned safely, although it is unlikely that they inflicted any telling damage. One Polish pilot distinguished himself by trying to shoot down barrage balloons over the target, and then shot up a Coastal Command aircraft before landing at Bircham Newton, a Coastal Command station! On the following night the Poles provided half of the twelve aircraft for another attack on shipping at Boulogne, and some bombs were observed to fall into the docks area. As the Battles were unsuited to any other kind of target, this remained the pattern of operations for 1 Group for the remainder of September and into October. The first casualties amongst the Polish units came on the night of the 24/25th, when a 301 Squadron crew was killed in a crash on return from one of the invasion ports.

Battle of Britain skirmishes continued into October, but the threat of invasion had diminished sufficiently by then to effectively end the operational career of the Fairey Battle in Bomber Command service. As an example of its limited employment, 12 Squadron, since its return from France, had logged just eight operations and thirty-six sorties. During the same period Hampdens, Whitleys and Wellingtons from the other groups had been much more active, playing their part in the defence of the country by also attacking marine craft, but mostly by targeting Ruhr industry and communications. A note in the ORB for September stated "the Polish squadrons have given a very good account of themselves, both by their enthusiasm and ability to learn and put into practice the British procedure in all of its ramifications."

W/C Falconer was posted from 142 Squadron on the 1st of October to take up duties as a liaison officer at HQ Bomber Command. He was succeeded at 142 Squadron by W/C Sadler on the same day. 103 and 150 Squadrons took delivery of their first Wellingtons on the 2nd of October, R3275 and T2610 going to the former, and L7870 to the latter. 103

Squadron would have a further eight on charge by the 24th, and 150 a total of nine more by the 9th. Battles remained on 12 Squadron charge while 1 Group went through the process of re-equipping with Wellingtons, and it would be the following month before it began conversion onto the Rolls-Royce Merlin powered Mk II along with 142 Squadron. 142 Squadron received its first Wellington, W5356, on the 8th, two days before W5353 and W5354 were taken on charge by 12 Squadron, but atrocious weather conditions slowed the progress towards operational status, and it would be spring of the coming year before Binbrook dispatched aircraft in anger.

It was a similar situation for the Polish units, and a number of inevitable incidents in training took the lives of a few airmen. On the night of the 9/10th the group provided eight Battles for an attack on le Havre, which was carried out from between six and ten thousand feet. All returned safely, five with claims of strikes in the docks area on Nos 6 and 2 basins. Most subsequently planned operations during the month were cancelled in the face of bad weather, and this was the end for the time being of 1 Group's contribution to the war effort. 300 Squadron took its first Wellington, L7789, on charge on the 18th, but would not be fully equipped until December. 301 squadron received its first Wellington, P9214, on the 20th, and a further eleven would arrive over the ensuing month.

November passed with no operations and no major incidents as training continued at Swinderby, Binbrook and Newton. It was noted, however, that Newton was unsuitable for night operations in Wellingtons, particularly when the wind blew from a north-westerly direction. On the 23rd W/C Dickens handed over temporary command of 103 Squadron to S/L Tait pending the appointment of a new commanding officer, and on the 27th, after just five months as A-O-C 1 Group, Air Commodore Breen was posted to the Air Ministry, and was succeeded by Air Commodore Oxland.

A third Polish unit joined 1 Group on the 2nd of December and took up residence at Syerston. 304 Squadron had been formed at Bramcote on the 22nd of August under W/C Bialy, with W/C Graham as his British advisor. Bialy had seen service in the Great War, and had been involved in the air battle for Poland before escaping to England through Romania and France. Initially equipped with Battles 304 Squadron had taken its first Wellingtons on charge, N2899 and N2989, on the 1st of November while still at Bramcote, and was now working up to operational status. The 3rd of December brought a change in leadership at 150 Squadron, when W/C Paul vacated his post at HQ 1 Group to swap roles with W/C Hesketh, who slid into W/C Paul's former seat on the 8th. The final Polish addition to 1 Group, 305 Squadron, moved into Syerston on the 4th under the command of W/C Jankowski, a navigator, who had W/C Drysdale as his British advisor. The squadron had been formed at Bramcote on the 29th of August, and like the other Polish units, had been equipped initially with Battles before converting to Wellingtons, the first of which, P2531, had been taken on charge on the 5th of November. S/L Littler was promoted to be W/C Dickens successor at 103 Squadron on the 5th, and S/L Tait reverted to his flight commander role.

On the 18th the group declared that it had twelve Wellingtons and crews available for operations, six each from Newton and Swinderby. On the 20th the figure was amended to eighteen, and that night the first six sorties by 1 Group Wellingtons were launched from Newton against Ostend. Earlier in the day W/C Bialy had vacated the helm of 304 Squadron, reputedly following some kind of misunderstanding with his British adviser, W/C Graham, and had been succeeded by W/C Dudzinski. In the early hours of the 22nd six Polish-crewed Wellingtons took off from Swinderby bound for Antwerp, and all returned safely. On the 23rd a leaving party was held at 103 Squadron for the departing W/C Dickens, during which he had his trousers removed before being thrown into the River Trent. His new posting was to 33 SFTS at Wilmslow, with which he moved to Canada. The Christmas period was allowed to pass without operations, but it was back to business for Newton and Swinderby on the 28/29th, when ports were the targets. Returning from Antwerp, 300 Squadron's R1035 crashed a mile short of Swinderby while trying to land, and P/O Krynski was killed outright, while one of his crew succumbed to his injuries later in station sick quarters.

1941

First Quarter

As the New Year dawned 150 Squadron was in the final stages of its preparations at Newton to join 103 Squadron in the war against Germany. Bremen occupied the bulk of the Command's attention during the first three nights of the year, while other small scale operations were carried out against a variety of targets in Germany and the occupied countries. Newton and Swinderby each dispatched six crews, and the three from 103 Squadron braved a freezing New Year's Night to reach the primary target. It became a sad night for 301 Squadron when two of its Wellingtons were stalked and shot down by enemy intruders over Lincolnshire while preparing to land. One of the pilots was a flight commander, and just one man survived from the two six-man crews. 1 Group sat out the Bremen operation on the night of the 2/3rd, but sent five aircraft to join an attack on the city on the 3/4th.

The battleship Tirpitz was believed to be at berth in Wilhelmshaven, and six operations of varying sizes were launched against the port during the course of January beginning on the night of the 8/9th. 1 Group's contribution to this first operation was cancelled because of doubtful weather conditions, but fourteen aircraft were made ready for the following night's effort, which would be the largest operation of the month. The target was the oil town of Gelsenkirchen in the Ruhr, for which a new record force of 135 aircraft was detailed, including a contingent of five aircraft each from Swinderby and Newton. It was on this night that 150 Squadron launched its first operational sorties in Wellingtons. In what would become a trend over the coming years, bombs were sprayed liberally around the Ruhr, and it was not possible to say how many found their intended target.

103 Squadron bade farewell to S/L Tait on the 15th, and he was succeeded as B Flight commander by S/L Mellor, who arrived from 15 O.T.U. Also on this day the commander-in-chief of Bomber Command, Sir Richard Peirse, who had been in post since succeeding Sir Charles Portal in October, received a new directive from the Air Ministry setting out the latest bombing policy. It was believed that Germany's oil situation was approaching a critical period, and that attacks on its synthetic oil production over the next six months would impact heavily upon its war effort. Accordingly a list of seventeen targets had been prepared, the top nine of which represented around 80% of output. These plants were at Leuna, Pölitz, Gelsenkirchen, Zeitz, Scholven-Buer, Ruhland, Böhlen, Magdeburg and Lützkendorf, and they represented the sole, primary aim for Peirse's forces until further notice. Peirse would wait until February before beginning the campaign, and would continue with his policy of one large scale attack per month against a major industrial city.

The attack on the Tirpitz at Wilhelmshaven on the night of the 15/16th caused significant damage to the town and buildings in the docks area. Of the ten Wellingtons dispatched by 1 Group, six reached and bombed the primary target and there were no losses. The second half of the month found 1 Group stations under snow for most of the time, and they were declared unserviceable as far as operations were concerned. French ports had been of interest during January, and this would continue into February with attacks on the likes of Boulogne, Brest, le Havre, Lorient, and Dunquerke, while mines were laid in the sea lanes around them.

12 Squadron's W5365 crashed in Nottinghamshire on the 8th of February while trying to land at Tollerton during training, and flight commander S/L Lawrence perished with his crew. This would be the first of an alarming loss rate among 12 Squadron flight commanders. The night of the 10/11th was devoted to the month's large-scale effort, for which

Hannover was selected. 222 aircraft, the largest force yet sent to a single target, took off for the city, and 183 returning crews claimed to have attacked their assigned aiming points. This was 103 Squadron's first operation of the month, and W/C Littler took the opportunity to lead the squadron's six participants. On return Sgt Crich was forced to ditch T2610 in the North Sea, and then endure a two day ordeal with his crew waiting for the rescue that eventually came at the hands of a Danish ship, SS Tovell, which was on hire to the Thompson Steamship Line. Having crashed on return from Gelsenkirchen a month earlier, this crew was in danger of using up its ration of luck. While this operation was in progress, more than forty other aircraft attacked oil storage tanks at Rotterdam, in the operation that saw the first sorties by 3 Group's new Short Stirling heavy bomber.

103 Squadron would spend the 11th to the 22nd at Lindholme, after the heavy February rains made Newton unfit for operations. During mid month, indeed, all of 1 Group's stations were declared unserviceable, and its squadrons sat out the start of the oil campaign, which began on the night of the 14/15th. The targets were Homberg, on the West Bank of the Rhine, a few miles to the north-west of Duisburg city centre, and Gelsenkirchen and Sterkrade-Holten further east, but it was a wasted effort as few aircraft reached their respective target areas. Twenty-four hours later a smaller force attacked Homberg again, while a greater number went back to the Holten plant at Sterkrade. 1 Group contributed eight aircraft to the night's proceedings, all launched from Waddington, and one overshot its landing there on return, and sustained considerable damage.

Düsseldorf was raided on the 22/23rd, when 103 Squadron's participation was cancelled because of the weather. 300 and 301 Squadrons each dispatched a freshman crew from the 3 Group airfield at Mildenhall on the 23/24th to join an attack on Boulogne, and they were the only 1 Group aircraft operating on the night. Düsseldorf was raided again on the 25/26th, for which 103, 150 and 300 Squadrons provided a total of twelve Wellingtons. The month's penultimate major operation took a force of over a hundred aircraft to Cologne on the night of the 26/27th, for which 300 and 301 Squadrons provided nine Wellingtons between them. Wilhelmshaven hosted the final operation of the month on the 28th, when a force of more than a hundred aircraft targeted the Tirpitz. 1 Group dispatched nine Wellingtons drawn from 103 and 150 Squadrons, and all returned safely. 103 Squadron had by now a strength of sixteen Wellington Mk ICs along with two Mk IAs. The pattern of operations for the period seemed to be set, although this would turn out to be an illusion. What was not in doubt, however, was that a steady rate of attrition would now become a fact of life as 1 Group faced a hard and uncompromising year. 150

Squadron operated on three occasions during the month and launched eleven sorties without loss.

Cologne opened the March account on the 1/2nd, following on from the attack a week earlier. Damage was quite considerable for the period, but just a pinprick compared with what was in store for this mighty city in the years to come. 1 Group sat this one out, and waited until the following night to next venture forth in anger. The target was Brest, to which 300 and 301 Squadrons each sent five Wellingtons. Another shot at Cologne occupied the night of the 3/4th, a smaller effort than that of the 1st, and this time 1 Group took part with ten aircraft from 103 and 150 Squadrons, and they contributed to slight superficial damage in a number of suburbs. On the 9th of March yet another new Air Ministry directive was received, which changed the emphasis of the Command's operations from oil to maritime matters. Unacceptably high shipping losses to U-Boots in the Atlantic forced the War Cabinet to order an all-out assault on this menace, and its partner in crime, the long range reconnaissance bomber, the Focke-Wulf Kondor. They were to be hunted down at sea, in their bases, and at the point of their manufacture, and this campaign was to be prosecuted as a priority. Kiel, Hamburg, Vegesack and Bremen all contained shipyards, and the last-mentioned was also home to a Focke-Wulf factory.

The new campaign began at Hamburg and Bremen on the night of the 12/13th, while another force targeted Berlin. 1 Group sent a contingent from Newton and Swinderby to bomb railway installations at Hamburg, while other elements of the eighty-strong force went for the shipyards. Destruction at Hamburg was significant, with the Blohm & Voss U-Boot yards sustaining damage to buildings and installations, and a number of high explosive bombs hit the Focke-Wulf aircraft factory in Bremen. At Berlin damage was confined to the southern districts, and no buildings were classed as destroyed. While these operations were in progress, four Polish crews attacked oil storage tanks at Rotterdam, a popular destination for fresher crews, and whenever weather conditions allowed, such small scale operations were a feature of operational activity, particularly during the Wellington era. W/C Littler led a 103 Squadron contingent back to Hamburg on the following night, in what was another effective raid that included five Polish crews. Further damage was inflicted upon the Blohm & Voss yards and more than a hundred fires were started. While this operation was in progress, four Polish crews slipped across the North Sea for another tilt at the oil storage facilities at Rotterdam.

The oil directive was not entirely shelved in favour of maritime considerations, and a hundred aircraft set out for Gelsenkirchen on the night of the 14/15th, when W/C Littler again led his men from the front.

Although a relatively ineffective attack, a number of bomb loads did fall upon the Hydrierwerk Scholven oil plant, and significant damage was inflicted. Thereafter during March the accent fell back onto German and French ports, but an attempt to hit the U-Boot base at Lorient on the 21/22nd was hampered by poor visibility. Even so, seven of the eight participating 103 Squadron crews reported bombing as briefed. R3288 became 150 Squadron's first Wellington operational casualty when crashing in Snowdonia on return, and only the rear gunner in F/O Elliot's crew survived. Fourteen Polish crews were scheduled for Berlin on the night of the 23/24th, using Langham as an advanced base. After the first four became airborne, the next two crashed while taking off, and forced the cancellation of the remaining sorties. All four did at least reach and bomb the target before returning safely. A change of leadership at 305 Squadron saw W/C Jankowski step aside in favour of W/C Kleczynski on the 29th.

Brest began to take on a particular level of importance from the 29th as the Scharnhorst and Gneisenau were spotted in its waters, and by the following day they had taken residence. Their presence over an extended period would be an unwelcome and costly distraction for the Command, which would ultimately end with little to show for the massive effort expended. On the night of the 30/31st more than a hundred aircraft took off to carry out the first of what would be a multitude of attempts over the next eleven months to incapacitate the newly arrived lodgers, and prevent them from going back to sea to threaten Allied surface shipping. 1 Group's effort was provided by fourteen Wellingtons from Newton, and until this night March had been a loss-free month for 103 Squadron. Sadly, R1043 crashed in Somerset during an attempted emergency landing, killing W/C Littler and injuring his crew. The B Flight commander, S/L Mellor, was attacked by an intruder as he returned from the same operation, but he force-landed W5612 near Newton without casualties. 150 Squadron operated four times during the month, and launched twenty-seven sorties with just the single casualty detailed above.

1941 Second Quarter

As April dawned, 12 Squadron was nearing the end of its conversion, but before it took to the skies again in anger five operations were directed at Brest during the first week of the month. The first one, a small effort by 5 Group, resulted in a recall, but larger attacks followed on the 3/4th and 4/5th. W/C Lowe was appointed to command 103 Squadron on the 4th, but the squadron did not take part in the operation that night which unwittingly produced consequences. The Continental Hotel sustained a number of hits, which killed several officers from one of the vessels, and a single bomb lodged in the bottom of the dry dock being occupied by the Gneisenau. The captain opted to remove his ship while the bomb was dealt with, and moored it out in the harbour. While there it was attacked in suicidal fashion by a lone Coastal Command Beaufort torpedo bomber, and suffered a direct hit requiring six months of repair work. The Beaufort was shot down with the loss of the entire crew, and the pilot, F/O Campbell, was a warded a posthumous Victoria Cross for his gallantry.

Another operation was mounted against the port and its guests on the night of the 6/7th, for which 1 Group dispatched twenty Wellingtons from Newton and Swinderby. Poor weather conditions prevented an accurate attack on this occasion, but, in contrast, good conditions attended a major assault on Kiel by over two hundred aircraft on the 7/8th. Ten Polish crews represented the group, and they contributed to the substantial damage inflicted upon housing and buildings in the eastern docks area, which led to several days' loss of production at two U-Boot construction yards. A follow-up raid twenty-four hours later involving eighteen crews from Newton and Swinderby was even more successful, and the number of civilian casualties was probably the highest of the war to date, as was the figure of more than eight thousand people bombed out of their homes. On the following night Berlin was the principal target, while two small-scale operations were directed at Vegesack and Emden.

The latter operation heralded the return to the Order of Battle of 12 Squadron, which dispatched four Wellingtons led by the commanding officer, W/C Blackden, in W5375. Sadly, he failed to return, having been shot down into the Ijsselmeer by a night fighter captained by the Ace, Oblt Egmont Prinz zur Lippe-Weissenfeld of 4/NJG/1, and there were no survivors. He would be succeeded on the 11th by W/C Maw. The night before his appointment the first of six further raids on Brest during the remainder of the month resulted in four bombs hitting the Gneisenau and killing fifty Germans. 1 Group missed that one, but eleven crews were dispatched there from Newton on the 12/13th and ten Polish crews followed suite two nights later. Kiel was attacked on four occasions, the first time on the night of the 15/16th, and the lack of effectiveness would prove to be a feature of the series and a reflection of the performance level of the period generally. A small-scale operation on the same night was directed at the docks at Boulogne, and involved the first four Wellington sorties by 142 Squadron at Binbrook. The Poles represented the group at Bremen on the following night, and then twelve crews set out from Newton for Berlin and Mannheim on the 16/17, only to fail to reach their objectives and bombing alternative targets instead.

It was again the Poles from Swinderby who went to Cologne on the 20/21st and Brest on the 23/24th, before Newton dispatched twelve Wellingtons for the second attack of the series on Kiel on the 24/25th, while crews from Binbrook went for Wilhelmshaven and le Havre. The third Kiel raid took place on the night of the 25/26th, when ten Polish crews represented the group. It was on this night that the Polish element was boosted by the operational debut of five fresher crews from 304 and 305 Squadrons at Syerston in Nottinghamshire. Their target was the oil storage tanks at Rotterdam, which four managed to locate, and all five returned safely. Another big effort from the Polish squadrons at Swinderby saw them dispatch fourteen Wellingtons to attack Mannheim on the 29/30th. The month's operational activity ended at Kiel on the last night of the month, when Newton and Binbrook put up seventeen Wellingtons between them. During the course of the month 150 Squadron managed forty-eight sorties during eleven operations without loss.

Hamburg was raided five times during the first week and a half of May, beginning on the night of the 2/3rd, when very modest damage was a scant reward for the effort of launching over ninety aircraft, sixteen of them crewed by Polish airmen from Swinderby. In an all-Polish effort for the group on this night, a further twelve from 300, 304 and 305 Squadrons carried out freshman sorties at Emden for the loss of one of their number. Cologne followed twenty-four hours later supported by a 1 Group contribution of twenty-three sorties from Newton and Binbrook, but cloud covered the target and the operation was a failure. The 4/5th became another all-Polish night, when crews from Syerston and Swinderby attacked le Havre and Brest respectively. On the 5/6th 141 aircraft were dispatched to Mannheim, where a house and a barn were destroyed by the twenty-five aircraft which reached the target area to bomb. The operation was supported by twenty-eight crews from Newton, Binbrook and Swinderby, and twenty-three of these claimed to have bombed as briefed through complete cloud cover. Over a hundred aircraft set off to return to Hamburg on the 6/7th, among them ten from Swinderby, but another disappointing operation ensued in poor visibility. A further eleven Polish crews from Syerston set off for le Havre on the same night, and one from 304 Squadron failed to return.

While a force of eighty aircraft attacked Brest on the night of the 7/8th, 103 and 150 Squadrons provided fifteen Wellingtons for an attack on St Nazaire, another of the ports containing a U-Boot base. Although having sustained casualties, up to this point 150 Squadron had not experienced the failure to return of one of its aircraft since converting to Wellingtons. It was a situation which had to end, and R1374 crashed in France on this night, killing F/L Savage and his crew. Hamburg hosted its third raid in the space of a week on the 8/9th, and this time eighty-three fires were started within the city, of which almost half were classed as large. Bremen was also attacked on this night by a force of 130 aircraft, including more than forty from the four 1 Group stations. A lack of concentration at the aiming point meant that it was the city rather than the U-Boot yards that received the bombs, and three aircraft from Polish squadrons were among the missing. An all British crew was on board 304 Squadron's R1473, which was captained by F/O Lynes, with the squadron's British adviser, W/C Graham, flying as second pilot. Both men were killed along with three others after flak brought them down in Germany, and just one man survived to be taken prisoner.

A moderately successful raid fell on the twin cities of Mannheim and Ludwigshafen astride the Rhine on the 9/10th, for which the bulk of the 1 Group effort was again provided by Polish crews. This was followed by two further attacks on Hamburg on the succeeding nights, each involving a 1 Group effort, and both operations left many fires burning. Having posted missing its first Wellington three nights earlier, 150 Squadron now lost a second, R1435 failing to make it back home with the crew of F/O Spiller, who all died. The busy schedule for the month continued with another trip to Mannheim and Ludwigshafen on the 12/13th, but this operation failed to find the mark, and then it was the turn of Hannover on the 15/16th, where the post office and telephone exchange were optimistically selected as the aiming points. Cologne was raided four times more before the end of the month, on the 16/17th, 17/18th, 23/24th and 27/28th, and on the final occasion a small force of Wellingtons and Whitleys also went to Boulogne. 150 Squadron's R1044 crashed in Leicestershire on return, and Sgt Huggett was killed with four of his crew. During the course of the month 150 Squadron carried out eight operations and launched sixty-five sorties for the loss of three aircraft and crews.

Düsseldorf, Cologne and Bremen dominated proceedings in June, and the first two-mentioned were attacked on the same night on no fewer than nine occasions during the second half of the month by forces of varying sizes, but not once with better than modest results. 1 Group's contribution to operations continued to grow, and there is insufficient space in this narrative to document all of its activity. 150 aircraft set off for Düsseldorf on the night of the 2/3rd, but only two thirds of the force reported bombing the city. Four 103 Squadron crews took part in a simultaneous raid by twenty-five Wellingtons on Duisburg, but the familiar ground haze prevented accuracy. Minor operations then held sway until the 10/11th, when a hundred aircraft were dispatched to Brest for another crack at the Scharnhorst and Gneisenau, which had now been joined by Prinz Eugen. Four railway targets ringing the Ruhr were the objectives for a combined total of over three hundred aircraft on the 12/13th. Of sixteen Wellingtons from Newton assigned to installations at Osnabrück, seven were provided by 150 Squadron. In addition, a single 103 Squadron freshman crew was sent to join others in bombing the docks at Boulogne and failed to return.

The German raiders at Brest continued to escape damage on the 13/14th, despite the attentions of around a hundred aircraft, including six from 150 Squadron. It was from this point that Cologne and Düsseldorf became the main focus of attention for the remainder of the month. While a combined total of 170 aircraft were divided between the two cities on the 16/17th, thirty-nine Wellingtons were sent to Duisburg. The solitary loss from this operation was 103 Squadron's N2849, in which B Flight commander S/L Kelly was killed along with his crew. Kelly was an experienced officer, who had been promoted from within the squadron and had been three times "Mentioned in Dispatches". W/C Paul was posted to Bomber Command HQ on the 17th, and was succeeded as commanding officer of 150 Squadron by W/C Carter. Cologne, Düsseldorf and Duisburg were back on twenty-four hours later, 150 Squadron providing five Wellingtons for the last-mentioned.

Another of Germany's capital ships, Tirpitz, now, since the recent loss of the Bismarck, the pride of the German fleet, was spotted at berth in Kiel, and a force of a hundred aircraft was sent to seek it out. It proved impossible for the crews to locate the ship, however, and the town was bombed instead. 150 Squadron put up eight aircraft for Cologne on the 23/24th and a further eight and five for Düsseldorf on the 26/27th and 30th respectively. During the former, 150 Squadron's R1644 fell victim to flak over Holland, and P/O Sievers and his crew died in the wreckage. An operation to Bremen on the night of the 27/28th by over a hundred Wellingtons and Whitleys took place in unfavourable weather conditions, and brought the heaviest loss to date on a single night of fourteen aircraft. 4 Group sustained the bulk of the casualties, but 12 Squadron posted missing another flight commander in the form of S/L Kitching, who disappeared without trace along with his crew in W5391.

1941 Third Quarter

Bremen featured again on the 2/3rd of July, when the sole loss from the twenty 1 Group participants was from 12 Squadron. Later on the 3rd

Elsham Wold officially opened for business, and the staff began preparations for the arrival of 103 Squadron a week hence. That night 1 Group put up twenty-nine Wellingtons from Swinderby and Newton for another attack on Bremen, from which two Polish crews failed to return. Binbrook and Syerston provided twenty-two aircraft for an operation to Lorient on the evening of the 4/5th, while a simultaneous assault went on at Brest. Conditions were fine at both targets, and the Lorient force produced some accurate bombing, but effective smoke screens kept the enemy warships safe. While over sixty aircraft targeted Münster on the 5/6th, the gas works at Bielefeld provided a change of objective for over thirty crews, twenty-four of which were launched from Newton and Swinderby. It appears that accuracy was achieved, as the gas works is believed to have blown up. Nineteen aircraft from Binbrook and Syerston took part in yet another attack on the warships at Brest on the 6/7th. 12 Squadron's flight commanders continued to be jinxed, and this time it was S/L Baird who failed to return in W5360, and again there were no survivors. On the night of the 7/8th an all Wellington force of more than a hundred aircraft delivered the most effective attack to date on Cologne, where housing and railway installations sustained the bulk of the damage and over sixty large fires were started. 1 Group provided more than half of the participants in response to a call for a maximum effort, and all returned. Thirty-three Wellingtons went back to Bielefeld on the 8/9th to attend to its power station, but only nineteen of the 1 Group element pressed on to bomb as briefed, while twelve others opted for alternative targets.

On the 9th a new Air Ministry directive signalled an end to the maritime distraction, and now called upon Peirse to concentrate his efforts against the German transportation system and the morale of its civilian population. From now on, during the moon periods, the major railway centres ringing and serving the Ruhr were to be attacked, while on moonless nights the Rhine cities of Cologne, Duisburg and Düsseldorf would be more easily identifiable. On dark nights offering less favourable weather conditions, Peirse was to send his forces to the more distant targets in northern, eastern and southern Germany. 103 Squadron operated for the final time from Newton on the night of the 10/11th, when dispatching eleven crews to Cologne as part of a force of 130 Wellingtons and Hampdens. They were unable to repeat the success of three nights earlier, however, and only five 103 Squadron crews bombed in the intended target area, five others finding alternative objectives to attack.

On the 11th 103 and 150 Squadrons completed their moves from Newton to Elsham Wolds and Snaith respectively, and for 103 its newly built north Lincolnshire station would be home for the remainder of the war. 150 Squadron returned to operations on the night of the 13/14th, but not one of the aircraft from Binbrook and Snaith located Vegesack. Three days after its move 103 Squadron was back on the order of battle, and sent six aircraft to Bremen without loss, although two were forced to turn back early with technical issues. Also on this day W/C Kippenberger was posted from 1 Group HQ to command 142 Squadron, while his predecessor, W/C Sadler was posted in the opposite direction to take up duties at 1 Group HQ. Over a hundred aircraft set off late on the 16th to attack Hamburg, among them six from 150 Squadron. In the event only seven of twenty 1 Group aircraft were able to identify the target in cloudy conditions, and damage was slight. 150 Squadron's R1495 failed to return after crashing in Germany, and P/O Bethridge-Topp died with four of his crew, the single survivor falling into enemy hands.

300 and 301 Squadrons completed their move to Hemswell on the 18th, and their former home of Swinderby was transferred to 5 Group. This was the opportunity for W/C Makowski to step down as commanding officer of 300 Squadron, and was succeeded by W/C Cwynar. On the following day 304 Squadron departed Syerston for Lindholme, where it was joined on the 20th by 305 Squadron, at which point Syerston was also transferred to 5 Group. On the same day HQ 1 Group moved out of Hucknall and took up residence at Bawtry Hall, near Doncaster in south Yorkshire, enabling Hucknall to be closed down next day. Scattered bombing attended a raid on Cologne on the 20/21st, for which Binbrook and Elsham put up a total of thirteen Wellingtons, while four more joined forces with twenty other aircraft to bomb the docks at Rotterdam. The first major raid on Frankfurt was mounted on the following night, when few bombs found the mark, but at least there were no losses from the seventy-strong force, which included a 1 Group element from Hemswell and Snaith.

The most complex operation for July was planned to be carried out at Brest in daylight on the 24th, when a concerted effort was to be mounted against the Scharnhorst and Gneisenau under the codename Sunrise. The plan had to be changed at the last minute after it was discovered that Scharnhorst had slipped away and was now at berth at la Pallice, some two hundred miles further south. It was decided to send the 4 Group Halifax element to attend to her, while the original plan went ahead at Brest. The 1 Group plan called for its aircraft to attack in eight sections of three aircraft each, 150 Squadron constituting sections 1 and 2 and 103 Squadron sections 3 and 4, with the final four sections provided by the Binbrook units. Three Fortress 1s of 2 Group's 90 Squadron went in at 30,000 feet to draw up the enemy fighters, while eighteen 5 Group Hampdens acted as further bait under the umbrella of a Spitfire escort. This was intended to leave the way clear for the seventy-nine Wellingtons of 1 and 3 Groups to sneak in and attack the objectives unescorted, but fierce flak and fighter opposition brought down ten of them, including 103 Squadron's N2770. It fell victim to fighters during the bombing run, and dropped out of formation with an engine on fire, losing height until crashing into the sea. Sgt Bucknole and his crew were killed, and theirs were the first names to be written on the Elsham Wolds Roll of Honour.

There were a number of unconfirmed hits on Gneisenau, but Scharnhorst suffered more severely while inflicting heavy casualties on the attacking Halifaxes, and she returned to Brest to take advantage of the superior repair facilities on offer. The final week of the month brought only minor operations, during which, on the 27th, W/C Rudkowski was posted from 301 Squadron to be succeeded as commanding officer by W/C Piotrowski. Rudkowski would move on to join 3 Group's highly secret 138 Squadron, which operated on behalf of the Special Operations Executive and the Special Intelligence Service, delivering agents into the occupied countries and supporting the various resistance organisations. The squadron was recruiting Polish crews to carry out operations to their homeland, and Rudkowski would drop a rank to take over command of the Polish Flight. On the night of the 30/31st more than a hundred aircraft were dispatched to Cologne. It was a night of bad weather characterised by thunderstorms and icing conditions, and only a handful of aircraft found the target area. Three aircraft failed to return, and six others crashed on arrival back in England. 150 Squadron's W5719 returned early after Sgt Parrott and his crew failed to find the target, and flew into high ground in Derbyshire killing all on board.

At this stage of the war the Wellington was very much the mainstay of the Command, equipping both 1 and 3 Groups, and almost without exception the operations undertaken thus far in 1941 had featured the type as the most numerous. This was certainly the case when major operations were mounted, as at Hamburg and Berlin on the night of the 2/3rd of August. Railway installations were the objectives at Hamburg for eighty aircraft on this night, including elements from Elsham and Lindholme. The Binbrook squadrons supported the Berlin operation, while eighteen freshmen from the group targeted the docks at Cherbourg. Frankfurt followed for sixty-eight aircraft on the 5/6th, the second of three raids on this city in the space of four nights. 4 Group Whitleys accounted for two-thirds of the force, and the 1 Group effort was provided by elements from Elsham, Snaith and Lindholme. Accurate bombing was claimed, and a large fire erupted close to the railway station, but some bombs also fell on Mainz, twenty miles away. It was, in fact, just one of three main operations on this night, the other targets being Mannheim and Karlsruhe, both also involving elements from 1 Group. 150 Squadron's W5721 failed to return from Frankfurt on the following night, and it was learned later that P/O Landreth and his crew had lost their lives. A 300 Squadron Wellington crashed into the North Sea, and two bodies were recovered by the Shipwash Lightship on the morning of the 7th.

That night Essen was the main target when Hampdens were predominant, but forty-five Wellingtons were sent to Hamm on the same night to attack railway installations. W/C Beill became the new commanding officer of 305 Squadron on the 8th, succeeding W/C Kleczynski. Forty-four Wellingtons went to Hamburg on the 8/9th to attack shipyards and the railway, and twenty-nine, including ten from 150 Squadron, targeted railway installations at Rheydt on the 11/12th, but were thwarted by cloud. Sixty-five and forty Wellingtons respectively were assigned to targets at Hannover and Berlin on the 12/13th, but doubtful weather conditions caused 1 Group to cancel all but the Binbrook element briefed for the Capital. On the night of the 14/15th eleven 150 Squadron aircraft departed Snaith for Hannover along with others from Elsham and Hemswell as part of an overall force of 150. The crews were briefed to use railway stations as aiming points, and some success was claimed in conditions of good visibility. Among the nine missing aircraft were two from 150 Squadron, R1394, which disappeared without trace with the crew of Sgt Perry-Keane, and R1016, which crashed in Holland killing one man, and delivering Sgt Elder and the remainder of his crew into enemy hands. On the same night an element from Binbrook joined others to attack Magdeburg with little success.

The 18th was the day on which Mr D M Butt presented his infamous report to the Air Ministry, and its disclosures sent shock waves reverberating around the halls of power. Having studied four thousand photographs taken during a hundred night raids in June and July, he concluded that only a fraction of the bombs delivered had fallen within miles of their intended targets. This swept away at a stroke any notion that the Command was having a materiel effect on the enemy's war effort, and demonstrated that its claims of success were without foundation. It also provided the detractors with a bountiful supply of ammunition to back up their calls for the dissolution of an independent bomber force, and for the redistribution of its aircraft to the U-Boot campaign and to redress reversals in the Middle East. Peirse had done his best to fulfil the often unrealistic demands of his superiors, but the damning Butt Report was a major blow to morale, and would forever unfairly blight his period of tenure as commander-in-chief.

Cologne and Duisburg were the objectives for forces of sixty and forty aircraft respectively on the night of the 18/19th, when the Cologne force was led astray by a decoy site. Bad weather was beginning to frustrate the Command's ability to hit its objectives, and a raid on Kiel on the 19/20th was thwarted by thick cloud and icing conditions. A force of Wellingtons and Hampdens failed totally at Mannheim on the 22/23rd, despite the claims made by returning crews. W/C Lowe concluded his tour as 103 Squadron's commanding officer, and was posted to Hemswell, and W/C Ryan succeeded him on the 25th. A new squadron joined 1 Group on this day in the form of 458 Squadron RAAF, which took up residence at Holme-on-Spalding-Moor under the command of W/C Mulholland, an Australian-born RAF officer. The unit had been formed in New South Wales Australia in July 1941, and was the second Australian unit to arrive in Bomber Command. *(In my book 4 Group Bomber Command I wrongly assigned 458 Squadron to 4 Group).* Its first two Wellingtons, R1490 and R1695, arrived on the 30th, and Z1272 and Z1273 were added on the following day. A further fifteen Wellingtons would arrive during September to bring the unit up to full strength.

There was little improvement in performance at Cologne on the 26/27th for which 1 Group launched nineteen sorties from Binbrook and Hemswell, or at Mannheim again on the following night supported by nineteen sorties this time from Elsham and Snaith. 150 Squadron's W5722 returned in poor visibility, and Sgt Nicholson ordered his crew to abandon ship before carrying out a successful forced-landing in Suffolk. A modest number of bombs found Duisburg on the 28/29th, when Binbrook alone represented 1 Group, and then the weather was blamed for a poor showing at Frankfurt twenty-four hours later and at Mannheim yet again on the same night, when Elsham, Snaith and Lindholme were on duty. The month's activities ended at Cologne on the night of the 31st in another ineffective operation, for which 1 Group provided thirty-two aircraft from Elsham, Hemswell and Binbrook. Also on this night six Wellingtons were sent to Boulogne, and there were no survivors from the 12 Squadron cosmopolitan crew of P/O Khosla, one of two members of the Indian Air Force on board W5577, which crashed off the French coast.

September began with operations to Frankfurt and Berlin on the night of the 2/3rd, with the Wellington contingent, including elements from Snaith and Lindholme, in attendance at the former. On return 150 Squadron's Z8851 crash-landed in Surrey, but Sgt Dickinson and his crew emerged unscathed from the wreckage. This would not to be this crew's only adventure of the month while returning from Frankfurt. 140 aircraft set off for Brest on the 3/4th, but the 1, 4 and 5 Group elements responded to a recall signal in deteriorating weather conditions. 3 Group pressed on with two 103 Squadron crews in tow, who had not picked up the recall signal, and they bombed through the anticipated smoke screen with inconclusive results. The attrition rate among 12 Squadron's flight commanders continued with the month's largest single effort, which was directed at Berlin on the night of the 7/8th. 197 aircraft were dispatched, among them nineteen from Binbrook and four each from Elsham and Snaith. By the standards of the period, the 130 or so which reported reaching the target area delivered what could be described as an effective attack for the loss of fifteen aircraft. This figure included 12 Squadron's W5598, captained by S/L Edinger, from whose crew just one man escaped with his life to become a PoW. Also failing to return was Z8328, from which S/L Fielden and his crew did at least all survive, and they too fell into enemy hands. The loss of so many flight commanders was indicative of the squadron's quality of leadership, which saw the senior officers operating regularly and sharing the lot of the rank and file.

The first large-scale attack on Kassel claimed some useful if not excessive damage on the 8/9th, and then it was off to Italy for contingents from Elsham and Snaith to target Turin, where good results were claimed on the 10/11th. The Baltic coast was the destination for elements of 1 Group on the night of the 11/12th, with aircraft from 12 and 142 Squadron assigned to Rostock and others from 150 Squadron to Kiel. Before take-off at Binbrook a 12 Squadron wireless operator walked into a propeller and was killed. 130 aircraft took off for Frankfurt on the 12/13th, with 103 Squadron providing the 1 Group contribution, and more than seventy high explosive bombs found the mark, mostly in residential areas. Almost 150 aircraft were committed to an attack on the three warships at Brest on the 13/14th, of which thirteen belonged to 150 Squadron and seven each to 300 and 301 Squadrons. Effective smoke screens hid the targets from view, and bombs were dropped on approximate positions. Six different types of bomber made up the force of 169 aircraft bound for Hamburg on the 15/16th, when Binbrook provided the 1 Group element. For once conditions were good, but despite that, crews found it difficult to pick up individual aiming points, and bombing was spread around the city to fairly good effect, and many fires were left burning as the force retreated. Also on this night an element from the group targeted le Havre, and 305 Squadron's W5526 failed to return having crashed in the target area. The squadron's British adviser, W/C Drysdale, was the pilot, and he perished with the rest of the crew.

Elements of 1 Group were present at two targets on the 20/21st, and both operations resulted in casualties for little if any gain. Of five 103 Squadron

Wellingtons sent to Berlin, two failed to return, one of them containing the A Flight commander, S/L Ingram, who joined the ever-growing ranks of RAF personnel on extended leave in German PoW camps. Four Wellingtons from 103 and eight from 150 Squadrons were assigned to Frankfurt, and returning from the latter 150 Squadron's X9811 struck a balloon cable at the Yorkshire coast and crash-landed. On board was the previously mentioned Sgt Nicholson and crew, who again walked away unscathed. To compound the 103 Squadron losses, another of its Wellingtons crashed near Holbeach while trying to make an emergency landing in fog, and all but the rear gunner were killed. A recall on the 26/27th involved aircraft from Elsham and Lindholme heading for Cologne, while other forces were making for Emden, Mannheim and Genoa. Three 103 Squadron crews heard the signal and two bombed alternative targets, but P/O Lawson pressed on obliviously and bombed Cologne. 1 Group provided eighteen aircraft from Elsham and Binbrook to join a force of over 130 bound for Stettin on the 29/30th, while twenty-one from Binbrook, Snaith and Hemswell were assigned to a ninety-strong force briefed for Hamburg. Good results were claimed at the former, but searchlight glare hampered efforts at the latter. The same two targets hosted smaller forces on the last night of the month, for which 1 Group put up a total of fifteen Wellingtons without loss.

1941 Fourth Quarter

Bad weather continued to hamper operations during October, and the first real night of large-scale activity came on the 10/11th, when seventy-eight aircraft were sent to the Krupp works at Essen, while a further sixty-nine targeted Cologne. 1 Group put up twenty-two Wellingtons for the latter, eleven of them from 150 Squadron, but only half of the force found the target area, and the unsatisfactory outcome was compounded by the loss of five aircraft. Two of these belonged to 12 Squadron, and the case of Z8397 was particularly unfortunate. Sgt Tothill had managed to crash-land the Wellington on a Norfolk beach, but it set off a mine as it slid across the sand, and all on board perished in the explosion. The night of the 12/13th brought a new record number of 373 sorties, 152 of which were sent to southern Germany to deliver the first large-scale assault of the war on Nuremberg. The operation was a dismal failure in which bombs were sprayed liberally over southern Germany, and few, if any, found the target city at a cost to the Command of eight aircraft. 1 Group put up just ten Wellingtons, but provided forty-seven of ninety aircraft involved in a simultaneous operation to Bremen. Of these eleven belonged to 150

Squadron, but they, like the rest of the force here and at a third operation to a chemicals factory at Hüls, encountered cloud cover that led to inconclusive outcomes. 103 and 150 Squadrons each sent nine Wellingtons to Düsseldorf on the 13/14th, when bombing was scattered and ineffective, but at least only one aircraft was lost out of sixty.

W/C Maw was posted from 12 Squadron at the end of his tour, and he was succeeded on the 14th by W/C Roberts. That night the new commanding officer dispatched seven crews as 1 Group's contribution to a force of eighty sent back to Nuremberg. Only fourteen crews reported reaching the target area, again having encountered unfavourable weather condition while outbound, and damage was slight. Sixteen 1 Group aircraft formed part of a force of eighty with Duisburg in their sights. Bombing took place through cloud, and some fires were observed, but an accurate assessment was not possible. The main target on the 20/21st was Bremen, for which 150 aircraft were detailed. 1 Group was not represented, but provided thirty-three aircraft from Elsham Wold, Snaith and Lindholme for Emden, along with the first two sorties by 458 Squadron at Holme-on-Spalding-Moor. 458 Squadron also contributed to a fresher operation to Antwerp docks, and one of its aircraft was the single failure to return from this target.

The night of the 21/22nd was again devoted to Bremen, for which 1 Group put up thirty-four aircraft, twenty of them from the Polish 300 and 301 Squadrons. It was always tragic when a crew completed its assigned task only to perish on return to base. 12 Squadron's Sgt Millar and four of his crew were killed in this manner, when W5393 crashed into the married quarters on return in the early hours of the 22nd. Thankfully, as it turned out, these were the final casualties of the year for "Shiney 12". Mannheim followed on the 22/23rd, with a contribution from 1 Group of nineteen aircraft, of which just eleven managed to battle through the severe conditions of cloud and icing to reach the target area. 150 Squadron posted missing the crew of Sgt Bradshaw, who were all killed in T2967.

Other major operations during the month were directed at Kiel on the 23/24th and Frankfurt on the 24/25th, but generally only half or even fewer of the crews reported reaching and bombing their briefed targets. 103 Squadron's P/O Keefer became lost on the way home from the last-mentioned in the early morning of the 25th, and eventually crash-landed T2506 in the Republic of Ireland, whereupon he and his crew were interned for a period. Twenty-five Polish crews from Hemswell and Lindholme provided the 1 Group effort for Hamburg on the 26/27th, and they contributed to some useful results. The warships at Brest were the objective for sixteen 1 Group crews drawn from 142, 301 and 458 Squadrons on the night of the 29/30th. The smoke screens did not operate, and bombs were seen to explode across the target area. Thirty-one Wellingtons from Binbrook, Elsham and Lindholme represented the 1 Group effort for Hamburg on the last night of the month, but only nineteen made it through the conditions to reach the target area.

The first night of November brought an operation to Kiel supported by elements of 150, 300 and 301 Squadrons, after which the group was stood down for five nights. In an effort to score a major success during what had been a frustrating period of unfavourable weather, Peirse planned a large-scale attack on Berlin for the night of the 7/8th. Although a record number of 392 aircraft set out for operations on that night, only 169 of the crews were briefed for Germany's capital city, including twenty-two from 1 Group. 5 Group's A-O-C, AVM Slessor, had expressed grave doubts about the continuing bad weather, and he had been allowed to send his force of seventy-five Hampdens and Manchesters to Cologne, while fifty-five other aircraft, including forty-six from 1 Group, went to Mannheim. The Berlin operation developed disastrously, and less than half of the force reached the target area to inflict a scant amount of damage, which was in no way commensurate with the massive effort expended. The disappointment was compounded by the loss of twenty-one aircraft, along with another seven from the Mannheim force, which failed to find the target with a single bomb. 150 Squadron contributed eleven Wellingtons, among them R1606, which crashed off the Dutch coast killing Sgt Atkins and crew. The 5 Group element came home unscathed from Cologne after destroying just two houses in the city, but nine other aircraft were missing from the night's minor operations, which included Boulogne, the destination for twelve 1 Group crews. The night's losses amounted to a new record total of thirty-seven, more than twice the previous highest for a single night. Of 1 Group's eighty aircraft, eight returned early and seven failed to return at all. This night of disaster was the final straw for the Air Ministry, and on the 13th Peirse was ordered to restrict further operations while the future of the Command was considered at the highest level. In the meantime Peirse was summoned to a personal meeting with Churchill to explain himself, but his time at the helm of Bomber Command was effectively over, and he would leave his post in January.

In the event, the continuing unfavourable weather would have placed its own restrictions on the Command's operational activity anyway. Just eight 1 Group aircraft, including two from 150 Squadron, took part in an operation to the Krupp works at Essen on the evening of the 8th, and they encountered the typical hazy conditions prevalent in the region. In contrast the visibility at Hamburg on the following night was excellent, but assessment of the results was hampered by searchlight glare. Seventeen of 1 Group's twenty participants found the target and bombed as briefed. Thereafter operations were restricted to freshman assaults on coastal targets, and it was during this lull that W/C Dudzinski stepped aside as commanding officer of 304 Squadron in favour of W/C Poziomek, who was a navigator rather than a pilot.

Another new squadron joined the ranks of Bomber Command at this time. Formed at Molesworth on the 15th 460 Squadron became the third Royal Australian Air Force unit to serve with Bomber Command, following in the footsteps of 455 Squadron in June and 458 Squadron in August. W/C Kippenberger was posted from the command of 142 Squadron on the 20th, and was succeeded by W/C Bertram, who had previously commanded 57 Squadron from late February to early May before being screened. W/C Hubbard was appointed as 460 Squadron's first commanding officer on the 21st, and on the 24th four officers and 117 other ranks were posted in from 458 Squadron to form the nucleus of the new unit. The first Wellington to be taken on charge was Z1284, which arrived on the 30th, and Z1334 followed on the 1st of December. By the end of the year, a total of nineteen aircraft had been received, and the business of working up to operational status got under way.

On the 26th 142 Squadron moved into the newly opened airfield at Waltham, which was a satellite of Binbrook. That night 1 Group was called into action for something other than freshman operations. Twenty-four of the Group's Wellingtons from Elsham Wolds and Hemswell joined a total force of a hundred bound for Emden, where an inconclusive raid was carried out through cloud. The month ended for the Command with a heavy raid on Hamburg on the last night of the month for which 181 aircraft were detailed. 1 Group contributed thirty-nine Wellingtons, including ten from 150 Squadron, and two-thirds of the force reached and bombed the target, while more than thirty others attacked alternative objectives. A further fifty aircraft were sent to Emden, and returning crews claimed good results.

The weather continued to hamper operations for the first half of December, and during this period, on the 6th, W/C Carter was posted to 1 Group HQ, and he was succeeded as 150 Squadron commanding officer by W/C Mellor, the former 103 Squadron flight commander, who was posted in from a similar role with 458 Squadron. It was the night of the 7/8th before the first major operation took place, when Aachen was the destination. 130 aircraft were dispatched, including fourteen from 1 Group, but only half reached it in difficult weather conditions. Meanwhile, twenty-two 1 Group aircraft were involved in minor operations directed at French and Belgian ports including Brest, where the German capital ships continued to take shelter. This would be the first of fifteen attacks of varying sizes sent against the port during the month, as the Command sought a conclusion to this annoying distraction. 150 Squadron's first operational activity of the month came on the night of the 11/12th, when four of its Wellingtons participated in an attack on Cologne conducted through cloud on estimated positions. Thirty-one crews from Elsham Wolds and Binbrook were briefed for Wilhelmshaven on the following night, and although visibility was generally good, ground haze made it difficult to pick out detail on the ground. Another attack on the warships at Brest involved thirty-two 1 Group aircraft, eleven from 150 Squadron and the remainder from Polish units. The overall force of 120 aircraft experienced problems with visibility, and this led to the bombing taking place on approximate positions.

Cologne was the target for over sixty aircraft on the night of the 23/24th, of which thirty-one from the Polish squadrons represented 1 Group. Most of the returning crews believed they had bombed the target, but the Cologne authorities recorded no bombs falling. Forty-one aircraft from the group, including twelve from 150 Squadron, contributed to an overall force of 130 bound for Düsseldorf on the night of the 27/28th. This was the final operation of the year for 458 Squadron, which launched nine aircraft. On his way home Australian acting S/L Don Saville attacked a Heinkel 111 as it was in the act of landing, and it was seen to take hits and veer off the runway. This was typical of Saville, who was a tough, no-nonsense character born in 1903 in Portland, New South Wales. Earlier in the year he had served with 12 Squadron, and in 1942 would command 104 Squadron in Malta, before being appointed commanding officer of 218 Squadron in 3 Group in March 1943. Sadly this inspirational officer would lose his life during the opening round of the Battle of Hamburg on the 23/24th of July after his Stirling is shot down by a night fighter. 103 Squadron posted its own new record on the 28/29th when launching sixteen Wellingtons in a 1 Group effort of forty-nine dispatched to Wilhelmshaven. This time the conditions were excellent and led to an effective attack that caused widespread damage, confirmed by local authorities.

It had not been a good year for Bomber Command, which had failed to make any significant advance on the previous year's performance. The past twelve months had been characterized by a disappointingly ineffective operational record, and the failure of the new bomber types to match expectations. The Stirling, Halifax and Manchester had all experienced major teething problems following their introduction to squadron service early in the year, and each had undergone annoying periods of grounding while essential modifications were carried out. Following the disastrous night of operations on the 7/8th of November, the Command's future had been left hanging in the balance, and there can have been little confidence of an improvement in prospects as the coming year beckoned. In fact, the Command's salvation was even now waiting in the wings in the shape of the new four-engine Lancaster, which was secretly undergoing proving trials with 5 Group's 44 Squadron. Put into the hands of a new and dynamic commander-in-chief, this "shining sword" was about to carve for itself a place in aviation history.

1942

January

The New Year began with Bomber Command still under the same cloud, and operational activity somewhat depressed. The weather also played its part in keeping the crews on the ground, and when flying was possible, it was French and German ports that received most of the attention. 460 Squadron moved to Breighton in Yorkshire on the 4th of January, and officially joined the ranks of 1 Group, which it would serve magnificently for the remainder of the war. As already mentioned an average of one raid every other day had been sent against Brest and its lodgers during December alone, and a further eleven would be mounted in January, eight of them during the first eleven days of the New Year. 1 Group put up forty-eight Wellingtons for the first one on the night of the 5/6th, and then thirty-one, thirty-five, forty-five and thirty-one on consecutive nights thereafter. W/C Roberts concluded his short spell as commanding officer of 12 Squadron, and he was succeeded on the 12th by W/C Golding.

There followed two raids on Hamburg on consecutive nights in mid month, the second of which, on the 15/16th, cost 103 Squadron R1395 and the crew of Sgt Dainton, who died with all but one of his crew. Neither of these operations achieved more than modest success, and this was the pattern for the remainder of the month, during which Bremen, Emden, Hannover and Münster were the principal targets. W/C Cwynar relinquished command of 300 Squadron on the 27th, and he was succeeded by W/C Sulinski. The Münster operation took place on the 28/29th, the night on which 1 Group dispatched twenty freshman crews to attack the docks at Boulogne. Among them were two from 458 Squadron, which was operating for the final time with Bomber Command. The honour of flying these final two sorties fell to F/O MacKellar and Sgt Cameron and their crews, who returned safely. January had proved to be 1 Group's most active of the war, with a record tally of 542 sorties, the highest number since July of the previous year, and the bomb tonnage delivered was also a new record.

February

Three more operations were mounted again Brest in early February, and just hours after the last one, on the evening of the 11th, the German cruisers slipped anchor, and headed into the Channel under a strong escort of destroyers and E-Boats. The fleet commander had chosen the most atrocious weather conditions for his audacious break-out, and it was 10.30 hours on the following morning before the enemy ships were spotted. Only 5 Group was standing by at four hours readiness to implement Operation Fuller, a plan devised for precisely this eventuality. 1 Group was alerted at 11.35, and dispatched its first wave of twenty-five aircraft at 13.30, followed later by a further twelve. A number of inconclusive attacks were carried out by 1 Group aircraft, and despite the commitment of a record 242 daylight sorties by the Command, the low cloud and squally conditions thwarted all attempts to halt the progress of the enemy flotilla. It passed through the Straits of Dover to make good its escape, and although both Scharnhorst and Gneisenau struck air-laid mines, the damage was insufficient to delay their arrival in home port on the following morning. 103 Squadron contributed five aircraft, of which only two made contact with the enemy. S/L Holford spent an hour jockeying for an advantageous position before making an inconclusive attack, and his Wellington sustained many holes from the flak shells being pumped up from below. It is believed that S/L Cross also delivered his bombs in Z8714, before being hit and having to ditch. Cross and three others were taken into captivity, which ended for Cross with his murder at the hands of the Gestapo following the "Great Escape" from Sagan PoW camp in 1944. The Channel Dash episode was a major embarrassment to the government and the nation, but at least, this annoying itch had been scratched for the last time, and the Command could now concentrate it resources against more suitable strategic targets.

On the 14th, a new Air Ministry directive opened the way to the blatant area bombing of industrial Germany, and an assault on the morale of its civilian population. This had, of course, been going on for more than a year, but now it could be conducted in the open, without the pretence of aiming for industrial and military targets. Waiting in the wings, in fact, at that very moment, on his way across the Atlantic from America in the armed merchantman Alcantara, was a new leader, who would pursue this policy with a will, and have the character and strength of personality to fight his corner against the critics. ACM Sir Arthur Harris took up his appointment on the 22nd, and set about the mammoth task of turning Bomber Command around. He arrived at the helm with firm ideas already in place on how to win the war by bombing alone. He recognized, that in order to destroy an urban target, it was necessary to concentrate his forces in time and space to overwhelm the defences. This was the birth of the bomber stream, and it brought an end to the former practice, whereby crews determined for themselves the details of their sorties. He also knew that built-up areas are most efficiently destroyed by fire rather than blast, and that by concentrating the effort, fires would have a chance to gain a hold before the emergency services could reach them through rubble-strewn streets. It would not be long before the bomb loads carried in Harris's aircraft reflected this thinking. It was a policy of the bludgeon over the scalpel, but the war to date had demonstrated that precision bombing was a dream still awaiting the scientific means to realise it.

The day of Harris's appointment also signalled the end in Bomber Command service for 458 Squadron. It had been told during the previous month to prepare to be sent overseas, and on the 22nd W/C Mulholland led a formation of three aircraft from Holme-on-Spalding-Moor on the 1,400 mile journey to Malta. Two arrived safely, but W/C Mulholland was shot down into the Mediterranean and died with all but one of his crew. The remainder of the squadron was ferried out over the ensuing days, but other units borrowed and stole 458's aircraft, and it would be September before it regained its identity and November before operations began from North African landing grounds.

For the remainder of February Harris continued with the small-scale attacks on German ports, and it was during one of these, aimed at the Gneisenau at Kiel on the 25/26th, that two 12 Squadron Mk II Wellingtons delivered the Group's first 4,000lb "cookies". It was at the same target on the following night that the war threw up one of its great ironies. While Wellingtons, Hampdens and Halifaxes were attacking the floating dock, a high explosive bomb struck the bows of the Gneisenau, now supposedly at safe haven after enduring eleven months of almost constant bombardment at Brest. The damage was sufficient to end her sea-going career for good, and her guns were removed for use as coastal defences.

March

460 Squadron was still engaged in training at this time, although it was close to being declared operational. Working up was rarely concluded without at least one major accident, and the squadron had suffered its first

wartime loss on the 17th of February, when Z1327 crashed in Yorkshire while descending after a night flying exercise, and Sgt Dutton and his crew were killed. The squadron was still not ready to operate at the start of March, and missed the first unmistakable sign of a new hand on the tiller. In a foretaste of future tactics, a plan was meticulously prepared for an attack on the Renault lorry factory at Billancourt in Paris. The operation was to take place in three waves, led by experienced crews, with extensive use of flares to provide illumination. Bombing would take place from low level, both to aid accuracy and to avoid civilian casualties in adjacent residential districts, and the number of aircraft over the target per hour would represent a 50% increase on the previous best. In the meantime, 103 Squadron welcomed a new commanding officer on the 1st of March, W/C Du Boulay succeeding W/C Ryan following his posting to Gibraltar. W/C Du Boulay was posted in from 27 O.T.U. at Lichfield. 235 aircraft were dispatched to Paris in the early evening of the 3rd, of which thirty-five Wellingtons represented 1 Group. This was the largest force yet sent to a single target, and 223 crews bombed as briefed, destroying 40% of the Renault factory buildings. Production of lorries was halted for four weeks, and the operation cost just a single Wellington. The satisfaction at this major success was marred only by the heavy casualties inflicted on French civilians, which amounted to 367 killed, and this was a problem which would never be satisfactorily addressed. It was somewhat paradoxical also, that Harris, as a champion of area bombing, should gain his first victory by way of a precision target.

Essen was to feature prominently in Harris's future plans, and he mounted three operations against this most important of industrial Ruhr cities on consecutive nights from the 8/9th. The leading aircraft were equipped for the first time with the new Gee navigation device, but the ever-present industrial haze made identification almost impossible, and all three raids were dismal failures. 1 Group contributed forty, sixty-two and thirty-one aircraft respectively, and lost a total of three. It was at this point that 460 Squadron was declared operational, and began what would be an illustrious career that few in the Command would surpass. Five of the squadron's aircraft joined up with thirty-five other Wellingtons and Whitleys on the night of the 12/13th to attack Emden. It was not a successful debut, and bombing photographs showed that no bombs fell within five miles of the target. However, a simultaneous attack on Kiel by sixty Wellingtons produced good results, including damage to two U-Boot construction yards. On the following night over a hundred aircraft took part in the first successful Gee-led raid on Cologne, while five freshman crews from 460 Squadron took part in a small-scale attack on Dunkerque.

This brought about the squadron's first operational loss after Z1251 crashed in Belgium, killing F/S Cooney and his crew. Thankfully, there would be no further losses for six weeks, and apart from a period of stand-down while it converted to Lancasters later in the year, this would be the squadron's longest ever break from casualties.

After a twelve-night stand-down through adverse weather conditions, the campaign against Essen continued on the 25/26th at the hands of a new record force of 254 aircraft. 109 of these were from 1 Group, and this represented its largest effort to date. Sadly, despite the commitment of such a large force, the result was the same as before, largely because of poor visibility, and only around sixty of the 1 Group participants reported bombing in the target area. 103 Squadron's R1393 was hit by flak and was ultimately ditched off the Suffolk coast without injury to the crew. A smaller force fared equally badly at Essen twenty-four hours later, and 12 Squadron lost its commanding officer, W/C Golding, whose Wellington W5372 was shot down by a night fighter over Holland on the way home, and there were no survivors.

The inability to identify Essen confirmed what Harris already knew, that navigating over a blacked-out, cloud-covered hostile country at night was a nightmare. However, he believed that if he could provide his crews with pin points on the ground, instead of forcing them to rely on dead-reckoning, they would do the rest. Coastlines offered the best reference points, and this was one of the considerations that led Harris to the Baltic port of Lübeck. Other inducements were the paucity of its defences, and the half-timbered construction of the buildings in its old centre, where the narrow streets would encourage the spread of fire. In a sign of things to come for Germany, Harris dispatched 234 aircraft on the night of the 28/29th, of which fifty-one represented 1 Group. The two-thirds incendiary bomb loads carried by the force reflected the fire-raising intention of the attack. The raid was conducted on similar lines to those employed against the Renault factory at the start of the month, and was equally effective. 30% of the city's built-up area was assessed as having been laid waste, and this amounted to over fourteen hundred buildings destroyed, with a further two thousand seriously damaged. This was the first major success for the area bombing policy, and it was achieved for the loss of twelve aircraft. Among them was 103 Squadron's R1061, which went into the sea and took with it P/O Ward and crew, who had crashed in the circuit on return from Emden at the end of November, and had clearly used up their ration of good fortune.

April

12 Squadron welcomed W/C Collard as its new commanding officer on the 1st of April, and that night he presided over his first operations and registered the squadron's first failure to return under his leadership. Five 12 Squadron Wellingtons took part in a small-scale attack on the Matford factory at Poissy, while a further four joined eleven other 1 Group aircraft in an overall force of fifty-six sent to bomb the docks at le Havre. It was from the latter operation that 12 Squadron's Sgt Woodhead and crew failed to return, although all survived, and one ultimately evaded capture. It was, in fact, a night of wildly varying fortunes in which 214 and 57 Squadrons of 3 Group lost seven and five aircraft respectively during operations against railway targets at Hanau and Lohr. Also on the 1st W/C Piotrowski concluded his term as commanding officer of 301 Squadron, and was succeeded by W/C Krzystyniak. Small-scale operations on the night of the 2/3rd involved twenty-seven Wellingtons from the Group attacking the Matford factory at Poissy again, while six others from 460 Squadron were detailed for le Havre. The 150 Squadron aircraft containing the crew of P/O Powell and the Snaith station commander, G/C Webb, failed to return from the former after crashing in France. The 1 Group ORB comments that X9814 was believed to have been shot down by or been in collision with an enemy night fighter, and only the rear gunner survived to be captured.

The first major operation of the month involved a new record force of 263 aircraft heading for Cologne on the 5/6th. 1 Group put up seventy-nine aircraft from all six of its operational stations, and their crews were briefed to aim at the Humbold Motoren A.G. This massive effort was not rewarded with success, however, and it left just a scattering of damage across the city. Essen again escaped lightly on the 6/7th, when appalling weather conditions prevented two thirds of the force from reaching the target area. Yet another new record was set on the 8/9th, when 272 aircraft took off for Hamburg, of which seventy-eight were provided by 1 Group. Icing conditions and electrical storms played their part in thwarting the crews, and only about fourteen bomb loads fell into the city. Two further raids were directed at Essen on the 10/11th and 12/13th, for which 1 Group put up seventy-five and seventy aircraft respectively, but each was a dismal failure, and this concluded a highly disappointing series of attacks on the home of the giant Krupp armaments producing concern. Another 103 Squadron Wellington, W5664, went into the sea during the last-mentioned operation, and took with it the crew of F/L Gillespie. Thus far, Harris had mounted eight heavy raids to Essen, amounting to 1,555 sorties for the loss of sixty-four aircraft, and although a thousand crews claimed to have bombed in the target area, little damage had been inflicted. 150 Squadron operated eight of its new Mk III Wellingtons on this night on a fresher operation to le Havre, and the crews expressed themselves delighted with the improvement in performance over the Mk1c.

Over two hundred aircraft took off for Dortmund on the 14/15th, and those reaching the Ruhr sprayed bombs over a wide area. The operation was repeated with similar results on the following night, before an attack on Hamburg on the 17/18th, which caused seventy-five fires, but no significant damage to war industry. Gee had proved useful as a navigation device, and in order to assess its potential as a blind bombing aid, an operation was mounted against Cologne on the 22/23rd employing sixty-four Wellingtons and five Stirlings. 1 Group's 150 Squadron was one of those newly equipped with the Gee or TR Wellington, and six of these participated in the operation. The experiment was deemed a failure when only about a quarter of the force found the mark, and the others dropped their bombs up to ten miles away.

In an attempt to repeat the success at Lübeck at the end of March, Harris dispatched the first of four raids on consecutive nights against Rostock, another port on the Baltic coast, on the 23/24th. The presence of a nearby Heinkel aircraft factory was an added attraction, and a small contingent was sent to attack it while the main raid was in progress. It was a disappointing start to the series, but matters were put right on the following night, when the centre of the town was heavily bombed, although the Heinkel factory again escaped damage. The third raid was equally successful, and this time, W/C Guy Gibson led a 106 Squadron element to the Heinkel factory, and scored some hits. 103 Squadron's DV579 failed to return with the crew of F/S Bray, and as no clue to their fate ever emerged, it must be assumed that the sea claimed them. The final raid took place on the night of the 26/27th, and this was also an accurate attack. Over the course of the four operations 1 Group launched 165 sorties, and these contributed to the destruction of over seventeen hundred buildings. This left an estimated 60% of the main town area in ruins for the modest overall loss of eight aircraft. While returning home close to the island of Sylt, the 460 Squadron Wellington captained by Sgt Kitchen was attacked by a BF110 night fighter, and two members of the crew sustained injuries. The aircraft also suffered severe damage to its flying surfaces, instruments and hydraulics, but despite this, the final four hundred miles across the sea were completed without further incident, and the aircraft was landed at base with punctured tyres. None of the crew received an award for their perseverance, and those returning uninjured would be lost in June. Such are the fortunes of war.

On the 27th W/C Bertram departed 142 Squadron on posting, and he was succeeded by W/C Simmons. Cologne hosted one of its more effective raids on the 27/28th at the hands of a predominantly Wellington force, and the type was also the most numerous employed against Kiel on the 28/29th, when all three shipyards were hit. The month's final operation was directed at the Gnome & Rhone aero engine works at Gennevilliers in Paris on the night of the 29/30th, for which 1 Group put up twenty-nine Wellingtons. Attacks were pressed home from altitudes varying from six thousand down to six hundred feet, and a number of hits were observed on the main target, and also on the power station, the Thompson-Houston works and the Goodrich Tyre factory. The total number of sorties dispatched by 1 Group for the month was 949.

May

May opened with a raid on Hamburg on the 3/4th by a modest fifty-four aircraft, out of the eighty-one originally dispatched, and the crews found the city completely cloud-covered, forcing them to drop their bombs on estimated positions. Despite this, over a hundred fires were started, and besides other damage, eleven blocks of flats were destroyed by the blast from a 4,000 pounder. This night brought the final sorties in Bomber Command by 304 Squadron, which was about to be transferred to Coastal Command. Three of its freshman crews were sent to deliver leaflets to the inhabitants of Paris, and all returned safely. On the following night the first of three raids on consecutive nights was mounted against Stuttgart, where the Bosch AG factory at Fuerbach was the main target for the twenty-four participating 1 Group aircraft. In the event, cloud thwarted all attempts to identify the target, and not one of the 1 Group crews found the aiming point. Under cover of this operation 103 Squadron sent F/S Arrowsmith and crew to drop nickels over Nantes, but on the way home Z8833 became the latest from the squadron to find the sea. When the Germans recovered the dinghy one week later, only the two gunners were alive to be taken into captivity. The second and third raids on Stuttgart were also disappointing in the extreme, for which ground haze was blamed, and the latter cost 460 Squadron two aircraft and one of its flight commanders. The 7th was the day on which 304 Squadron departed Bomber Command on transfer to Coastal Command.

On the 8/9th, almost two hundred aircraft, half of them Wellingtons, set out for the Baltic port of Warnemünde. Thirty-four aircraft from 1 Group were assigned to the town and its port facilities, while twelve others targeted the nearby Heinkel works. A further element was sent in to supress searchlight activity, and three of these were from 1 Group. All in all the night was a disaster, with inconclusive results and heavy losses amounting to nineteen aircraft, four of which were 44 Squadron Lancasters. Happily, 103 Squadron's contingent of eight all made it home safely. Minor operations occupied most of the next ten nights while 103 Squadron was stood down, and 300 Squadron moved from Hemswell to Ingham on the 18th. The first major operation for more than a week saw around two hundred aircraft fail almost entirely to hit the city of Mannheim on the 19/20th. A freshman crew was dispatched by 103 Squadron on this night to deliver leaflets to the occupants of Paris, while two others joined a mining effort in French waters and four more raided St Nazaire. The last-named cost the squadron F/L Rees and crew, who were killed when Z1141 was shot down in the target area.

Apart from the isolated notable successes already mentioned, the Command had failed to impress thus far under Harris, and voices in high places, particularly at the Admiralty, were still calling for bomber aircraft to be diverted to other theatres. When Harris took up the reins of command, he had asked for four thousand bombers with which to win the war. While there was not the slightest chance of getting them, he needed to ensure that those earmarked for him were not spirited away to what he considered to be less deserving causes. He required a major victory, and, perhaps, a dose of symbolism to silence the critics, and out of this was born the Thousand Plan, Operation Millennium. This called for the commitment of a thousand aircraft in one night to erase from the map an important German city, for which Hamburg had been pencilled in. Harris did not have a thousand frontline aircraft at his disposal, and he needed the support of other Commands, principally Coastal and Flying Training, to make up the numbers. This was forthcoming in letters to him on the 22nd and 23rd respectively, but following an intervention from the Admiralty, Coastal Command underwent a change of heart, and withdrew its contribution.

Undaunted as always, Harris, or more likely his able Deputy, AM Sir Robert Saundby, set about scraping together every airframe capable of controlled flight, or something close to it, and pulled in the screened crews from their instructional duties. Come the night, not only would the magic figure of one thousand be achieved, it would be comfortably surpassed. There was little operational activity after Mannheim, and the arrival on bomber stations from Yorkshire to East Anglia of aircraft from the training units during the final week of the month gave rise to much speculation. Only the weather remained in question, and as the days ticked by inexorably towards the end of May, it was showing no signs of cooperating. Harris was aware of the genuine danger, that such a large fleet of aircraft might draw attention to itself, and compromise security, and the point was fast being reached when the operation would either have to be launched, or be abandoned for the time being. On the 29/30th, he allowed seventy-seven aircraft to carry out another raid on the Gnome & Rhone aero-engine factory at Gennevilliers in Paris, to follow up the attack there a month earlier. As before, the operation failed, and five aircraft would not be available for Operation Millennium after failing to return. Two of these were 460 Squadron Wellingtons, both of which crashed in France. 103 squadron contributed four aircraft led by the commanding officer, and these all returned.

It was in a tense atmosphere of uncertainty and frustration that "morning prayers" began at Harris's High Wycombe HQ on the 30th, with all eyes turned on the chief meteorological adviser, Magnus Spence. After deliberating for some time, he was able to give a qualified assurance of clear weather over the Rhineland after midnight, while north-western Germany and Hamburg would be concealed under buckets of cloud. Thus did the fickle finger of fate swing away from Germany's Second City, and point unerringly at Cologne as the host for the first one thousand bomber raid in history. One of the concerns for the planners had been the risk of collisions over the target as the unprecedented concentration of at least ten aircraft per minute funnelled towards the aiming point during the intended ninety-minute duration of the raid. At the pre-op briefings crews were informed that the experts had predicted that just two aircraft would collide over the target. It is reported, that at least one "wag" asked whether the statisticians knew which two aircraft would be involved! Whether or not they did, their prediction proved to be accurate.

On the 27th 103 Squadron had been joined at Elsham Wolds by eleven Wellingtons from 22 O.T.U. at Wellesbourne Mountford in Warwickshire, and the latter were among the first of 1047 assorted aircraft to take off for Germany at around 22.30 hours. Some of the older training hacks took somewhat reluctantly to the air, and were lifted more by the enthusiasm of their crews than by the power of their engines. A few of these, unable to climb to a respectable height, would fall easy prey to the defences, or just drop from the sky through mechanical failure. 1 Group's effort was significant, 12 Squadron making the greatest contribution of the night when putting up a magnificent twenty-eight Wellingtons from Binbrook. Inevitably, a number of these aircraft would return early for a variety of reasons. 103 Squadron contributed nineteen Wellingtons, one of them containing the station commander, G/C Constantine, who had volunteered to stand in for a sick flight commander. 150 Squadron launched seventeen Wellingtons from Snaith, 460 Squadron put up a creditable eighteen, one of which returned early, and the Polish element of 300, 301 and 305 Squadrons contributed a combined total of forty-one Wellingtons from Ingham, Hemswell and Lindholme respectively. 1,400 tons of bombs reigned down on the target during the three wave operation, which was an outstanding success by any standards, and resulted in the destruction of over 3,300 buildings, with a further two thousand seriously damaged.

A new record of forty-one aircraft failed to return, but in conditions favourable to both attackers and defenders alike, and in the context of the size of the force, this was an acceptable loss of 3.9%. 12 Squadron sustained the heaviest losses of any individual unit that night, Sgt Everatt and crew perishing before they even reached the English coast outbound after Z8598 blew up over Norfolk and crashed. F/L Payne and crew were shot down over Holland in W5361 and all died, and P/O Waddell and his crew were also killed when Z8376 crashed in Germany. As Z8643 crossed over from Holland into Germany it experienced an overheating engine, which soon burst into flames. P/O Shearer ordered the bomb load to be jettisoned before calling for the mixed Australian/Kiwi crew to abandon ship. Three got away without difficulty, but the rear gunner "Kid" Gane was beginning to panic as he struggled to release his harness. Composing himself he eventually succeeded, but before he had time to evacuate his turret the Wellington pitched into a dive and spin, trapping him against his guns. Suddenly the spinning stopped, and he was thrown out backwards, hitting the ground almost immediately, but, miraculously, without sustaining injury. Later on he was invited to identify the body of his captain, which was shown to him sympathetically by his captors. Shearer had been the last to leave the Wellington, and did so with too little height for his parachute to deploy. Like so many pilots before and after him, he died trying to ensure the safety of his crew.

103 squadron was not exempt from the casualties, Sgt Onions and crew failing to return in DV452, and it was later learned that all had died. Perhaps the loneliest death on this night was that of Sgt Roberts, a new man flying as a "spare bod" with S/L Saxilby. He was killed by a flak splinter while standing in the astrodome, the only fatality in the aircraft, which, despite a fierce fire in the fuselage, made it home in one piece. On return Sgt Flowers diverted to Kirmington in R1234, and took off on the following morning to return to Elsham Wolds. Almost immediately an engine failure caused the Wellington to stall and crash, killing the pilot and three of his crew. 460 Squadron came through unscathed, and the ground crews busied themselves in preparations for another maximum effort raid two nights hence. The total number of 1 Group sorties for the month was 504.

June

Wishing to capitalize on his success, Harris determined to use the Thousand force again as soon as possible, and selected Essen as the target for the night of the 1/2nd of June. Only 956 aircraft were available to answer the call to arms, and 12 Squadron again put up the largest effort in 1 Group with twenty-three Wellingtons in an overall total of 137. In contrast to the raid on Cologne, this operation followed the same pattern as past attempts on Essen, and bombs were distributed all over the Ruhr, with few falling where intended. Only eleven houses were destroyed at a cost of thirty-one aircraft, three of them from 1 Group, and while all eighteen 103 Squadron crews came home, 460 Squadron was represented among the missing by two aircraft. A follow-up raid by under two hundred aircraft twenty-four hours later failed to bring any improvement, and 460 Squadron again posted missing two crews. Harris switched his force to Bremen on the 3/4th, and produced the best result yet at this target, but he was determined to nail Essen, and returned there on the 5/6th with 180 aircraft to register yet another failure. 103 Squadron posted missing F/L Morison and crew in DV699, which crashed in Germany after colliding with another aircraft, and only the pilot survived.

Before Harris tried again at Essen, he sent over two hundred aircraft to Emden on the 6/7th, where three hundred houses were destroyed. He would attempt to capitalize on this success with three further raids later in the month. 170 aircraft set out for Essen on the 8/9th, and they produced another widely scattered raid for the loss of nineteen aircraft. This target had already cost 460 Squadron four aircraft during the month, before a fifth was lost raiding it on this night. 103 Squadron also registered a failure to return in the form of P/O Firman and crew, who were all killed when DV773 was shot down by a night fighter over Holland. Thus far during the month 1,600 sorties had been launched against Essen for the loss of eighty-four aircraft, and there was little to show for it. After a period of minor operations, 106 aircraft were detailed for a return to Essen on the 16/17th, but only sixteen crews reported bombing as briefed, and many of the others found alternative targets, mostly Bonn.

After two hugely disappointing series of operations against Essen since becoming C-in-C, Harris would now turn his attention elsewhere, and he carried out three attacks on Emden in the space of four nights beginning on the 19/20th. Neither this operation nor the one on the following night repeated the success of the earlier raid, and the former cost 460 Squadron the crew of the previously mentioned Sgt Kitchen, who were all killed in Z1486. W/C Beill concluded his tour in command of 305 Squadron on the

21st, and he was replaced by W/C Sniegula. On the 21/22nd, fifty-six crews were dispatched to lay mines in French coastal waters off St Nazaire, and the single loss was another 460 Squadron Wellington. The night of the 22/23rd brought the third of the current series against Emden, and it cost 103 Squadron it's A Flight commander, S/L Godfrey, who was killed with four of his crew when DV818 was shot down off the Dutch coast. Mining operations were a constant feature of activity, particularly for freshman crews, and two were posted missing from 103 Squadron during an effort in Frisian waters on the 23/24th. T2921 crashed into the sea with no survivors from the crew of Sgt Emmott, and Sgt Vickery and crew were lost without trace in DV831.

The final outing for the Thousand force was to Bremen on the 25/26th, when 960 aircraft and crews answered the call for a maximum effort, among them 111 from 1 Group. This time 150 Squadron topped the Group's effort with twenty-one Wellingtons. Ordered by Churchill to participate, Coastal Command contributed 102 aircraft, in what was classed as a separate operation, but the numbers converging on the target exceeded those going to Cologne at the end of May. While not achieving the success of that operation, the results at Bremen far surpassed the Essen debacle, and 572 houses were destroyed, while over six thousand others sustained varying degrees of damage, and a number of shipyards and other war industry factories were hit. The Command registered a new record loss of forty-eight aircraft, but only two were from 1 Group. The Wellington of 301 Squadron's commanding officer, W/C Krzystyniak, was hit by flak over the target, and he and his crew were forced to parachute into the arms of their captors. 103 and 460 Squadrons dispatched fifteen and twenty Wellingtons respectively, and all made it home, although 460's P/O Falkiner was attacked first by a JU88, which the rear gunner claimed as destroyed, and then by two single engine fighters. W/C Brzozowski became the new commanding officer of 301 Squadron on the 26th, but would barely have time to settle in. The month ended with two smaller-scale follow-up raids on Bremen on the 27/28th and 29/30th, both of which resulted in some useful industrial damage. W/C Mellor stepped down as commanding officer of 150 Squadron on the 29th, and he was succeeded by W/C E J Carter. *(Not to be confused with the earlier c.o. W/C RAC Carter)*. The group launched 930 sorties during the month.

July

It fell to Bremen also to open the July account on the 2/3rd, for which 1 Group contributed ninety-one aircraft. Damage was again quite widespread, and a number of ships were hit in the port, but the operation cost 1 Group seven aircraft, among them the 301 Squadron Wellington containing the commanding officer and his crew. Badly damaged by a night fighter over Holland, the Wellington had to be abandoned, and once on the ground W/C Brzozowski managed to evade capture for four days. W/C Kolodziejek became the new commanding officer, and his period of tenure would last less than three months. June had been an expensive month for 460 Squadron, with the loss of seven aircraft and crews, and when two more failed to return on this night, it boded ill for the new month. 103 Squadron also posted missing two of its own after R1617 was caught by a night fighter, and Sgt Spooner and two of his crew were killed, and P/O Little and three of his crew lost their lives in DV611. As events were to prove, this was the final operation undertaken by the squadron on Wellingtons.

By the middle of 1942 plans were afoot to convert the whole of 1 Group to the Halifax, and 103 Squadron was selected as the first to receive the type. A little later 460 Squadron would also begin training on Halifaxes, but would not achieve operational status before a change in policy decreed that the group would operate Lancasters instead. On the 7th 103 Squadron Heavy Conversion Unit was formed under S/L Holford, and the process of working up got under way in earnest. There was little further operational activity during the first half of the month, other than a raid on Wilhelmshaven on the 8/9th, which 1 Group supported with fifty-eight Wellingtons. Some damage was inflicted, but generally the bombing missed the target. On the 9th W/C Sulinski was succeeded as commander of 300 Squadron by W/C Dukszto, who unlike his predecessors was a navigator rather than a pilot. 460 Squadron lost another Wellington to mining on the 12/13th, and no trace of it was ever found.

On the 13/14th, Harris began a five raid series against Duisburg over a three and a half week period, and found it equally as elusive as its neighbour Essen. The weather was partly responsible on this night, and only eleven houses were destroyed by the force of almost two hundred aircraft, which included seventy-five from 1 Group. Daylight cloud-cover operations on the 16th, 17th and 19th involved two, seven and seven aircraft respectively from 150 Squadron carrying out nuisance raids on Essen. Only four sorties were completed as briefed, and no results were observed. The second operation to Duisburg was mounted on the 21/22nd, when 253 crews reported bombing as briefed, of which sixty-six were from 1 Group. Ninety-four buildings were destroyed, which represented an improvement, but was still a poor return for the effort expended. It was a similar story on the 23/24th and 25/26th, and the latter occasion brought more casualties for 460 Squadron. Both crashed in Germany, and flight commander S/L Leighton was among those to lose their lives. This operation also cost 12 Squadron its commanding officer, W/C Collard, whose Z8591 was damaged by flak in the target area. It became necessary to part company with the Wellington over Holland on the way home, pitching him and three of his crew into enemy hands, where they were joined by one of the Squadron's flight commanders, S/L Lemon, and four of his crew. On the 26/27th Hamburg was the victim of perhaps the most effective attack of the war after Cologne, and suffered the destruction of over eight hundred houses, while more than five hundred large fires had to be dealt with. 1 Group contributed eighty-three Wellingtons to the four hundred strong force, of which seven were among the twenty-nine failures to return, two of them from 460 Squadron at Breighton. On the 27th the former commanding officer of 142 Squadron, W/C Kippenberger, was promoted to group captain and posted from HQ 1 Group to become station commander at Wattisham.

Rarely was conversion training accomplished without accidents, and 103 Squadron's first loss of a Halifax occurred on the 28th, when W1218 stalled and crashed near Louth in Lincolnshire, killing Sgt Stockford and his crew. The month ended with two very effective operations, the first against Saarbrücken on the 29/30th, when almost four hundred buildings were destroyed, and Düsseldorf on the night of the 31st. This raid included a sizeable contribution from the training units, enabling an overall figure of 630 aircraft to take part, of which 484 crews claimed to have bombed in the target area. 1 Group provided eighty-four aircraft, including seven Halifaxes of 103 Squadron on its return to operations following conversion. Some of the bombing spilled over into nearby Neuss, and a total of 453 buildings were destroyed in the two locations, and over nine hundred fires were started.

It was a promising start for 103 squadron, whose aircraft all returned safely, but it would turn out to be a false dawn. The Halifax would not find favour with the crews, and none would complete a tour on the type. It had been another expensive month for 460 Squadron, with the loss again of seven crews, and the coming month would be only marginally better. It had been even worse for 12 Squadron, which had lost a total of twelve aircraft and nine crews. It now also had a new commanding officer in the form of W/C Dabinett, who had been appointed on the 30th. He had previously commanded 3 Group's 115 Squadron between June 1940 and January 1941. The group sortie total for the month reached 796.

August

It was not long before August claimed its first 460 Squadron crew, and this was another one lost to a mining sortie. The final raid of the Duisburg series came and went on the 6/7th without any improvement in bombing accuracy. 1 Group dispatched forty-two aircraft, of which two failed to return, and this night also brought the first operational loss of a 103 Squadron Halifax. It seems that W1225 suffered technical difficulties shortly after take-off, and crashed in the Humber while P/O Gilby was attempting to return to base. There were no survivors. The next operation was a useful attack on Osnabrück on the 9/10th, for which 1 Group dispatched forty-six aircraft. The attack left over two hundred houses destroyed, but another 460 Squadron Wellington was one of six missing aircraft. Two effective raids fell on Mainz on the 11/12th and 12/13th, supported by thirty-three and thirty-seven 1 Group aircraft respectively. Central districts and industrial areas were heavily damaged, and it was estimated that 135 acres of the town had been destroyed. 460 Squadron posted missing yet another crew, which, it was later learned, had failed to survive the crash in Belgium.

A new era began on the 15th, with the formation of the Pathfinder Force under the then G/C Don Bennett, an Australian with unparalleled experience as an airman and navigator. Harris had been opposed in principle to the formation of an elite target finding and marking force, a view shared by all but his 4 Group commander, AVM Roddy Carr. Among Harris's supporters was AVM Baldwin of 3 Group, under whose control the new outfit would nominally fall, and upon whose stations it would lodge somewhat uneasily for the time being. The four founder heavy squadrons, which each represented a group from which they would draw fresh recruits, were 7, 35, 83 and 156 Squadrons, and they moved into their new stations on this day to begin preparations for their operational debut. Once overruled by higher authority, Harris, in typical fashion, gave the Pathfinders his unstinting support, and his choice of Bennett, a relatively junior officer as its leader, although controversial, would prove to be inspired. A matter of great significance for the future success of the Command was the posting to the Pathfinders at the same time of 109 Squadron, which would spend the remainder of the year marrying the Oboe blind-bombing device to its Mosquitos, and ironing out the technical problems. This magnificent pioneering work under W/C Hal Bufton would bear fruit in the coming year, and enable the Command to hit effectively at the hitherto elusive Ruhr towns and cities.

On the night of the new force's formation 1 Group contributed forty-two aircraft to an attack on Düsseldorf, where few found an aiming point in the hazy conditions, and most bombed on D.R. (dead reckoning). It was on the night of the 18/19th that the fledgling Pathfinder Force led its first raid on Germany, for which the port of Flensburg was selected. A force of a little over a hundred aircraft included eighteen from 1 Group. The target's location in Schleswig-Holstein, on the narrow neck of land where Germany and Denmark meet, should have made it relatively simple to find, but in the event, no bombs fell within miles, while a number of Danish towns reported being hit. It was an inauspicious beginning to what would become an illustrious career for the Pathfinders, and matters proceeded equally disappointingly at Frankfurt on the 24/25th, when 1 Group put up fifty aircraft. It was not until the third Pathfinder-led operation, to Kassel on the 27/28th, that the target was identified and illuminated sufficiently for the main force crews to find the mark, and a moderate amount of damage was inflicted. Any sense of success was marred by a 10% loss rate, and there were fourteen aircraft missing from the ninety-three dispatched by 1 Group. 12 Squadron posted missing four aircraft, two of them the first Wellington Mk IIIs to be lost by the squadron, and 103 squadron's F/L Frith and crew were all killed when W1270 was shot down by a night fighter over Holland. This was not a happy night either for 460 Squadron, which posted missing two more crews.

On the following night, while a force of 159 aircraft was engaged over Nuremberg, 113 others targeted Saarbrücken, and failed to inflict more than scattered superficial damage. 103 Squadron sent seven Halifaxes to the main target, and two of them failed to return. BB204 was shot down by a night fighter over Belgium on the way home, and W/O Telfer died with three of his crew, while the three survivors were soon captured by the enemy. They were joined as PoWs by Sgt Dryhurst and two of his crew after BB214 also fell victim to a night fighter. Meanwhile, another 460 Squadron Wellington did not return to Breighton, and was lost without trace. Back in June, 460 Squadron had been told to prepare to convert onto Halifaxes, and the 460 Squadron Conversion Flight had been established at Holme-on-Spalding-Moor on the 22nd of May. This organisation would move to Breighton in September, having received its first Halifaxes in late August, but operations with Wellingtons would continue into October. 516 sorties were mounted by the group during the month.

September

The Pathfinders posted a "black" on the 1/2nd of September, when marking the non-industrial town of Saarlouis in error for nearby Saarbrücken, and much to the chagrin of its inhabitants, the main force bombing was unusually accurate. It could have been an ill-omen for the month, but from this point on, the Command embarked on an unprecedented series of effective operations, which would take it through the first two weeks. 460 Squadron began the month with a new commanding officer, after the long standing W/C Hubbard was posted out. W/C Keith Kaufman was one of hundreds of Australians serving with the RAF before the war, and on that fateful morning almost three years to the day before he took up his appointment as the new commanding officer, he had been stooging around at 2-3,000 feet between base and the airfield at Carew Cheriton. He was basking in the sunshine, when the wireless operator passed up a note, which read, "war declared 11.02 hours." Kaufman's immediate reaction was to question his presence in England with a war on, when he should be back home in Australia. Never-the-less, like the rest of his countrymen, he remained over here to give magnificent service to this country and to Bomber Command.

Kaufman presided over his first operation as the 460 Squadron commander on the night of his appointment, the 2/3rd, when Karlsruhe was the destination for two hundred aircraft, forty-six of them from 1 Group. The Pathfinders identified and illuminated the target, and returning crews claimed to have seen two hundred fires burning in the city. Two nights later at Bremen, the Pathfinders introduced the three-phase system of illuminators, visual markers and backers up, and 470 buildings were destroyed, while thousands of other sustained varying degrees of damage. The losses continued for 103 Squadron with the failure to return of W1220 and its crew captained by Sgt Davies, none of whom survived the crash in Holland. 114 buildings were destroyed in Duisburg on the 6/7th, and while this was a modest return, it still represented something of a victory at this target. 103 Squadron posted missing the experienced flight commander, S/L Saxilby, but he and all but two of his eight-man crew survived, and one ultimately evaded capture.

The run of successes was temporarily halted at Frankfurt on the 8/9th, when most of the bombs missed the mark altogether, but a return to winning ways would come with the next operation. On the 9th W/C Du Boulay was posted to 1 Group HQ at the end of his tour in command of 103 Squadron, and he was succeeded by W/C Carter, who went in the opposite direction. He was already an experienced squadron commander, having been at the helm of 1 Group's 150 Squadron between June and December 1941. 479 aircraft took off for Düsseldorf on the 10/11th, a number which included sixty-two 1 Group aircraft as well as an element from the training groups. The Pathfinders employed pink pansies as target indicators for the first time, and the result was the destruction of over nine hundred houses and eight public buildings in the city and nearby Neuss. Many industrial premises also sustained damage, but it was not a one-sided affair, and it turned into a good night also for the defenders. Thirty-three aircraft failed to return, and among them was a 460 Squadron Wellington, which was actually the squadron's second loss of the night, after R1695 suffered engine failure while outbound, and crashed into the sea fifteen miles off Cromer ninety minutes after take-off. The pilot and two others went down with the Wellington, but the remaining two were rescued with only slight injuries.

The 13/14th brought Bremen's second heavy raid of the month, in which over eight hundred houses were destroyed, and its industry suffered extensive damage. Delivered by a force of something over four hundred aircraft, of which fifty-seven were supplied by 1 Group, this surpassed the level of destruction achieved by the thousand force back in June. 460 Squadron's Z1385 failed to return to Breighton, and it was later established that F/S Brasher and his crew had lost their lives. It was a particularly tragic loss, this crew having brought back a badly damaged Wellington from the Düsseldorf raid, after it was attacked by a night fighter. The rear gunner had seen their assailant fall away in flames, and the pilot was awarded an immediate DFM for his airmanship. This was, at least, the final Wellington casualty for the squadron, which was shortly to be stood-down to allow full conversion training to take place.

The run of successes continued at Wilhelmshaven on the 14/15th, which registered its most destructive raid of the war to date, and this was the final operation for 460 Squadron as a Wellington unit. Even Essen did not escape when attacked on the 16/17th, reporting its worst night of the war thus far, although the Command suffered the heavy loss of thirty-nine aircraft for its troubles. Four of the missing were from among the thirty-two dispatched by 1 Group, and 142 Squadron had to post missing three of its crews. The group's final operation of the month against a German target came on the night of the 19/20th, when thirty-five aircraft joined elements from other groups to attack Saarbrücken. Thereafter there was a steady diet of mining operations to see the month out. It can be no coincidence that the highly effective series of operations during the first two weeks of the month came at a time when the Pathfinders were emerging from their shaky start, and the crews were coming to terms with the complexities of their demanding role. It would not be an overnight transformation, and failures would continue to outnumber successes for some time to come. The encouraging signs were there, however, and it boded ill for Germany's industrial heartland in the coming year.

The almost inevitable first loss of a 460 Squadron crew undergoing Halifax conversion training involved DT481, a new aircraft delivered around the 22nd of August. It crashed in Lincolnshire on the 19th of September, killing Sgt Solomons and the other seven men on board, all but one of whom were RAAF. Happily, this would be one of only two major incidents during the working up period, which, as far as the Halifax was concerned, was to be short-lived. The more experienced 460 Squadron pilots were able to undergo their conversion training at Breighton, once the Conversion Flight moved there on the 24th of September, while the others were dispatched to 1656 Conversion Flight at Lichfield, where a number of Manchesters were in use. On the day after the Conversion Flight's move to Breighton, it was ordered to dispose of its Halifaxes, and to prepare to receive Lancasters, the type now selected to re-equip 1 Group. It was a popular move, and the crews over at 103 Squadron shed no tears at the departure of the much disliked "Halibag", on which no crews had survived to complete a tour. On the 25th 12 Squadron completed its move from Binbrook, where it had been in residence for two years, and settled in at Wickenby, which would be its home for the remainder of the war. 301 Squadron, meanwhile, was welcoming a new commanding officer on this day, as W/C Dabrowa succeeded W/C Kolodziejek, and as events were to prove, he would be the unit's final commander. On the 29th, the 460 Squadron Conversion Flight was absorbed into 1656 HCU, and its eight Halifaxes were transferred to 460 Squadron proper, until the arrival of Lancasters. On this same day 101 Squadron moved into Holme-on-Spalding-Moor with its Wellingtons under the command of W/C Eaton, and officially joined the ranks of 1 Group. On the following day ten crews were packed off to 1654 HCU at Wigsley to begin training on Lancasters, while the remainder stayed behind to continue operations on Wellingtons. 101 Squadron had begun the war as a 2 Group Blenheim unit, before converting to Wellingtons and transferring to 3 Group early in July 1941. The group launched 662 sorties during the month.

October

101 Squadron's Stirling Conversion Flight was absorbed into 1657 HCU on the 1st of October, and when Lancaster R5842 arrived on the 11th, the squadron would become the twelfth to receive the type. In the meantime, operations continued for the rest of the Command, and the month's bombing account began at Krefeld on the night of the 2/3rd. 101 Squadron launched its maiden sorties under 1 Group, when providing four Wellingtons to an overall contribution by the group of fifty-eight aircraft.

103 Squadron was soldiering on with its Halifaxes, and it lost another of these to a poor raid on Aachen on the night of the 5/6th, when W1216 was shot down by a night fighter over Belgium on the way home. W/O Edwards and two of his crew lost their lives, but four others survived as PoWs and a fifth evaded capture. The first 460 Squadron Lancaster, W4273, was taken on charge later on the 6th, and the squadron thus became the eleventh operational unit to receive the type. 103 Squadron posted missing the crew of Sgt Porter following a raid on Osnabrück on the 6/7th, and it was later established that W1189 had fallen victim to a night fighter off the Frisians.

A modestly effective attack on Kiel on the 13/14th was followed by a disappointing effort at Cologne two nights later, the latter claiming two more 103 Squadron Halifaxes and crews. There were no survivors from the crew of F/L Parker in W1213, and just one man escaped with his life from the crew of F/L Winchester in W7850. This operation was the last to be conducted by 101 Squadron on Wellingtons, and as it had not been screened during the Lancaster working up period, a total of eight operations involving thirty-seven sorties had been undertaken on Wellingtons since joining the group. Despite being away from the operational scene, death continued to stalk 460 Squadron. On the 19th one of the 1656 C.U. Manchesters, R5780, crashed on the main Lichfield to Burton-on-Trent road, killing P/Os Wood, Forrester and Murphy. 101 Squadron's converted crews returned to Holme-on-Spalding-Moor on this day, and there would be fourteen Lancasters on charge by the end of the month.

It was at this juncture that a campaign began in support of Operation Torch, the Allied landings in North Africa, which would ultimately lead to Montgomery's victory over Rommel at El Alamein. Bomber Command's role was to carry out an assault on the major cities in Italy, and fifteen such operations would be mounted between the 22/23rd of October and the 11/12th of December. The 103 Squadron Halifax swansong came at Milan on the night of the 24/25th, in what proved to be an unsatisfactory operation, that cost the squadron two more crews. It was during this period also that Australian navigator Don Charlwood was serving with the squadron as a member of Geoff Maddern's crew. They had arrived in the Autumn, late in the Halifax period, and in his superb book, No Moon Tonight, Charlwood describes the lead up to this final Halifax operation, and talks about S/L Fox, the young flight commander, whose life was about to end. It had been Fox who had announced to an ecstatic and uproarious briefing room that the Halifax was about to be replaced by the Lancaster. Charlwood would later admit that the belief in the invulnerability of the Lancaster was somewhat misplaced, but it would prove to be a considerable improvement on the Mk II Halifax. Fox's W1188 was caught by a night fighter over France, and Fox and four of his crew were killed. Two of the survivors were picked up by the enemy, but Dizzy Spiller, the squadron character and reputedly the scruffiest man at Elsham Wolds, managed to evade capture, and return to the squadron some months later, when the Maddern crew was one of only two left who had been present at Fox's momentous announcement. Prior to his temporary disappearance, Spiller had often recounted the tale of how he had guided "Connie" or G/C Constantine, the incumbent station commander, to Cologne on the night of the first one thousand bomber raid at the end of May. Also missing from Milan was Sgt Claridge and his crew, who failed to survive the crash in France of W1223. This night also brought 12 Squadron's final loss of a Wellington, when W5394 failed to return from a mining sortie in French waters.

On the 26th 150 Squadron moved out of Snaith and took up residence at Kirmington, from where it would mostly be required to carry out mining and moling duties, and launched its first sorties from its new home on the 28/29th. Moling was a pointless exercise that involved sending small numbers of aircraft by daylight to carry out nuisance raids. The squadron sent three Wellingtons to Emden on the 31st, and not one completed its assigned task. Two were shot down by fighters over Holland, and all ten crew members were killed. W/C Dukszto completed his tour as commanding officer of 300 Squadron on the 31st, and he was succeeded by W/C Kropinski. The number of sorties by the group during the month dropped to 554.

November

W/C Simmons was posted from 142 Squadron on the 1st to take up duties at the Department of the Chief of the Air Staff. He was succeeded on the same day by W/C Bamford, who arrived from 27 O.T.U. W4318 became the first Lancaster to be taken on charge by 103 Squadron on the 1st of November, making it the thirteenth in the Command to be so equipped, and would be fully up to strength and ready for operations by the 21st. Lancaster ED386 was the first of the type to join 12 Squadron, which it did on the 8th, making 12 Squadron the fourth in the group and fourteenth in the command to be so equipped. Although 460 Squadron got its hands on Lancasters a few days before 101 and 103 Squadrons, it would be 101 Squadron that won the unofficial race to carry out the first 1 Group Lancaster operation. In the meantime the month began with mining operations, and during this period on the 7th, five Wellington squadrons were either formed or reformed within Bomber Command. Of these 199

Squadron was destined for 1 Group, and took up residence at Blyton, whither acting S/L Hattersley was posted from HQ 1 Group to take command as an acting wing commander. It would operate the Wellington Mk X, and the first examples, BJ819, BJ960, BK366 and BK367, arrived on the 10th, to be followed by eleven more by the 22nd.

The first bombing operation of the month against a German target came on the 9/10th, when Hamburg was the destination. 1 Group contributed forty-five Wellingtons, including eleven each from 142 and 150 Squadrons, whose time with Bomber Command under their present guise was approaching its end. On the 13th 150 Squadron dispatched three crews to Emden for another moling operation. One actually completed its assigned task, the first to do so from thirteen sorties wasted on this type of operation thus far, and, thankfully, there would be no more for this squadron. On the 16th 101 Squadron suffered its first Lancaster casualty, when W4236 crashed in Wales while on a training flight, and Sgt Spinney and his crew were killed. They had survived a crash-landing back in August when returning from Kassel. The operational debut for 101 Squadron Lancasters should have come on the night of the 18/19th, when eight aircraft were made ready for a trip to Turin, but it was cancelled. Two nights later the same target was the destination for a force of over two hundred aircraft, thirty-five of them from 1 Group, including eight Lancasters of 101 Squadron led by W/C Eaton. All of the Lancasters reached and bombed the target, and two thirds of the Wellington element, which had departed from forward bases in southern England, also attacked as briefed. On the following night 103 Squadron sent six crews mining in the Bay of Biscay to begin its Lancaster career. It was also the first time that 1 Group had used Lancasters to deliver mines.

It was a further twenty-four hours before 460 Squadron went to war in Lancasters for the first time, and this was as part of a 220-strong force bound for the difficult target of Stuttgart. The squadron contingent was led into the air by flight commander S/L Osborn DFC, who returned safely from what was a disappointing debut effort, after haze over the target prevented precision marking by the Pathfinders. In a foretaste of the heavy losses to be suffered by the squadron during its Lancaster career, its very first casualty occurred on this night. W4273, the first Lancaster to be taken on charge, failed to return home, but happily, P/O Galt and his entire crew survived. The pilot and two others ultimately evaded capture, and Galt returned home six weeks later to be posted to Coastal Command, with which he was lost on his first operation. The final major operation of the month was again directed at Turin, when 1 Group put up a record twenty-six Lancasters from 101, 103 and 460 Squadron. On the 28th W/C Carter concluded his period in command of 150 Squadron. He would rejoin the operational scene in January 1944 when appointed to command 97 Squadron of the Pathfinders, but, sadly, he would be lost with his crew during the early hours of D-Day, on the 6th of June. The number of sorties for the month fell again to 446, of which 265 were in support of mining operations.

December

On the 1st 142 and 150 Squadrons were stood down from operations, and W/C Barclay succeeded W/C Carter as the new commanding officer of the latter. An echelon was prepared for overseas duties in North Africa, and on the 9th W/C Kirwan led thirteen crews as they departed England via Portreath in tropicalized Wellingtons. They were bound for Blida in Algeria, where they would become established by the 19th and joined by similar numbers from 142 Squadron, which set out from England on the 18th. The remnants of the two squadrons remained at home and began the task of rebuilding. The first loss of a 103 Squadron Lancaster occurred on the night of the 2/3rd of December, when Frankfurt was the intended target for a force of over a hundred aircraft, of which fourteen were from Elsham Wolds. In hazy conditions most of the bombing found wooded and open country, and W4339 was lost with the crew of F/O Cumming. Mannheim escaped serious damage at the hands of 250 aircraft, including twelve from Elsham Wolds, on the night of the 6/7th, when 101 Squadron registered its first operational Lancaster casualty. ED322 crashed off the Welsh coast on return, and there were no survivors from the crew of P/O Dabbs. 199 Squadron made its operational debut on this operation, and all seven of its aircraft returned safely. Ten 103 Squadron crews returned to the Baltic to lay mines on the 8/9th, and twelve went to Turin on the 9/10th as part of a 1 Group contingent of thirty-nine Lancasters and Wellingtons. W/C Hattersley was piloting BK514, one of two participating 199 Squadron aircraft on this night. It was hit by flak shortly after crossing the French coast outbound, causing an engine fire, and it became necessary to abandon it to its fate thirty miles or so south of Paris. One man died, but Hattersley and four others were taken into captivity, and this was the squadron's first operational casualty. He was succeeded as commanding officer by W/C Blomfield. Turin was again the target for seven Lancasters each from 101 and 460 Squadrons on the 11/12th, but it was a less effective operation than that of forty-eight hours earlier.

A new squadron joined 1 Group's ranks on the 15th at Walsham, which was a satellite of Elsham Wolds, and would eventually have its name changed to Grimsby. 100 Squadron became the 17th in the Command to receive the Lancaster, and its first example, ED553, was received on the 12th of January. W/C Swain was posted in from 27 O.T.U., and installed as the first commanding officer on Boxing Day, having stopped off at 1656 HCU to convert to Lancasters. He was an experienced officer, whose Mention in Dispatches had been gazetted in September 1941. It was during another mining operation that 103 Squadron's next loss occurred, P/O Smith and crew perishing when W4786 crashed on Danish soil on the 17/18th, and many houses were wrecked by the detonation of a mine. 142 Squadron completed its move from Grimsby on the 19th to make way for 100 Squadron, and joined up with 150 Squadron at Kirmington. When Duisburg provided the target on the 20/21st, returning crews claimed a successful operation. Absent from debriefing, however, was the crew of 103 Squadron's F/S Moriarty, whose W4334 had been shot down over Holland without survivors.

Almost unnoticed while this main operation was in progress, six 109 Squadron Mosquitos carried out the first Oboe raid, for which a power station at Lutterade in Holland was the target. The operation was to serve as a calibration exercise, but this was thwarted, when photographic reconnaissance revealed a mass of craters left by misdirected bombs from a recent attack on Aachen, and it proved impossible to plot those delivered by Oboe. The Oboe trials would continue into the New Year, and would ultimately prove to be vital in the success of the Command's spring offensive. Most, if not all, of the bombs intended for Munich on the following night fell into open country, and Sgt Bayliss was the sole survivor of his crew after 103 Squadron's W4820 crashed in France. Suffering a similar fate, all of F/L Rose's crew died in the wreckage of W4787, and these were 103 Squadron's final casualties of the year. W/C Kaufman concluded his brief spell in command of 460 Squadron, and was succeeded on the 14th by W/C Dilworth. It had been a testing year for 460 Squadron in particular, which registered the loss of twenty-nine Wellingtons and one Lancaster from nine months of operations. This, however, was but a foretaste of things to come for the Australians in 1943, when Bomber Command would embark on a series of major campaigns against industrial Germany. 276 sorties were carried out during the month, broken down as six day bombing, 170 night bombing and a hundred mining.

1943

January

The first two weeks of January were dominated by the continuing Oboe trials program, involving the Mosquitos of 109 Squadron and Lancasters from 1 and 5 Groups. Essen would feature on seven occasions during this period, and Duisburg once, but the group's first operational activity involved twelve Wellingtons of 199, 301 and 305 Squadrons laying mines off the French coast on the night of the 2/3rd. The first of the small-scale operations against Essen took place on the following night, when only nineteen Lancasters were employed. 1 Group was not involved, but instead sent seventeen Lancasters and fourteen Wellingtons on mining sorties. The ten sorties by 12 Squadron Lancasters represented its operational debut on the type. On the following night twenty-nine 1 Group Lancasters formed the main force at Essen, and forty-two buildings were destroyed for the loss of two aircraft. One of these was 101 Squadron's W4796, which disappeared without trace with the crew of F/S Waterhouse. 1 and 5 Groups each provided twenty-five Lancasters for Essen on the 9/10th, when over 120 buildings were either destroyed or seriously damaged. On this occasion a 103 Squadron Lancaster was one of three aircraft failing to return. Essen was again the target for 1 and 5 Groups on the 11/12th, 12/13th and 13/14th, for which 1 Group put up thirty-three, twenty-one and eighteen Lancasters respectively.

A new Air Ministry directive was issued on the 14th, which authorized the area bombing of those French ports providing bases and support facilities for U-Boots. A list of four such targets was drawn up accordingly, headed by Lorient, which that night received the first of its eight raids over the ensuing month. Main force Lancasters were not involved at this stage, and the 1 Group effort amounted to fifteen Wellingtons, of which one failed to return. The home echelon of 142 Squadron operated for the first time during the month, sending one Wellington on the main raid and six others mining. It was not until the following night that 150 Squadron's home echelon dispatched its first three sorties of the year on mining duties. Lorient was attacked again twenty-four hours later, and this time eleven 1 Group Wellingtons took part. The Lancasters were out in strength on the 16/17th for the first of two operations to Berlin on consecutive nights. The force of two hundred aircraft included forty-seven from 1 Group, but twelve of these returned early for a variety of reasons. Germany's Capital lay beyond the range of Gee and Oboe, and the H2S navigation and blind-bombing device was not yet quite ready for its operational debut, and this was reflected in the scattered nature of the attack. Despite good visibility and the first use by the Pathfinders of genuine target indicators, the only building of note to be hit was the ten thousand-seat Deutschlandhalle, the largest covered arena in Europe, and this was completely wrecked. A bonus was the loss of just one aircraft, but this was redressed somewhat on the following night, when a slightly smaller force returned to Berlin, and lost twenty-two of its number in return for another disappointing raid. 1 Group dispatched forty-five Lancasters, and 101 Squadron's W4321 was one of six from the group to fail to return, and no trace of it or the crew of P/O Duffill was ever found. Between these two operations on the 17th 305 Squadron exchanged commanding officers, as W/C Sniegula was posted out in favour of W/C Czolowski. A raid on Essen on the 21/22nd by over seventy Lancasters, including twenty-nine from 1 Group, was hampered by cloud, and another 101 Squadron Lancaster, ED443, crashed in Germany killing Sgt Wiltshire and his crew.

The next stage of the Oboe development programme brought a raid by eighty Lancasters from 1 and 5 Groups on Düsseldorf on the 23/24th. 1 Group dispatched twenty-eight, but losses and the usual crop of early returns reduced those reaching the target to nineteen. The attack was delivered through complete cloud cover on estimated positions, as few if any crews caught a glimpse of the "Wanganui" flares, and the operation was inconclusive. Two aircraft failed to return, and 460 Squadron was represented by one of them. W4308 contained the crew of the A Flight commander, S/L Osborn, and was on the return flight over the sea when it was raked by cannon fire from a BF110. The pilot was wounded in the upper arm, the starboard wing trailed a long ribbon of flame, and the intercom was put out of action. The crew believed themselves to be over the North Sea, but were, in fact, over the Ijsselmeer, and, as the pilot prepared to turn back towards Holland to carry out a forced-landing, the night fighter attacked again, knocking out the hydraulics and killing the rear gunner. Remarkably, in the absence of instruments, S/L Osborn belly landed the stricken Lancaster, and together with four members of his crew, scrambled away from the burning wreckage to fall into enemy hands. On the following day, the body of the bomb-aimer was found with his unopened parachute, and it became clear, that in the absence of the intercom system, he had baled out from too low an altitude only seconds before the landing. In September 1944, S/L Osborn would be repatriated.

During week ending Friday the 26th, W/C Eaton was posted from 101 Squadron to 1 Group HQ pending an eventual posting in April to 1662CU as chief instructor. After a year away from the operational scene W/C Eaton would return as the commanding officer of 156 Squadron, a Pathfinder unit. Sadly, this popular and highly respected officer would lose his life while leading his men into battle at Friedrichshafen on the 27/28th of April 1944. He was succeeded at 101 Squadron by W/C Reddick, who was promoted from within from his flight commander role. Lancasters were still playing a minor role in the assault on Lorient, and only eleven took part in the fourth raid on the 26/27th, three of these carrying freshman crews from 1 Group. The group also provided fifty-one Wellingtons, including eighteen from 166 Squadron, which was operating for the first time on the day of its formation from the marriage of the C Flights of 142 and 150 Squadrons under the command of W/C Barclay, formerly of 150 Squadron. The single casualty of this operation was a 301 Squadron aircraft, which crash-landed at Langar injuring the crew. This was to be the final operational casualty for 301 Squadron, which would soon be disbanded. Only three aircraft failed to return from Lorient on this night, and the single missing Lancaster was from 460 Squadron at Breighton.

On the following night, Düsseldorf was selected as the objective for the first ground marking by Oboe Mosquitos, a method far more reliable than the parachute flares employed thus far. A force of 160 aircraft set off, of which twenty-six Lancasters were provided by 1 Group. Despite the presence of thin cloud, the bombing was concentrated, and over four hundred houses were destroyed, while many public and industrial premises sustained serious damage. A 1, 4 and 6 Group Wellington and Halifax assault on Lorient took place on the 29/30th, for which 1 Group put up twenty-eight aircraft and lost one. The month closed at Hamburg on the 30/31st, when Stirlings and Halifaxes of 7 and 35 Squadrons respectively, carried H2S into battle for the first time. Although it would become a useful device as the war progressed, it required great skill on the part of the operator to interpret the light and dark blotches on the cathode-ray tube, and its maiden operation was not an outstanding success. Twenty-five 1 Group Lancasters took off, but more than a quarter of them returned early or failed to bomb the primary target. Dozens of large fires were started, but there was no significant industrial damage, and the destruction of a railway bridge, which brought the city's network to a standstill, was an unanticipated bonus. 101 Squadron's ED447 was brought down by flak at the Dutch coast, and F/S Campbell died with his crew. It had been a sobering start to the year for 101 Squadron, which had lost four aircraft from a not particularly hectic period, and although it had not yet been established, there was not a single survivor. 300 Squadron moved back to Hemswell from Ingham on the 31st, but the competition between the two stations to be home to the Poles was not yet over. The summary for the month showed 571 sorties, of which six were day bombing, 434 night bombing and 131 mining.

February

The new month began with a raid on Cologne on the 2/3rd, to which 1 Group contributed twenty-six Lancasters. The Pathfinders used a combination of Oboe and H2S to mark the target on this night, as attempts continued to find a reliable system. The attack again failed to achieve any degree of concentration, and no significant damage was inflicted. 199 Squadron completed its move from Blyton to Ingham on the 3rd, and this was probably the day on which W/C Blomfield handed command of the squadron to W/C Wynn-Powell. That night icing conditions over the North Sea made life difficult for the crews, and twenty-one of the thirty-five 1 Group Lancasters and Wellingtons turned back early from Hamburg, where over forty large fires were started, but damage was still not commensurate with the effort expended. The night of the 4/5th brought a change of scenery for 156 crews, who crossed the Alps to bomb Turin, and returned to confirm an accurate and destructive attack. 1 Group provided twenty-one Lancasters for this operation, and a single Lancaster and twenty-five Wellingtons for a simultaneous attack on Lorient.

The campaign against Lorient continued twenty-four hours later, when Lancasters were employed against it in numbers for the first time. 1 Group provided 25% of the eighty of the type and twenty-six Wellingtons that made up a force of over three hundred aircraft for a successful two wave assault. Complete cloud cover forced the use of skymarking at Wilhelmshaven on the 11/12th, but despite this, the bombing was concentrated, and at least one bomb load hit a naval ammunition depot, which blew up, and laid waste to 120 acres of the town and dockyard. 1 Group dispatched forty-two Lancasters for this operation, from which only three aircraft failed to return. Among these was 101 Squadron's W4313, which was lost without trace with the crew of Sgt Hiley. The heaviest raid on Lorient thus far involved over four hundred aircraft on the 13/14th, when Lancasters were the most populous type. 1 Group's forty-four Lancasters and forty-two Wellingtons helped to deliver over a thousand tons of bombs accurately onto the target, in what was the penultimate raid of the series. Another disappointing raid was directed at Cologne on the 14/15th, when less than a quarter of the 240 strong force found the mark. Meanwhile the Lancaster brigade was elsewhere, pounding Milan to good effect, and starting fires that could be seen from a hundred miles away. 101 Squadron contributed twelve aircraft to this operation, led by W/C Reddick.

On the way home Sgt Hazard's Lancaster was damaged by an Italian biplane, and the rear gunner was wounded, but his colleague in the mid-upper position took revenge by shooting the assailant down.

W/C Dabinett was posted from 12 Squadron to 1662CU on the 15th, and was succeeded at 12 Squadron by W/C Wood, who arrived from 1656CU. W/C Dilworth completed his tour of operations at 460 Squadron with thirty-one to his credit, and was posted to Breighton, possibly as station commander. He would return later to the operational scene with sad consequences. He was succeeded at 460 Squadron on the 16th by W/C Martin, who arrived from 20 O.T.U. as a squadron leader. W/C Martin was the first graduate from the Empire Training Scheme to lead a Bomber Command squadron. That night, the final attack on Lorient was delivered by a force of 363 aircraft, which included forty-one Lancasters and eighteen Wellingtons from 1 Group, and they left the town little more than a deserted ruin. 101 Squadron's ED374 crashed on return with flak damage, and P/O Harrower and one of his crew sustained injuries. Of three disappointing raids on Wilhelmshaven on the 18/19th, 19/20th and 24/25th, 1 Group participated in the first two and contributed thirty-nine Lancasters and thirty-two Wellingtons respectively. The night of the 21/22nd was devoted to Bremen, when a force of 140 aircraft included forty-three Lancaster from 1 Group. Those reaching the target bombed through cloud, and no assessment of the results could be made. On the 24th Air Commodore Edgar Rice was installed as the new A-O-C., and his two year tenure would prove to be controversial. He had joined the RFC in 1915, and had commanded a number of squadrons by the end of the Great War. When the Second World War began he was the station Commander at Hemswell.

Nuremberg was the next destination on the 25/26th, where poor weather conditions hampered the marking, and although three hundred buildings were damaged within the city, most of the bombing from the three hundred strong force fell around the northern suburbs and in outlying communities. 1 Group put up forty-five Lancasters, and all returned safely. A force of over four hundred aircraft again failed to make its mark at Cologne on the 26/27th, when much of the bombing missed the target altogether. 1 Group dispatched forty-three Lancasters and twenty-eight Wellingtons, and again all returned without major incident. Having dealt with Lorient, the Command's attention was now turned upon St Nazaire on the last night of the month, when over four hundred aircraft destroyed an estimated 60% of the town's built-up area. 1 Group provided forty-five Lancasters and twenty-six Wellingtons, and for the fourth operation in a row there were no losses. The tally of sorties for the month climbed to 807, of which 708 were night bombing and 99 mining.

March

March would bring the start of the year's first major offensive, against the industrial Ruhr, but first, Berlin was attacked on the 1/2nd by a mixed four-engine force of under three hundred aircraft, for which 1 Group dispatched forty-two Lancasters. The problems of interpreting H2S returns were demonstrated by the lack of accuracy and concentration in the marking, and this led to widely scattered bombing, and the main weight of the attack falling into the south-western districts. Despite the failings the total of 875 buildings destroyed represented the best result yet at the Capital. Hamburg came next on the 3/4th, when a force of four hundred aircraft included forty-three Lancasters and thirty-one Wellingtons from 1 Group. Similar difficulties were encountered to those at Berlin, but a hundred fires were, never the less, started in the city. However, it was the small town of Wedel, downstream of the Elbe, which received the bulk of the main force effort, and heavy damage was inflicted. On the following night 100 Squadron undertook its maiden operation when sending eight Lancasters on mining sorties. Sadly, one of these was lost in the sea, and another was diverted to Langar on return, and crashed while trying to land, killing six of the crew. Within weeks three more of the eight crews involved in this maiden operation would have paid the ultimate price.

Two nights after Hamburg, Harris embarked on what would become a five month long offensive against Germany's industrial heartland. Within two weeks of his appointment as C-in-C a year earlier, he had made his intentions clear with regard to the likes of Essen and Duisburg, but had failed repeatedly to deliver a telling blow at either. Düsseldorf, alone of the Ruhr cities, had experienced a number of effective operations, but now the means were to hand to negate the ever-present blanket of haze, which had so often frustrated the best endeavours of the crews. The Ruhr campaign would be the first for which the Command was genuinely well equipped and prepared, and with Oboe demonstrating a reasonable degree of reliability, the time was right to strike. Essen, with its giant Krupp armaments complex, was the obvious choice to open proceedings, and on the night of the 5/6th, 442 aircraft took off either side of 19.00 hours and headed towards the east to deliver the three wave attack.

1 Group contributed forty-one Lancasters and thirty-eight Wellingtons, and 460 Squadron dispatched ten of the former for this momentous occasion, led by S/L Speare. S/L Speare was an experienced officer, who

had served as a flight commander with 7 Squadron during 1941, and had arrived to fulfil a similar role at 460 after a period away from the operational scene. In May, he would be appointed to the command of 138 Squadron, one of the two "moon" squadrons at Tempsford in Bedfordshire, from where top secret operations were mounted on behalf of the Special Operations Executive. 101 Squadron provided eleven Lancasters led by S/L Fisher. An unusually high number of early returns, and the bombing of alternative targets reduced those attacking as briefed to 362, but after accurate marking of the city centre, first by the Oboe Mosquitos, and then by the heavy backers-up, the main force delivered a concentrated assault. Over three thousand houses and apartment blocks were destroyed, while fifty-three buildings within the Krupp works were hit, and this was by far the most successful raid of the war on this target. Among fourteen missing aircraft was the 300 Squadron Wellington containing F/O Romaniszyn and his crew, which included on this night S/L Jankowski, the first commanding officer of 305 Squadron. He was killed when BK150 crashed in Germany, but the other four occupants survived as PoWs.

Before launching round two of the campaign, Harris turned his attention to southern Germany, and raided Nuremberg, Munich and Stuttgart over the succeeding week. The first mentioned operation took place on the 8/9th, at the hands of a force of over three hundred aircraft, including forty-eight Lancasters, of which 100 Squadron contributed eight for its first bombing operation. The force experienced the usual problems with marking beyond the range of Oboe, and visual identification proved difficult in the face of ground haze. As a consequence the markers delivered by H2S were not concentrated, and much of the bombing fell short. Even so, six hundred buildings were destroyed, and a number of important war industry factories were damaged. It was a similar story at Munich on the 9/10th, when 1 Group provided forty-seven Lancasters to an overall force of 260 aircraft. On this occasion it was the wind that influenced the outcome of the raid, and a more modest 291 buildings suffered destruction, mostly in western districts. The Stuttgart raid on the 11/12th was disappointing in comparison, despite accurate marking, and it is possible that the first recorded use of dummy target indicators caused most of the bombs to fall into open country. 1 Group put up forty-one Lancasters, and all returned safely.

The second operation of the Ruhr offensive took place on the 12/13th, and was also directed at Essen. A force of 450 aircraft took off, among them forty-five Lancasters and thirty-nine Wellingtons from 1 Group. The Krupp works was in the centre of the bombing area on this night, and sustained 30% more damage than a week earlier, although substantially less housing was destroyed. Twenty-three aircraft failed to return, five from

1 Group, and among them was 101 Squadron's W4862, which was brought down in the target area with no survivors from the crew of P/O Kee. A period of minor operations followed, during which 101 Squadron lost Sgt Hazard and crew, who all died after ED446 crashed on the Yorkshire coast during an air test. It was around this time that S/L Kennard concluded his tour at 103 Squadron, and was succeeded as a flight commander by S/L O'Donoghue, an officer with a distinct dislike of night operations. He preferred daylight, even though it meant going alone, and on the 20th he went to Leer in Germany and carried out an accurate attack.

Later on that day W/C Wynn-Powell concluded his short spell at the helm of 199 Squadron, and he was succeeded by W/C Howard. W/C Wynn-Powell would later command 623 and 620 Stirling Squadrons in 3 Group and later after they were transferred to 38 Group. The next assault on St Nazaire was carried out on the 22/23rd, when 283 crews bombed as briefed for the loss of a single Lancaster, 101 Squadron's ED375, which fell in the target area, killing Sgt Lewis and his crew. The Ruhr campaign continued at Duisburg on the 26/27th, when 455 aircraft were dispatched, among them fifty-two Lancasters and forty-three Wellingtons from 1 Group. Five of the Oboe Mosquitos returned early with technical problems, while a sixth was lost, and this was partly responsible for the disappointing outcome, which reflected previous attempts at this target.

The month ended with raids on Berlin on the 27/28th and 29/30th, and another one on St Nazaire in between. Both attacks on the Capital were highly disappointing, the former involving fifty-one Lancasters from 1 Group and costing 101 Squadron W4322, which crashed in Germany with the loss of Sgt Bell and his crew. The latter Berlin operation took place in unfavourable weather conditions at the hands of three hundred aircraft, of which twenty-six were contributed by 1 Group. Most of the bombing on this night fell into open country, and the failure was compounded by the loss of twenty-one aircraft. For the first time since the arrival of Lancasters, 460 Squadron had to post missing two crews. A simultaneous operation against Bochum involved thirty-eight aircraft from 1 Group, and it proved to be the final operation for 301 Squadron, which, because of a lack of available Polish airmen was about to be disbanded. While these operations were in progress 101 Squadron's ED522 crashed in Yorkshire during a night training sortie, and there were no survivors from among the crew of P/O Hobday. The month's 824 sorties were broken down as 1 day bombing, 714 night bombing and 109 mining.

April

April would prove to be the least rewarding month of the Ruhr period, but this was largely because of the number of operations directed against targets in other regions of Germany, and consequently beyond the range of Oboe. 103 Squadron's S/L O'Donoghue took off at 04.00 on the 1st with the oil town of Emmerich on the banks of the Rhine as his objective. He failed to return after being shot down in broad daylight by a fighter, and all on board ED626 were killed. 1 Group's first conventional operational activity involved ten Lancasters and four Wellingtons with freshman crews aboard mining the sea lanes around St Nazaire and Lorient on the 2/3rd. The bombing campaign against Germany began in encouraging fashion with the third attack of the series on Essen on the following night, and this left over six hundred buildings in ruins, and five hundred more displaying signs of serious damage. 1 Group dispatched seventy-two Lancasters in an overall force of almost 350 aircraft, and 101 Squadron's ED736 became the group's single casualty when it crashed in Germany killing the crew of F/O Johnson. A new record non-1,000 force of 577 aircraft sent against Kiel on the 4/5th included a contingent from 1 Group of sixty-seven Lancasters and twenty-seven Wellingtons. In the event the massive effort was not rewarded with success, for which strong winds and decoy fires may have been to blame. Only a few bombs fell within the built-up area of the town, and twelve aircraft were lost to this failure. The end came for 301 Squadron when it was disbanded on the 7th, and its personnel were posted to other units.

Almost four hundred aircraft set off for Duisburg on the 8/9th, among them thirty-eight Lancasters and twenty-nine Wellingtons from 1 Group. On arrival over the target they encountered thick cloud, which led to inaccurate marking and bombing, and nineteen aircraft failed to return. 104 Lancasters and five Mosquitos returned to Duisburg twenty-four hours later, but the city's apparently charmed life continued, and a modest fifty houses were destroyed. 1 Group lost three of the thirty-four Lancasters it dispatched, and for the first time 101 Squadron had two missing from one operation. ED608 fell victim to flak in the target area, but P/O Nelson and four of his crew escaped with their lives to fall into enemy hands. ED618 was caught by a night fighter over Holland, and this time there were no survivors from among the crew of F/S Steele.

The run of ineffective operations included Frankfurt on the 10/11th, when five hundred aircraft failed to find the mark in the face of complete cloud cover, and just a few bombs fell into the suburbs. 1 Group contributed forty-six Lancasters and twenty-eight Wellingtons, of which four failed to return. Matters improved somewhat on the 13/14th, when an all Lancaster main force successfully bombed the docks area in the Italian town of La Spezia. 1 Group had two of its seventy-five Lancasters fail to return, and the 101 Squadron freshman crew of Sgt Fee crashed while trying to land at base following an early return, and all on board were killed. The night of the 14/15th brought a useful raid on Stuttgart, the success of which was largely the result of the almost inevitable creep-back, a feature of most heavy raids. It could work in favour of, or against the Command, and on this occasion it fell across the industrial suburb of Bad Canstatt and into nearby residential districts, where almost four hundred buildings were destroyed. 1 Group contributed forty-six Lancasters to the overall force of 450 aircraft, and among the twenty-three failing to return was 101 Squadron's W4951, which went down in France with the crew of Sgt Hamilton.

When Germany took Czechoslovakia under its wing, it acquired for itself the huge Skoda armaments works at Pilsen, and this was the target for the Lancaster and Halifax squadrons on the night of the 16/17th. While this was in progress, a predominantly Wellington and Stirling raid on Mannheim was intended to provide a diversion to split the night fighter defences. 327 aircraft took off for the former, where the plan was to identify the target visually in bright moonlight, and for the Pathfinder markers to provide a route-marker reference for the start of the bombing run. Unfortunately, many main force crews became confused and bombed on the route markers seven miles short of the Skoda works. Many loads fell onto an asylum, and the intended target escaped damage. The failure was compounded by the loss of thirty-six aircraft, split evenly between the two types, and these had to be added to the eighteen missing from the moderately effective attack on Mannheim, making it the heaviest losses to date in a single night. 1 Group put up sixty-five Lancasters for the main operation and thirty-four Wellingtons for the diversion. It turned into a bad night for 460 Squadron, its worst so far, and there were three empty dispersals to contemplate at Breighton on the following morning. ED379 was the missing 101 Squadron aircraft, and it was eventually established that only one member of Sgt Menzies crew had survived to fall into enemy hands. Later on the 17th W/C Carter handed command of 103 Squadron to W/C Slater, and took up his new post as station commander at Waltham (Grimsby) on the 28th.

The heavy losses from Pilsen were still fresh in the mind for the next two long-range operations, to the naval base at La Spezia again on the 18/19th and the Baltic port of Stettin on the 20/21st. 170 Lancasters took part in the former, and there were no losses from among the sixty-two sent by 1 Group. The latter involved a force of over three hundred aircraft, of which seventy Lancasters were provided by 1 Group. They helped to lay waste to a hundred acres in the centre of the town at a cost of twenty-one aircraft. It was a bad night for 100 Squadron, which lost two aircraft, one of them containing the squadron commander. ED709 crashed off the Danish coast, and W/C Swain died with the rest of his crew, which included the squadron navigation officer. *(Ammunition from this Lancaster is on display in the Stradingsmuseum St George in Ulfborg, Denmark.)* History repeated itself for 460 Squadron, when another three aircraft failed to make it back home, and twenty-one more once familiar faces became a receding memory. It soon emerged that the casualty rate could so easily have been greater, when it was discovered that six further Lancasters had returned to Breighton with battle damage. Among them was the one containing F/S Fuhrmann and his crew, which suffered from the attentions of a flak ship in the Baltic, seriously wounding the pilot and navigator. The aircraft was eventually crash-landed at base, whereupon, F/S Fuhrmann collapsed, and was rushed off to hospital. Both he and F/O Anderson survived the experience to receive the immediate award of the DFM and DFC respectively, and they would return to operations in due course, although sadly, it seems, they had already used up their ration of good fortune. Of 101 Squadron's sixteen participants ED422 was hit by flak while crossing the Dutch coast at low level, and F/S Gray was forced to jettison the bomb load and turn back.

On the 24th W/C McIntyre was posted in from 1656CU and installed as the new commanding officer of 100 Squadron, and S/L Preston was posted to Binbrook on the 25th to occupy a wing commander post, although it would be October before he took command of his first squadron. The next major operation was against Duisburg on the 26/27th, and although it was the most effective raid yet on this city, destroying three hundred buildings, it still fell short of what might have been expected from a force of 561 aircraft. 1 Group dispatched sixty-two Lancasters and thirty-one Wellingtons, and, for once, all returned home. The largest mining effort to date took place on the night of the 27/28th in French and Dutch coastal waters, and the single missing aircraft from the force of 160 was 101 Squadron's ED728, which went into the sea off the French coast, taking with it Sgt Margerum and his crew. An even larger force of 207 aircraft was committed to the mining of northern waters on the following night, and although the number of mines laid was a new record, at twenty-two aircraft, so was the scale of losses from this type of operation. This time 1 Group counted the cost of six missing aircraft, four of them from 12 Squadron, the second time this year that "Shiney" 12 had lost four from a single operation. The month ended with a tilt at Essen on the last night, which produced more modest returns than the previous raids on this target during the campaign. 1 Group contributed sixty-five Lancasters, of which just one failed to return. The month produced a record 1030 sorties, of which one was day bombing, 865 were night bombing and 164 were mining.

May

May would bring a return to winning ways, with a number of records and spectacular successes. It began for 300 Squadron with a change at the top on the 4th, as W/C Kucharski took over from W/C Kropinski. That night a new record non-1,000 force of 596 aircraft, which included seventy-six Lancasters and thirty-four Wellingtons from 1 Group, carried out the first genuinely heavy raid of the war on Dortmund. Only about half of the force managed to bomb within three miles of the aiming point after some of the backers-up dropped their markers short, and a decoy fire site also attracted some attention. Never-the-less, it was a very successful operation, which destroyed over twelve hundred buildings, and inflicted useful damage on industrial premises and dock facilities. The defenders fought back to claim thirty-one aircraft, and it turned out to be a testing night for 101 Squadron. Two of its eighteen Lancasters failed to return, W4784 disappearing without trace with the crew of Sgt Nicholson, who was leading his crew for the first time, and W4888 falling to a night fighter over Holland, killing all but one of the experienced crew of F/O Stanford. Four more of the squadron's aircraft crashed on return, ED776 just short of the runway at base, and ED830 after colliding with trees near Linton-on-Ouse, but happily there were no casualties among the crews of F/S Kelly and Sgt Smith respectively. Two other crews were less fortunate, however, and when W4863 crashed in Yorkshire, Sgt Browning and three of his colleagues perished in its wreckage. A flak damaged ED835 claimed the lives of F/S Hough and two of his crew when it also came down in the county.

The main force and Pathfinder crews were rested over the succeeding week, and it was on the night of the 12/13th that they were next called to arms, for yet another crack at the elusive city of Duisburg. 572 aircraft took off, among them sixty-one Lancasters and thirty-two Wellingtons of 1 Group. This time Germany's largest inland port succumbed to an outstandingly accurate and concentrated assault, which destroyed almost sixteen hundred buildings, and sank or damaged sixty thousand tons of shipping. Again this was not a one-sided affair, and the enemy defences claimed thirty-four bombers, a new record for the campaign thus far. It was a relatively good night for 1 Group, however, which registered just three failures to return. On the following night over four hundred aircraft targeted Bochum, for which operation 1 Group managed a new record of eighty-three Lancasters along with thirty-four Wellingtons. They contributed to the destruction of almost four hundred buildings, for the loss of twenty-four aircraft. The Lancaster of 100 Squadron's commanding officer, W/C McIntyre, received a burst of flak in the belly, which wounded the wireless operator, but he managed to nurse it home to a crash-landing in Norfolk without further casualties. W/C McIntyre was awarded a DFC, which was Gazetted on the 4th of June in a joint citation with his wireless operator. 5 Group and a Pathfinder element, meanwhile, were engaged over Czechoslovakia, attempting in vain to rectify the recent failure at the Skoda works at Pilsen.

Another nine day break allowed the squadrons to rest and replenish, during which, on the 14th, 460 Squadron moved to a new home at Binbrook in Lincolnshire, where it would remain for the rest of the war. Binbrook had just reopened after having concrete runways installed, and there to meet the 460 Squadron crews was the Australian station commander, G/C Hughie Edwards VC, who had been in post since February, and had twice commanded 2 Group's 105 Squadron earlier in the war. Edwards would revel in the opportunity to be among his fellow countrymen, and would use his experience to instil confidence into sprog crews by taking them into battle, whether unofficially or with the approval of his superiors. With the move to Binbrook, the 460 Squadron code letters changed from UV to AR. It was also during this period of inactivity, that 617 Squadron earned its place in bomber folklore, with its epic attack on the dams on the 16/17th.

When the rest of the Command returned to action on the 23/24th, it was for a record breaking operation to Dortmund by the largest non-1,000 force to date. The 826 aircraft included another new record for 1 Group of 122 Lancasters and fifty-eight Wellingtons, which took off in favourable weather conditions, and headed eastwards to the Ruhr. Those reaching the target contributed to a massively successful raid, which destroyed two thousand buildings and inflicted serious damage on the city's industry. The defenders fought back and claimed their biggest haul for the campaign of thirty-eight aircraft, of which nine were from 1 Group. 166 Squadron lost three Wellingtons, while 460 Squadron posted missing two Lancaster crews. When F/S Stevens and his entire crew escaped by parachute to be taken captive, they were, remarkably, the first to survive from a shot down 460 Squadron Lancaster, since S/L Osborn and four of his crew had been taken prisoner exactly four months earlier. During that intervening period, fifteen of its Lancasters had failed to return, and each had resulted in a total loss of life. 101 Squadron's W4919 fell victim to a night fighter over Holland, and F/S Hayes and his crew all died. ED775 crashed in Norfolk on return, and one member of Sgt Fry's crew later succumbed to his injuries.

Another very large force of 759 aircraft was dispatched to Düsseldorf on the 25/26th, but this mammoth effort was not blessed with success, possibly because of cloud and decoy fires and markers. 1 Group dispatched 116 Lancasters and forty-seven Wellingtons, and seven of these were among the twenty-seven aircraft missing. It was a high price to pay for little return, and 101 Squadron was represented among them by ED660. This became yet another victim of an enemy night fighter interception over Holland, and there were no survivors from the crew of Sgt Tindale. The next attack on Essen came on the 27/28th, when a force of five hundred aircraft included 104 Lancasters and twenty-nine Wellingtons from 1 Group. Almost five hundred buildings were destroyed, mostly in central and northern districts, and twenty-three aircraft failed to make it home. This time all twenty-one from Holme-on-Spalding-Moor arrived back safely, but four others from the group did not.

The final operation of the month took place on the 29/30th, and was directed at Barmen, one of the twin towns known jointly as Wuppertal. The force of seven hundred aircraft included ninety-six Lancasters and thirty-one Wellingtons from 1 Group. They became involved in one of those relatively rare occasions when all facets of the plan came together in perfect harmony, and it spelled catastrophe for the unfortunate inhabitants of the doomed town. Concentration of marking and bombing had always been the key to success, and it was achieved completely on this night, gutting by fire the centre of the town, and destroying in all four thousand houses and over two hundred industrial premises. Unusually, the number of buildings classed as completely destroyed was double the number seriously damaged, and the level of devastation was reflected in the estimate, that 80% of the town's built-up area lay in ruins. The death toll, at 3,400 people, was also many times higher than in any previous raid on an urban target, but Bomber Command's losses were high as well. Among the thirty-three failures to return were just three from 1 Group, and of these two belonged to 460 Squadron. 999 sorties were dispatched during the month, broken down as 923 night bombing and 76 mining.

June

The moon period at the start of June kept the heavy brigade on the ground until the 11/12th, when Düsseldorf was the target for over seven hundred aircraft. Included in this figure was a new record for 1 Group of 128 Lancasters along with fifty Wellingtons. An errant Oboe marker persuaded a proportion of the force to bomb open country, but the remainder delivered an accurate attack on central and southern districts. The fires covered an area of forty square kilometres, and over forty war industry factories suffered a complete stoppage of production, while almost thirteen hundred people were killed, and 140,000 others were rendered homeless. The Command had to contend with the loss of thirty-eight heavy bombers, however, another new record for the campaign, and "Happy Valley's" evil reputation was now set for all time. 1 Group lost ten aircraft, and worryingly, half of these were from 12 Squadron. On the following night a force of almost five hundred aircraft destroyed 130 acres of built-up area in the centre of Bochum. 1 Group sent a contingent of 106 Lancasters, of which five failed to return out of an overall missing total of twenty-four aircraft. 460 Squadron lost two Lancasters, and 101 Squadron posted missing ED987 with the crew of Sgt Claydon, who all perished.

199 squadron operated for the final time with 1 Group on the night of the 13/14th when dispatching six mining sorties. Thereafter the squadron was stood down pending its transfer to 3 Group and conversion to Stirlings. Two nights later, a relatively modest main force of 197 Lancasters, almost half of them from 1 Group, took off for Oberhausen, and those arriving over the target accurately bombed the Oboe markers, and destroyed 267 buildings. The seventeen failures to return represented an 8.4% loss, and for the third operation running, 460 Squadron suffered casualties on an escalating scale. One crew had been lost from Düsseldorf, two from Bochum, and now three from Oberhausen, and the month was only half way through. On the 15th 101 Squadron completed its move from Holme-on-Spalding-Moor and took up residence at Ludford Magna, where it would remain until the end of hostilities. Thirty-one Lancasters were involved in the move, and C Flight was rather unique in 1 Group in having a navigator, acting S/L Greig, as its flight commander.

In a further effort to fine-tune target marking techniques, sixteen H2S equipped Pathfinder heavy aircraft led a raid on Cologne on the 16/17th, for which 1 and 5 Groups provided the main force of two hundred Lancasters. This would be the first of four attacks on the city over a three week period. A high level of equipment failure on this night led to late and sparse skymarking, and the resultant bombing was scattered, although moderately effective. Four hundred houses were destroyed, many public buildings and railway stations were hit, and sixteen industrial premises sustained damage. Fourteen Lancasters failed to return, five of them from 1 Group's contingent of seventy-six, and 460 Squadron's already expensive month took another turn for the worse. One of its crews went missing, later to be pronounced killed in action, and another crashed while trying to land at Elsham Wolds on return, with similar consequences for the crew.

A hectic round of four major operations in the space of five nights began at Krefeld on the 21/22nd, and involved a force of seven hundred aircraft, of which 110 Lancasters and thirty-seven Wellingtons were provided by 1 Group. The Pathfinder marking was near perfect, and the main force crews exploited the situation to deliver most of the 2,300 tons of bombs within three miles of the aiming point. The whole centre of the town was engulfed in flames, and over 5,500 houses were reduced to ruins, a new record for the war, while more than a thousand people lost their lives. The bomber losses were also a new record for the campaign, however, and the seventy-two thousand people made homeless by the raid would have been cheered to know, that over three hundred of their assailants in forty-four aircraft would not be returning home either.

This was 101 Squadron's first operation from its new station, and it was marked with a missing aircraft. ED650 crashed in Germany close to its frontier with Holland, and there were no survivors from among the crew of Sgt Brook. 1 Group lost seven aircraft in all, three of them Wellingtons from the Polish Squadrons. Later on the 22nd 300 Squadron departed Hemswell to return to Ingham, where it would remain for more than eight months. On the following night Mülheim suffered the destruction of over eleven hundred houses, while dozens of public buildings sustained damage, and many industrial premises suffered loss of production. The Command's losses remained high at thirty-five of the original 557 participating aircraft, but just three came from 1 Group's contribution of 102 Lancasters. 103 and 460 Squadrons each posted missing one, as did 101 Squadron, whose LM325 was dispatched by a night fighter over Holland, with just one survivor from the crew of Sgt Waterhouse.

After a night's rest, 630 aircraft took off for Wuppertal, to attack the Elberfeld half, having destroyed its twin Barmen a month earlier. 1 Group dispatched ninety-five Lancasters and thirty-three Wellingtons, and they participated in a raid even more devastating, that resulted in the destruction of three thousand houses and 171 industrial premises, with a further 2,500 buildings suffering serious damage. Over 90% of the town's built-up area was laid waste on this one night, and eighteen hundred people were killed. Another thirty-four Bomber Command crews paid the price for this success, five of them from 1 Group, and among these was that of Sgt Lane from 101 Squadron, who all died when W4311 became yet another victim of enemy night fighters over Holland. An attempt by a force of 450 aircraft to hit the important oil town of Gelsenkirchen foundered on the 25/26th, when a proportion of the Oboe aircraft experienced equipment failure. In an echo of the past, bombs were sprayed all over the Ruhr, and the disappointment was compounded by the loss of thirty aircraft. 1 Group had put up eighty-eight Lancasters and ten Wellingtons, and seven of these were among the missing. 101 Squadron's LM318 came down in Germany without survivors from the crew of Sgt Hay, and ED373 was abandoned by its crew over the Dutch coast after a night fighter had rendered it incapable of continuing on. Tragically, F/S Banks and five of his crew landed in the sea and were drowned, while one man fell into the arms of the enemy and became a PoW. The squadron sent a freshman crew mining in French waters on the night of the 27/28th, and it didn't come back. ED377 crashed in France with the loss of F/O Buck and five of his crew, the sole survivor ultimately evading capture.

Either side of midnight on the 28/29th over six hundred aircraft departed their stations for the first of three raids on Cologne in the space of ten nights spanning the turn of the month. 1 Group sent eighty-nine Lancasters and twenty-seven Wellingtons, and those reaching the target found the skies heavy with cloud, making it necessary to employ the less reliable skymarking method. Only half of the Oboe Mosquito crews were able to mark as briefed, and did so some seven minutes late, but despite these setbacks, the operation developed into the most awesomely destructive assault yet visited upon a German city. 6,400 buildings were totally destroyed, including forty-three industrial premises, and 4,377 people lost their lives, while a further 230,000 were rendered homeless. In return, a slightly more modest twenty-five aircraft were shot down, and among those missing from 1 Group were two from 100 Squadron at Grimsby. The group put up 1,146 sorties during the month, 1,039 of which were night bombing and 107 mining.

July

The month began for 166 Squadron with some changes in leadership, beginning with the departure of W/C Barclay to 1667 HCU on the 3rd. He was succeeded by the B Flight commander, S/L Twamley, who was promoted to acting wing commander. He in turn was replaced as B Flight commander by S/L Powley, who was posted in from 1667 HCU. It fell to Cologne to open the July account that very night, and during the bombing up process at Binbrook, some incendiaries were accidently jettisoned from 460 Squadron's DV172, and the Lancaster exploded in the ensuing fire, showering R5745 with burning debris. This aircraft also then caught fire, and was torn asunder in its own explosion shortly afterwards. This night of the 3/4th was the occasion on which the Luftwaffe introduced its new Wilde Sau (Wild Boar) night fighter tactic, in which single engine day fighters were employed over the target city to pick off bombers silhouetted against the fires below. Over six hundred RAF aircraft were detailed for the operation, of which one hundred Lancasters and twenty-nine Wellingtons represented 1 Group. Those reaching the target helped to deliver another stunning attack, which destroyed a further 2,200 houses and twenty industrial premises for the loss of thirty of their number. Seven of these were from 1 Group, and included two each from 12 and 103 Squadrons. Also missing was the A Flight commander of 166 Squadron, S/L Cookson, and he and his crew all died. As a result yet another change in leadership was required at the squadron, and the experienced acting S/L "Pip" Pape was posted in from 18 O.T.U at Finningley as the new A Flight commander.

The Cologne series was concluded on the 8/9th, when an all-Lancaster heavy force from 1, 5 and 8 Groups destroyed almost 2,400 more houses and apartment blocks, along with nineteen industrial premises. A modest seven aircraft failed to return, among them two from 101 Squadron. ED697 was probably returning early when it went down in the sea, taking with it F/L Fleming and his crew, and W4275 was shot down by a night fighter over France on the way home. Four of the crew lost their lives, but the pilot, P/O Ager, and two others survived, and one of these managed to evade capture. When the Cologne city authorities were able to assess the cost of the three raids, they catalogued eleven thousand buildings destroyed, 5,500 people killed, and a further 350,000 made homeless.

Another failure at Gelsenkirchen on the 9/10th effectively brought an end to the Ruhr campaign, although two further operations to the region would be mounted at the end of the month. Harris could look back over the past five months with genuine satisfaction at the performance of his squadrons, and point to Oboe as the crucial factor. Most of the operations attended by Oboe Mosquitos had been a major success, while those beyond the device's range had continued to be something of a lottery. Losses had been grievously high, and "Happy Valley's" reputation had been justifiably earned, but much of Germany's industrial heartland now lay in ruins, and the aircraft factories at home had more than kept pace with the rate of attrition. The training units were continuing to feed fresh crews into the fray to fill the gaps, and a gradual expansion was taking place to further strengthen Harris's hand. With confidence high, Harris now sought to rock the very foundations of Nazi morale, by erasing from the map one of Germany's most important cities in a short, sharp series of raids until the job was done. In the meantime, 1, 5 and 8 Groups carried out a highly destructive attack on Turin, in which almost eight hundred people were killed, but the Command also lost one of its favourite sons. W/C Nettleton, the commanding officer of 44 Squadron, who had earned a Victoria Cross for his part in the epic daylight raid on the M.A.N. diesel engine factory at Augsburg in April 1942, was shot down into the English Channel on the way home, and died with his crew.

Having been spared by the weather from hosting the first one thousand bomber raid in May 1942, Hamburg became Harris's choice for Operation Gomorrah, to be mounted during the final week of July. As Germany's Second City, its political status was undeniable, and as a centre of U-Boot construction and other important war industries, it had always been at the top of the Command's list of priority targets. There were other considerations of an operational nature, however, which also made it an attractive proposition, chief among which was its location. Close to a coastline, it could be approached from the sea, without the need to traverse large tracts of hostile territory, and would be fairly easy to pinpoint. It was also close enough to the bomber stations to allow a large force to approach and withdraw in the few hours of total darkness afforded by mid summer. Finally, beyond the range of Oboe, it boasted the wide River Elbe to provide a strong H2S signature for the navigators high above. Operation Gomorrah would also benefit from the first use of Window, the tinfoil-backed strips of paper, which, when dispensed into the slipstream, produced radar-reflecting clouds. The effect was to swamp the enemy night fighter, searchlight and gun-laying radar with false returns, making it impossible to pick out a genuine hostile aircraft. The device had actually been available for a year, but its use had been vetoed in case the enemy copied it. Germany had, in fact, already developed a similar system under the code name Düppel, which it too had withheld for the same reason.

Briefings for the opening round of what might be termed the Battle of Hamburg, took place on the 24th, and that evening 791 aircraft took off between 22.00 and 23.00 hours, 158 of them from 1 Group. 103 Squadron led the way with a magnificent twenty-seven Lancasters, closely followed by 460 Squadron with twenty-six, 100 Squadron with twenty-five and 101 Squadron with twenty-three. An early indication of the effectiveness of Window was the relatively low number of combats before the target was reached. A number of aircraft were shot down during this stage of the operation, and, in fact, the first two losses involved 103 Squadron

Lancasters, which were shot down into the sea off the Dutch coast by night fighters. Both were well off track, one by sixty miles and the other by a hundred, and one was flying at only five thousand feet when intercepted. It seems likely that they were returning early with technical difficulties, and were, therefore, outside of the protection of the bomber stream.

The efficacy of Window became clearly apparent in the target area, where the usually efficient co-ordination between the searchlight and flak batteries was absent, and anti-aircraft defence was at best random. The Pathfinder marking was slightly misplaced and scattered, but close enough to the aiming point to make little difference to the outcome, had the main force crews produced concentrated bombing. This they failed to do, and an extensive creep-back developed, which cut a swathe of destruction from the city centre along the line of approach, out across the north-western districts and into open country, where a substantial number of bomb loads were wasted. Fifteen hundred people on the ground lost their lives, but in terms of the heavy damage inflicted, it was an encouraging start to the campaign. A bonus was the loss of just twelve aircraft, including a third one from 103 Squadron, one from 460 Squadron and a 166 Squadron Wellington.

On the following night Harris planned another attack on Hamburg, but a combination of lingering smoke over the target and the proximity of a cold front persuaded him to switch his force to Essen, where he could take advantage of the body blow dealt to the enemy's defensive system by Window. 705 aircraft took off, including 148 from 1 Group, and those reaching the target destroyed over 2,800 houses and fifty industrial premises, while the Krupp works suffered its worst night of the war. It was another bad night for 103 Squadron, which posted missing two Lancasters, including one captained by flight commander S/L Carpenter, who survived with two members of his crew as PoWs. A night's rest preceded the second round of Operation Gomorrah, for which 787 aircraft were dispatched on the night of the 27/28th, including a contribution of 159 from 1 Group. What followed their arrival over Hamburg was both unprecedented and unforeseeable, and was the result of a combination of factors. A spell of unusually hot and dry weather during July had left tinderbox conditions within parts of the city, and when the Pathfinders dropped their markers, they did so with unaccustomed concentration two miles to the east of the planned city centre aiming point, and into the densely populated working class residential districts of Hamm, Hammerbrook and Borgfeld.

729 main force crews followed up with uncharacteristic accuracy and scarcely any creep-back, and delivered most of their 2,300 tons of bombs into this relatively compact area. The individual fires took hold, and joined

together to form one giant conflagration, which sucked in oxygen from surrounding areas at hurricane velocity to feed its voracious appetite. Such was the ferocity of this meteorological phenomenon, that trees were uprooted and flung bodily into the flames, along with debris and people. The temperature at the seat of the inferno reached a thousand degrees Celcius, and it was only once all of the combustible material had been consumed, that the fire began to subside. An estimated forty thousand people perished on this one night alone, and on the following morning the first of an eventual 1.2 million inhabitants began to file out of the tortured city. Of the seventeen missing aircraft just three were from 1 Group, and among these was 101 Squadron's JA863, which fell to a night fighter near the target without survivors from the crew of F/S Hurst. Earlier in the day W/C Carey-Foster had arrived from 1656 HCU to become the new commanding officer of 101 Squadron on the departure to Lindholme of W/C Reddick.

305 Squadron changed leaders for the final time as a Bomber Command unit on the 28th, when W/C Czolowski was succeeded by W/C Konopasek. The assault on Hamburg continued on the 29/30th at the hands of another force of over seven hundred aircraft, to which 1 Group contributed 150 Lancasters and Wellingtons. The Pathfinders made their approach from the north, and again dropped their markers to the east of the city centre, and a little south of the districts afflicted by the firestorm. The main force reverted to type on this night, and allowed a four mile creep-back to develop, which spread across the devastation from the previous raid, before hitting other residential districts beyond, and creating a large area of fire. Another 2,300 tons of bombs continued the torment, but as the Luftwaffe began to recover from the effects of Window, so the bomber losses began to escalate. Twenty-eight were missing on this night, but only three of them came from 1 Group, two Lancasters from 460 Squadron and a 166 Squadron Wellington, and there was not a single survivor. Before the final assault on Hamburg took place, a relatively modest force of under three hundred aircraft destroyed over 80% of Remscheid's built-up area on the 30/31st, to finally bring down the curtain on the Ruhr campaign. 1 Group was called upon to provide thirty aircraft, and all returned safely. The group registered a new high of 1,159 sorties during the month, of which 1,095 were bombing and 64 mining.

August

The group provided 153 aircraft towards the 740 that took off for the final assault on Hamburg on the night of the 2/3rd of August. The crews

encountered severe icing conditions and electrical storms over the North
Sea, and many were persuaded to bomb alternative targets, or to jettison
their loads. Those pressing on to the target produced a widely scattered
attack, which inflicted no significant new damage but cost thirty aircraft.
Eight of these were from 1 Group, the two Polish squadrons losing three
Wellingtons between them, while 100 and 103 Squadrons each posted
missing two Lancasters. In addition to the loss of a Wellington at Hamburg,
166 Squadron also had one fail to return from a mining sortie. This proved
to be the final operation in Bomber Command for 305 Squadron, which
would join the 2nd Tactical Air Force in the following month. 1 Group's
contribution to the four raids of Operation Gomorrah amounted to 473
sorties by Lancasters and 159 by Wellingtons for the loss of fourteen and
six respectively. 460 Squadron dispatched ninety-eight sorties across the
campaign, the second highest number in the Group and the Command, and
ninety-five of these had been completed as briefed, the highest in the Group
and the Command, and this was accomplished for the loss of three aircraft
and crews.

Italy was by now teetering on the brink of capitulation, and the second
week of August was devoted largely to nudging it over the edge. The
campaign began on the 7/8th, with attacks on Genoa, Turin and Milan by
1, 5 and 8 Groups, G/C Searby of 83 Squadron using the Turin raid as a
trial run for the Master Bomber role, which he would be assuming for a
very important operation ten nights hence. 1 Group put up fifty Lancasters
for Turin, seventeen of them from 101 Squadron, and twenty-two for
Genoa, and all returned safely from what were reported to be very effective
attacks. Before the next trip across the Alps, over four hundred aircraft
destroyed thirteen hundred buildings in Mannheim on the 9/10th, despite
the presence of cloud, which made identification of the Pathfinder markers
very difficult. Of 1 Group's contingent of 114 Lancasters, just a single one
from 103 Squadron failed to return. This was followed by an attack on
Nuremberg twenty-four hours later by a force of six hundred aircraft, which
included 114 Lancasters from 1 Group. Again cloud intervened to prevent
an accurate assessment of the outcome, but the glow of fires visible from
up to 150 miles away suggested an effective attack, and there were no
losses from the Group. While this operation was in progress 166 and 300
Squadrons sent eighteen Wellingtons on mining sorties, and these too all
returned safely.

111 Lancasters from 1 Group joined an attack on Milan on the 12/13th,
while a simultaneous assault on Turin was delivered by a predominantly
Stirling force. The attack at Milan proceeded in perfect weather conditions
following accurate Pathfinder marking, and the defences were described

in the 1 Group ORB as "well up to their standard of hoplessness". No aircraft were lost from the group, although a 166 Squadron Wellington failed to return from a mining sortie. 1, 5 and 8 Groups returned to Milan on the 14/15th, when twenty-eight of the forty-four 1 Group participants were assigned to attack the Breda Pirelli works just outside the city. In the event it proved difficult to identify, and most crews opted to join in the main raid. The group put up sixty-seven Lancasters for a return to Milan on the 15/16th, and the ensuing attack was described as even more destructive than the previous efforts, with smoke rising to ten thousand feet. This concluded the main force Lancaster interest in Italy. The final raid by the Command on the country came on the 16/17th at the hands of a 3 and 8 Group force, and then all attention turned to a target of great significance for the security of Britain and the free world.

Since the start of hostilities, intelligence had been filtering through to London concerning German research into rocket weapons. As the war progressed and the Enigma codes were broken, it became possible to identify Peenemünde, on the island of Usedom on the Baltic coast, as the centre of such activity. It was here that the V-1 first came to light, when the photographic interpreters at Medmenham were searching for an aircraft with a twenty foot wingspan, and having discovered it, dubbed it the Peenemünde 20. Through the interception and decoding of signals traffic, it was possible for the brilliant scientist, Dr R V Jones, to monitor the V-1 trials taking place over the Baltic, and thereby to assess the weapon's range capability, and use this data to feed disinformation to the enemy. Reconnaissance flights over northern Germany frequently passed, as if by accident, over the research and development establishment, to enable a picture of its activities to be built up, and by the summer of 1943, enough evidence was to hand to cause alarm. Curiously, Churchill's chief scientific adviser, Professor Lindemann, or Lord Cherwell as he became, steadfastly refused to give credence to rocket weapons, and even when confronted with a photograph of a V-2 on a trailer at Peenemünde, taken by a PRU Mosquito in June, he remained unmoved. It required the combined urgings of Dr Jones and Duncan Sandys to impress upon Churchill the need to act, and it was at last decided to attack the site at the first suitable opportunity. This arose on the night of the 17/18th, for which a complex and detailed plan was prepared under the code name Operation Hydra.

Three specific areas of the establishment required attention, the housing estate, wherein lived the scientists and technical staff, the V-2 assembly buildings, and finally the experimental site, each of which was to be assigned to a wave of bombers. The Pathfinders were charged with the task of shifting the point of aim accordingly, and a heavy burden of responsibility rested upon their shoulders. The entire operation would be overseen by G/C Searby, acting as Master of Ceremonies in the manner pioneered by Gibson at the dams, and his role would be one of monitoring the marking, instructing the main force crews on which markers to bomb, and encouraging all to press home their attacks. It was a demanding role, which would require him to remain within range of the defences throughout the attack, or at least, for as long as his fuel reserves allowed. In an attempt to lure the night fighters away from the Peenemünde area, 139 Squadron was to send eight Mosquitos to Berlin to carry out a spoof raid, and this contingent would be led by the commanding officer, G/C Slee, a former 5 Group stalwart and 49 Squadron commander.

597 aircraft were made ready during the course of the 17th, the number somewhat depleted by the late return to their stations of a proportion of the Stirling force, following their trip to Italy the night before and enforced diversion to various non 3 Group airfields on their return. 1 Group's contribution amounted to 113 Lancasters from 12, 100, 101, 103 and 460 Squadrons, led by 12 Squadron with an impressive twenty-five aircraft, closely followed by 103 and 460 Squadrons with twenty-four each. 3 and 4 Groups were assigned to the first aiming point, the housing estate, while 1 Group would target the assembly buildings in phase two, and 5 and 6 Groups were to bring up the rear to attack the experimental site. The 5 Group crews were authorized to adopt their "time and distance" method of bombing, should the aiming point be obscured by smoke and dust.

Most aircraft departed their stations between 21.00 and 22.00 hours, and notably absent from among 101 Squadron's twenty participants were the squadron and flight commanders. This contrasted sharply with the trend for the night, when a high number of senior officers put themselves on the order of battle for such an important operation. The attack opened in good conditions, and the main defence from the ground was in the form of a very effective smoke screen. The initial marking of the housing estate went awry, and some stray markers fell onto the Trassenheide forced workers camp more than a mile beyond. The error was quickly rectified, but in the meantime, severe casualties were inflicted on the friendly foreign nationals trapped inside their wooden barracks. 3 and 4 Groups dealt effectively with the housing area, and a number of important members of the technical staff were killed. 1 Group's attack on the assembly buildings was hampered by a cross-wind, but substantial damage was inflicted, and all of the 460 Squadron crews bombed as briefed.

It was while predominantly 5 and 6 Group aircraft were in the target area that the night fighters belatedly arrived from Berlin, some of them carrying the new "Schräge Musik" (jazz music) upward firing cannons.

Once on the scene they proceeded to take a heavy toll of bombers, both in the skies above Peenemünde, and on the route home towards Denmark. Of the forty-one missing aircraft, twenty-nine were from the final wave, and seventeen of these were from 5 Group. 12 Squadron posted missing one of its flight commanders, S/L Slade, who died with his crew, and 100 and 103 Squadrons also lost one aircraft each. 460 Squadron came through unscathed, something which it rarely achieved, but a testing time lay ahead for the remainder of the year. The operation against Peenemünde was sufficiently successful to delay the development of the V-2 by a number of weeks, and the assembly of secret weapons would be continued underground, while the rocket's flight testing was moved eastwards into Poland.

Harris had long believed that Berlin, as the seat and symbol of Nazi authority, held the key to ultimate victory, and that its destruction would bring an early end to the war. In a minute to Churchill on the 3rd of November, he would state that he could "wreck Berlin from end to end", if the Americans were to join in, and, although he estimated it would cost between them four to five hundred aircraft, it would cost Germany the war. Harris was holding firm to the belief that a victory could be achieved by bombing alone, and he was the first commander in history to put this theory to the test. Having personally witnessed the carnage of the trenches in the Great War, he wished to avoid a protracted and bloody land campaign this time round. The Americans, of course, were committed to victory by land invasion, where the film cameras could be present to record the heroic actions, and there was never the slightest chance of enlisting their support. The first phase of his assault on Germany's Capital would begin during the last week of August, but in the meantime, he dispatched over four hundred aircraft to Leverkusen on the 22/23rd, wherein lay an important I G Farben chemicals plant. The operation degenerated into something resembling the raids on Ruhr targets in 1942, and bombs were sprayed over twelve other towns in the region. All five 1 Group Lancaster squadrons contributed twenty-one aircraft, and one from 103 Squadron failed to return after being brought down by a night fighter.

On the following night 727 aircraft were prepared for the first raid on Berlin since the end of March, and this number included 107 Lancasters from 1 Group. A contingent of Pathfinder Mosquitos was also on hand to lay route markers at predetermined points. The difficulties associated with identifying an aiming point by H2S in an urban sprawl the size of Berlin were made manifest on this night. Instead of the city centre, the Pathfinders marked the southern outskirts, and much of the bombing fell onto outlying communities, something which would become a feature of the entire campaign. Never the less, over 2,600 buildings were destroyed or seriously damaged, and this was the best result yet at the Capital. On the debit side a new record of fifty-six aircraft failed to return in the face of a spirited defence, and eight of the casualties belonged to 1 Group. It turned into a shocking night for 100 Squadron at Grimsby, which had one Lancaster crash on take-off, happily without crew casualties, and four others fail to return. In human terms it left twenty-two men dead, five in enemy hands and one on the run, ultimately to evade capture. 101 squadron lost two aircraft, ED328, which crashed in Germany killing F/S Naffin RAAF and crew, and EE192, which was lost without trace with the crew of F/O Mahoney.

While this operation was in progress twelve 166 Squadron Wellingtons laid mines in two areas and all returned safely. On the 25th W/C Wood was posted from 12 Squadron to Lindholme, and he was succeeded by W/C Towle, who had arrived from 1656CU on the 19th, and would not be around for long. On the following two nights the group's Lancasters stayed at home while Wellingtons of 166 and 300 Squadrons continued with the mining campaign.

On the 27/28th Nuremberg was the target for over six hundred aircraft, including 105 Lancasters of 1 Group. Although the initial marking was accurate, many of the backers-up experienced problems with their H2S sets, and this allowed a creep-back to develop. Despite the attentions of a Master Bomber, it proved impossible to rescue the attack, and much of the bombing was wasted in open country, a disappointment compounded by the loss of thirty-three aircraft, of which two belonged to 1 Group. In contrast, a raid on the twin towns of Mönchengladbach and Rheydt on the 30/31st was highly successful, and resulted in the destruction of over 2,400 buildings for the loss of twenty-five aircraft. 1 Group contributed 134 aircraft, including fourteen Wellingtons each from 166 and 300 Squadrons. Two Lancasters and three Wellingtons failed to return, but 166 Squadron's two missing crews would be the last to be lost on Wellingtons as conversion to the Lancaster was imminent. In nine months of operations the squadron had lost forty-six aircraft, either missing or destroyed in accidents, and this was the highest attrition rate in the Command among Wellington units. 12 Squadron's W/C Towle elected to join the crew of F/L Booth as 2nd pilot, and they were all killed when ED972 was shot down in the target area.

The last night of the month brought the second raid of the series on Berlin, and involved a force of over six hundred aircraft, of which 102 Lancasters were provided by 1 Group. Again the marking was inaccurate as the H2S sets proved to be temperamental, and many crews undershot the city, some by up to thirty miles. Less than a hundred houses were destroyed, while Berlin's industry escaped altogether, and the defenders hacked down forty-seven bombers, including 16% of the Stirlings. Berlin was to be a costly target for many squadrons, but none was to suffer as grievously as 1 Group's 460 Squadron, which lost another crew on this night. 101 Squadron's JB150 was another of the group's five casualties, and disappeared without trace with the crew of F/S Edis. 1,469 sorties were flown during the month, of which 1,336 were night bombing and 133 mining.

September

12 Squadron welcomed W/C Craven as its new commanding officer on the 1st of the month, and he presided over the squadron's involvement in the final raid on Berlin before the autumn recess. It was delivered by three hundred Lancasters on the night of the 3/4th, of which 109 were from 1 Group. The marking and bombing again fell short, but some loads were deposited in the industrial Siemensstadt district, where a number of war industry factories suffered a serious loss of production. Twenty-two Lancasters were missing from this operation, and it was a bad night for 1 Group in general and the stations of Ludford Magna and Binbrook in particular. 460 Squadron posted missing three crews, including that of flight commander S/L Kelaher, and 101 Squadron suffered similarly. ED410 crashed in Germany, killing F/O Carpenter and all but one of his crew, and ED659 also crashed on German soil and took with it W/O Tucker and his crew. JB149 was shot down by a night fighter, and although F/S Hammond and one of his crew survived in enemy hands, the precise location of his Lancaster and fallen crew mates has never been established. 305 Squadron was posted from Bomber Command on the 5th, and became part of the 2nd Tactical Air Force, with which it would fly Mosquitos. This left just 300 Squadron to represent Poland in the heavy bombing war.

The Command's persistently heavy losses continued at the twin cities of Mannheim and Ludwigshafen on the 5/6th, when thirty-four aircraft failed to return from a highly successful operation. The location of the cities astride the Rhine made them ideal for a dual attack, in which the creep-back tendency could be incorporated into the plan. An approach from the west with the aiming point on the eastern side of Mannheim on the eastern bank, guaranteed the spread of the bombing across the city and onto the western bank of the river, where lay Ludwigshafen. Mannheim reported a catastrophe, while the Ludwigshafen authorities recorded almost two thousand fires, and over a thousand buildings destroyed. Of the 1 Group contingent of 102 Lancasters just four were missing on the following morning, including JA926 of 101 Squadron with the crew of F/O Graham. The Lancaster was a notoriously difficult aircraft to evacuate in an emergency, because of its narrow confines and inadequate and poorly designed escape hatches. Never the less, on this night no fewer than twenty-five of the twenty-eight airmen involved in the four crashes escaped with their lives, eighteen of them in captivity and seven on the run, ultimately to evade capture.

On the following night, four hundred aircraft were sent to Munich, eighty-six of them representing 1 Group. Most of the crews bombed on estimated position after a timed run from the Ammersee. Results were inconclusive, but at least the losses amounted to a more modest sixteen aircraft. The single 1 Group casualty was a 12 Squadron Lancaster, which suffered engine failure and was in the process of jettisoning its bombs when a fierce fire erupted in the engine. The pilot's only course of action was to ditch immediately, which he did off Spurn Head. Such was the urgency of the situation that he was unable to contact base, and the crew was initially listed as missing. Sadly, two members of the crew went down with the aircraft, but the pilot and four others were found floating in their dinghy on the following morning and were picked up.

The main force Lancaster squadrons remained off the order of battle thereafter for two weeks, and, in the meantime, one of the most fascinating aspects of the bomber war was taking another step forward. The field of electronics was championed by Harris as the tool by which Bomber Command could at last overcome the difficulties of accurate bombing by night, and thwart the enemy's attempts to make it an uneconomical undertaking. Every gain, however, was temporary, as the enemy always seemed to find a countermeasure. Now that the effectiveness of Window was waning, it was decided to equip a squadron with frequency-jamming apparatus, and 100 Squadron was earmarked to be the recipient of the device code named "Jostle". However, as 101 Squadron was not included in the first phase of H2S conversions, and 100 Squadron was, it was to Ludford Magna that the highly secret equipment was delivered.

The device provided an opportunity to jam three frequencies simultaneously, with the aim of interfering with ground-to-air night fighter communications. An extra crew member was required to operate Jostle, which was renamed Airborne Cigar or ABC in 101 Squadron usage, and rather than being a German speaker capable of broadcasting spurious instructions to enemy pilots, he needed only sufficient knowledge of the language to be able to recognise genuine German transmissions. A number of trials were carried out in a 101 Squadron Lancaster in early September, overseen by radar specialist, F/L Collins, who was on secondment from

Bomber Command. A trials flight actually approached to within ten miles of the enemy coast on the 8th, and F/L Austin was the pilot selected for all proving flights. Two aircraft, JA965 and JA977, arrived on squadron charge from the Signals Intelligence Unit, both fitted with ABC, and such aircraft were easily identifiable by the three seven foot-long aerials which sprouted from the top of the fuselage. The ABC equipment was to be carried in addition to, and not instead of, a bomb load, and the only concession was a reduction in payload of a thousand pounds to compensate for its 605lbs of weight and the extra man. Once the ABC Flight became operational, a minimum of eight of its aircraft would accompany every major Bomber Command operation, spread through the stream not more than ten miles apart, whether or not the rest of 1 Group was on the battle order. To accommodate the increased activity, the complement of aircraft on charge would exceed thirty, and at one time would reach forty-two including reserves.

166 Squadron carried out its final Wellington mining operation on the night of the 18/19th, and was then stood down to begin conversion to the Lancaster. To help it along the way it received an influx of crews and Lancasters from 103 Squadron's C Flight on the 20th. The night of the 22/23rd brought the first of a month-long four raid series against Hannover. This first operation would prove to be the largest of the series, and involved over seven hundred aircraft, including 101 Lancasters and twelve Wellingtons from 1 Group. Eight of the Lancasters represented 166 squadron at Kirmington, which was carrying out its maiden operation on the type. 101 Squadron put up nineteen Lancasters, of which eight were of the ABC variety, operating against Germany for the first time. Unfortunately, the crews' efforts were effectively wasted, when stronger than forecast winds pushed the marking and bombing beyond the city's south-eastern quadrant, and little significant damage was inflicted. The cost of the disappointment was twenty-six aircraft, and another expensive month was in prospect for 460 Squadron following the failure to return of two more of its Lancasters. 101 Squadron lost W4324, which crashed near Bremerhaven killing Sgt Green and his crew.

Mannheim received its second heavy assault of the month on the 23/24th, when well over nine hundred buildings were destroyed, and some of the later bombing spilled across the Rhine into Ludwigshafen, and the small towns of Oppau and Frankenthal. 104 Lancasters of 1 Group took part, and six were among the thirty-two aircraft that failed to return. W/C Craven of 12 Squadron chose this operation as his first with the squadron, and he returned safely. 101 Squadron's JA977 was the only ABC Lancaster involved in the operation, and it was damaged by enemy action before exploding over France. F/O Turner and five of his crew were killed, and two others survived to fall into enemy hands. This was, therefore, the first of many ABC Lancasters to fail to return from operations.

The second Hannover raid took place on the 27/28th, for which 1 Group put up 108 Lancasters and fifteen Wellingtons. The post raid assessment suggested a successful attack, and the bombing was, indeed, concentrated, however, wrongly forecast winds had caused it to be concentrated outside of the city and onto outlying communities and open country. Five of the group's aircraft were missing, and it was a black night for 166 Squadron, to which three of them belonged. 101 Squadron's ABC equipped JA965 was homebound over Lincolnshire, when it was spotted by an enemy intruder and shot down. The appropriately named pilot, P/O Skipper, and his seven crew colleagues all died in the wreckage. Another sad loss was that of 103 Squadron's S/L Kennard DFC, who had been screened back in March, and had just returned to operations. Killed with him was another holder of the DFC and three holders of the DFM. Seventy-seven 1 Group Lancasters were called into action on the 29/30th to join in an attack on the Ruhr city of Bochum, and 166 Squadron lost yet another aircraft and crew, the group's only casualty of the night.

October

On the 1st of October, on paper at least, 100 Squadron donated its C Flight as the nucleus of 625 Squadron, which was forming at Kelstern, although it would be the 13th before any crews actually transferred over. JB122 was the first Lancaster to be taken on charge. The month began in hectic fashion for the Lancaster squadrons, which were called on to operate six times in the first eight nights. 460 Squadron bade farewell to W/C Martin on a posting, and he was replaced by W/C Norman, who had arrived from 1663 HCU on the 9th of September, and whose time with the squadron, sadly, would be brief. 1, 5 and 8 Groups opened the month's account at Hagen in the Ruhr on the 1/2nd with a force of 240 aircraft. The eighty-five 1 Group participants to reach and bomb the primary target helped to devastate the town's industry. On the following night, the same groups went to Munich with 290 aircraft and destroyed over three hundred buildings, although the 5 Group "time and distance" effort resulted in much of its bombs undershooting the city. 1 Group dispatched ninety-three Lancasters, of which 101 Squadron's contribution was a modest nine aircraft. Only eight Lancasters were lost, but three of them were from 1 Group, and two belonged to 460 Squadron at Binbrook.

For the third night running a major operation was mounted on the 3/4th, and this time the Halifaxes and Stirlings joined in to make up a force of 540 aircraft. The target was Kassel, for which 1 Group provided fifty-seven aircraft, of which eight belonged to 101 Squadron as the ABC conversion continued at Ludford Magna. They contributed to a partially successful operation that resulted in the devastation of one of the city's eastern districts, and damage to two aircraft factories. For once the group sustained no losses, but there was to be no rest, and the following night brought an operation to Frankfurt, where all previous efforts had achieved only modest results. To operate on four successive nights was a new record for the group, but the ground crews worked hard to prepare for what turned out to be two operations. Twenty-seven Lancasters from the group joined forces with 370 others to hit the primary target, while fifty-four acted as the main force for a "spoof" raid on Ludwigshafen. The Frankfurt operation was the most effective yet on the city, and the eastern half and the inland docks area were left a sea of flames.

After a two night rest 340 Lancasters of 1, 3, 5, 6 and 8 Groups went to Stuttgart on the 7/8th, the night on which 101 Squadron employed its ABC communications-jamming Lancasters in numbers for the first time. In all the squadron put up nineteen Lancasters in a 1 Group effort of 107, and they enjoyed moderate success at a cloud-covered target. It cannot be determined whether the two tiny 8 Group diversions at Munich and Friedrichshafen were responsible for the low loss figure, or the presence of the ABC Lancasters, but just four aircraft failed to return from Stuttgart, and for the third operation in a row 1 Group had no losses to report.

The third of the series against Hannover followed twenty-four hours later, for which 1 Group contributed ninety-six Lancasters and twelve Wellingtons to an overall force of five hundred aircraft. The operation was an outstanding success, the first at this target, and almost four thousand buildings were totally wrecked, while thirty thousand others were damaged to some extent. W/C Norman led 460 Squadron into battle, and this proved to be his first and last operation as commanding officer. Lancaster EE202, which had been borrowed from 12 Squadron at nearby Wickenby, was shot down by a night fighter west of the target, and Norman was one of three survivors from the eight on board to be taken into captivity. A second 460 squadron crew failed to return along with two from 12 Squadron, and a 166 Squadron aircraft crashed after returning early with an engine fire. W/C Arthur was installed as the new commanding officer of 460 Squadron. 625 Squadron officially came into existence at Kelstern on the 13th under the command of W/C Preston, although, as mentioned earlier, it had existed on paper at least at Grimsby since the 1st. W/C Preston had previously served as a flight commander with 12 Squadron, before being posted to a training station on the 1st of September 1942, and later spending time at 1 Group HQ.

The crews were allowed a welcome break from operations until the night of the 18/19th, when the fourth and final Hannover raid was carried out, and like the first two, it was a disappointing failure. 360 Lancasters took part, of which 108 were provided by 1 Group, including nine from 625 Squadron on its maiden operation. The Pathfinders failed to achieve concentration in conditions of complete cloud cover, and most of the bombs found open country. Eighteen aircraft failed to return home, of which seven represented 1 Group. 103 Squadron was hardest-hit with three failures to return, which must have been a blow to W/C Nelson, who had only succeeded W/C Slater earlier on the 18th. 101 Squadron had two aircraft missing, among them DV230, which was shot down by a night fighter twenty miles north-west of the target, killing F/O Humphries and the other eight occupants. DV266 also went down close to the target with fatal consequences for Sgt Daye and all but one of his crew.

The first major operation against Leipzig took place on the night of the 20/21st, when appalling weather conditions conspired to render the attack ineffective. 1 Group put up 104 Lancasters, five of which failed to return, and among them was the first to be lost from 625 Squadron. In contrast to this dismal failure, a second attack during the month on Kassel on the 22/23rd produced outstanding results. 569 Lancasters and Halifaxes took off, of which 105 represented 1 Group. 101 Squadron provided fourteen aircraft, and it was the first time that all carried ABC. The marking and most of the bombing were stunningly accurate, and achieved the kind of concentration that inevitably led to massive destruction. It also led to a firestorm, and although not as extensive as that experienced in Hamburg in July, it contributed to the destruction of 4,349 apartment blocks, containing 26,782 flats, and serious damage to a further 6,700 blocks. More than 3,500 fires were dealt with and at least six thousand people lost their lives, but the defenders fought back to claim the high figure of forty-three bombers, among which were seven from 1 Group. 103 Squadron was again the hardest-hit with three failures to return, one of them captained by a flight commander. There were no other major operations to occupy the crews during the month, but it should be remembered that while the major offensives had been taking place, Wellingtons of the Polish 300 Squadron were busy mining the enemy sea lanes, and they conducted nine such operations during October. 908 sorties were dispatched by the group during the month, of which 841 were night bombing and 67 mining.

November

For the crews of 1 Group there was only one major operation to negotiate during the first half of November, and this was to Düsseldorf on the night of the 3/4th. 140 Lancasters of 1 Group joined 440 other Lancasters and Halifaxes heading towards the Ruhr city in conditions of heavy cloud. As if by royal command the cloud disappeared when the force was twenty-five miles from its destination, and the residents braced themselves for what was destined to be a torrid time. The Pathfinder marking was both punctual and accurate, and the main weight of the attack was delivered onto central and southern districts, where substantial damage was inflicted on housing and industry. Eighteen aircraft failed to return, of which five were from 1 Group, including two each from 12 and 101 Squadrons. The latter's DV265 was attacked by a night fighter over the target, and a fierce fire developed in the fuselage aft of the navigator's compartment. Both gunners, the wireless operator and the ABC specialist were cut off, and all perished with their pilot, Sgt Evans, when the Lancaster crashed into a north-eastern suburb. LM365 crashed in Germany close to the Dutch frontier killing Sgt Cummings and his seven comrades.

There would be little further activity for the heavy brigade for the next two weeks, and it was during this period, on the 7th, that 12 Squadron's C Flight of eight Lancasters was transferred across the station at Wickenby to form the nucleus of 626 Squadron under the command of W/C Phillip Haynes, an officer who had been commissioned as far back as 1930. He had served on the North-West Frontier and had been posted to command the Air Observers School in the month that war was declared. The nucleus of experienced crews meant that there would be no delay in declaring the squadron operational. The group was alerted on the 10th to provide aircraft for an attack on the distant Baltic port of Königsberg. At midday the target and bomb load were changed, and the ground crews worked frantically to prepare 102 Lancasters to join more than two hundred others from 5 and 8 Groups for an attack on the railway tunnel at Modane in southern France, which linked Turin and Grenoble through the Alps. It was at this juncture that the newly-formed 626 Squadron entered the fray, dispatching seven crews, among them P/O Jack Currie in his favoured Charlie Two, a Lancaster he had brought over from 12 Squadron. *(Jack Currie wrote a number of books about his experiences, as well as fronting a documentary or two)*. The Pathfinder marking was slightly off, but over two hundred aircraft brought back aiming point photographs showing serious damage. W/C Kucharski concluded his six month tour of duty as commanding officer of 300 Squadron, and he was succeeded on the 18th by W/C Kuzian.

As Harris's recent hint to Churchill concerning an American involvement in the Berlin campaign had generated no positive response, he resolved to go alone. On the night of the 18/19th, the Lancaster squadrons were made ready for the Capital, while a predominantly Halifax and Stirling effort at Mannheim and Ludwigshafen was intended to act as a diversion. Among the 440 Lancasters heading for Berlin was a 1 Group record contribution of 153 of the type. Complete cloud cover over the target necessitated blind marking and bombing, and in the absence of any concentration, a modest 169 houses were destroyed, along with four industrial premises, while a further five hundred buildings were seriously damaged. One useful victim of the operation was the Daimler-Benz car factory, which suffered a 90% loss of production for a period. The diversionary raid was moderately effective, and may well have contributed to the relatively low loss of nine aircraft. 460 Squadron contributed a very creditable twenty-eight Lancasters, the largest effort of the night by a clear five aircraft, and only one of these returned early. Berlin generally meant losses, but there were just three from the group, including another 101 Squadron ABC Lancaster, LM370, which crashed in Holland killing P/O McManus and his entire crew.

The Lancaster squadrons sat out a disappointing raid on Leverkusen on the 19/20th, and later on the 20th W/C David Holford was posted from 1656CU, where he had been a flight commander and senior instructor since February, to take command of 100 Squadron at Grimsby. His predecessor, W/C McIntyre, had completed eleven operations during his tour, and would be awarded a Bar to his DFC early in the coming year. He was posted to HQ 1 Group, where he would assist in preparing North Killingholme for the arrival of its first operational squadron. W/C Holford was a highly experienced officer, who had been awarded a DFC back in 1940 for service with 99 Squadron. Following a period as an instructor at 11 O.T.U., he returned to the operational scene in October 1941 and completed twenty-nine operations with 103 Squadron, during which he earned a DSO for his fortitude during the already mentioned Operation Fuller on the 12th of February 1942. At the conclusion of his tour he commanded 103 Squadron's Conversion Flight, which, during his tenure, ultimately merged with that of 460 Squadron to form 1656 CU. Although officially screened, he managed two trips to Berlin in January 1943, and was also involved in the testing of the Vickers Warwick at Boscombe Down. Holford had gained the rank of wing commander in February 1943 at the age of twenty-one, and he was the youngest man ever in the RAF to hold this rank. Sadly, his time with 100 Squadron would be quite brief.

The Lancaster brigade returned to the fray on the 22/23rd, for a maximum effort assault on Berlin. 764 aircraft set out either side of 17.00 hours for the long slog eastwards on a relatively direct route, in weather conditions that were generally unfavourable for night fighters. Complete cloud cover over the target prevented the crews from making an immediate assessment of their work, but beneath the clouds, Berlin was undergoing its worst night of the war. From the city centre westwards, three thousand houses and apartment blocks were reduced to ruins, along with twenty-one industrial premises, and a number of fire areas developed with firestorm characteristics. Around two thousand people lost their lives, while 175,000 others were rendered homeless. This outstanding success was gained at a cost of twenty-six aircraft, and not a single one of the 169 contributed by 1 Group failed to return, although 101 Squadron's DV291 had crashed on take-off without injury to the crew. Five of the fifty participating Stirlings were among the casualties, and after a succession of disproportionately high losses, Harris decided to withdraw them from future operations over Germany.

On the following night an all Lancaster main force set off to return to Berlin with 111 of their number provided by 1 Group. Perhaps the strain of back-to-back Berlin operations had something to do with the twenty-three early returns experienced by the group, but those pressing on continued the good work of the previous night, guided by the glow of fires still burning beneath the clouds. Another two thousand houses were destroyed, along with eight industrial premises, and around fifteen hundred people were killed. The main defence in the target area was provided by single engine day fighters operating in the Wilde Sau role, and these probably accounted for many of the twenty shot-down Lancasters, six of which were from 1 Group, two of them belonging to 460 Squadron.

1 Group's expansion program continued on the 25th with the posting of 103 Squadron's C Flight to form the nucleus of 576 Squadron, which would share the facilities at Elsham Wolds for the next eleven months. W/C Gareth Clayton was installed as the commanding officer, having previously occupied the role of flight commander at 100 Squadron. Also on this day 100 Squadron, having already spawned 625 Squadron in the previous month, now donated its C Flight again to form the nucleus of 550 Squadron, with which it would share the station at Grimsby for the next six weeks. W/C J J Bennett was installed as the unit's first commanding officer, and he came with a wealth of experience, having completed two tours of operations with 5 Group. While serving with 50 Squadron in April 1940, the then flight lieutenant Bennett took part in the first mining operation of the war, having earlier become the first Bomber Command

pilot to be awarded the DFC for night bombing. He commanded 144 Squadron between February and July 1942, before undertaking a period of duty at 1 Group HQ.

Halifaxes provided the main force for an ineffective attack on Frankfurt on the 25/26th, before the fourth raid on Berlin since the resumption took place on the 26/27th. This was by an all Lancaster heavy force numbering over four hundred aircraft, including 153 from 1 Group, among which were eight representing 550 Squadron on its maiden operation. Also in the 1 Group contingent was the magnificent total of thirty Lancasters from 103 Squadron, only a day after shedding a whole flight, and this was the largest number by a single squadron during the entire campaign. It was a busy night for 101 Squadron, which provided seventeen aircraft for the main operation and six ABC Lancasters for a diversionary attack on Stuttgart by a Halifax main force. Approaching Berlin from the south in clear conditions, the Pathfinders overshot the aiming point by many miles, and marked an area in the north-west of the city, where a number of industrial suburbs were situated. More by luck than judgement, therefore, thirty-eight war industry factories were destroyed, but there was less damage to housing. Sadly, the zoo was hit, and although some animals had been evacuated, most of those remaining were killed.

Twenty-eight aircraft failed to return home, and many more crashed in England. 1 Group lost eleven from Berlin and one from Stuttgart, and 103 Squadron once again suffered the highest casualties with four failures to return. 101 Squadron's DV268 and DV289 both crashed in Germany, the former a non-ABC aircraft in which Sgt Zanchi and all but one of his crew lost their lives. The latter was an ABC aircraft captained by F/S Bennett, who died with all but two of his crew, who were captured. DV285 was shot down by a night fighter over Belgium during the Stuttgart diversion, but P/O Walker and two others escaped by parachute, and the navigator evaded capture to eventually arrive home in October 1944. 550 Squadron registered its first casualty on this, its first operation, after LM379 caught fire in the target area, and was partially abandoned, ultimately with just two survivors. This series of three raids on Berlin had inflicted terrible damage, with fatalities in the city amounting to 4,330, but its modern layout with wide thoroughfares and open spaces created natural firebreaks, and from now on the law of diminishing returns would apply and further successes would have to be ground out at a high cost in Bomber Command lives. 460 Squadron had lost four crews since the resumption of the campaign, but this was just a foretaste of the casualties it would sustain during operations to the Capital over the coming month. The month's tally of sorties by the group amounted to 989, of which 834 were night bombing and 155 mining.

December

1 Group now consisted of ten Lancaster units, while 300 Squadron would continue to soldier on with Wellingtons until well into the coming year. It fell to the "Big City" to open Bomber Command's December account on the 2/3rd, when over four hundred Lancasters represented the main force. 1 Group put up 144, including seven from 576 Squadron on its maiden operation. War correspondents are very courageous people, who place their lives at risk in the pursuit of their art, and two such men boarded two of the twenty-five 460 Squadron Lancasters taking off for this night's attack. No one could have known that they had chosen to fly on the squadron's blackest night of the war thus far, and that the aircraft to which they had been assigned would be among those failing to return. The direct route to the target helped the Luftwaffe night fighter controller to identify the destination of the bomber stream in good time, and he was able to assemble a proportion of his aircraft in the target area. Wrongly forecast winds scattered the stream, and presented the Pathfinders with great difficulty in establishing their position. This led to a scattering of bombs from east to west, and across southern districts, where some useful industrial damage occurred, but many bomb loads were wasted in open country.

Night fighters continued to be active on the return flight, and a massive forty aircraft were lost, eighteen of them from 1 Group. Five of these were from Binbrook, and all fell within the Berlin defence zone. W4881 exploded in the air after being attacked by a night fighter, and the war correspondent from the Sydney Sun, Norman Stockton, was among the five fatalities. A Norwegian war correspondent, Capt Grieg, was on board LM316, from which there were no survivors. In all twenty-seven 460 Squadron airmen were killed, including a flight commander, and eight others ended up as PoWs. Three more of the squadron's Lancasters returned to Binbrook on three engines, but the war would go on amidst the tragedies, and men hardened themselves to the loss of comrades. 101 Squadron posted missing three crews for the second operation running, and the only bright spot was the survival of S/L Robertson and his seven crew mates in JB128. LM363 and LM364 both crashed in Germany, and there were no survivors from the two eight-man crews captained by F/L Frazer-Hollins and F/S Murrell respectively. 12 and 103 Squadrons also each registered three failures to return, and only 100 Squadron welcomed all of its aircraft home.

On the following night over five hundred aircraft were detailed for a raid on Leipzig, and the famous American broadcaster, Ed Murrow, hitched a lift in a 619 Squadron Lancaster of 5 Group. 1 Group provided ninety-six Lancasters for what turned out to be a highly successful and destructive operation, despite the presence of complete cloud cover. The operation demonstrated that skymarking under favourable conditions could be as effective as visual marking. It helped that the Luftwaffe controller had wrongly identified Berlin as the target, and had sent the night fighters there. As a result the operation proceeded without undue interference from the defences, and much residential and industrial property was destroyed. Twenty-four aircraft failed to return, at least half of them as the result of flying into the Frankfurt defence zone on the way home. Just three 1 Group aircraft were missing, including one captained by a 625 Squadron flight commander, who survived, as did Ed Murrow, who returned safely from what was the most successful raid of the war on this eastern city.

On the 15th, during a two week period when minor operations held sway, 166 Squadron welcomed a new commanding officer in the shape of the American W/C Scragg. He was posted in from 103 Squadron at Elsham Wolds on promotion to succeed W/C Twamley, who took over command of 1667 HCU. Colin Scragg was a pre-war officer, and was a chief flying instructor in Canada from 1940. Even then he was a wing commander, and had to drop a rank to stand a chance of getting into the war proper. He got to England by ferrying a Mitchell across the Atlantic, and after time at 18 O.T.U and 1656 HCU he was posted to 103 squadron in early October as A Flight commander.

After the lengthy stand-down the main force and Pathfinder Lancaster crews were briefed on the 16th for the next trip to Berlin. 483 Lancasters took off in the late afternoon of what would become known as "Black Thursday", and this number included a new record of 161 aircraft from 1 Group. Matters began to go awry immediately as a 103 Squadron Lancaster collided with another from 576 Squadron three minutes after take-off, and both crashed into the Lincolnshire countryside without survivors. Sgt Cull, the flight engineer on board the 576 Squadron Lancaster, was just eighteen years old, and was amongst the youngest to lose his life on Bomber Command operations. Gradually, a further twenty aircraft made their way back without completing the operation. A direct route took the remainder across Holland and Germany, and night fighters remained in contact from the Dutch coast, all the way to the target. Berlin was cloud covered, but most of the bombs found the mark in central and eastern districts, although there was no recognizable point of concentration. Housing, railway installations and public buildings were the chief victims of the attack, but the defences claimed twenty-five aircraft, of which seven were from 1 Group.

The real problems arose when the tired crews arrived back over England to encounter a blanket of fog concealing their airfields, principally in the 1, 6 and 8 Group regions. Most had insufficient fuel reserves to even contemplate the long flight to a diversionary station, and as they stumbled around in the murk in search of somewhere to land, accidents were inevitable. Twenty-nine Lancasters either crashed or were abandoned by their crews, and around 150 airmen lost their lives in these most tragic of circumstances. It was a particularly bad night for 100 Squadron, which had all of its aircraft return safely to home airspace, before two collided in the circuit at 00.40 and crashed just south of Waltham with just one survivor between them. This tragedy occurred an hour and forty minutes after another 100 Squadron aircraft had come down within five miles of Grimsby, killing the pilot and three others. The biggest blow, however, was the loss of the squadron's popular commanding officer, W/C Holford, whose Lancaster crashed near Kelstern killing four of the crew. Holford actually survived the crash, but the heavy demand for ambulances on this night resulted in a delay, and he died before one arrived. It was another torrid night for 101 Squadron also, which lost DV300 to an enemy night fighter at the Dutch coast while outbound, and there were no survivors from the eight man crew of F/L MacFarlane. DV299 also failed to return, and was lost without trace with the crew of F/S Head.

Losses to enemy action were part and parcel of the job, but to have to battle the weather on return to base at the end of an exhausting seven or eight hour slog was asking too much. Two 101 Squadron crews became caught up in the frantic search for a landing site, and one such episode ended happily, while the other did not. DV283 arrived back desperately short of fuel, and in the absence of somewhere to put down it was successfully abandoned by F/O Lazenby and his crew. Sgt Cooper and his crew were less fortunate and LM389 crashed in Yorkshire killing all but one of the occupants. 166 Squadron had one failure to return, and two others crash in Lincolnshire, and all twenty-one airmen perished. At 23.12, a message was received from 460 Squadron's JB657 to say that it had clipped a tree, and about forty minutes later it came down in Lincolnshire, killing the crew. At 23.57, JB704 crashed next to the airfield without crew casualties, and twenty minutes later, DV173 crashed near Caistor, killing one of the gunners. The highly experienced W/C Dilworth became 100 Squadron's new commanding officer, having previously commanded 460 Squadron between December 1942 and February 1943. He was posted in from 576 Squadron, where he had been for just three weeks as a flight commander, and had spent the three months before that at 101 Squadron. The drop in status after his time at 460 Squadron suggests that his rank while there was acting, and he had reverted to his substantive rank of squadron leader on his departure.

On the 20/21st, Frankfurt was the objective for over six hundred Lancasters and Halifaxes, while a small 1 and 8 Group raid on Mannheim acted as a diversion. 1 Group contributed 103 Lancasters to the main operation and twenty-eight to the diversion. The crews had been briefed to expect clear skies and ground marking, but in the event, marking had to take place through gaps in the cloud, and the confusion was exacerbated by a decoy fire site some miles away. Some of the creep-back fell across residential districts, and 466 houses were destroyed, while many cultural and historic buildings sustained severe damage. It was a costly night for the attackers, and it was the Halifax brigade that sustained the bulk of the casualties among the forty-one missing aircraft. 1 Group came off lightly with just three missing aircraft.

Over 350 Lancasters made up the main force for Berlin on the night of the 23/24th, of which 128 represented 1 Group. The bombers failed to make a major impression on the Capital, after many Pathfinder crews experienced technical failures with H2S. Under three hundred buildings were destroyed, but at least the losses were substantially down on recent operations, and a more modest sixteen were absent from their dispersals on the following morning. Six of these belonged to 1 Group, but tragically, two others, both from 550 Squadron, had collided at twelve thousand feet about half an hour after take-off from Grimsby, and crashed near Louth without survivors.

The fifth wartime Christmas came and went in relative peace, and it was not until the 29th that the crews were ushered once more into the briefing rooms, to learn that they must endure yet another trip to the Capital. This was a maximum effort operation, involving over seven hundred aircraft, and would be the first of three against Berlin in the space of five nights spanning the turn of the year. 1 Group provided 136 Lancasters for this operation, and like the rest of the force the crews found the city again concealed beneath a layer of cloud, forcing them to bomb on skymarkers. As they retreated westwards at the end of the attack, they remained uncertain as to the effects of their efforts. Reconnaissance later showed the main weight of the attack to have fallen into southern and south-eastern districts, where around four hundred buildings were destroyed. Twenty aircraft were brought down by the defences, and among these were five from 1 Group. 101 squadron's LM371 crashed in Germany, but not before F/S Shearer and six of his crew had escaped by parachute to fall into enemy hands. 460 Squadron ended 1943 with two more failures to return, and it had now lost seventy aircraft on operations during the year, more than any other Lancaster unit, and the coming year was not about to bring any respite.

The frequent operations to Berlin were by now having an effect on the resolve of all crews, and this would be reflected in the rate of early returns. It was not the most opportune time for new crews to be beginning their first tour of operations, and in the minds of most of them, there can have been little prospect of surviving to complete thirty sorties. It had, of course, been a tough year for all squadrons, but, on balance, a highly successful one, which had seen the enemy's industrial heartland devastated, and many cities in other regions bearing the scars of battle. Both sides must have known that the future promised nothing other than more of the same. 832 sorties were launched by the group during the month, of which 796 were night bombing and 36 were mining.

1944

January

The beleaguered citizens of Berlin and the hard-pressed crews of Bomber Command doubtless shared a common hope as the New Year dawned, that Germany's Capital would cease to be the main focus of Harris's attention. For their part, the Berliners were a hardy breed, and just like their counterparts in London during the blitz of 1940, they would bear their trials with fortitude and humour, and develop a strong sense of community. They were proud of their status as Berliners first and Germans second, and during this, their "winter of discontent", they taunted their tormentors by parading banners through the shattered streets, proclaiming, "you may break our walls, but not our hearts". The radio played endlessly the melodic strains of the most popular song of the period, Nach jedem Dezember kommt immer ein Mai, After every December comes always a May, the lyrics catching the mood of the time, and hinting at a change of fortunes with the onset of spring. Harris, however, remained single-minded in his purpose, and both camps would have a long wait before their hopes were realized.

As the last few minutes of New Year's Day passed, the first of 421 Lancasters took off for the rendezvous over the North Sea, among them 117 from 1 Group. Cloud began to build up as they left the English coast behind, and by the time the bombers reached the Continent it was ten-tenths with tops at ten to twelve thousand feet. The force proceeded almost due east to pass south of Hamburg, and on reaching the "Big City" the crews found it impossible to pick out the Pathfinder ground markers. As a result they delivered most of their bombs into wooded and open country, and managed to destroy only twenty-one houses and one industrial building. It was a poor return for the loss of twenty-eight Lancasters, and the death toll among RAF airmen was greater than that suffered on the ground. Six 1 Group Lancasters failed to return home, among them two from 101 Squadron with a G suffix to their serial numbers, denoting that they were carrying secret equipment. One of these was captained by a flight commander. 460 Squadron registered its first loss of the year after JB606 crashed in Germany, without survivors from the crew of F/S Rowley.

The crews were late to bed on the morning of the 2nd, but that didn't prevent many of them from being on the order of battle for that night, for the third trip to Berlin in five nights. Such back-to-back long range flights were exhausting, and many men must have been incredulous at the prospect of another seven or eight hour round trip. This was reflected in the very high number of sixty early returns, which amounted to almost 16% of the 383 aircraft dispatched. Twenty-eight of 1 Group's contingent of 116 Lancasters returned early, but fifteen of these resulted from a recall signal to a simultaneous Wellington mining operation, which used the group's collective call sign for Lancasters. The operation began badly for 460 Squadron, when JB738 crashed in Lincolnshire just six minutes after take-off, killing F/L Knyvett and his crew. It was once the Bomber stream had reached the target area that the night fighters caught up, and they contributed to the loss of twenty-seven Lancasters, in return for another very disappointing operation. A modest eighty-two houses were destroyed in the scattered attack, and again, there were more fatalities among the bomber crews than on the ground. 1 Group posted missing five crews, including another from 101 Squadron in a G suffix aircraft.

This was the final operation for 550 Squadron while stationed at Grimsby, and it completed its move to North Killingholme on the 3rd. Here it would remain for the rest of the war as the only resident unit. In a change from Berlin, over three hundred Lancasters provided the main force for a raid on Stettin on the 5/6th, in the first major operation to the Baltic port since the previous April. 1 Group contributed 113 aircraft, whose crews encountered ten-tenths cloud most of the way to the target area, but found it clear over the city, with just a little haze. As always seemed to happen at this target, the marking and bombing were accurate, and much damage was inflicted on housing and industry, while eight ships were sunk in the harbour. Two 12 squadron aircraft were among five from the group to fail to return, and one of these force-landed in Sweden, where the crew was interned for a period to enjoy the legendary hospitality of their hosts. It was at this time, during w.e.f 15th that W/C Arthur was posted out of 460 Squadron, and was succeeded as commanding officer by W/C Marsh.

A period of rest extended through to mid month, and when briefings took place on the 14th, there must have been a degree of relief when the target was revealed to be Brunswick, and not Berlin. Brunswick was an historic town to the east of Hannover, and some crews would doubtless have recalled the expensive series of operations against that city during the autumn. Almost five hundred aircraft, all but two of them Lancasters, took off either side of 17.00 hours, among them 151 from 1 Group. The city was cloud covered and the marking scattered, and this virtually virgin target escaped with only light superficial damage, after most of the bombs fell onto outlying communities to the south. The bombers did not escape lightly, however, having been under attack from night fighters from the moment they crossed the enemy coast near Bremen, and thirty-eight Lancasters were shot down. 1 Group lost eleven aircraft, including three more from 101 Squadron, and 166 Squadron posted missing its commanding officer, W/C Scragg, who had been in post for just one month. The crew had lost the main intercom system early on because of a fault with the Monica enemy fighter warning device, but they pressed on, and moments after the bombs went down the Lancaster was raked by cannon fire, and the starboard-inner engine burst into flames. With all control lost the aircraft plunged towards the ground, the starboard wing now also on fire, and somehow Scragg managed to squeeze his way through the sliding window on that side. Within seconds of his parachute snapping open he was on the ground, the only survivor of his crew. He made every effort to evade capture, but was caught in a railway station on the following day. S/L Francis Powley was immediately promoted from B Flight commander to succeed him as commanding officer.

Losses had been high since the turn of the year, and the Pathfinders in particular were taking a beating. 156 Squadron alone lost fourteen aircraft and crews during these first two weeks of the year, a figure equivalent to almost a full two-flight squadron, and it was putting a terrible strain on the force. It was now struggling to find adequate resources to fill the gaps, and the original intention to recruit only experienced tried and tested crews would no longer sustain 8 Group. The opportunity to become Pathfinders became opened up to the leading crews leaving training units, the prospect of a straight-through tour of fifty operations balanced out in part by the one step up in rank enjoyed by all of its aircrew. Many sideways postings took place between the squadrons to maintain a leavening of experience, but the situation was becoming critical.

There were no operations at all over the succeeding five nights, and during this period, on the 18th, W/C Alexander succeeded W/C Carey-Foster as commanding officer of 101 Squadron. At 300 Squadron also there was a change of leadership as W/C Kuzian stepped aside after a two month period of tenure, and was succeeded by W/C Kowalczyk. A maximum effort was called on the 20th, for which Berlin was to be the destination. 769 aircraft and crews answered the call, of which 144 represented 1 Group, and almost 10% of them returned early to face interrogation from their commanding officers, to ascertain that they had a cast-iron reason to abort their sorties. The others pressed on, passing into enemy territory a little south of Denmark, and shortly thereafter the night fighters made contact, and remained with the bomber stream all the way to the target and part of the way home. Berlin was cloud-covered, and it was impossible for the crews to make an immediate assessment of the outcome of the raid. It was later learned that the main weight of bombs had fallen into the hitherto less severely afflicted eastern districts, where a moderate amount of damage was achieved, and this was paid for by the loss of thirty-five aircraft, two-thirds of them Halifaxes. 460 Squadron's JB739 was one of three aircraft missing from the group, and was shot down by a night fighter over Germany during the outward flight. F/S Lynch and his flight engineer were killed, while the remaining five men fell into enemy hands.

On the following night, 132 Lancasters from 1 Group joined more than five hundred other aircraft setting out for the first major raid of the war on Magdeburg. On this occasion, some night fighters infiltrated the bomber stream even before it crossed the German coast. The two combatant forces remained in contact all the way into eastern Germany, where stronger than forecast winds drove some main force crews to the target ahead of the Pathfinders. Some of these bombed before Zero Hour, and the resultant fires attracted bomb loads, while decoy fires lured others away, and the Pathfinders were unable to bring the attack back on track. The early bombing fell into the south-eastern quadrant of the city before a degree of concentration was achieved. In return for this disappointing outcome, a new record of fifty-seven aircraft was lost, three only from 1 Group, but among them was another from 460 Squadron. JB702 crashed in Germany, and there were no survivors from the crew of F/S Allan. To compound this, ND366 arrived back short of fuel, and crashed in Lincolnshire after two engines cut, injuring two members of the crew of F/S Teece who were on their fifth operation.

A few days of rest would allow the Command to lick its wounds, but the end of the month was to bring a major effort against the Capital in the form of three operations in an unprecedented four nights. This would test the resolve of the crews to the absolute limit, and would prove to be the last concerted attempt to bring Berlin to its knees. The series began on the night of the 27/28th, and involved an all Lancaster heavy force numbering 515 aircraft, of which 149 were from 1 Group. 7% of the force returned early, which was about average, while the others pressed on to deliver a scattered attack through complete cloud cover, with more bombs falling into the south of the city than the north. A number of important war industry factories sustained serious damage and loss of production, and twenty thousand people were bombed out of their homes, but there was a large wastage of bombs onto dozens of outlying communities. Thirty-three Lancasters were brought down, and, on a bad night for 1 Group, it posted missing twelve, more than a third of the overall loss figure. 12 and 460 Squadrons in particular experienced a testing time, each losing three aircraft and a flight commander. 460 Squadron's JA860 crashed east of Berlin, presumably after bombing, and F/S McLachlan died with three of his crew, while the three survivors were taken into captivity. They were joined by flight commander S/L Simpson and his entire crew, who abandoned JB296 somewhere over hostile territory, after experiencing problems with the fuel supply. Finally, JB637 went down over Germany, and there were no survivors from the crew of W/O Power.

The Halifax squadrons joined in on the following night to create a force of 670 aircraft, of which 125 belonged to 1 Group. Berlin lay under ten-tenths cloud with tops at ten thousand feet, but the Pathfinders seemed to achieve a degree of concentration, and the consensus was of an effective assault. Western and southern districts bore the main weight of the attack, and 180,000 people were bombed out of their homes. A high number of public and administrative buildings were also hit on this night, as were seventy-seven communities outside of Berlin. The defenders also enjoyed a successful night, hacking down forty-six bombers, although only four from 1 Group, including two from 166 Squadron, one of which exploded in the air following a collision. After a night's break, a predominantly Lancaster heavy force of over five hundred aircraft returned to Berlin, and caused heavy damage in central and south-western districts in particular, where fires raged out of control. A thousand people died under the bombs, and thirty-three aircraft were shot down, all but one of them Lancasters. 129 aircraft took part from 1 Group, of which thirty were assigned to Pathfinder support duties, and nine failed to return home. 100 Squadron suffered the highest casualties with three missing aircraft, and only two of the twenty-one crew members survived to be captured.

This concluded the current round of operations against Germany's Capital, and there is no question that it had been sorely afflicted as a result of these three latest assaults, but it was still a functioning city, the seat of government, and nowhere were there signs of collapse. 1,232 sorties were flown by 1 Group during the month, of which 1,176 were night bombing and 56 mining.

February

Had bad weather not kept most of the Command on the ground for the first two weeks of February, Harris would have followed up the recent successes at Berlin with another attack early in the month. As it was, 300 Squadron kept the war mobile by carrying out mining operations on four nights during the period. It was at this time, on the 8th, that W/C Haynes stepped down as commanding officer of 626 Squadron, and was posted on the following day to Sandtoft on promotion to Group Captain. He would soon be back at Wickenby, however, as the new station commander. In December he would be awarded the DFC, the citation for which made the following mention. "Group Captain Haynes has completed numerous sorties, including two attacks on the German capital and one on Mannheim. He has displayed high qualities of skill, courage and leadership, setting an example which has inspired all with whom he has flown. In addition to his gallant work in the air, Group Captain Haynes has rendered most valuable service as station commander. By his outstanding ability, great drive and unfailing devotion to duty, this officer has contributed in a large way to the operational efficiency of all under his command." (AMB No 16740. 22.12.44.) Arriving from 11 Base on the 8th as 626 Squadron's new commanding officer was W/C Quentin Ross, but his time at the helm would be all too brief.

It was not until the night of the 15/16th that Harris could mount another heavy raid on the Capital, and this was a record breaking effort in a number of ways, and would be the penultimate raid of the war on Berlin by RAF heavy bombers. The 891 aircraft represented the largest non-1,000 force to date, and those reaching the target would deliver an unprecedented 2,640 tons of bombs. It was also the first time that over five hundred Lancasters and three hundred Halifaxes had operated as part of the same force. It was a record night also for 1 Group, which dispatched 161 Lancasters, of which 139 are known to have bombed the primary target. Despite the long lay-off, during which the crews had rested and recuperated, seventy-five aircraft turned back early, more than 8% of the force, and twelve of these were from 1 Group. The remainder pressed on and the bomber stream was left largely unmolested by night fighters during the outward flight, which took place in cloud. Berlin itself lay under a blanket of ten-tenths cloud with tops at eight thousand feet, into which the Pathfinder markers quickly disappeared.

The bombing was most heavily concentrated in central and south-western districts, and over eleven hundred fires sprang up, half of them classed as large. Around a thousand houses were destroyed, along with over five hundred temporary wooden barracks, and many important war industry factories sustained damage. Forty-three aircraft failed to return home, and nine of these belonged to 1 Group. For the third Berlin raid running, 460 Squadron operated without loss, but apart from 576 Squadron each of the others in the Group posted missing one crew, and 166 Squadron two. The 625 Squadron casualty was the veteran Lancaster R5702, which had begun its career with 50 Squadron back in July 1942. After numerous operations it was damaged by flak and spent time under repair. Spells with 106, 460 and 100 Squadrons preceded its arrival at 625 Squadron, and on this fateful night it was shot down by a night fighter over Denmark, killing Sgt Ashurst and all but one of his crew. Berlin was planned as the destination on each of the following three nights, but each was cancelled by late afternoon.

A slimming down of the Halifax contribution reduced the size of the force taking off for Leipzig on the 19/20th to 823 aircraft, but 1 Group put up another record of 170 Lancasters. They departed their stations either side of midnight for the long trek into eastern Germany, and headed in broken cloud towards the greatest disaster to afflict the Command thus far. A proportion of the night fighter force met the bomber stream as it crossed the Dutch coast, and the two camps remained in contact all the way to the target. The meteorologists had been experiencing difficulty in predicting the winds over Germany, and this had hampered a number of recent operations. So it was on this night, when an unanticipated strong tail wind led to some crews reaching the target area ahead of the Pathfinders, where they were forced to orbit and await the opening of the attack. Around twenty of these fell victim to the local flak batteries, while four others were involved in collisions. The attack was delivered through cloud, and many returning crews described seeing the glow of fires and heavy columns of smoke rising towards them. Never the less, the cloud prevented an assessment of the results, but the performance of the enemy defences was all too clear to see.

When all returning aircraft had been accounted for, there was an unbelievable shortfall of seventy eight, the heaviest loss to date by a clear twenty-one. Seventeen 1 Group aircraft failed to return, and 166 Squadron was the hardest-hit, losing three Lancasters, with a fourth crash-landing at Manston after returning early with battle damage and crew casualties. 625

Squadron also suffered the loss of three aircraft and crews, while 103 lost two and had two others collide in the Elsham circuit, one crashing and killing five of the crew and the other crash-landing safely. 460 Squadron posted missing two crews, those of W/O Godwin and F/S Mackrell in JB610 and ND569 respectively, both navigators surviving along with the bomb-aimer from the former, and the wireless operator from the latter, and they all fell into enemy hands. The Halifaxes suffered a 13% casualty rate, and from this point, the less efficient Merlin powered Mk II and V variants were withdrawn from operations over Germany, as had been the Stirlings in November.

Despite the prohibitive losses, almost six hundred aircraft set out on the following night for Stuttgart, among them 130 from 1 Group. Cloud in the target area varied from three to ten-tenths, and inaccurately forecast winds led to some aircraft arriving early. The Pathfinders opened proceedings on time, and the impression was of concentrated marking and bombing in the built-up area until the later stages, when it spread to the north. Photo reconnaissance confirmed extensive damage in central districts and in the northern quadrant, and this was achieved for the modest loss of nine aircraft, none of which was from 1 Group. 460 Squadron's misfortune happened at home, when ND419 hit trees and crashed south of Grantham in Lincolnshire while trying to establish its position in blizzard conditions, and F/O Cleveland and his crew were killed. The group lost another aircraft on this night, 300 squadron Wellington JA117, which disappeared without trace while mining. This was the very last Wellington to be lost on operations with Bomber Command.

A new tactic was employed for the next two operations to Germany in an attempt to address the problem of unacceptably high losses. This involved splitting the force into two waves, with a two hour gap in between, to catch the enemy night fighter force on the ground refuelling and rearming as the second phase force passed through. 392 aircraft represented the first wave for Schweinfurt on the night of the 24/25th, taking off after 18.00 hours, and 342 others followed after 20.00 hours. 1 Group provided seventy Lancasters for the first wave and eighty-six for the second, and each found similar conditions of cloud over France and clear skies in the target area. The impression was of a successful initial assault, which set fires burning that were visible by the approaching second phase crews from 150 miles away. Heavy smoke tended to obscure the ground for the second phase attack, and there was some undershooting and a gradual spreading of the bombing towards the north.

Photo reconnaissance suggested that the operation was not as effective as at first believed, but the second phase lost 50% fewer aircraft than the first, in an overall casualty figure of thirty three. 1 Group lost five from the first phase, and among them was 100 Squadron's commanding officer, W/C Dilworth, who was mid way through his second tour and died with five of his crew. One of two other sad losses for the Grimsby unit on this night was that of F/S Wadge and crew, who had returned early after the pilot became too ill to continue. On arrival back over the station he was told to jettison his bombs and fuel over the sea, and the Lancaster was never seen again. Only days earlier this gallant crew had collided with an enemy night fighter while returning from Stuttgart, and had lost six feet of wing and eighteen inches of fin along with other damage sufficient to prompt a call to prepare to abandon ship. In the event, the pilot regained control, and through a supreme effort of crew co-operation, the battered Lancaster was nursed home to a landing at Ford, for which Wadge received the immediate award of a DFM.

460 Squadron's ND394 was another victim of the first phase attack, and fell to a night fighter over France, killing four of the crew. The pilot, W/O Baxter, and his bomb-aimer survived to ultimately evade capture, but one of the gunners was taken prisoner. The Squadron's LM315 was one of two 1 Group aircraft missing from the second phase, and there were no survivors from the crew of Sgt Yates. During the late afternoon, JB547 had taken off from Binbrook for a cross country exercise in the hands of F/S Stitt, and on the way back it collided with a 166 Squadron Lancaster, which was outbound for Schweinfurt. Both aircraft crashed in Lincolnshire, but the 460 Squadron crew parachuted at the last moment, and all survived, although two suffered serious injury. The other crew was less fortunate, and four died in the crash, while a fifth succumbed to his injuries on the following day.

On the following night, Augsburg became the victim of another of those rare occasions beyond the range of Oboe, when an operation proceeded almost entirely according to plan. 590 aircraft took part in the two-phase attack, 1 Group contributing 102 Lancasters to the first and thirty-nine to the second. The operation was characterised by highly accurate and concentrated marking and bombing, which left the old centre of this beautiful and historic city ravaged by fire, destroying forever centuries of irreplaceable culture. Almost three thousand houses were wrecked, as were many public buildings, and millions of pounds worth of art treasures were also lost. For its part, the bomber force returned home without twenty-one of its number, which suggested that there was some merit in splitting the force, and this would become a regular feature of operations from the coming autumn. 1 Group's losses were again five and two respectively, with 550 Squadron posting missing two crews. 460 Squadron's JB742 was absent from Binbrook having crashed in Germany during the second phase assault, and it was later established that none had survived from the crew of F/S Martin. 100 Squadron's ND595 was approaching the target at 23,000 feet when it was hit by flak, wounding the bomb-aimer. F/O Smith, who was on his 13th operation, ordered the crew out and was the last to leave the Lancaster, which blew up seconds later. The entire crew landed in neutral Switzerland, where they were treated with great hospitality during their period of internment. Sadly, the bomb-aimer did not survive his descent by parachute. 811 sorties were carried out by the group during the month, of which 758 were bombing and 53 mining.

March

The opening of Sandtoft at the start of March enabled 1667 HCU to leave Faldingworth and make room for 300 Squadron to move over from Ingham. The month's operations began on the night of the 1/2nd with a return to Stuttgart by over five hundred aircraft, the majority of which were Lancasters. Eighty of these were provided by 1 Group, and they set out in clear conditions, which persisted until the force was south of Paris, where ten-tenths cloud developed with tops as high as fifteen thousand feet. At the target the Pathfinder markers disappeared quickly into the cloud, forcing the crews to bomb on release point flares. Some H2S equipped crews became aware that the marking was concentrated too much in the south and south-western districts, but it did spread towards the north in the later stages of the attack. The cloud prevented an immediate assessment of results, but it was a successful operation, which caused fresh damage in central, western and northern districts. One bonus was the loss of just four aircraft, none from 1 Group, and another was a stand-down for most of the Lancaster squadrons thereafter until mid month. W/C Pattison was posted in from 11 Base on the 3rd and installed as the new commanding officer of 100 Squadron following the loss of his predecessor.

During this lull in major operations, 300 Squadron went to war for the final time as a Wellington unit, sending three aircraft to mine the waters around Lorient on the 3/4th. Also, the first salvoes were fired in the pre-invasion campaign, when Halifaxes were the predominant type in attacks on railway yards at Trappes and le Mans on the 6/7th and 7/8th respectively. These raids would continue throughout the month, and would be stepped up when the rest of the main force joined in at the conclusion of the winter offensive. W/C Craven was posted from 12 Squadron to 9 ITW at Stratford-upon-Avon, and was succeeded on the 6th by W/C Nelson, who would prove to be a popular leader. Nelson had been with the squadron since the previous month, and flew his first two operations with the unit as second pilot to P/O Adams on the Leipzig disaster and the Stuttgart raid twenty-four hours later. His first operation as crew captain came at Schweinfurt four nights after that. On the 7th, 460 Squadron's ME646 blew up on the ground at Binbrook with a cookie on board, and JA687 was written off by flying debris.

The Command was up in unprecedented strength on the 15/16th, when 823 aircraft took off for the third raid in three weeks on Stuttgart, 140 Halifaxes, Stirlings and Mosquitos went to Amiens to target the railway yards, and a small 5 Group raid was directed at an aero-engine factory at Woippy. 1 Group dispatched a record number of 190 Lancasters, which took off in conditions of thin broken cloud, which had thickened to seven to ten-tenths by the time they reached the target area. The enemy night fighters arrived at the same time and remained in contact with the bombers until they were well on their way home. The cloud prevented an assessment of results, but it would become clear that it had not been as effective an attack as that at the start of the month. Thirty-seven aircraft were brought down, eight of them from 1 Group, 550 and 625 Squadron's each losing two. Tragically, a returning 625 Squadron Lancaster collided with another from 463 Squadron as they approached their respective stations, and they crashed four miles south of Lincoln with total loss of life. 460 Squadron also posted missing an aircraft and crew, ND393 disappearing without trace with the crew of F/S Parkinson.

The first of two heavy and successful operations against Frankfurt took place on the night of the 18/19th, when more than eight hundred aircraft took part. The 194 Lancasters from 1 Group represented a new record, and they contributed to the destruction of or serious damage to over six thousand buildings. Of the twenty-two missing aircraft just two were from 1 Group, and this enabled it to put up another 194 Lancasters for the second assault on this southern city on the night of the 22/23rd. The outcome was even more catastrophic for the residents, who came out of their shelters to find half of the city without electricity, gas and water, a situation that would persist for an extended period. Fires could be seen from up to two hundred miles by returning crews, all but four of those from 1 Group making it back home. 460 Squadron suffered no losses, and it was able to claim a new Bomber Command record of 131 tons of bombs delivered.

W/C Preston was posted from 625 Squadron to Lindholme on the 27th at the end of his tour, and was succeeded by the twenty-eight-year-old W/C Haig who was promoted from his role as flight commander. That night Harris mounted what would be the final raid of the war by RAF heavy bombers on Berlin, and the sixteenth since the resumption of the campaign in November. 1 Group put up 184 Lancasters in an overall force of 811 aircraft, of which fifty-three returned early. Having set course at cruising altitude, the crews encountered an unusually strong wind from the north, which broke up the cohesion of the bomber stream and pushed the aircraft continually south of the intended track. This inevitably led to the Pathfinders' skymarkers being driven to the south-west of the city, as a result of which two areas of concentration developed. The release point flares were identified as being five to eight miles north of the ground markers, and the Master Bomber could be heard clearly exhorting the crews to aim for these. A feature of Berlin operations had been the number of outlying communities finding themselves under the bombs, and on this night more than a hundred reported bombs falling around them. The part of the attack that hit the city inflicted moderate damage in residential districts, but no important industrial concerns were hit.

Many crews found themselves straying over heavily defended areas of the Reich on the way home, as it remained difficult to resist the jetstream wind, and over two-thirds of the seventy-two missing bombers were claimed by flak batteries. After a recent period of light casualties 1 Group registered the loss of nineteen aircraft on this night, with 12 and 166 Squadrons each posting missing four and 625 Squadron three. 460 Squadron's ME640 was certainly a victim of flak, and crashed in Germany with just one of the gunners surviving from the crew of F/L McKinnon. ND463 also crashed on German soil, killing P/O Cusick and all but his wireless operator, who, like the survivor from the other crew, was taken prisoner. From now on, it would be left to the Mosquitos of 8 Group to maintain the pressure on the Capital, and this they would do right up to the end of hostilities.

626 Squadron posted missing its commanding officer, W/C Ross, who had been in post for just one month. He died along with his crew after HK539 was shot down over Germany on the way home. They had almost reached the frontier with Holland when misfortune arrived in the shape of the "Ace" night fighter pilot Major Heinz-Wolfgang Schnaufer, for whom, it is believed, this was his fiftieth kill. It is also believed that this was Ross's thirtieth operation. The crew had actually begun its tour under the captaincy of Sgt Fred Blaydon, who had just received a commission after five operations, and for whatever reason, was reluctantly kept on the ground on this night. Ross was succeeded by W/C Rodney, a Canadian in the RAF, who had been commissioned in 1936. He was awarded the AFC in January 1939, and was Mentioned in Despatches in January 1944. He took over the squadron at a time when morale was at a low ebb, but by force of personality, and by leading his men from the front, he was able to pick the

squadron up and develop an esprit de corps which would see it through to the end. The gunnery leader at the time was F/L Whitehouse, who recalls that whenever W/C Rodney flew an operation, it was always with a "sprog" crew, and with his gunnery leader in the rear turret.

It is interesting to take stock of the eight month period from August 1943 to March 1944, during which nineteen major operations were directed at Berlin. In his superb book, The Berlin Raids, Martin Middlebrook provides many statistics, which allow a clear picture of the fortunes of respective groups and squadrons to emerge. The 1 Group A-O-C, AVM Rice, believed fervently that the way to win was to deliver the maximum possible bomb tonnage to the enemy. He undertook trials to ascertain just how much a Lancaster could carry before its undercarriage showed signs of failure while taxying to the runway. The answer was around four hundred pounds more than that carried by 5 Group aircraft. This meant that 1 Group Lancasters were less able to reach the safer higher altitudes, and were less manoeuvrable in a combat situation. As a result 1 Group's rate of early returns was greater than 5 Group's, and it was noticed that 1 Group crews were guilty of jettisoning bombs over the sea, thus negating the point of loading them to the maximum. It is worth noting that four 1 Group squadrons featured in the top ten table of sorties dispatched, 460 and 101 Squadrons in first and second place respectively, while 103 and 100 Squadrons occupied sixth and seventh spot. 460 Squadron, as an example, participated in all nineteen of the main operations, and the 385 sorties launched by the squadron was the highest in the Command. It lost a total of twenty-eight Lancasters to operational causes, the highest in the Command, and the twenty-three of these failing to return represented the second highest in the Command and the highest in 1 Group. 135 airmen lost their lives, while forty-one others were languishing in PoW camps.

Two other records belonged to 460 Squadron crews, those of W/O Douglas and F/L Wales. Both completed fourteen of the sixteen Berlin raids from the November resumption, the former capturing the record for the highest number by a first tour crew, and the latter by a second tour crew. 1 Group as a whole dispatched 2,598 sorties for the loss of 143 Lancasters, 5.5%, and this represented the highest loss figure for any group participating in the campaign. A further twenty-nine Lancasters were destroyed in crashes at home. 899 of the group's crewmen were killed, 231 became PoWs and ten evaded capture. (The Berlin Raids. Martin Middlebrook.)

Although the Berlin offensive was now over, the winter campaign still had a week to run, and two more major operations for the crews to negotiate. The first was against Essen on the 26/27th, for which over seven hundred aircraft took off, 165 of them from 1 Group. The benefits of returning to a target within range of Oboe were made manifest by the destruction of over seventeen hundred houses, and the serious damage to forty-eight industrial buildings. Thus was continued the remarkable run of successes against this once elusive city since the introduction of Oboe to main force operations a year earlier. The defences were caught napping by the sudden switch to a Ruhr target, and only nine aircraft were lost. Three of these were from 1 Group, including 460 Squadron's JB598, which crashed in Belgium, killing F/O Burnell and his crew.

The winter offensive was brought to a conclusion on the night of the 30/31st, when a standard maximum effort raid was planned for Nuremberg. A 5 Group inspired route was offered for consideration, which would take the bomber stream on a long, straight leg from Belgium across Germany to a point about fifty miles north of Nuremberg, from where the final run-in to the target would begin. During a planning conference, the Lancaster Group A-O-Cs unanimously expressed a preference for this, rather than a more circuitous route as prepared by 8 Group, and 4 Group's AVM Roddy Carr was the lone dissenting voice. AVM Bennett, the Pathfinder A-O-C, blew a gasket and predicted a disaster, but his warning went unheeded, as did a report from a Met Flight Mosquito crew, which cast grave doubts on the accuracy of the cloud forecast. More than a few crews expected the operation to be scrubbed, but it was not to be, and no one could have predicted the extent to which the conditions would blight the forthcoming proceedings.

795 aircraft took off either side of 22.00 hours, among them 180 from 1 Group. They converged on the rendezvous point over the North Sea, before setting a south-easterly course for Charleroi in Belgium, and then an almost due easterly heading into Germany. Once at cruising altitude, the crews became aware of some unfamiliar meteorological characteristics, which left many of them feeling distinctly uneasy. Although relatively new, the moon cast an unusual brightness, and the visibility possessed a crystal clarity that enabled the crews to see the other aircraft in their part of the sky. The forecast high cloud failed to materialize, but formed instead beneath the bombers, to silhouette them like flies on a table cloth. As if this were not enough, condensation trails began to develop to further advertise their presence over hostile territory, and as the final insult, the jetstream winds, which had so adversely effected the Berlin raid a week earlier, were also evident, only this time from the south. These conditions and the route served to hand the bomber force on a plate to the night fighters, which were waiting at their control beacons close to the chosen route.

The carnage began at Charleroi, and from there to the target the track was clearly marked out by the burning wreckage of bombers on the ground. Over eighty were shot down before the target was even reached, and these included three of the twenty-four Lancasters from Binbrook. ND750 was one of the few to be lost to flak, and this fell near the Rhine, killing P/O Anderson and three of his crew, who were on their fifth operation. ND360 was shot down by a night fighter in central Germany, and only the navigator in the crew of S/L Utz DFC* survived to fall into enemy hands. This was a particularly sad loss of a flight commander, who, had he returned, would have been only two operations short of completing his second tour. Finally, ND738 crashed on final approach to the target, having also been dispatched by a night fighter, and there were no survivors from the crew of F/S Hargreaves.

The jetstream wind, meanwhile, was breaking up the bomber stream, and those crews who were either unaware of its strength, or simply refused to believe the evidence, were blown up to fifty miles north of track. In every operation certain crews were designated as wind-finders, and it was their task to gauge the strength and direction of the wind, and pass that on by W/T to the raid controllers, who would broadcast the findings back to the whole force. In the event, the wind-finders found it difficult to believe what they were seeing, and modified the readings they sent back to group for fear of being disbelieved. In turn, the groups were disbelieving even of the modified readings, and modified them further before transmitting them back to the bomber stream. As a result navigators were working from wildly inaccurate data, and this led to numerous crews turning towards Nuremberg from a false position. Many of these were among more than a hundred, who bombed Schweinfurt in error, and together with the fifty-two early returns and the losses already sustained, this dramatically reduced the numbers available to bomb as briefed to something over five hundred aircraft. In the face of heavy cloud cover, these failed to find the mark, and much of the bombing was wasted in open country.

Nuremberg escaped lightly, but Bomber Command had suffered by far its heaviest defeat of the war, amounting to ninety-five aircraft, and others were written off in crashes at home, or with battle damage too severe to repair. 101 Squadron experienced an horrendous night, which saw six aircraft shot down, one of them by a Halifax, and a seventh crash in Berkshire on return without survivors. 166 Squadron was also devastated by the loss of four aircraft, three of them containing eight-man crews, but perhaps there was slight consolation when it was learned later that twelve of the thirty-one men had survived and were in enemy hands. The full 1 Group casualty figure amounted to twenty-one failures to return, and it was a tragic ending to a long and bitterly fought first quarter of the year. It had been a testing period also for 460 Squadron, which had seen twenty of its crews either posted missing or killed in crashes at home.

April

That which now lay before the crews was in marked contrast to what had been endured over the preceding months. The new priority was the Transportation Plan, the systematic dismantling by bombing of the French and Belgian railway networks in preparation for the forthcoming invasion. In place of the long slog to distant German targets on dark, often dirty nights, shorter range trips to the occupied countries would become the order of the day in improving weather conditions. These would prove to be equally demanding in their way, however, and would require of the crews a greater commitment to accuracy, to avoid unnecessary civilian casualties. The main fly in the ointment was a pronouncement from on high, which decreed that most such operations were worthy of counting as just one-third of a sortie towards the completion of a tour, and until this flawed policy was rescinded, an air of discontent pervaded the bomber stations.

Despite the prohibitive losses over the winter, the Command was in remarkably fine fettle to meet its new challenge, and Harris was in the enviable position of being able to achieve that which had eluded his predecessor. This was, to attack multiple targets simultaneously, with forces large enough to make an impact, and he could now assign objectives to individual Groups, to Groups in tandem or to the Command as a whole, as dictated by operational requirements. Although pre-invasion considerations would always take priority, with Harris at the helm, his favoured policy of city-busting would never be entirely shelved, and whenever an opportunity presented itself, he would strike. As mentioned earlier, elements from 3, 4, 6 and 8 Groups had already begun bombing French railway installations, and with the availability now of the rest of the main force squadrons the time had arrived for the campaign to get into full swing.

During the absence of operations 300 Squadron changed its commanding officer yet again, when W/C Kowalczyk stepped aside on the 1st after just ten weeks at the helm. He was succeeded by W/C Pozyczka, who would remain in post for ten months. Two days later LL856 became the first Lancaster to be taken on charge by the Poles, and the process of working up to operational status began. On the 4th Operational Instruction No 19 was issued by 1 Group HQ, stating that it was the intention to "train and operate suitable crews to act as target markers and assembly point markers for precision attacks by small forces of exclusively 1 Group aircraft". The instruction went on to state that these operations would be carried out "chiefly during moonlight periods", and generally when the bulk of the Command's main force squadrons were inactive.

It is interesting to note that 5 Group had been working on its own target marking system in the preceding months, pioneered by W/C Cheshire at 617 Squadron. Frustrated by the inability of Oboe to mark small, precision targets such as V-1 launching and storage sites, Cheshire had tried diving his Lancaster towards the aiming point and releasing spot fires from low level. So successful was the experiment, that 5 Group A-O-C Cochrane sanctioned a series of operational trials against selected targets in France. As a direct result of this, 617 Squadron trained four crews and took on a number of Mosquitos to perform the low level visual marking role. What would become a spectacularly successful method was soon to be introduced to 5 Group operations as a whole, with an entire Mosquito squadron, 627, dedicated to the low level marking role. This was a move that would ultimately lead to the Group's independence. This reflected a general policy to develop each group where possible to a degree of autonomy. 3 Group had begun to experiment with G-H during the autumn of 1943, and although the trials were suspended after a short time, the autumn of 1944 would see its successful return. Operational Instruction No 19 was a move in this direction for 1 Group.

The first major night of operations since Nuremberg came on the 9/10th, when elements of 3, 4, 6 and 8 Groups attacked the Lille-Delivrance goods station, while 225 aircraft from all groups targeted the railway yards at Villeneuve-St-Georges in Paris. 1 Group supported the latter with thirty-six Lancasters, and provided forty-seven others as part of a 1 and 5 Group force of 103 sent to lay mines in the Baltic. 460 Squadron supported both 1 Group operations, and any hopes that the new campaign would be less hazardous were quickly dashed. The mining force ran into fierce night fighter activity as it withdrew from the target area, and nine Lancasters were lost, seven of them from 1 Group, of which three belonged to 460 Squadron. All three were shot down over Denmark, with no survivors from the crew of W/O Proud in JB734, just one from the crew of P/O Burke in JB600, and two from the crew of F/O Crosby in ME663. The two last-mentioned crews were experienced, and were on their 22nd and 23rd operations respectively. Just six minutes after taking off from Binbrook for Villeneuve, ME727 crashed five miles east of the airfield, killing P/O McKenzie and his crew.

Both of the main operations were claimed as successful, the Lille force destroying over two thousand items of rolling stock, and seriously damaging buildings and track, but heavy casualties were inflicted on French civilians at each location. It was a sobering start to the new phase of operations, which carried over into the following night, when five railway yards were attacked in France and Belgium. 130 Lancasters of 1 Group were assigned to those at Aulnoye, where the marking was carried out by Oboe Mosquitos. The attack resulted in damage to the engine shed and thirty locomotives, but 340 houses were also destroyed or damaged, and fourteen civilians lost their lives. Seven Lancasters were lost, including 460 Squadron's ND568, which fell to a night fighter over France, killing the entire crew of F/O Probert. On the 11/12th over three hundred Lancasters from 1, 3 and 5 Groups provided the main force for an attack on railway installations at Aachen. Ninety-five 1 Group Lancasters took part in what became a highly destructive area raid that resulted in the deaths of over fifteen hundred people.

It was a week before the heavy brigade was in action again, and in the meantime, on the 14th, the Command officially became subject to the authority of SHAEF, and would remain thus shackled until the Allied armies were sweeping towards the German frontier at the end of the summer. On the 15th 300 Squadron was declared operational on Lancasters with sixteen on charge and four in reserve. On the 18th 1 Group's Special Duties Flight, or SDF as it became known, was formed at Binbrook under the command of S/L Breakspear, an experienced flight commander from 100 Squadron. He was a man to whom taking the war to the enemy was a point of principle and pride. The London Gazette carried an announcement of the award of his DFC, which read;

"An excellent captain of aircraft and flight commander, Squadron Leader Breakspear has continually displayed a fine fighting spirit and an outstanding devotion to duty. On no fewer than eleven occasions this officer has taken part in attacks on Berlin, undeterred by the most intense enemy opposition. In November 1943, two engines of his aircraft were set on fire when over the German capital, and on another occasion half of a rudder was shot away. Each time by superb airmanship and captaincy, this officer has extricated his aircraft and crew from their perilous situations."

F/L Gillam and crew also of 100 Squadron were posted in on that day along with the crews of F/L Hull from 101 Squadron, F/L Russell-Fry from 103 Squadron, P/O Marks from 625 Squadron and P/O Stewart from 626 Squadron. F/S Daley and P/O Knowles and their crews from 460 and 625 Squadron's respectively would be added to the unit's strength in three weeks time.

The night of the 18/19th was devoted to attacks on four railway yards, and 1 and 3 Groups acted as the main force at Rouen, for which 1 Group dispatched 140 Lancasters, seven of them from 300 Squadron on its maiden Lancaster operation. The attack took place in clear conditions, which allowed concentrated bombing without loss to the defences. A 460 Squadron crew had a narrow escape, however, when JB662 crashed on take-off, but W/O White and his crew walked away. The first major raid on Cologne since its pounding during the Ruhr offensive was mounted on the 20/21st, and involved a force of more than 370 Lancasters from 1, 3 and 6 Groups. 1 Group contributed a record 196 aircraft, and they helped to inflict massive destruction on industrial and residential property, while railway installations and public buildings also featured in the extensive catalogue of damage. Two nights later it was the turn of Düsseldorf to suffer similarly at the hands of 590 aircraft from all but 5 Group, which, as mentioned above, was now effectively an independent entity with its own target marking force. 1 Group provided 178 Lancasters, of which seven failed to return. 460 Squadron's run of losses continued after LM525 was shot down by a night fighter over Germany, killing the pilot, F/S Allen. His crew all successfully abandoned the stricken Lancaster, and were taken into captivity. Earlier in the day the SDF had begun training at the Misson bombing range close to the 1 Group HQ at Bawtry.

On the 24/25th Karlsruhe was the destination for more than six hundred aircraft, of which 179 were provided by 1 Group. In addition a simultaneous operation by 5 Group against Munich was supported by ten ABC Lancasters from 101 Squadron. Cloud and a strong wind led to only the northern part of Karlsruhe being bombed, but even so, over nine hundred houses were destroyed or seriously damaged. Seven 1 Group aircraft failed to return, among them the first two to be lost by 300 Squadron. 626 Squadron also posted missing two aircraft and a third was caught by an intruder over East Anglia on the way home, and crashed with total loss of life. Essen hosted an operation on the 26/27th that involved almost five hundred aircraft, of which 175 were provided by 1 Group. The raid took place in good visibility with only slight ground haze, and returning crews were enthusiastic about the degree of concentration. Four 1 Group aircraft failed to return, and among them was 460 Squadron's ND652, which succumbed to a night fighter over Germany, killing F/O Sharpe and his crew. 101 Squadron again supported a 5 Group operation to Schweinfurt, and one of its nine ABC Lancasters failed to return.

On the following night 322 Lancasters of 1, 3, 6 and 8 Groups set off for the long flight to the highly industrialized town of Friedrichshafen, on the northern shore of the Bodensee near the Swiss frontier. I Group dispatched 162 Lancasters, and they contributed to a highly concentrated and effective attack, which, because of the relatively small size of the town, necessitated an attack in moonlight. An estimated 67% of the built-up area was left in ruins, while a number of factories sustained severe damage, and the destruction of a tank gearbox plant had a major effect on Germany's tank production. The night fighters arrived on the scene as the attack was in progress, and benefiting from the bright conditions, contributed to the loss of eighteen Lancasters in the target area and on the way home. Two Pathfinder squadron commanding officers were among those shot down, and the 1 Group casualty figure reached ten. 166 and 460 Squadrons each lost three Lancasters, as the month went from bad to worse for the Australians. LL906 was a night fighter victim, and was sent crashing to earth close to the Franco-German border with no survivors from the crew of F/O Brown. LM523 suffered a similar fate over southern Germany, and only a gunner escaped with his life from the crew of flight commander S/L Jarman. Finally, ND364 blew up over France, and W/O Leary died with his crew.

The month had not quite done with the squadron yet, and the final incident took place in tragic circumstances on the afternoon of Sunday the 30th. F/L Healey DFC, a 49 Squadron pilot, took off from Binbrook in the afternoon for a proving flight in 460 Squadron's ND553, with a 460 Squadron crew and F/O Brian Jagger DFM of the Bombing Development Unit, which was based on the Pathfinder station at Gransden Lodge. Brian Jagger had been David Shannon's front gunner on the Dams raid in May 1943. The purpose of the flight was to trial the new "Village Inn" system, also known as AGLT - Automatic Gun Laying Turret, with an RAF fighter making dummy attacks on the Lancaster to test the new system. The Lancaster was being thrown around the sky in evasive action, and it was during these strenuous manoeuvres that the dinghy began to inflate while still in the Lancaster's wing. It broke free from its stowage in the wing, when it had inflated too much to remain physically contained. It burst out with disastrous consequences, tangling around the tail and forcing the Lancaster over onto its back, and despite the best efforts of the pilot, the aircraft crashed near Witchford at 16.55. In the light of similar incidents involving dinghies and Lancasters during this period, it was decided to reduce the pressure in the CO_2 bottles used to inflate the dinghy. Such was the secrecy surrounding AGLT at the time, that the accident card referred to the flight simply as fighter affiliation.

The 30th was also the day on which W/C Powley relinquished command of 166 Squadron on posting to No 1 Lancaster Finishing School (LFS). He was succeeded by W/C Donald Garner, who had been a flight commander at 576 Squadron.

That night the SDF carried out its first operation, against a German ammunition dump at Maintenon, close to the village of Chartres, south west of Paris. Under bright, full moon conditions S/L Breakspear and the SDF carried out very accurate marking of the target with yellow target indicators (TIs), and Breakspear continued to circle the target providing bombing instructions to the 109 main force crews, who released their bombs from eight thousand feet. The three-wave attack produced several large explosions, and returning crews claimed that the ammunition dump had been totally destroyed, and this was backed up by post-raid photographic reconnaissance. F/L Gillam's flight engineer, Ken Talbot, recorded it as a "wizard prang!!" The A-O-C, AVM Sir Edgar Rice, sent a personal message to the SDF crews, which read;

> "My hearty congratulations on your magnificent work last night. The job was done with precision and complete efficiency. The loss of so much ammunition is a great disaster for the enemy, and will be of tremendous assistance to our invading forces when the time comes."

With this operation F/L Middlemiss and his crew became the first from 625 Squadron to complete a tour of operations, and just five months after its formation, 550 Squadron now stood proudly at the top of the group bombing ladder.

May

April had been a disastrous month for 460 Squadron, in which twelve aircraft had been lost, and only one crew had survived intact, and the events at the beginning of May suggested that the new month could be even worse. The month's operations began for the Command with attacks against six separate targets on the night of the 1/2nd. A 1 Group main force of sixty-nine Lancasters was assigned to the Merliet Motor Vehicle Works at Lyons, where the six SDF crews carried out the marking at 00:47. One of the TIs was judged to be wide of the aiming point, but this was quickly corrected, and the first wave of main force aircraft was called in at 01.02. Acting as Master Bomber and circling the target at just a few thousand feet, S/L Breakspear quickly corrected the initial creep-back, and called for remarking of the smoke-obscured target before the second wave bombed. The operation was concluded without loss, and returning crews claimed another successful operation.

The night of the 3/4th became one of high drama, when the target was a German army Panzer training camp and motor transport depot at Mailly-le-Camp, in the Aube region of north-central France. Its presence posed a potential threat to the Normandy landings now only a month away. The two phase operation by 1 and 5 Groups was to be led by G/C Deane of 83 Squadron as Master Bomber, with 617 Squadron's W/C Cheshire acting as the Mosquito marker leader. The two men attended separate briefings, and this may have contributed to some of the confusion that later characterized the operation. Neither seems to have been fully aware either of the part to be played by 1 Group's SDF, which was assigned to a specific target of its own. The plan was for 617 Squadron Mosquitos to mark two aiming points, one for each group, and for Cheshire to hand proceedings over to Deane at the appropriate junctures.

Cheshire and Shannon were in position before midnight, and as soon as the illuminating flares went down from the 83 and 97 Squadron Lancasters, Cheshire released two red spot fires onto the first aiming point from fifteen hundred feet at 00.00½, which Shannon backed up from four hundred feet thirty seconds later. As far as Cheshire was concerned, the operation was now bang on schedule, and he called up Deane to bring the main force first phase in. It was at this stage that Deane became unable to pass on the necessary instructions, and it seems that some crews, noticing the red markers burning clearly on the ground, decided to go in and bomb. These were predominantly 5 Group crews, who, according to the plan, should have completed their part in the operation by 00.16, leaving the way clear for the second pair of 617 Squadron Mosquitos to mark the camp for the 1 Group main force of 140 Lancasters. In the event, 5 Group bombs were still falling, and Cheshire asked for a pause in the bombing to allow the marking to take place. Eventually, Deane's deputy, S/L Sparkes of 83 Squadron, found a clear channel and called for a halt, but chaos reigned and bombs were still falling as the 617 Squadron Mosquitos flew across the target to mark the aiming points at 00.23 and 00.25. At two thousand feet they were lucky to survive the blast of the cookies going off below them. Their efforts were backed up by a stick of markers from a 97 Squadron Lancaster, and Sparks was at last able to call 1 Group in. It would be discovered later that interference from an American Forces broadcasting station, and a wrongly tuned VHF transmitter prevented the instructions from getting through.

Four SDF aircraft, led by F/L Hull, were specifically tasked with marking Target "B", a Panzer depot to the east of the main camp. The initial green spot flare was judged by Hull to have overshot by a thousand yards, and a second was misplaced by five hundred yards. The deputy marker leader laid a third marker which was judged to be accurate, and at eleven minutes past midnight the first dozen of twenty-nine Lancasters from 460 and 625 Squadrons followed up with accurate bombing, before the target became obscured by smoke. As a result of this, and the fact that the 5 Group attack had commenced close by, the remaining seventeen 1 Group aircraft assigned to the "special target" were diverted to assist in that.

During the ten minute delay caused by the communications difficulties, enemy night fighters took advantage of the bright, moonlit and cloud-free conditions to get amongst the bombers as they circled a fighter beacon just a few miles from the target. They began to pick off Lancasters with impunity, Hpt Helmut Bergmann alone downing no fewer than six bombers in thirty minutes. As burning Lancasters were seen to fall out of the sky in large numbers, some crews succumbed to their anxiety and frustration, and a number of uncomplimentary comments were broadcast in a rare breakdown of R/T discipline. Once under way, the bombing was accurate, and much damage was inflicted on barracks and transport sheds, and thirty-seven tanks were among the hundred vehicles destroyed.

Forty-two Lancasters were shot down, twenty-eight of them from the 1 Group second phase, and 460 Squadron was most sorely afflicted of all, losing five aircraft. LM531 was a victim of the delay, and was dispatched by a night fighter while F/S Gritty was awaiting instructions. He and three others lost their lives, but the navigator, bomb-aimer and a gunner ultimately evaded capture. JB741 was approaching the aiming point when it fell, and there were no survivors from the crew of P/O Baker. ME740 and ND630 were both on their way from the target area when the end came, and neither produced a survivor from the crews of F/S Fry and W/O Smart respectively. ME728 was also on the way home when it crashed in France, and the crew of P/O Lloyd perished to a man. 101 Squadron posted missing five crews, as did 12 Squadron four, while 103, 166, 625 and 626 Squadrons each lost three. F/L Hull was flying in ND860, and rather than marking for the SDF was carrying a bomb load, and operating below the main force to issue instructions to aid the accuracy of the attack. He reported being hit, and handed over to his deputy before his Lancaster crashed in the target area without survivors. F/L Hull and his crew were on the final operation of their second tour, and it is believed that ND860 fell victim to "friendly" bombs. After this operation recriminations abounded, with much of the vitriol unjustly directed at W/C Cheshire, and there is still a mistaken belief among some veterans that he was to blame for the delay and the consequent heavy losses.

A number of small scale operations occupied elements from the Group over the succeeding week, and during this period, on the 6th, W/C Goodman succeeded W/C Nelson as commanding officer of 103 Squadron.

The latter was posted to Ingham, probably to take command of 1481 Bombing and Gunnary Flight. That night the 13 Base commander, Air Commodore Ivelaw-Chapman, was lost in a 576 Squadron Lancaster during an operation against an ammunition dump at Aubigne Racon in France. He survived, and became the most senior Bomber Command officer to be taken prisoner. Seven coastal batteries were attacked in the Pas-de-Calais on the 9/10th, to maintain the deception concerning the true location of the landings. 1 Group was assigned to targets at Merville and Mardyck, and all of its one hundred aircraft returned. Five railway yards provided the objectives for five hundred aircraft on the 10/11th, and four similar targets were attacked on the following night.

The 1 Group raid on the yards at Hasselt was thwarted by cloud, and the Master Bomber sent two-thirds of the crews home with their bombs. 460 Squadron's ND674 failed to arrive back at Binbrook with P/O McCleery and his crew, and it was later established that they had all escaped by parachute after being shot down by a night fighter over Belgium. Another casualty on this night was 103 Squadron's new commanding officer, W/C Goodman, who had taken ND700 and the crew of the hospitalised "Mad Belgian", S/L Van Rollegan. All on board were killed when the Lancaster blew up over Belgium following an encounter with a night fighter. He was succeeded by W/C St John. On the 15th 460 and 550 Squadrons also welcomed new commanding officers, in the form of W/Cs Douglas and Connolly respectively. Jack Douglas was a highly experienced officer, who had commanded 467 Squadron in 5 Group for four months spanning the turn of the year.

Minor operations then held sway until the 19/20th, when five railway yards and two gun emplacements provided the main fare. Over a hundred Lancasters of 1 Group carried out an accurate attack on the yards at Orleans, for the loss of just one of their number. The first major raid on Duisburg for a year was delivered by over five hundred Lancasters of 1, 3, 5 and 8 Groups on the 21/22nd, and 350 buildings were destroyed in return for the loss of a hefty twenty-nine aircraft. 1 Group dispatched a record 207 Lancasters, and twelve of these failed to return. 550 Squadron was hardest-hit with three missing aircraft, and 460 Squadron's LL951 was shot down near the Dutch/Belgian border, with only the flight engineer and bomb-aimer from the crew of F/O McDougall escaping with their lives to fall into enemy hands. Dortmund was similarly honoured with its first major raid for a year on the following night, when 6 Group substituted for 5 Group. Of over 370 aircraft taking part 183 were provided by 1 Group. The attack destroyed more than 850 houses and six industrial premises, mostly in south-eastern districts, and for a change, no 460 Squadron aircraft were among the eleven missing from 1 Group in an overall loss of eighteen.

Two railway yards were the aiming points in Aachen on the 24/25th, but the town and outlying communities also suffered at the hands of over four hundred aircraft from all but 5 Group. Elements of 1, 3 and 8 Groups returned on the 27/28th for another tilt at the Rothe Erde yards at the eastern end of the town, and all though-traffic was halted. Nine 1 Group aircraft failed to return, among them three from 166 Squadron. Also on this night 1 Group Lancasters were involved in attacks on a military camp at Bourg Leopold in Belgium and a coastal battery at Merville. The single missing Lancaster from the latter was 460 Squadron's LM545, which crashed into the sea just off the French coast, and there were no survivors from the crew of F/S Kirkland. On the last night of the month, the group participated in attacks on railway yards at Trappes and Tergnier.

June

The first few nights of June were dominated by preparations for the invasion, which was being delayed by bad weather. 1 Group joined others in maintaining the deception by sending 166 Lancasters to bomb coastal batteries in the Pas-de-Calais and a signals station at Berneval on the 2/3rd. On the 3/4th a battery at Wimereux was the target, and another one at Sangatte was the group's destination on the 4/5th. Over a thousand aircraft were aloft on D-Day Eve, the 5/6th, to bomb ten batteries on the Normandy coast, for which 1 Group contributed 191 aircraft along with a further twenty-four ABC Lancasters from 101 Squadron engaged in special patrol duties. In the face of complete cloud cover the SDF carried out skymarking for the 1 Group effort, and although returning crews claimed to have concentrated their bombing on the markers, it was impossible to assess the results. No direct reference was made at briefings to the invasion, but crews were given strict flight levels, and were instructed not to jettison bombs over the sea. Aircraft were taking off throughout the night, and those crews returning at low level in dawn's early light were rewarded with a glimpse of the armada ploughing its way sedately across the Channel below.

That night another thousand aircraft concentrated their efforts against road and rail communications in or near nine towns on the approaches to the beachhead. 1 Group sent ninety-seven aircraft to attack marshalling yards at Acheres, but less than fifty had bombed before the master bomber called a halt to proceedings. Another 107 from the group were active at Vire, and 460 Squadron's P/O Knight and crew all died when JB700 was brought down to crash in France. Similar targets occupied large sections of the Command over the following two nights, before 1, 4, 6 and 8 Groups attacked airfields south of the battle area on the 9/10th. A hundred 1 Group crews were briefed to attack the airfield at Flers on this night. A railway junction at Acheres was one of four railway targets in the bomb sights on the 10/11th, and the operation included a 1 Group contingent of a hundred aircraft. 460 Squadron's ME696 failed to return to Binbrook, and news eventually came through, that it had crashed with no survivors from the crew of P/O Nicholson.

Elements from 1, 3, 4 and 8 Groups bombed four different railway yards on the following night, and this preceded the start of a new oil campaign, which began at the hands of a 1 and 3 Group main force at Gelsenkirchen on the 12/13th. The availability of an improved version of Oboe enabled the marking of the Nordstern synthetic oil refinery to take place with great accuracy, and a large proportion of the bombs fell within the plant. All production was brought to a halt for several weeks, at a cost to the German war effort of a thousand tons of aviation fuel per day. A spirited defence could always be guaranteed, however, and seventeen Lancasters were shot down, ten of them from among the 193 dispatched by 1 Group. 166 and 300 Squadrons each lost three aircraft, and among the others was ME785 of 460 Squadron, which crashed in Holland, killing P/O Roche and his crew. Earlier on the 12th a second flight had been formed at 300 Squadron, where a lack of Polish crews had restricted the squadron's development. It was decided to use British crews as a stopgap until more Poles became available, and three crews each were posted in from 550 and 101 Squadrons, two from 626, one from 576 and four from 1 Lancaster Finishing School.

The first daylight operation since the departure of 2 Group a year earlier was mounted against E-Boats and other light marine craft at le Havre on the evening of the 14th. It was a two phase operation, in which a predominantly 1 Group force of 198 Lancasters took the first shift, followed by 3 Group at dusk. The attack was entirely successful, and few if any craft remained to pose a threat to the Allied shipping supplying the beachhead. 1 Group contributed 101 aircraft to a similar and equally effective attack on Boulogne twenty-four hours later, although, on this occasion there were many civilian casualties.

A second new campaign was opened by elements of 1, 4, 5, 6 and 8 Groups on the 16/17th, when four flying bomb launching sites were accurately bombed in the Pas-de-Calais. These and V-1 storage sites would feature prominently over the next two months, alongside the Command's other responsibilities to the Transportation Plan, oil and tactical support for the land forces. Also on this night, 1 Group contributed a hundred

Lancasters to a raid on the Ruhr oil plant at Sterkrade/Holten. The attack was rendered generally ineffective by cloud, and thirty-one aircraft were lost, most of them Halifaxes. 5 Group entered the oil offensive on the 21/22nd, when sending separate forces to Wesseling, near Cologne, and Scholven-Buer in the Ruhr, with Pathfinder support at the latter, and a sprinkling of 101 Squadron ABC Lancasters at both. Cloud prevented use of the normally highly effective 5 Group low level visual marking method, and the Wesseling force was badly mauled by night fighters, losing thirty-seven aircraft, in return for modest damage to the plant.

A V-Weapon site at Mimoyecque was the target for a 1 Group contingent by daylight on the 22nd, and that night, a second element attacked the railway yards at Reims. Of the four Lancasters missing, two were from 460 Squadron, and both LM547 and NE116 crashed in France, with no survivors from the crew of F/O Lamble in the former. NE116 was twice coned by searchlights while outbout, but managed to escape, before being attcked by a night fighter. F/S Pearson gave the order to bale out, but only the navigator and bomb-aimer managed to do so before the Lancaster exploded, and they ultimately evaded capture. The 23rd brought a new commanding officer to 576 Squadron, as W/C Clayton was posted to Faldingworth as deputy station commander, and was succeeded by W/C Boyd "Shrub" Sellick who arrived from 12 Squadron. He was another highly experienced officer, who had served with 214 Squadron pre-war, and commanded 7 Squadron at Oakington between April and October 1942.

Three flying bomb sites were accurately bombed by daylight on the 24th, and a further seven were attacked that night, and three more on the following day, and 1 Group supported each with a hundred Lancasters. On the 27/28th the targets were flying bomb sites and railways, and 460 Squadron's ME793 disappeared without trace while attacking the marshalling yards at Vaires, taking with it the crew of P/O Israel. Returning from a flying bomb construction site at Domleger on the 29th with two dead engines courtesy of flak, 460 Squadron's F/L Critchley put ME784 down on its belly at Manston, and the occupants were able to walk away. On the last night of the month, the group's Special Duties Flight marked the railway yards at Vierzon with great accuracy, and the 1 Group main force of over a hundred Lancasters inflicted heavy damage for the loss of fourteen Lancasters. Among these was ND975, which was on duty with the SDF and contained the crew of P/O Knowles formerly of 625 Squadron, who was on his fifteenth operation. There were no survivors. This was the second and, as it turned out, the final loss of an SDF crew.

July

July would follow a similar pattern, and it began for 1 Group with raids on flying bomb construction sites at Domleger and Oiscmont/Neuville on the 2nd. 460 Squadron's first casualty of the month occurred on the evening of the 4th, when NE139 suffered an undercarriage collapse while taking off for a training flight, but no injuries were reported among the crew of P/O Hanrahan. That night 156 aircraft from 1 Group were assigned to the railway yards at Orleans, and 460 Squadron registered its first missing crew of the new month. NE174 crashed in France, and there were no survivors from the crew of P/O Solomon. No aircraft were lost from a 1 Group raid on railway installations at Dijon on the 5/6th, and then it was back to a V-Weapon site in the Foret de Croc by daylight later on the 6th. The first major operations in direct support of the land forces took place on the evening of the 7th. 1 Group provided almost half of the force of over four hundred aircraft sent to bomb open ground between Caen and a number of fortified villages north of the town, ahead of advancing British and Canadian forces. 1 Group elements returned to the railway yards at Vaires without loss on the 7/8th and 12th, and in between, another joined forces with 3 Group for what was an ineffective attack on a flying bomb site at Nucourt on the 10th.

An important railway junction at Revigny was assigned to 1 Group on the 12/13th, but cloud in the target area hampered both the SDF attempt to mark accurately, and the subsequent bombing. The Master Bomber called proceedings to a halt after only half of the crews had bombed, and ten Lancasters failed to return. 103 and 166 Squadrons each lost four aircraft, one of the Elsham Wolds contingent colliding in the air with another from 550 Squadron over France, and all fourteen occupants lost their lives. 460 Squadron did not take part in the operation, but was called into action when it was rescheduled for the 14/15th. On this occasion, for which Pathfinder markers replaced the SDF, haze prevented any bombing from taking place, and a further seven Lancasters were shot down for their trouble. W/C Connolly was on his sixth operation since taking command of 550 Squadron, and he had among his crew S/L Fuller, who had arrived less than a week earlier from 12 Squadron as gunnery leader. Their Lancaster LL837 was shot down over France by a FW190, and all on board were killed. 460 Squadron's ME755 was dispatched by a night fighter over France on the way home, killing P/O Vaughan and four of his crew, while the wireless operator and a gunner survived to evade capture. W/C Sisley, an Australian, became 550 Squadron's new commanding officer on the 16th. He was an experienced officer, who had previously commanded 3 Group's 115

Squadron between December 1942 and the following March. It was left to 5 Group to finally complete the job at Revigny on the 18/19th, but at a cost of twenty-four Lancasters.

In the early morning of that day, over nine hundred aircraft had been employed against five fortified villages east of Caen, in support of the British Second Army, which was about to launch Operation Goodwood. American bombers also took part, and 6,800 tons of bombs were delivered in a highly effective assault. Of this figure, 5,000 tons were delivered by aircraft of the RAF. While the third Revigny raid was in progress that night, 1 Group was active over the oil refineries at Wesseling and Scholven-Buer, the scene of the 5 Group mauling a month earlier. Both operations were successful, and each plant suffered loss of production, the latter completely so for an extended period. It was from this contingent that 460 Squadron's LL957 failed to return to Binbrook, having been shot down by a night fighter over Holland. F/O Carr and five of his crew died in the Lancaster's wreckage, but the navigator survived to be taken prisoner. A more encouraging outcome attended the loss of ND654 during an operation to bomb the railway yards and a junction at Courtrai on the 20/21st. The Lancaster was shot down over Belgium, but the entire crew escaped by parachute, P/O Jopling and five others ultimately evading capture, while one of the gunners was rounded up and packed off to a PoW camp.

The first major raid on a German urban target for two months took place on the 23/24th, when Kiel was the destination for a force of over six hundred aircraft, of which 189 were provided by 1 Group. They appeared suddenly and with complete surprise from behind a 100 Group RCM screen, and inflicted severe damage on the town and port area, where all of the U-Boot yards were hit. On the following night, the first of three raids in five nights took place on Stuttgart. The last raid, on the 28/29th, was intercepted by night fighters, and a massive thirty-nine Lancasters were lost, eight of them from Elsham Wolds. There were four failures to return each from 103 and 576 Squadrons, and another from 103 was written off with battle damage after crash-landing at an airfield in Buckinghamshire. By this time Stuttgart's central districts lay in ruins, with most of its public and cultural buildings reduced to rubble, and eleven hundred of its inhabitants killed. The month ended with support for the ground forces in the Villers Bocage-Caumont area on the 30th, and further attacks on railways and flying bomb sites on the 31st. W/C Alexander concluded his tour in command of 101 Squadron, during which he had operated twelve times, and was succeeded on the 31st by W/C Everest.

August

The first week of August was dominated by the campaign against flying bomb sites, and operations were mounted daily from the 1st to the 6th. The largest effort was on the 3rd, when over eleven hundred aircraft were involved in attacks on three sites. 1 Group provided 180 Lancasters for the one at Trossy-St-Maximin, among them 460 Squadron's PB125, which was shot down over France with fatal consequences for F/O Fidock and his crew. Happily, from this point almost until the end of the month, 460 Squadron would enjoy a rare loss-free period. On the 7/8th, over a thousand aircraft took off to bomb five enemy strong points ahead of Allied ground forces in the Caen area of Normandy. The attacks, which involved 204 Lancasters from 1 Group, including six from the SDF, were carefully controlled by Master Bombers, and in the event only 660 crews were allowed to bomb. The group was involved in attacks on oil and fuel storage dumps on the 8/9th, 9/10th and 10th, and a railway target at Douay on the 11th. On the last-mentioned occasion, the SDF operated for the final time, and it was in a bombing rather than marking role. The flight was ultimately disbanded without ceremony a few days later with little recognition of its contribution to 1 Group's war effort.

The principal operation on this night was a raid by all but 8 Group on Brunswick, to ascertain the ability of main force crews to identify and attack a target on the strength of H2S alone without Pathfinder marking. Supported by eighty Lancasters from 1 Group, it was not an entirely successful experiment, and while a proportion of the bombing did fall within the town, there was no concentration, and much of the effort was wasted on other towns and communities. Meanwhile, a second force of almost three hundred aircraft attempted to hit the Opel motor works at Rüsselsheim, but succeeded in inflicting only slight damage. Also that night a modest number of Lancasters and Halifaxes bombed a German troop concentration near Falaise. This was the town upon which the Third Canadian Division was advancing, and on the afternoon of the 14th, eight hundred aircraft took off to attack seven German positions. Halfway through the raid some bombs fell among Canadian soldiers, and thirteen were killed, while fifty-three others were wounded. A number of Squadron commanders were carpeted as a result of this "friendly fire" incident, for not adequately briefing their crews.

In preparation for his new night offensive against industrial Germany, Harris launched a thousand aircraft on the morning of the 15th to bomb nine night fighter airfields in Holland and Belgium. 1 Group sent a hundred Lancasters each to Volkel and le Culot airfields, and all of the day's operations were believed to be successful. On the night of the 16/17th 1 Group joined others to raid Stettin for the first time since January, and as always was the case at this target, heavy damage was inflicted. Fifteen hundred houses and twenty-nine industrial premises were destroyed, and thirteen ships were either sunk or seriously damaged in the harbour. A simultaneous raid on Kiel was moderately successful, and caused particular damage in the docks area. Bremen suffered its most catastrophic night of the war on the 18/19th at the hands of 5 Group, in which over 8,600 apartment blocks were left gutted, and eighteen ships were sunk in the harbour. 1, 3, 6 and 8 Groups returned to Rüsselsheim on the 25/26th, and parts of the factory were put out of action for several weeks, although most of the machine tools escaped damage, and production was not badly effected. 1 Group put up 189 Lancasters for this operation, and there were claims from returning crews of two FW190s and a JU88 destroyed. W/C Nelson was posted from 12 Squadron to 11 Base, and he was succeeded as commanding officer by W/C Stockdale, who came in from 166 Squadron. As events were to prove, he would remain in post until the end of hostilities. That night Kiel was attacked for the second time in the month, when 1 and 3 Groups provided the main force, and much further damage was visited upon the town.

The final acts of the flying bomb campaign were played out on the 28th, and shortly afterwards, the Pas-de-Calais region fell into Allied hands. Stettin became the third German city to receive a second visit during the month, when attacked by almost four hundred aircraft from 1, 3, 6 and 8 Groups on the 29/30th. Over fifteen hundred houses and thirty-two industrial premises were added to the previous catalogue of buildings destroyed, but twenty-three Lancasters were claimed by the defences. 101 and 300 Squadrons each lost three aircraft, and this night also brought to an end 460 Squadron's casualty free period, a fact made manifest by two empty dispersals at Binbrook. NE144 crashed in the Baltic, taking with it three of the crew, but F/O Humphries and three others survived to become PoWs. There was good news all round concerning the other errant crew, that of F/O Aldred, who had abandoned a fuel starved PB379 to its fate over Sweden on the way home, and were now enjoying the hospitality of their hosts as internees. On the 31st, six hundred aircraft were dispatched to attack nine suspected V-2 storage sites in northern France, and 460 Squadron's PB176 crashed into the sea, taking with it to their deaths the crew of P/O Grey. It was a sad end to the month for 460 Squadron, but ahead lay an entirely loss-free September, the first fully operational month since early 1942 to produce a clean sheet. It was a sad end also for 550 Squadron, which had sent twelve aircraft to the Argenville site led by W/C

Sisley. He and the other seven occupants of NF962 were killed when the Lancaster crashed in France, and this was the squadron's second commanding officer in a row to be lost on operations.

September

September would be largely devoted to clearing enemy resistance from the three French ports still unavailable to the Allies. 550 Squadron flight commander, S/L Raymond, stepped up to take temporary command of the squadron on the 1st, pending a permanent appointment. The first major activity of the month came on the 3rd, when over six hundred aircraft carried out heavy raids on six airfields in southern Holland. 1 Group targeted Gilze-Rijen and Eindhoven with ninety-nine and fifty-one Lancasters respectively. The first of six raids on enemy strong points around le Havre took place on the 5th, and this was followed up on the 6th, 8th, 9th, 10th and 11th, with a 1 Group participation in all but two of them, during which a total of 679 sorties were launched. Shortly after the final attack, the German garrison surrendered to British forces. The final major raid of the war on Frankfurt was delivered by 1, 3 and 8 Groups on the 12/13th, in which 198 Lancasters from the group took part. Severe damage was caused in the city's western districts, where much of the industry was located. A simultaneous raid on Stuttgart by a predominantly 5 Group force was also highly destructive, and a firestorm afflicted one of the central districts. The dismantling of Kiel continued on the 15/16th at the hands of 4, 6 and 8 Groups and nine ABC Lancasters from 101 Squadron, and further heavy damage was inflicted on central districts and the port area.

W/C Haig concluded his tour as commanding officer of 625 Squadron, and was succeeded by W/C Mackay. The attacks on enemy airfields continued on the 16/17th, with 1 Group elements active over Rheine, Leeuwarden, Steenwijk and Hopsten with a total of two hundred Lancasters. Boulogne was returned to Allied control after three thousand tons of bombs were dropped onto enemy positions on the 17th, 1 Group's one hundred aircraft assigned to three coastal batteries and an ammunition dump. 550 Squadron finally acquired a new commanding officer on the 18th, with the appointment of W/C Bryan Bell, who was posted in from 100 Squadron, where he had been a flight commander.

On the 19/20th ten ABC Lancasters of 101 Squadron joined a 5 Group force to raid the twin towns of Mönchengladbach and Rheydt, for which 617 Squadron's now famous first commanding officer, W/C Guy Gibson VC, was selected for the role of Master Bomber. He was serving as an operations officer at 54 Base Coningsby, and was desperate to get back to operational flying before the war ended. Although his time away from the operational scene had left him listless, frustrated and lacking direction, he retained the arrogance that had made him the ideal choice to lead Operation Chastise. He was not experienced as a Master Bomber, however, but brushed aside the advice freely given by those who were, and as the home of the 5 Group Master Bomber fraternity, Coningsby was, at the time, bristling with qualified men. Gibson also, unaccountably, refused to accept the 627 Squadron Mosquito prepared for him, and insisted on another, which he was duly given. After initial difficulties with the complex marking arrangements, the operation proceeded more or less according to plan, although a number of crews bombed markers not assigned to them. Gibson was heard to send the crews home at the end, but did not arrive back himself, and it was later established that his Mosquito had crashed on the outskirts of the Dutch town of Steenbergen, where he and his navigator lie side-by-side in the local Catholic cemetery.

W/C Pattison concluded his period in command of 100 Squadron on the 20th, and was posted to 12 O.T.U. for instructional duties. He was succeeded by W/C Hamilton, who was promoted from within, having been with the squadron since June. It was also on this day that the first operation to liberate Calais took place, and over six hundred aircraft delivered an accurate attack in good visibility. Before the second raid 1 Group contributed a record 204 Lancasters to a 1, 3, 4 and 8 Group operation against the Ruhr town of Neuss on the 23/24th, and heavy damage resulted. Cloud interfered with the second raid on Calais on the 24th, and some crews came below the cloud base to bomb from two thousand feet, suffering the consequences from the light flak. Further operations against enemy positions around Calais were mounted daily from the 25th to the 28th, for which 1 Group put up a total of over five hundred Lancasters, and Canadian ground forces took control of the area shortly afterwards.

October

A number of attempts had been made during September to bomb heavy gun emplacements on the island of Walcheren in the Scheldt Estuary, which were barring the approaches to the much needed port of Antwerp. They proved to be difficult targets, and it was decided instead to breach the sea walls, and inundate the batteries, while also creating difficult terrain for the enemy to defend against ground forces. On the 3rd eight waves of thirty Lancasters each attacked the sea walls at Westkapelle, and the fifth wave, which included a 1 Group element, created a breach, which was widened by those following behind. On the 5/6th, Saarbrücken was raided for the first time in two years, and suffered a catastrophe. The force of over five hundred aircraft of 1, 3 and 8 Groups included a new 1 Group record to a single target of 239 Lancasters. They contributed to the destruction of almost six thousand houses in what was now a frontier town, and it would not be necessary for the bombers to return. A further thirteen ABC aircraft from 101 Squadron joined a simultaneous 5 Group attack on the town's marshalling yards.

A new Ruhr campaign began at Dortmund on the 6/7th at the hands of 3, 6 and 8 Groups, and from this point on, an unprecedented weight of bombs would fall on Germany's urban centres. On the morning of the 7th a new squadron came into existence, or rather, was reformed at Kirmington. 153 Squadron received twenty-seven crews and eighteen Lancasters from 166 Squadron, and W/C Francis Powley was installed as the commanding officer. Powley was a Canadian in the RAF, and had just completed a spell at No1 Lancaster Finishing School (LFS) following his period in command of 166 Squadron from January to the end of April. There was no time to settle in, as the squadron found itself on the order of battle that very afternoon. The frontier towns of Cleves and Emmerich were earmarked for destruction, and the latter was assigned to elements of 1, 3 and 8 Groups, which, under an umbrella of escorting Spitfires, left over 2,400 houses in a state of ruin. 153 Squadron managed a creditable eleven sorties, and all returned safely. 460 Squadron's PB254 was hit by incendiaries from above while over the target, and this caused a fire to break out in the fuselage. Three of the crew baled out, but the bomb-aimer failed to survive, and the Lancaster was eventually crash-landed at Hawkinge by F/O Gratton and his three remaining colleagues, who were able to walk away. PB407 also failed to return, and it was later learned that F/L Greenacre and his crew were in enemy hands. A rare failure for the period occurred at Bochum on the 9/10th, when a 101 Squadron element joined 4, 6 and 8 Groups to produce a scattered attack that caused only modest damage in southern districts.

On the 11th, Lancasters and Mosquitos of 1 and 8 Groups attacked the Fort Frederik Hendrik gun battery at Breskens on the south bank of the Scheldt, but dust and smoke forced an abandonment after less than half of the crews had bombed. It was on this day that W/C Rodney was posted away from 626 Squadron at the conclusion of his highly successful tour, and he took up a staff appointment. He would return to the operational scene in April 1945 when taking command of 153 Squadron, and would remain in that post until the squadron's disbandment in September. The new commanding officer was W/C Molesworth, who arrived from 11 Base. He had begun his operational career as a sergeant, before being commissioned in 1940, and was awarded the DFC in 1941 for service with 77 Squadron. On the following day, 460 Squadron bade farewell to W/C Douglas on his posting to take over the reins at 5 Group's Australian 467 Squadron at Waddington. Sadly, on the night of the 7/8th of February 1945, at the tender age of twenty-three, he would lose his life during a 5 Group attack on the Dortmund-Ems Canal at Ladbergen, on what was reputedly his 124th sortie. His replacement at 460 Squadron was W/C Parsons, whose period of tenure would be brief.

The new Ruhr offensive led inexorably to Operation Hurricane, a demonstration to the enemy of the overwhelming superiority of the Allied air forces ranged against it. At first light on the 14th over a thousand aircraft took off for Duisburg, and delivered more than 4,500 tons of bombs into the already shattered city. 1 Group provided 243 Lancasters for three aiming points, including the Thyssen Steel Works. 153 Squadron had been due to move to Scampton on this day, but that was postponed while thirteen of its Lancasters participated in the action at Duisburg. It turned out to be a sad occasion, when two of its aircraft failed to return, its first casualties since being reformed, and it was learned later that no crew members had survived. Also involved in this operation was broadcaster Richard Dimbleby, who was a passenger in a 12 Squadron Lancaster flown by W/C Stockdale. That night similar numbers returned to Duisburg to press home the point about superiority, and remarkably, these 2018 sorties in less than twenty-four hours were achieved without a contribution from 5 Group.

153 Squadron's delayed move to Scampton took place on the 15th. Scampton had become famous as the launch pad for 617 Squadron's attack on the Ruhr dams in May 1943, but had a grass runway at the time, which was unsuitable for ever increasing bomb loads, particularly in winter. When 617 and 57 Squadrons moved out in August 1943, the station was closed down to have concrete runways laid. The station also passed from 5 Group to 1 Group, and 153 Squadron had the privilege of being the first to sample the benefits of life on this pre-war permanent airfield, with all of the creature comforts that were lacking from the many wartime-built stations thrown together out of necessity. On the same day 170 Squadron was reformed at Kelstern from C Flight of 625 Squadron, and W/C Hackforth was installed as the commanding officer. The role of the squadron was entirely different now, having been formed in June 1942 as a fighter reconnaissance unit operating Mustangs, before being disbanded in January 1944.

The Independent Air Force, or "Lincolnshire Poachers", as 5 Group had been dubbed by 8 Group, was also absent from what the Command claimed was a successful raid by almost five hundred aircraft on Wilhelmshaven on the 15/16th, for which 1 Group contributed seventy Lancasters. 1, 3, 6 and 8 Groups carried out a two phase attack on Stuttgart on the 19/20th, and although the bombing was scattered, damage in central and eastern districts was heavy. It was on this operation that 170 Squadron made its operational debut with thirteen sorties. Two 460 Squadron aircraft failed to return, and only one of the fourteen men involved survived as a PoW. He was the navigator in the crew of P/O Fontaine, whose PB152 crashed in southern Germany. Also falling in that region was PB175, which took to their deaths the crew of F/O Hamilton. After just one week at Kelstern 170 Squadron moved into Dunholme Lodge near Lincoln, another station, which, like Scampton, had formerly belonged to 5 Group, and had been vacated just three weeks earlier by 44 (Rhodesia) Squadron.

The Hurricane force moved on to Essen in the early evening of the 23rd, and returned on the afternoon of the 25th, destroying a combined total of over seventeen hundred buildings and killing almost fifteen hundred people. 1 Group took part in the former with 229 Lancasters, among them 460 Squadron's PB351, which was damaged by a flak shell exploding beneath the rear turret. The occupant, the appropriately named F/S Jack Cannon, woke up some time later lying on the ground amongst trees. He had sustained a painful hip injury, and sat for a while smoking cigarettes cupped in his hands to avoid giving his position away. On the following morning he heard an approaching aircraft, which he identified as a Beaufighter, and using a branch as a crutch, he began to hobble in the direction of its path. He estimates, that his evasion went on for about thirty-six hours, probably spent going round in circles, before he chanced upon a Germanic-looking mansion, beside which, a gardener was tending his vegetable patch. Cannon approached him, and reading from his escape kit language card, he asked where he was in German, Dutch and French. Eliciting no response, he shouted in English, "where the **** am I?", to which the elderly man answered that he was on the estate of the Lord High Chancellor, Lord Cholmondly, near Norwich. Cannon later established that his Lancaster had lost one engine to the flak, and that another had caught fire. On approaching the Norfolk coast, F/O Richins had been unable to make height, partly through icing, and the Lancaster hit an oak tree with a bomb still on board. In the ensuing explosion, Cannon's turret was catapulted a massive distance from the rest of the aircraft, and landed in a tree in a wood, before disgorging him as the sole survivor. In confirmation of this, his unopened parachute was discovered later.

Cologne's turn at the hands of the Hurricane force came on the 28th, and again on the evenings of the 30th and 31st, by which time the city was descending into a state of chaos. 1 Group supported all three operations with a combined total of 719 sorties, of which just two failed to return from the final one. 460 Squadron's F/O Reid and his crew were all killed when PB567 was brought down. In between, on the 29th, 1, 3, 4 and 8 Groups carried out the penultimate attack on enemy positions on Walcheren, and on the 31st, ground forces went in, and took the island after a week of heavy fighting. The following four weeks were spent clearing mines from the estuary, and it was the end of December before the first convoy arrived at Antwerp. 576 Squadron completed its move from Elsham Wolds to Fiskerton on the 31st, and it would remain at this station until its eventual disbandment.

November

On the 1st C Flight of 550 Squadron moved from North Killingholme to Fiskerton, and was renumbered 150 Squadron. It will be recalled that an overseas echelon of the previous incarnation of this unit had been sent to North Africa, and eventually Italy, where it had only recently been disbanded, and that the home-based echelons of 150 and 142 Squadrons had been combined to form 166 Squadron. Thus this famous number plate found itself once again operating under the banner of 1 Group, which it had served so well until the end of January 1943. W/C Avis was installed as commanding officer, and he would have the privilege of taking on charge the first Lancasters equipped with the new Rose rear turret, which was roomier than its predecessor, and boasted two .50 calibre guns rather than the four puny .303. The rate of fire was slower, but the range infinitely better, and that was the selling point.

Düsseldorf became the next victim of Operation Hurricane, when over nine hundred aircraft destroyed or seriously damaged five thousand houses and twenty-five industrial premises on the night of the 2/3rd. 1 Group dispatched 252 Lancasters, of which just four failed to return. Two nights later, Bochum wilted under a very heavy blow delivered by seven hundred aircraft from 1, 4, 6 and 8 Groups, of which 1 Group contributed 235 Lancasters. The force destroyed or severely damaged four thousand buildings, and killed almost a thousand people in return for the loss of twenty-eight aircraft. The Halifax brigade took a beating on this night, losing twenty-three of their number, and the 5 missing Lancasters all belonged to 1 Group. Seven hundred aircraft bombed either the Nordstern oil plant or the town of Gelsenkirchen itself on the 6th, for which 1 Group again put up over two hundred aircraft. Another 228 from the group set out for the oil town of Wanne-Eickel on the 9th, but cloud hampered the attack and it was deemed a failure.

The group produced a better performance at the Hoesch Benzin plant at Dortmund on the 11/12th, when it dispatched over 180 Lancasters, among them six from 150 Squadron, which was making its Lancaster operational debut. The 16th was devoted to the destruction of the three towns of Heinsberg, Jülich and Düren, which lay in a line from north-west to south-east behind enemy lines, north-east to east of Aachen. The last mentioned was assigned to 1 and 5 Groups, which all but erased it from the map, and left over 3,100 of its inhabitants dead. On the 18th W/C Mackay was posted from 625 Squadron at the conclusion of his tour, and was succeeded by W/C Barker, who had arrived on the 10th from 1LFS, after converting to the Lancaster. Barker was an experienced pilot and pre-war officer, whose previous command experience had been with 241 Squadron, a Lysander unit, from August 1941, but until joining 625 Squadron he had gained no operational experience on bombers. The Group returned to Wanne-Eickel on the 18/19th, when all but two of its 253 participating Lancasters bombed as briefed and inflicted some fresh damage on the Krupp synthetic oil refinery. A single Lancaster failed to return, and this was 460 Squadron's PB541, in which F/O Carter and his crew lost their lives. The night of the 21/22nd brought a hive of activity involving 1,345 sorties against five main targets and others in various support and minor operations. 1 Group's main effort was against the marshalling yards at Aschaffenburg, for which 238 crews were briefed, and while this target was hit, it was the town itself that sustained the heaviest damage, with five hundred houses destroyed and fifteen hundred others seriously damaged. Only two Lancasters failed to return, but both of these were from 460 Squadron, and crashed in southern Germany. There were no survivors from the crew of P/O McMaster in NE141, and only one of the gunners escaped with his life from the crew of F/O Ottaway in PB469.

As worthwhile targets became increasingly difficult to find, some seemingly strategically insignificant towns and cities began to find themselves in the bomb-sights. Freiburg was a minor railway centre, deep in south-western Germany close to the Swiss border, and until the night of the 27/28th, it had never been attack by the RAF. Now that mobile Oboe stations were located in France, these hitherto inaccessible targets were now within range, and in a twenty-five minute orgy of destruction, the 292-strong record 1 Group main force destroyed two thousand houses, and killed a similar number of people, while missing the railway installations altogether. This was the last operation in which G/C Edwards VC, the station commander, flew with the squadron, accompanying on this occasion the freshman crew of P/O Whitmarsh. 170 Squadron completed its move from Dunholme Lodge to Hemswell on the 29th, and was not required to take part that afternoon in an operation to Dortmund by almost 250 aircraft from the group. Unfavourable weather conditions contributed to a scattered attack, during which, 460 Squadron's PB459 crashed in the target area, with no survivors from the crew of F/O Gray.

December

The new month began for 103 Squadron with a change at the top, as W/C St John was posted out and was succeeded by W/C MacDonald, who would remain in post for the remainder of the war. G/C Edwards also moved on, departing Binbrook in early December to take up a new post as an operations officer in the Far East. He was succeeded by the newly promoted 460 Squadron commanding officer, G/C Parsons, and until a replacement was appointed, S/L Clark stepped into his shoes. The first large-scale 1 Group effort of the month was directed at Karlsruhe, in company with 6 and 8 Groups on the night of the 4/5th. 1 Group provided 259 Lancasters, of which just one failed to return. This highly destructive raid was followed on the 6/7th by the first of a concerted campaign against the synthetic oil refineries in eastern Germany. The target was a plant at Leuna, near Merseburg, west of Leipzig, and the operation was carried out by 1, 3 and 8 Groups with moderate success in cloudy conditions. 460 Squadron's ND971 collided with another Lancaster over Germany, and as ND703 from 635 Squadron was lost in similar circumstances, it would seem to be the other aircraft involved. As the two aircraft fell, an explosion threw the 460 Squadron pilot, P/O Walter, clear, and he alone of his crew survived to be taken prisoner, along with the two gunners from the other aircraft.

1 Group contributed over 260 aircraft for the final heavy night raid of the war on Essen, which was mounted by over five hundred aircraft from 1, 4 and 8 Groups on the 12/13th. Despite the already massive damage inflicted on this city since March 1943, there were still buildings standing, and almost seven hundred of them were destroyed on this night, while the Krupp works was among the war industry factories to be hit again. Losses among the bomber force were very modest, but 150 Squadron registered its first failure to return since its reformation, and 460 Squadron posted missing its temporary commanding officer. S/L Clark and his crew were all killed when PB542 was shot down by flak while outbound over Germany. W/C Roberts became the new commanding officer, but he also would not remain long in post. 166 Squadron, likewise, had a new commanding officer after W/C Garner was posted out to take up a place on a Staff College course. His successor was W/C Vivian, a rather curious

choice, as he had no operational experience, and was not even qualified on four-engined aircraft. He was given instruction by a number of the more experienced pilots on the squadron, but results were not encouraging. Never the less, he would remain in post for the remainder of the war and beyond.

Ludwigshafen was one of the cities associated with the important I G Farben chemicals company, and contained one factory in a northern suburb, and another in the nearby town of Oppau. Over three hundred Lancasters of 1, 6 and 8 Groups provided the main force for the raid on the 15/16th, and production was halted at both sites. The old city of Ulm in southern Germany became the latest virgin target to suffer a catastrophe at the hands of Bomber Command, when attacked by a 1 Group main force of over 260 aircraft on the 17/18th. Twenty-nine industrial premises were hit, a square kilometre was engulfed in flames, and over 80% of the city's buildings were damaged to some extent. Railway installations at Coblenz and Cologne were the targets for 1 Group forces on the 22/23rd and 24/25th respectively, and the latter resulted in 460 Squadron's final casualty of the year. PB255 crashed in Holland, and the crew of F/O Skarratt were all killed. The final wartime Christmas Day was observed in peace, but representatives from all Groups were in action on Boxing Day, to attack German troop positions at St Vith, following their breakout in the Ardennes ten days earlier.

A full programme of operations resumed thereafter, and 1 Group rounded out the year against oil and railway targets. On the 28/29th, the group sent forces of 103 and 133 aircraft respectively to marshalling yards at Mönchengladbach and Bonn, and 166 Squadron's W/C Vivian flew to the former as second pilot to Norwegian Capt Schyberg. On the following night an element from the group joined 6 and 8 Groups to deliver an accurate Oboe attack on the oil refinery at Scholven-Buer, which also caused major damage in the towns themselves. On New Year's Eve, the Group sent 130 Lancasters to attack the railway yards at Osterfeld, where moderate success was achieved. It had been a year of steady losses for 460 Squadron, which had seen sixty-nine Lancasters lost as a result of operations, and this was the second highest in the Group after 166 Squadron. For many squadrons 1945 would bring a reduction in casualty figures, but the high rate of attrition would continue for 460 and particularly 166 Squadron right up to the end of the bombing war.

1945

January

Despite the unmistakable scent of victory wafting in from the Continent, much remained to be done before the proud, resolute and resourceful enemy finally laid down his arms. Although stretched beyond their capability to protect all corners of the Reich, the defenders were still able on occasions to take a heavy toll of Bomber Command aircraft. The Luftwaffe did itself no favours when launching its ill-conceived and ultimately ill-fated Operation Bodenplatte at first light on New Year's Morning. The intention to destroy large numbers of Allied aircraft on the ground at the recently liberated airfields in France, Holland and Belgium was only modestly realized, and in return, the day fighter force lost around 250 aircraft. More importantly, a large proportion of the pilots were killed, wounded or taken prisoner, and this was a setback from which the Tagjagd would never fully recover.

1 Group opened its account on the night of the 2/3rd, when a new record of 296 of its Lancasters joined forces with 3, 6 and 8 Groups to carry out what must have been a highly satisfying assault on Nuremberg, the target for the Command's heaviest defeat of the war eight months earlier. This time the tables were turned, and the birthplace of Nazism wilted under a massively accurate attack, which left over 4,600 houses and apartment blocks in ruins, and destroyed a further two thousand preserved medieval houses. Industrial districts and railway areas also sustained heavy damage, and a modest six aircraft were lost, five of them from 1 Group. 166 Squadron's fortunes did not alter with the advent of the new year, and three aircraft failed to return from this operation. LM687 was hit by flak over the battle front on the way home, and the crew of P/O Buck was forced to bale out over France. Sadly, it appears the rear gunner struck the tail as he exited his turret, and he was killed. All but one of the crew arrived back in England three days later. There was less good news concerning the fate of the other crews, those of P/O Chittim and F/O Burgoyne in ND635 and PB635 respectively. The former came down in Germany with just the rear gunner surviving as a PoW, and the latter was brought down by flak over France with total loss of life. The other two losses resulted from a tragic mid air collision between Lancasters of 150 and 153 Squadrons just north of Lincoln as they neared their home stations, and all fourteen crewmen died.

In the early hours of the 4th, ninety-eight Lancasters from 1 Group joined others from 5 Group to carry out what became a controversial attack on the French town of Royan. This was in response to a request from Free French forces, which were laying siege to the town on their way through to Bordeaux. Many of the residents had declined an offer by the German garrison commander to evacuate the area, and they suffered terrible consequences under the weight of over fifteen hundred tons of bombs. In the event, the French did not take the town, and it was mid April before the garrison finally surrendered. On the 5/6th, Hannover received its first major raid since the series in the autumn of 1943. 163 Lancasters from 1 Group joined elements from 4, 6 and 8 Groups to destroy almost five hundred apartment blocks. Three 1 Group Lancasters failed to return, among them JB603 of 100 Squadron, which carried a flying duck as nose art and the legend "Take it easy". She was a veteran, and was lost on her 113th operation. The same Groups attacked Hanau on the following night, destroying 40% of the town's built-up area, while a smaller element from 1 and 3 Groups destroyed or seriously damaged almost eighteen hundred buildings while attacking the marshalling yards at Neuss. The final raid of the war on Munich came at the hands of an all Lancaster force of over six hundred aircraft from 1, 3, 5, 6 and 8 Groups on the 7/8th, of which 235 were provided by 1 Group. Eight of these failed to return, among them NG290 of 166 squadron, which crashed south of Stuttgart, killing F/O Soper and his crew. This concluded a busy first week of the new year.

There was little to occupy the crews of 1 Group thereafter until mid month, when 235 of its Lancasters joined forces with elements of 5, 6 and 8 Groups on the 14/15th for a return to the oil refinery at Leuna. The attack was conducted in two phases separated by three hours, and a highly successful outcome was achieved for the loss of ten Lancasters, three of which belonged to 1 Group. Two nights later 232 Lancasters from the group joined elements of 6 and 8 Groups to attack the Braunkohle-Benzin synthetic oil plant at Zeitz, and left its northern half severely damaged. 166 Squadron's ME296 failed to return, and it transpired that F/O Burke and his flight engineer were killed, while their crew mates were taken into captivity. On the 21st W/C Gundry-White succeeded W/C Everest as commanding officer of 101 Squadron. A synthetic oil plant in Duisburg was targeted by 1, 3 and 8 Groups on the 22/23rd, and the nearby Thyssen steel works was also hit be five hundred high explosive bombs. Another two phase operation was directed at an aero-engine factory in Stuttgart-Zuffenhausen and the railway yards at nearby Kornwestheim on the 28/29th. Cloud led to a scattered attack, which fell mainly into the city's northern and western districts, but Kornwestheim suffered severe damage, while a decoy site attracted some bomb loads. During the course of the month, W/C Roberts was posted from 460 Squadron, and was succeeded by W/C Cowan, who became the squadron's final wartime commanding officer.

February

The weather conditions at the start of February were not ideal for marking and bombing, and complete cloud cover over many targets led to a number of failures. Despite this problem at Ludwigshafen on the night of the 1/2nd, 260 aircraft from 1 Group and others from 6 Group produced an accurate attack on Pathfinder skymarkers, and nine hundred houses were destroyed or seriously damaged. Eight Lancasters were lost from the 1 Group element, and six of them were shared between 101 and 166 Squadrons. The latter's NE648, PD385 and NG391 all crashed in Germany killing the crews of F/L Spankie and F/L Pollock respectively, while P/O Smithers and two of his crew survived as PoWs. One of the two remaining missing Lancasters belonged to 100 Squadron, and was carrying a nine man crew, all of whom were killed. On a brighter note this operation brought up a century for the squadron's ND458 "Able Mable", which would go on to complete 130, the final few in support of the humanitarian Operation Manna. 300 Squadron swapped commanding officers for the final time during the war on the 2nd, when W/C Jarkowski replaced W/C Pozyczka, who was posted to liaison duties.

The first and only large raid of the war on Wiesbaden was also conducted through cloud on the 2/3rd, but most of the 1, 3 and 6 Group bombs found the mark. Of the 233 aircraft dispatched by 1 Group, seven failed to return, among them two each from 460 and 576 Squadrons. The former's ME328 was on the way home over France, when it collided with PD286 of 626 Squadron, and both aircraft plunged to the ground. The 460 Squadron Lancaster was being piloted by the station commander, G/C Parsons, and he landed safely by parachute in Allied territory, while five others were killed, and a gunner later succumbed to his injuries. On the following night a 1 Group main force of 160 aircraft attacked the Prosper Coking plant at Bottrop, causing severe damage for the loss of four of their number. The frontier towns of Goch and Cleves were pounded on the 7/8th, in preparation for the impending crossing into Germany of the British XXX Corps. The latter was assigned to a 1 Group force of 250 aircraft, and when the bombing was over, little of the town remained standing. On the following night, a two phase attack on the oil refinery at Pölitz was opened by 5 Group, employing its low level marking method, and 1 Group followed up with 180 aircraft two hours later with a Pathfinder element to complete a successful operation. AVM "Bobby" Blucke became the new

A-O-C 1 Group on the 12th, succeeding AVM Rice, who would be posted to HQ 7 Group on the 21st.

The Churchill inspired series of raids on Germany's eastern cities under Operation Thunderclap began at Dresden on the 13/14th, in another two phase assault opened by 5 Group. A layer of cloud hampered the marking and bombing, but 244 Lancasters delivered over eight hundred tons of bombs into the beautiful and historic city, and started fires burning. These acted as a beacon to the 529 Lancasters of 1, 3, 6 and 8 Groups following three hours behind, by which time the skies had cleared. A further eighteen hundred tons of bombs rained down onto the city and its hapless population, which had been swelled by a massive influx of refugees fleeing from the eastern front. The same chain of events that had devastated parts of Hamburg in July 1943 was unleashed, and somewhere between twenty-five and thirty-five thousand people died in the ensuing firestorm. American bombers arrived on the following morning, and escort fighters are alleged to have strafed the streets and open spaces where the survivors were sheltering. Twenty-four hours later a similar two phase attack on Chemnitz, which included 200 Lancasters from 1 Group, was spoiled by complete cloud cover, and the city escaped serious damage. 166 Squadron's PD394 crashed in Germany killing F/O Kemp and his crew.

On the 20/21st, 1, 3, 6 and 8 Groups set out to destroy the southern half of Dortmund, and Bomber Command claimed that this was achieved, in what was the penultimate heavy raid of the war on this city. 1 Group contributed 270 Lancasters, and eleven of the fourteen missing aircraft were among these. 166 Squadron's NG183 crashed in the target area, and F/L Hill died with his crew. S/L Collinson was killed with his crew in PA179, and S/L Walters brought home a flak-damaged RA501, which he wrote-off in a crash-landing at Manston. On the following night 1, 6 and 8 Groups carried out the final raid of the war on Duisburg, and left extensive further damage. 1 Group lost five of its 245 aircraft, and among them was the 550 Squadron commanding officer, W/C Bell, who survived with five members of his crew after they were brought down over Germany. Two others died, and it seems the rear gunner was burned to death, trapped by jammed doors in his turret. The same groups went to Pforzheim on the 23/24th, for the first and only major raid of the war on this city. The marking and bombing took place from medium level, and in twenty-two minutes of horror, eighteen hundred tons of bombs left the built-up area a sea of flames, which was captured for posterity by a Film Unit Lancaster, and 17,600 people lost their lives. 258 Lancasters took part from 1 Group, and eleven failed to return, among them two each from 101, 103 and 300

Squadrons. 166 Squadron's ND506 crashed in Germany, killing F/O Ellis and four of his crew.

550 Squadron welcomed W/C McWatters as its new commanding officer on the 25th, and he would remain in post for the rest of the war. He had previously completed a tour of operations with 4 Group's 78 Squdron. W/C Hackforth was posted out of 170 Squadron on the same day, and he was succeeded by W/C Templeman-Rooke, known to all as Rookie Templeman-Rooke began his operational career in April 1943 as a sergeant pilot with 100 Squadron. During the course of his first tour he discovered that empty beer bottles produced an eerie sound as they fell, and he made a practice of taking them on operations to drop over Germany. During an operation to Gelsenkirchen he lost two engines to flak, which killed his rear gunner and severely damaged the tailplane. After nursing the crippled Lancaster back to Grimsby he and his crew counted ninety holes, and this episode no doubt contributed to the award of the DFC. He began a second tour in May 1944 when joining 576 Squadron as a flight commander, and it was at this time that he began to return from operations at low level to avoid the enemy defences. He was awarded a Bar to his DFC for "pressing home his attacks with utmost determination and accuracy", and for displaying "outstanding leadership, sustained courage and initiative".

March

Mannheim hosted its final heavy raid of the war on the afternoon of the 1st of March, delivered by over four hundred aircraft from 1, 6 and 8 Groups, and 166 Squadron's ME447 crashed in Germany killing F/O Phelps and his crew. Cologne was likewise bombed for the last time on the morning of the 2nd in a two-phase operation. The first phase involved seven hundred aircraft, 240 of them from 1 Group, and the second was to have been by 155 Lancasters of 3 Group, but only a handful bombed after the failure of a G-H station in England. Never-the-less, the much bombed city was left in a state of paralysis, and was taken by American forces four days later. On the night of the 3/4th the Luftwaffe mounted its highly successful Operation Gisella, in which around two hundred aircraft carried out intruder sorties as bombers returned from Kamen, the Dortmund-Ems Canal, various support and minor operations and training. Twenty Bomber Command aircraft were lost in this manner, including two 12 Squadron Lancasters, which were shot down over Lincolnshire while training, and all fourteen crewmen were killed. A 460 Squadron Lancaster was also shot down into the Lincolnshire countryside as it was carrying out a training flight, but the pilot and four others were able to walk away. The JU88 responsible for its demise then attacked a car, killing a member of the Royal Observer Corps, before itself colliding with telephone wires and crashing with fatal consequences for its crew. (Bomber Command Losses, 1945, Bill Chorley.)

Having failed to inflict a telling blow on Chemnitz on the night after Dresden, over seven hundred aircraft returned on the 5/6th and left central and southern districts in flames. 1 Group put up 239 aircraft for this operation, eight of which failed to return. W/C Morton took over the reins at 100 Squadron on the 7th, arriving from 15 Base to succeed W/C Hamilton. He had spent some time at 576 Squadron during February, presumably to gain operational experience, and had flown to Dresden as second pilot to F/O Hardman. He would prove to be the squadron's final wartime commander. The eastern town of Dessau had never before been bombed when five hundred aircraft from 1, 3, 6 and 8 Groups arrived overhead on the 7/8th, and the now familiar catalogue of damage to residential, industrial and railway property resulted. 1 Group provided a force of 243 Lancasters, and the crew of one of them claimed an enemy jet fighter as destroyed. Thirteen aircraft from the group failed to return, and 550 Squadron was hardest-hit with three missing crews. On the 8/9th, Kassel was raided for the first time since its ordeal by firestorm in October 1943, and this attack by a 1 Group main force of 235 aircraft proved to be its last of the war.

An all-time record was set on the 11th, when 1,079 aircraft, including 240 from 1 Group, took of in the late morning to bomb Essen for the final time. A little over twenty-four hours later, 1,108 aircraft departed their stations in the early afternoon, for the final raid of the war on Dortmund, and this new record would stand to the end of hostilities. A record 4,800 tons of bombes rained down into mainly central and southern districts, and all production it its factories ceased. 1 Group put up 243 Lancasters for this operation, during which a 103 Squadron aircraft was hit by a bomb, which embedded itself in a wing. The crew baled out after arriving in home airspace, but sadly, the flight engineer died after his parachute failed to deploy. 1 Group continued its involvement in the oil offensive by attacking two Ruhr Benzol producers on the 13/14th. Seventy-five Lancasters were involved at the Erin plant at Herne, while eighty others targeted the Dahlbusch works at Gelsenkirchen. Cloud at the former compelled the crews to bomb on navigational aids, and around 50% of the loads fell in the general target area, but visibility was clearer at the latter and bombing was accurate until smoke obscured the aiming point towards the end of the attack. Two nights later over two hundred 1 Group Lancasters were involved in a raid on the Deurag refinery at Misburg on the outskirts of

Hannover. Conditions were excellent in the target area, and most of the bombing hit the mark.

Nuremberg was visited for the last time on the 16/17th by a force of 230 Lancasters from 1 Group with 8 Group Mosquitos to provide the marking. Enemy night fighters were active during the outward flight, and they were largely responsible for the loss of twenty-four Lancasters. Heavy damage was caused in the southern half of the city, and over five hundred people were killed. It was a shocking night for 12 Squadron, which posted missing four aircraft, and had a fifth written-off with battle damage after landing at Juvincourt in France. 166 Squadron had PA234, PB153 and RF154 all crash in Germany, with the crews of F/O Muncer, Sgt Hilder and F/O Churchward respectively. F/O Muncer survived with one member of his crew, but lost his left arm, and F/O Churchward and five of his crew also came through their ordeal, but Sgt Hilder and five of his crew lost their lives. 103, 170 and 576 Squadrons also each had three fail to return, while 100 and 625 Squadrons both lost two. Among the 100 Squadron casualties was ND644, which crashed in the target area on its 115th sortie. At least, these were the final wartime casualties to be sustained by the squadron. In human terms the 1 Group losses amounted to ninety-four men killed, thirty-eight in captivity and one evader. Hanau was devastated by a 1 Group force of 230 aircraft on the 18/19th, and the tally of destruction included over 2,200 houses and fifty industrial premises, while around two thousand people were killed. An operation to Bremen in the morning of the 21st involved a hundred Lancasters from 1 Group, and they attacked in fine conditions to produce accurate and concentrated bombing.

It was after midnight on the 22nd when 117 Lancasters from 1 Group took off for Bochum and the Bruchstrasse Benzol plant. They found the target clear of cloud, and another accurate and concentrated attack ensued. Hildesheim was one of a number of Germany's cities to escape attention almost until the end of hostilities, but when its one and only raid came on the afternoon of the 22nd, it did so with terrifying fury at the hands of a 1 Group main force of just a hundred aircraft. 3,300 apartment blocks were destroyed or seriously damaged, the cathedral and many other public buildings were reduced to rubble, and over sixteen hundred people were killed. 166 Squadron's PD365 failed to return, and F/S Moore died with his crew. Over ninety Lancasters from the group joined others from 5 Group on the morning of the 23rd to target a bridge at Bremen. Bombing took place either side of 10.00 hours, and was confined to the immediate target area, where a number of direct hits were observed before smoke obscured ground detail. Both missing Lancasters were from 101 Squadron, and DV245 was on its 119th or 122nd operation. It was hit by flak and exploded, killing four of the crew. These and those on board LL775 were the last from the squadron to lose their lives during the war.

As Allied forces began their crossing of the Rhine on the 24th, the Command continued its attacks on oil related targets. The Harpenerweg oil plant at Dortmund was the objective for the afternoon of the 24th, for which 1 Group provided eighty Lancasters, with other aircraft in support from 6 and 8 Groups. Visibility was excellent, enabling the target to be easily identified and attacked with great accuracy. 166 Squadron's NG114 was brought down over Germany, and only one man survived from the crew of F/O Defraigne. 150 Squadron lost one of its ten participants, and it was a particularly sad one. F/O Morris and his crew were on the thirtieth and final operation of their tour when they were forced to parachute into the hands of the enemy. With Germany in ruins and on the point of defeat it was a bad time to be a bomber crewman on enemy soil. All landed safely on the ground, but the pilot and four others were murdered, and just two survived as PoWs. Thankfully, this would prove to be 150 Squadron's final loss of the war.

1, 6 and 8 Groups went to Hannover for the last time on the 25th, for which 1 Group contributed 150 aircraft. Good conditions again prevailed, and the bombing was concentrated in the built-up area of the city. 166 Squadron's ME521 was struck by bombs from above and crashed in the target area, killing S/L Laverack and two of his crew. Also on the 25th the highly popular G/C Donkin was posted to Andover from his station commander role at Kelstern, and 625 Squadron's W/C Barker stepped up to combine the roles of squadron and station commander. 1 Group was involved in the destruction of Paderborn on the 27th, when sending 220 Lancasters to soften up the area ahead of advancing American ground forces. On the 31st the group launched two hundred aircraft as part of an overall 1, 6 and 8 Group force of more than four hundred aircraft targeting the Blohm & Voss U-Boot yards at Hamburg, where the new Type XXI vessel was under construction. In conditions of complete cloud cover, most of the bombing fell into the city and nearby Harburg, and another attempt would be mounted in April. Eleven aircraft failed to return, although none from 1 Group, and this was the last double figure loss from a single city target. W/C Sellick was posted from 576 squadron during the course of the month, and he was succeeded by W/C McAllister as the unit's last wartime commander.

April

April would prove to be the final month of the bombing war for the heavy brigade, but before the action got under way, 100 Squadron completed its move from Grimsby to Elsham Wolds. Waltham had been a happy station, and a close bond had developed between it and the people of the local area. Operations began for 1 Group on the 3rd, with a daylight attack by more than two hundred aircraft on what was believed to be a military barracks at Nordhausen. It was, in fact, a camp for forced workers at the underground secret weapons factory, which had been established after Peenemünde, and heavy casualties were inflicted on these friendly foreign nationals. 5 Group added to the discomfiture of the hapless inmates with a follow-up attack twenty-four hours later.

On the night of the 4/5th a 1 Group force of 230 aircraft teamed up with an 8 Group element to inflict moderate damage on the Wintershall oil refinery at Lützkendorf, a target which would be finished off by 5 Group on the following day. On return 166 Squadron's LM289 crashed west of Kirmington, and although F/O Ayton and one of his crew survived with injuries, five of those on board lost their lives. By this time ND909 had already crashed in Germany with fatal consequences for F/O Day and his crew. These would be the squadron's final operational casualties of the war. 153 Squadron dispatched twelve aircraft on the main operation, and five more for mining duties. W/C Powley was available to fly that night, and opted for the mining operation, from which he did not return. RA544 was lost without trace, but it is believed to have been shot down by a night fighter over the Kattegat. S/L Tom Rippingale took temporary command of the squadron until the arrival of a permanent replacement for the popular Powley. 625 Squadron's A and B Flights completed their move to Scampton on the 6th to join 153 Squadron. C Flight had been hived off now that the end was in sight, and it was transferred to Fiskerton. W/C Guy Rodney arrived at Scampton on the 9th to take over 153 Squadron, and like his recently deceased predecessor, W/C Powley, he was another Canadian in the RAF who had completed two tours, and had commanded 626 Squadron at Wickenby from April to September.

W/C Dixon was posted in to 626 Squadron from 1656 CU on the 9th as commanding officer elect. That night an accurate raid on Kiel by 250 Lancasters from 1 Group in company with others from 3 and 8 Groups inflicted severe damage on the Deutsche Werke U-Boot yards, capsized the surface raider Admiral Scheer, and damaged the Admiral Hipper and the Emden. On the 11th 150 Squadron's W/C Avis reported sick, and S/L Rippon, who had joined the squadron from 166 Squadron, stepped into his shoes as temporary commanding officer. In the event he was confirmed as the permanent occupier of the office on the 19th, and he was thus the squadron's last wartime commander. That night the railway yards at Plauen were the specific target for another 250 aircraft from the group with 8 Group support, but 50% of the town's built-up area was also destroyed. The final area raid on a city target was directed at Potsdam by 1, 3 and 8 Groups on the 14/15th, and this was the first time since March 1944 that RAF heavy bombers had conducted an operation within the Berlin defence zone. 1 Group contributed over two hundred Lancasters to this operation, while twenty-four from 576 Squadron carried out a spoof raid on Cuxhaven as a diversion. Severe damage occurred at the main target, and some of the bombing spilled over into Berlin itself. On the 16th W/C Molesworth was posted to 1661 CU at the conclusion of his tour in command of 626 Squadron, and he was succeeded by W/C Dixon.

Over nine hundred aircraft took part in a lunchtime attack on the island of Heligoland on the 18th, for which 1 Group contributed a record 311 Lancasters assigned to two aiming points. The first involved the docks and U-Boot pens on the southern end of the Island, and the whole area erupted under the bombardment. A few minutes later the northern half received similar treatment in fine weather conditions, and many crews noted a huge explosion, believed to be from an ammunition dump. As the massive force retreated it left behind it a heavily cratered and scarred surface that resembled a moonscape. As the British XXX Corps prepared to enter Bremen, 1, 3, 6 and 8 Groups were sent to attack its south-eastern suburbs. The raid was halted after 195 aircraft had bombed, when smoke and dust obscured the aiming point, and the 270 strong 1 Group contingent along with that of 6 Group returned home with bombs still on board. The 25th brought the final offensive operations by the heavy squadrons, and the day's activities began in the morning with an attack by 1, 5 and 8 Groups on the SS barracks at Hitler's Eaglesnest retreat at Berchtesgaden in the Bavarian mountains. Only two Lancasters were lost from the entire force, and one of them was from the 1 Group element of 247. 460 Squadron's NX585 surrendered three engines to flak, and had to be crash-landed in enemy territory by F/O Payne, after it was discovered that one of the crew had rendered his parachute unusable.

Offensive operations had now ended for 1 Group, and the remaining two weeks of war would see it involved in humanitarian duties. The first flights under Operation Exodus, to ferry PoWs back home, took place on the 27th, when forty-six Lancasters were sent to Brussels. Bad weather intervened, however, and only twenty-two sorties were successful, bringing home 503 men. On the following day forty aircraft brought back another 901 former PoWs. On the 29th 145 Lancasters from the Group took part in Operation Manna, and successfully carried out food drops to the starving Dutch people still under enemy occupation. 269 returned on the 30th, and efforts to feed the Dutch continued on each day thereafter, except for the 6th of May, up to and including the 8th, the day on which the war in Europe officially came to an end. Operations to repatriate PoWs continued throughout the month of May.

From its reconstitution in July 1940, 1 Group took its place on the Command's order of battle, and once equipped with the Wellington it embarked on an operational career that saw it at the forefront of the Command's campaigns right through to the end. Its record of service bears comparison with any group, and stands as a memorial to all those who served within its ranks.

CHAPTER TWO

Quick Reference

Facts, Figures and General Information

AIR OFFICER COMMANDING

Air Commodore	J. J. Breen	27.06.40. to 27.11.40.
Air Vice Marshal	R.D. Oxland	27.11.40. to 21.02.43.
Air Vice Marshal	E.A.B. Rice	24.02.43. to 12.02.45.
Air Vice Marshal	R.S. Blucke	12.02.45.

OPERATIONAL STATIONS

Binbrook	Blyton	Breighton
Dunholme Lodge	Elsham Wold	Faldingworth
Fiskerton	Grimsby	Hemswell
Holme-On-Spalding-Moor	Ingham	Kelstern
Kirmington	Lindholme	Ludford Magna
Newton	North Killingholme	Scampton
Snaith	Swinderby	Syerston
Wickenby		

AIRCRAFT TYPES

Battle	Wellington	Halifax	Lancaster

FULL LIST OF OPERATIONAL 1 GROUP SQUADRONS BETWEEN 3.9.39. and 8.5.45.

12, 100, 101, 103, 142, 150, 153, 166, 170, 199, 300, 301, 304, 305, 458 RAAF, 460 RAAF, 550, 576, 625 and 626.

GROUP STRENGTH

As of 30th of September 1940
12, 103, 142, 150, 300 and 301 Squadrons, all operational

As of April 1945
12, 100, 101, 103, 150, 153, 166, 170, 300, 460 RAAF, 550, 576, 625
and 626 Squadrons.

QUICK REFERENCE STATION/SQUADRON

Binbrook	12, 142, 460 RAAF.
Blyton	199
Breighton	460 RAAF.
Dunholme Lodge	170
Elsham Wolds	100, 103, 576
Faldingworth	300
Fiskerton	150, 576
Grimsby	100, 142, 550
Hemswell	150, 170, 300, 301, 305
Holme-On-Spalding-Moor	101, 458 RAAF
Ingham	199, 300, 305
Kelstern	170, 625
Kirmington	153, 166
Lindholme	304, 305
Ludford Magna	101
Newton	103, 150
North Killingholme	550
Scampton	153, 625
Snaith	150
Swinderby	300, 301
Syerston	304, 305
Wickenby	12, 626

QUICK REFERENCE STATION/SQUADRON
DATES

Binbrook	12, 142	03.07.40. to 07.08.40.
	142	07.08.40. to 12.08.40.
	142	06.09.40. to 07.09.40.
	12, 142	07.09.40. to 26.11.41.
	12	26.11.41. to 25.09.42.

	460 RAAF	14.05.43. to 27.07.45.
Blyton	199	07.11.42. to 03.02.43.
Breighton	460 RAAF	04.01.42. to 14.05.43.
Dunholme Lodge	170	22.10.44. to 29.11.44.
Elsham Wolds	103	11.07.41. to 25.11.43.
	103, 576	25.11.43. to 31.10.44.
	103	31.10.44. to 02.04.45.
	100, 103	02.04.45. to 26.11.45.
Faldingworth	300	01.03.44. to 28.12.46.
Fiskerton	576	31.10.44. to 01.11.44.
	150, 576	01.11.44. to 22.11.44.
	576	22.11.44. to 13.09.45.
Grimsby	142	26.11.41. to 15.12.42.
	100, 142	15.12.42. to 19.12.42.
	100	19.12.42. to 25.11.43.
	100, 550	25.11.43. to 03.01.44.
	100	03.01.44. to 02.04.45.
Hemswell	300, 301	18.07.41. to 18.05.42.
	301	18.05.42. to 23.07.42.
	301, 305	23.07.42. to 31.01.43.
	300, 301, 305	31.01.43. to 07.04.43.
	300, 305	07.04.43. to 22.06.43.
	150	22.11.44. to 29.11.44.
	150, 170	29.11.44. to 07.11.45.
Holme-On-Spalding-Moor	458 RAAF	25.08.41. to 22.02.42.
	101	29.09.42. to 15.06.43.
Ingham	300	18.05.42. to 31.01.43.
	199	03.02.43. to 20.06.43.
	300, 305	22.06.43. to 05.09.43.
	300	05.09.43. to 01.03.44.
Kelstern	625	13.10.43. to 15.10.44.
	625, 170	15.10.44. to 29.10.44.
	625	29.10.44. to 06.04.45.
Kirmington	166	27.01.43. to 15.10.44.
	153, 166	15.10.44. to 28.09.45.
Lindholme	304	19.07.41. to 20.07.41.
	304, 305	20.07.41. to 10.05.42.
	305	10.05.42. to 23.07.42.

Ludford Magna	101	15.06.43. to 01.10.45.
Newton	103, 150	03.07.40. to 10.07.41.
	103	10.07.41. to 11.07.41.
North Killingholme	550	31.01.44. to 31.10.45.
Scampton	153	15.10.44. to 06.04.45.
	153, 625	06.04.45. to 28.09.45.
Snaith	150	10.07.41. to 26.10.42.
Swinderby	300	22.08.40. to 28.08.40.
	300, 301	28.08.40. to 18.07.41.
Syerston	304	02.12.40. to 04.12.40.
	304, 305	04.12.40. to 19.07.41.
	305	19.07.41. to 20.07.40.
Wickenby	12	25.09.42. to 07.11.42.
	12, 626	07.11.42. to 24.09.45.

QUICK REFERENCE
SQUADRON/AIRCRAFT/PRINCIPAL DATES

12 SQUADRON
Wellington

First received		10.11.40.
First operation	EMDEN	9/10.04.41.
Last operation	MINING	21/22.11.42.

Lancaster

First received		8.11.42.
First operation	MINING	3/4.04.43.

100 SQUADRON
Lancaster

First received		12.01.43.
First operation	MINING	4/03.43.

101 SQUADRON
Wellington

First operation	KREFELD	2/3.10.42.
Last operation	MINING	14/15.10.42.

Lancaster

First received		11.10.42.
First operation	TURIN	20/21.11.42.

103 SQUADRON
Wellington

First received		2.10.40.
First operation	OSTEND	20/21.12.40.
Last operation	BREMEN	2/3.07.42.

Halifax

First received		c7.07.42.
First operation	DÜSSELDORF	31.7/1.08.42.
Last operation	MILAN	24/25.10.42.

Lancaster

First received		1.11.42.
First operation	MINING	21/22.11.42.

142 SQUADRON
Wellington

First received		8.12.40.
First operation	BOULOGNE	15/16.04.41.
Last operation	LORIENT	15/16.01.43.

150 SQUADRON
Wellington

First received		2.10.40.
First operation	GELSENKIRCHEN	9/10.1.41.
Last operation	MINING	15/16.01.43.

Lancaster

First received		1.11.44.
First operation	DORTMUND	11/12.11.44.

153 SQUADRON
Lancaster

First received		7.10.44.
First operation	EMMERICH	7.10.44.

166 SQUADRON
Wellington

First received		26.01.43.
First operation	LORIENT	26/27.01.43.
Last operation	MINING	18/19.09.43.

Lancaster

First received		20.09.43.
First operation	HANNOVER	22/23.09.43.

170 SQUADRON
Lancaster

First received		15.10.44.
First operation	STUTTGART	19/20.10.44.

199 SQUADRON
Wellington

First received		10.11.42.
First operation	MANNHEIM	6/7.12.42.
Last operation	MINING	13/14.06.43.

300 SQUADRON
Wellington

First received		18.10.40.
First operation	ANTWERP	22/23.12.40.
Last operation	MINING	3/4.03.44.

Lancaster

First received		3.04.44.
First operation	ROUEN	18/19.04.44.

301 SQUADRON
Wellington

First received		20.10.40.
First operation	ANTWERP	22/23.12.40.
Last operation	BOCHUM	29/30.03.43.

304 SQUADRON
Wellington

First received		1.11.40.
First operation	ROTTERDAM	25/26.04.41.
Last operation	LEAFLETING	3/4.05.42.

305 SQUADRON
Wellington

First received		5.11.40.
First operation	ROTTERDAM	25/26.04.41.
Last operation	HAMBURG	2/3.08.43.

458 SQUADRON RAAF
Wellington

First received		30.08.41.
First operation	EMDEN/ANTWERP	20/21.10.41.
Last operation	BOULOGNE	28/29.01.42.

460 SQUADRON RAAF
Wellington

First received		30.11.41.
First operation	EMDEN	12/13.03.42.
Last operation	WILHELMSHAVEN	14/15.09.42.

Lancaster

First received		6.10.42.
First operation	STUTTGART	22/23.11.42.

550 SQUADRON
Lancaster

First received		25.11.43.
First operation	BERLIN	26/27.11.43.

576 SQUADRON
Lancaster

First received		25.11.43.
First operation	BERLIN	2/3.12.43.

625 SQUADRON
Lancaster

First received		13.10.43.
First operation	HANNOVER	18/19.10.43.

626 SQUADRON
Lancaster

First received		7.11.43.
First operation	MODANE	10/11.11.43.

QUICK REFERENCE RECORDS

1 GROUP SORTIES AND LOSSES

Aircraft	Sorties	Losses
Battle	287	6 (2.1%)
Wellington	12,170	395 (3.2%)
Halifax	137	12 (8.8%)
Lancaster	43,836	1016 (2.3%)
Total	56,430	1429 (2.5%)

Most Overall Operations	103 Squadron	519
Most Bombing Operations	103 Squadron	486
Highest Aircraft Operational Losses	103 Squadron	179
Highest Percentage Losses	12 Squadron	3.3%
Most Sorties	460 Squadron	6238
Highest Bomb Tonnage	460 Squadron	24,000

Battle

Most Overall Operations	103/142/150 Squadrons	16
Most Sorties	142 Squadron	63
Highest Aircraft Operational Losses	142 Squadron	4
Highest Percentage Losses	142 Squadron	6.3%

The first presentation of DFC's to Polish bomber pilots S/L Sulinski of 300 Squadron and W/C
Piotrowski of 301 Squadron on New Year's Day, 1942. (Greg Korcz)

The 300 Squadron crews who took part in the first Polish attack on Berlin on the 23/24 March, 1941. W/C Makowski stands centre front row. (Greg Korcz)

103 Squadron's W/C Dickens with other squadron officers at Rheges, May 1940. (David Fell)

103 Squadron Battles over Betheniville 1940. (David Fell)

103 Squadron Battle and bomb train at Betheniville. (David Fell)

A 103 Squadron Wellington demonstrating the strength of its construction. (David Fell)

103 Squadron aircrew in front of a Halifax at Elsham Wolds in August, 1942. (David Fell)

'Mad Belgian' S/L Van Rolleghem and his crew of 103 Squadron at Elsham Wolds. (David Fell)

576 Squadron at Fiskerton in early 1944. (Fiskerton Airfield Association)

LL804 BH-F at Faldingworth in August 1944. This was the squadron's longest serving Lancaster and completed 70 sorties before being transferred to 1660 CU in March 1945. (Greg Korcz)

ED327 BH-R of 300 Squadron displaying artwork symbolising Polish and Allied friendship. This Lancaster belonged to the British B Flight that existed within the squadron between June and September 1944 during a shortage of Polish personnel. It was one of three from the squadron to fail to return from Stettin on the night of 29/30 August 1944 and P/O Harry Lupton and crew all died. (Greg Korcz)

The wreckage of 103 Squadron's ND363 PM-A on the Dutch Frisian island of Texel on the morning of 16 February 1944, following the penultimate heavy attack on Berlin. F/L Ken Barry DFM and his crew were killed. Berry had just embarked on his second tour with the Squadron. (Andreas Wachtel)

G/C Constantine, Station Commander at Elsham Wolds and later A-O-C 5 Group. (Steve Smith)

103 Squadron's W4340 PM-A taken from Ken Berry's W4337 PM-K en-route to Turin 12.12.42. (Andreas Wachtel)

Sgt Ken Berry at the start of his operational career with 103 Squadron. (Andreas Wachtel)

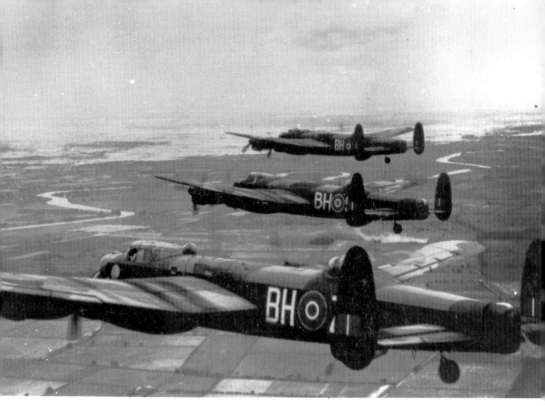

Lancasters of 300 Squadron over Holland during Operation Manna, May 1945. (Greg Korcz)

576 Squadron's LM227, a veteran of 100 operations, at Fiskerton, April 1945. (Fiskerton Airfield Association)

S/L Hamilton and Crew of 100 Squadron. (The Greg Harrison collection)

The bombing-up of Wellington Ic R1006 GR-H of 301 Squadron at Swinderby in July 1941. (Greg Korcz)

W/C Gardner addresses aircrew of 166 Squadron. (Steve Smith)

Wellington Ic Z1112 NZ-M of 304 Squadron at Lindholme in 1941. (Greg Korcz)

Wellington IV Z1260 SM-B of 305 Squadron at Ingham in June 1943. (Greg Korcz)

The crew of Wellington IV Z1407 BH-Z of 300 Squadron stand in front of their flak-damaged aircraft on return from Bremen on 5.9.42. (Greg Korcz)

S/L Tommy Wright (3rd left) and crew of 170 Squadron with Lancaster TC-N. (The Greg Harrison collection)

100 Squadron, May 1943, left to right; Sgt Jefraney, Sgt Cooper, Sgt McRae, W/O Fletcher, Sgt Jackson, Sgt Clark, Sgt Manyweather. (The Greg Harrison collection)

100 Squadron aircrew at Waltham (Grimsby), Summer of 1944. (The Greg Harrison collection)

F/L Sheriff and crew of 100 Squadron, 1943. (The Greg Harrison collection)

W/C J. D. Nelson (front row, centre), Commanding Officer of 12 Squadron between March and August 1944, pictured with his crew. Back row, left to right; Sgts Kent, Owen, Smith and Davis. Front row left F/S Hyland, right F/S Hearn. (The Wickenby Museum)

Merlin-powered MK11 Wellingtons WS361 of 12 Squadron. (The Wickenby Museum)

Crew of Wellington II PH-M W5419 of 12 Squadron. Pilot F/L Baxter, 3rd from left. (The Wickenby Museum)

Wellington

Most Overall Operations	300 Squadron	323
Most Bombing Operations	300 Squadron	218
Most Sorties	300 Squadron	2421
Highest Aircraft Operational Losses	12 Squadron	59
Highest Percentage Losses	460 Squadron	5.4%

Halifax

Most Overall Operations	103 Squadron	15
Most Sorties	103 Squadron	137
Highest Aircraft Operational Losses	103 Squadron	12
Highest Percentage Losses	103 Squadron	8.8%

Lancaster

Most Overall Operations	103 Squadron	344
Most Bombing Operations	103 Squadron	317
Most Sorties	460 Squadron	5700
Highest Aircraft Operational Losses	460 Squadron	140
Highest Percentage Losses	103 Squadron	3.0%

A-HAA-HA

Chapter Three

THE SQUADRONS

In the interests of uniformity commanding officers are listed without decorations.

12 SQUADRON

Motto: **Leads The Field**   Code **PH**

12 Squadron was formed in February 1915 and moved to France in that September to carry out a reconnaissance and bombing role. In early 1916 it became solely an artillery-spotting and reconnaissance unit, and saw out the war accordingly. It joined the army of occupation in Germany until disbandment in July 1922. The squadron reformed in April 1923 as a day bomber unit, and remained in that role, at home and in the Middle East, until the eve of WWII, by which time it was equipped with Fairey Battles and stationed at Bicester. For the first nine months of hostilities it served with the AASF in France, and after withdrawal to the UK in mid-June 1940 became a founder member of the reconstituted 1 Group in Bomber Command.

STATIONS

BERRY-au-BAC	02.09.39. to 08.12.39.
AMIFONTAINE	08.12.39. to 16.05.40.
ECHEMINES	16.05.40. to 08.06.40.
SOUGE	08.06.40. to 16.06.40.
FINNINGLEY	16.06.40. to 03.07.40.
BINBROOK	03.07.40. to 07.08.40.
THORNEY ISLAND	07.08.40. to 12.08.40.
EASTCHURCH	12.08.40. to 07.09.40.
BINBROOK	07.09.40. to 25.09.42.
WICKENBY	25.09.42. to 24.09.45.

COMMANDING OFFICERS

Squadron Leader	R W G Lywood	16.05.38. to 28.09.39.
Wing Commander	A G Thackray	28.09.39. to 28.06.40.
Wing Commander	V Q Blackden	28.06.40. to 10.04.41.
Wing Commander	R H Maw	11.04.41. to 14.10.41.
Wing Commander	B J R Roberts	14.10.41. to 12.01.42.
Wing Commander	A Golding	12.01.42. to 27.03.42.
Wing Commander	R C Collard	01.04.42. to 26.07.42.
Wing Commander	H I Dabinett	30.07.42. to 15.02.43.
Wing Commander	R S C Wood	15.02.43. to 25.08.43.
Wing Commander	J G Towle	25.08.43. to 31.08.43.
Wing Commander	D M H Craven	01.09.43. to 06.03.44.
Wing Commander	J D Nelson	06.03.44. to 26.08.44.
Wing Commander	M Stockdale	26.08.44. to 31.05.45.

AIRCRAFT

Battle	02.38. to 11.40.
Wellington II	11.40. to 11.42.
Wellington III	08.42. to 11.42.
Lancaster I/III	11.42. to 08.46.

Operational Record

Operations	Sorties	Aircraft Losses	% Losses
484	5160	171	3.3%

Category Of Operations

Bombing	Mining	Other
427	51	6

Battles

Operations	Sorties	Aircraft Losses	% Losses
8	36	1	2.8%

Wellingtons

Operations	Sorties	Aircraft Losses	% Losses
167	1242	59	4.8%

Category Of Operations

Bombing	Mining	Other
137	24	6

Lancasters

Operations	Sorties	Aircraft Losses	% Losses
309	3882	111	2.9%

Category Of Operations

Bombing	Mining
282	27

18 further Lancasters were destroyed in crashes.

TABLE OF STATISTICS
(Heavy squadrons)

23rd highest number of overall operations in Bomber Command.
22nd highest number of sorties in Bomber Command.
10th equal (with 101Sqn) highest number of aircraft operational losses in Bomber Command.
24th highest number of bombing operations in Bomber Command.
16th highest number of mining operations in Bomber Command.

Out of 42 Wellington squadrons.

12th highest number of Wellington overall operations in Bomber Command.
10th highest number of Wellington sorties in Bomber Command.
4th highest number of Wellington operational losses in Bomber Command.

Out of 59 Lancaster squadrons.

10th highest number of Lancaster overall operations in Bomber Command.
14th highest number of Lancaster sorties in Bomber Command.
9th equal (with 9Sqn) highest number of Lancaster operational losses in Bomber Command.

Out of 20 squadrons in 1 Group.

2nd highest number of overall operations in 1 Group.
3rd highest number of sorties in 1 Group.

2nd highest number of aircraft operational losses in 1 Group.

Out of 6 Battle squadrons in 1 Group.

4th equal (with 301Sqn) highest number of overall Battle operations in 1 Group.
Lowest number of Battle sorties in 1 Group.
2nd equal (with 103Sqn) highest number of Battle operational losses in 1 Group.

Out of 13 Wellington squadrons in 1 Group.

5th highest number of Wellington overall operations in 1 Group.
3rd highest number of Wellington sorties in 1 Group.
highest number of Wellington operational losses in 1 Group.
2nd highest Wellington percentage loss rate in 1 Group.

Out of 14 Lancaster squadrons in 1 Group.

2nd highest number of Lancaster overall operations in 1 Group.
6th highest number of Lancaster sorties in 1 Group.
5th highest number of Lancaster operational losses in 1 Group.

AIRCRAFT HISTORIES

BATTLE.	**To November 1940.**
K9212	From XVSqn. to 6MU.
K9274	From 150Sqn. to 142Sqn.
K9275	From 150Sqn. to 101Sqn.
K9276	From 150Sqn. Abandoned in France May 40.
K9277	From 150Sqn. to 3Gp TTF.
K9279	From 150Sqn. to 1 Salvage Section.
K9280	From 150Sqn. Abandoned in France May 40.
K9284	From 150Sqn. to 6 RSU.
K9285	From 150Sqn. to 22MU.
K9286	From 150Sqn. to 8MU.
K9288	From 150Sqn. to 22MU.
K9290	From 150Sqn. to 1 AACU.
K9291	From 150Sqn. to CGS.

K9368	PH-F	From XVSqn. to 20MU.
K9375		To 3 Go TTF via Mildenhall.
K9376		To 6MU.
K9414		From 63Sqn. to 98Sqn.
K9415		From 63Sqn. to 22MU.
K9417		From 63Sqn. to 150Sqn.
K9421		From 63Sqn. to 98Sqn.
K9423		From 63Sqn. to 22MU.
K9485		To 105Sqn.
K9486		To 105Sqn.
L4944	PH-R	Abandoned in France 16.5.40.
L4949	PH-V	FTR Luxembourg 10.5.40.
L4950	PH-V	FTR Sedan 14.5.40.
L4951		To 13 OTU.
L4952	PH-X	FTR Sedan 14.5.40.
L4960		From 63Sqn. to 22MU.
L4961		From 63Sqn. to 1 AACU.
L5011		From 103Sqn. to 7 AACU via 27MU.
L5076		From 20MU. to 38MU.
L5100		From 20MU. to 38MU.
L5127	PH-K	Damaged beyond repair in taxying accident at Eastchurch while training 25.8.40. Became ground instruction machine.
L5188	PH-O/C	From 88Sqn. FTR Sedan 14.5.40.
L5190	PH-P	From 16Sqn. FTR Luxembourg 10.5.40.
L5220		From 20MU. to 38MU.
L5227	PH-J	From 142Sqn. FTR Veldwezelt 12.5.40.
L5240		From 20MU. to 27MU.
L5241	PH-G	From 40Sqn. FTR Vroenhoven 12.5.40.
L5249		From 40Sqn. Damaged during operation to Luxembourg 10.5.40. and abandoned in France.
L5324	PH-A	From 10MU. FTR Foret de Gault 13.6.40.
L5328	PH-A	From 10MU. Lost in France May 40. Details uncertain.

L5359		From 27MU. to 20MU.
L5383	PH-F	From 10MU. FTR Evreux 14.6.40.
L5391		From 27MU. to 142Sqn.
L5396		From 10MU. FTR Evreux 14.6.40.
L5398	PH-G	From 27MU. to 38MU.
L5399		From 27MU. to 38MU.
L5400		From 27MU. to Fairey.
L5404		To 20MU.
L5415	PH-O	From 6MU. to 20MU.
L5420	PH-N	From 6MU. to 20MU.
L5439	PH-N	From 8MU. FTR Veldwezelt 12.5.40.
L5451	PH-C	From 20MU. to 20MU.
L5458		From 20MU. to 18MU.
L5491	PH-Z	From 27MU. to Fairey.
L5493		From 27MU. SOC 31.8.40.
L5495		From 27MU. to 20MU.
L5520	PH-N	From 6MU. Lost in France June 40. Details uncertain.
L5521		From 6MU. to Fairey.
L5531		From 27MU. FTR Foret de Gault 13.6.40.
L5538	PH-R/A	From 10MU. FTR Hannogne 19.5.40.
L5546	PH-U	From 142Sqn. FTR from attack on troops and Panzers 8.6.40.
L5568		From Andover. Shot down by friendly night fighters near Skegness during operation to bomb invasion ports 31.7/1.8.40.
L5580		From 6MU. FTR Foret de Gault 13.6.40.
L5629		From 98Sqn. to 103Sqn.
L5630		From 150Sqn. to 4Gp TTF.
N2020		From 6MU. to 8MU.
N2150	PH-Y	From 6MU. Destroyed on evacuation from France 18.6.40.
N2166		From 20MU. to 18MU.
N2178	PH-I	From 6MU. FTR Hannogne 19.5.40.
P2162		From 6MU. FTR Poix 7.6.40.

P2174		To 22MU.
P2175		To 22MU.
P2176		To 105Sqn.
P2177		To XVSqn.
P2178		To 22MU.
P2179		To 150Sqn.
P2180		To XVSqn.
P2181		To 22MU.
P2182		To 150Sqn.
P2183		To 150Sqn.
P2184		To 150Sqn.
P2204	PH-K	From 105Sqn. FTR Veldwezelt 12.5.40. Posthumous VCs awarded to F/O Garland and Sgt Gray.
P2243	PH-U	From 105Sqn. FTR Luxembourg 10.5.40.
P2262		From 20MU. to 38MU.
P2308		From 103Sqn via 27MU. to 27MU.
P2311		From 103Sqn. to Austin.
P2331		From 226Sqn. Destroyed by enemy action at Eastchurch 19.8.40.
P2332	PH-F	From 20MU. FTR Vroenhoven 12.5.40.
P5229	PH-O	From 6RSU. FTR Sedan 14.5.40.
P5231		From 27MU. Abandoned in France June 40.
P5236		From 150Sqn. to 20MU.
P5237		From 103Sqn. to 38MU.
P6571		From 20MU. to Binbrook.
P6597	PH-V	From 6MU. FTR Boulogne 19/20.8.40.
WELLINGTON.		**From November 1940 to November 1942**.
W5353		To OADU.
W5354		Destroyed by fire at Binbrook 18.6.41.
W5355		From 142Sqn. FTR le Havre 11/12.2.42.
W5356		From 142Sqn. Force-landed in Worcestershire on return from Cherbourg 9.1.42.
W5358		To 158Sqn.

W5360	PH-U	FTR Brest 6/7.7.41.
W5361	PH-C	FTR Cologne 30/31.5.42.
W5363		From 142Sqn. to OAPU.
W5365		Crashed on approach to Tollerton while training 8.2.41.
W5366		To OAPU.
W5367		FTR Hamburg 26/27.7.42.
W5368		From 405Sqn. to 1446Flt.
W5371		FTR Essen 26/27.3.42.
W5372	PH-D	FTR Essen 26/27.3.42.
W5373		To 142Sqn.
W5375	PH-D	FTR Emden 9/10.4.41.
W5376		To OAPU.
W5377		From 142Sqn. to 1443Flt.
W5379	PH-O	FTR Cologne 10/11.10.41.
W5380	PH-L	FTR Brest 24.7.41.
W5381		Crashed in Lincolnshire during an air-test 18.6.42.
W5382		To OADU.
W5383		From 142Sqn. to 311FTU.
W5387		From 142Sqn. to 158Sqn.
W5391	PH-A	FTR Bremen 27/28.6.41.
W5393		From 142Sqn. Crashed on approach to Binbrook on return from Bremen 22.10.41.
W5394	PH-H	From 104Sqn. FTR from a mining sortie 25.10.42.
W5395		From 142Sqn. FTR le Havre 1/2.4.42.
W5397		FTR Duisburg 13/14.7.42.
W5399		From 149Sqn. SOC 17.8.43.
W5401		To OAPU.
W5414		FTR from mining sortie 19/20.7.42.
W5419	PH-H	FTR Bremen 2/3.7.41.
W5421	PH-G	FTR Aachen 5/6.8.41.
W5422		To 104Sqn.

W5424	PH-D	From 158Sqn. Crashed on take-off from Binbrook when bound for Saarbrücken 29.7.42.
W5427		To 405Sqn.
W5428		To 305Sqn.
W5430		To 1446Flt.
W5437		From 158Sqn. Crash-landed at North Coates following early return from Duisburg 26.7.42. SOC. 9.42.
W5440		From 142Sqn. FTR Kiel 25/26.2.42.
W5442	PH-B	From 214Sqn. FTR Essen 9/10.3.42.
W5444	PH-T	Force-landed in Norfolk on return from Cologne 17.8.41.
W5447		From 305Sqn. Returned to 305Sqn.
W5458		From 99Sqn. FTR Mannheim 19/20.5.42.
W5460		From 99Sqn. SOC 29.3.43.
W5484		From 405Sqn. SOC 22.6.43.
W5495		From 405Sqn. to 1446Flt.
W5514	PH-S	From 142Sqn. Force-landed in Derbyshire on return from Brest 6.1.42.
W5523		To 104Sqn and back. FTR Brest 6/7.1.42.
W5528		To 1443Flt.
W5536	PH-M	Shot down by intruder near Grimsby on return from Rotterdam 14.8.41.
W5552		FTR Nuremberg 12/13.10.41.
W5570		FTR Essen 10/11.4.42.
W5571		To 1443Flt.
W5574		FTR Warnemünde 8/9.5.42.
W5575		To 158Sqn.
W5577	PH-U	FTR Boulogne 31.8/1.9.41.
W5578		FTR St Nazaire 25/26.3.42.
W5585	PH-D	From 142Sqn. Crashed on take-off from Binbrook when bound for Hannover 26.1.42.
W5587		To 1FCP.
W5598	PH-N	FTR Berlin 7/8.9.41.

W5611		To 104Sqn and back. Crashed in Lincolnshire on return from Wilhelmshaven 10.1.42.
X3553		To 425Sqn.
X3802	PH-J	FTR Kassel 27/28.8.42.
X3812		From 142Sqn. to 101Sqn.
X3987		To 142Sqn.
X3988	PH-X	FTR Kassel 27/28.8.42.
Z1728	PH-U	FTR Bremen 13/14.9.42.
Z1748		From 101Sqn. to 199Sqn.
Z8328		FTR Berlin 7/8.9.41.
Z8342	PH-Z	FTR Kiel 28/29.4.42.
Z8356		To 1446Flt.
Z8370		FTR Emden 20/21.1.42.
Z8375		From 158Sqn. to 1FP.
Z8376		FTR Cologne 30/31.5.42.
Z8397		Force-landed on Norfolk beach during an operation to Cologne 11.10.41.
Z8398		FTR Hamburg 17/18.4.42.
Z8400		From 158Sqn. SOC 19.11.44.
Z8402		To 1446Flt.
Z8403	PH-Z	From 57Sqn. FTR Kassel 27/28.8.42.
Z8407		To RAE.
Z8409	PH-H	From 214Sqn. FTR Essen 8/9.3.42.
Z8410		FTR Kiel 25/26.2.42.
Z8412		From 158Sqn. to 1446Flt.
Z8420	PH-G	From 158Sqn. FTR Duisburg 21/22.7.42.
Z8429		From 158Sqn. to FAA.
Z8431		From 405Sqn. SOC 25.3.44.
Z8435		From 305Sqn. SOC 25.4.44.
Z8437		From 405Sqn. Became ground instruction machine.
Z8489		To 1443Flt.
Z8491		Crashed near Sheffield on return from Brest 6/7.2.42.

Z8493		From 405Sqn. to 311FTU.
Z8495		From 305Sqn. FTR Stuttgart 5/6.5.42.
Z8499		FTR Düsseldorf 31.7/1.8.42.
Z8501		To 12FPP.
Z8502		FTR Duisburg 25/26.7.42.
Z8505	PH-F	FTR Wilhelmshaven 14/15.9.42.
Z8517	PH-C	FTR Duisburg 6/7.9.42.
Z8523	PH-Y	From 305Sqn. FTR Bremen 13/14.9.42.
Z8526		From 158Sqn. Caught fire after landing at Binbrook on return from Hamburg 27.7.42.
Z8529	PH-U	FTR Karlsruhe 2/3.9.42.
Z8531	PH-P	Force-landed in Norfolk on return from Bremen 3.7.42.
Z8532	PH-P	From 158Sqn. Force-landed in Yorkshire on return from mining sortie 12.10.42.
Z8533	PH-V	FTR Essen 2/3.6.42.
Z8535		To Manufacturers and back. to 301FTU.
Z8538	PH-O-	FTR Flensburg 18/19.8.42.
Z8539		To RAE.
Z8578		FTR Dunkerque 13/14.3.42.
Z8579		FTR Bremen 2/3.7.42.
Z8585	PH-W	From 158Sqn. FTR Duisburg 6/7.8.42.
Z8587		From 305Sqn. to 1 ECDU.
Z8591	PH-O	FTR Duisburg 25/26.7.42.
Z8595		From 305Sqn. Crashed in the North Sea while returning early from Bremen 5.9.42.
Z8598	PH-B	Crashed in Norfolk while bound for Cologne 30.5.42.
Z8643		FTR Cologne 30/31.5.42.
Z8644	PH-A	FTR Frankfurt 8/9.9.42.
Z8648		SOC 14.7.44.
Z8652		FTR Essen 8/9.6.42.
Z8656	PH-E	FTR Kassel 27/28.8.42.
Z8660		SOC 12.4.44.
BJ606	PH-S	From 101Sqn. FTR Cologne 15/16.10.42.

BJ609		To 199Sqn.
BJ653	PH-R	FTR Kiel 13/14.10.42.
BJ691	PH-T	FTR Duisburg 6/7.9.42.
BJ692		Crashed on landing at Wheaton Aston 1.10.42.
BJ776	PH-V	From 150Sqn. FTR from mining sortie 26/27.9.42.
BJ777		From 150Sqn. FTR from mining sortie 7/8.9.42.
BJ780	PH-W	From 142Sqn. FTR from mining sortie 8/9.10.42.
BJ819		From 142Sqn. to 199Sqn.
BJ821		To 142Sqn.
BJ889		To 199Sqn.
BJ960		To 199Sqn.
BJ964	PH-R	FTR from mining sortie 30.9.42.
BK198		To 142Sqn.
BK273		To 18 OTU.
BK366		To 199Sqn.
BK367		To 199Sqn.
BK460		From 142Sqn. to 166Sqn.
LANCASTER.		**From November 1942**.
R5549		From 1661CU. to 1667CU.
R5688	PH-G	From 50Sqn. Ditched in North Sea on return from Bochum 13/14.5.43.
W4328		From 103Sqn. to 1656CU.
W4366	PH-R	FTR Bochum 13/14.5.43.
W4368	PH-U	FTR Berlin 17/18.1.43.
W4369	PH-Z	FTR Essen 11/12.1.43.
W4370	PH-N	FTR Mannheim 5/6.9.43.
W4371	PH-C	FTR from mining sortie 8/9.1.43. Sqn's first Lancaster loss.
W4372	PH-G	FTR Berlin 17/18.1.43.
W4373	PH-F	FTR Düsseldorf 11/12.6.43.
W4374	PH-D	Force-landed near Wickenby while training 18.6.43.

W4380	PH-E	From 50Sqn. to 9Sqn.
W4788		To 103Sqn.
W4789	PH-E	To 61Sqn.
W4790	PH-B	To 1667CU.
W4791	PH-W	FTR Düsseldorf 11/12.6.43.
W4792	PH-M	FTR Cologne 26/27.2.43.
W4793	PH-H	To 1656CU.
W4794	PH-V	To 1667CU.
W4836	PH-P	From 100Sqn. Crashed in Lincolnshire on return from Lorient 13.2.43.
W4855	PH-D	FTR Hamburg 3/4.3.43.
W4858	PH-A	FTR Berlin 29/30.3.43.
W4861	PH-M	FTR Dortmund 23/24.5.43.
W4881	PH-C	To 460Sqn.
W4925	PH-N	FTR Essen 30.4/1.5.43.
W4954	PH-V	From 100Sqn. FTR from mining sortie 28/29.4.43.
W4958	PH-B	From 100Sqn. FTR Cologne 3/4.7.43.
W4990	PH-V	To 626Sqn.
W4991	PH-Q	FTR Mannheim 23/24.9.43.
W4992	GZ-A/A-	FTR Oberhausen 14/15.6.43.
W4994	PH-T	To 166Sqn.
DV157	GZ-Z	FTR Düsseldorf 11/12.6.43.
DV158	GZ-A^2 PH-Y	FTR Berlin 23/24.8.43.
DV164	PH-W	From 1667CU. FTR Gelsenkirchen 9/10.7.43.
DV168	PH-F	FTR Peenemünde 17/18.8.43.
DV171	PH-K	To 626Sqn.
DV177	PH-K^2	To 626Sqn.
DV185	PH-D	FTR Berlin 31.8/1.9.43.
DV187	PH-A	FTR Nuremberg 27/28.8.43.
DV190	PH-B^2	To 626Sqn.
DV200	PH-F^2	To 550Sqn via 1LFS.
DV218	PH-S	FTR Düsseldorf 3/4.11.43.

DV219	PH-G²	FTR Hannover 22/23.9.43.
DV222	PH-G²	FTR Munich 2/3.10.43.
DV224	PH-G	FTR Hamburg 2/3.8.43.
DV225	PH-H	FTR Mannheim 23/24.9.43.
DV241	PH-F	FTR Berlin 31.8/1.9.43.
DV244	PH-E	To 626Sqn.
DV295		To 100Sqn.
ED325	PH-J	FTR from mining sortie 28/29.4.43.
ED326	PH-K	First off on Sqn's first Lancaster operation. FTR Stettin 20/21.4.43.
ED357	PH-S	FTR Düsseldorf 11/12.6.43.
ED386	PH-A	FTR Düsseldorf 23/24.1.43.
ED388	PH-Y	From 50 Sqn. FTR Berlin 17/18.1.43.
ED392	PH-D²	From 57Sqn. Crashed in sea near Spurn Head following early return from Munich 6.9.43.
ED408	PH-A	FTR from mining sortie 28/29.4.43.
ED424	GZ-E	To 626Sqn.
	PH-E²	
ED476	PH-N	From 9Sqn. FTR Duisburg 12/13.5.43.
ED522	PH-U	FTR Düsseldorf 11/12.6.43.
ED548	PH-V/X-/J²	Exploded over Firth of Forth while training 6.7.43.
ED629	PH-K	FTR Cologne 16/17.6.43.
ED714	PH-K	From 103Sqn. FTR Spezia 13/14.4.43.
ED818	PH-Y	FTR Stettin 20/21.4.43.
ED820	PH-A	FTR Cologne 3/4.7.43.
ED821		To 100Sqn.
ED824		To 100Sqn.
ED967	GZ-F	FTR Düsseldorf 25/26.5.43.
ED968	GZ-G	Crashed in Lincolnshire during training 25.6.43.
	PH-P-	
ED972	PH-R	FTR Mönchengladbach 30/31.8.43.
ED993	PH-J	To 166Sqn.
ED995	PH-X	FTR Hannover 8/9.10.43.

ED996	GZ-J	FTR Wuppertal 29/30.5.43.
EE133	PH-P	To 626Sqn.
EE142	GZ-E- PH-G	FTR Hamburg 27/28.7.43.
EE195	GZ-B	FTR Cologne 28/29.6.43.
EE199	PH-U	Crashed soon after take-off when bound for Cologne 29.6.43.
EE202	PH-L	FTR Hannover (460Sqn crew) 8/9.10.43.
JA864	PH-B	To 626Sqn.
JA865	PH-U	To 166Sqn.
JA922	PH-J^2	To 626Sqn.
JB145		To 166Sqn.
JB281	PH-R	To 5LFS.
JB283	PH-W	FTR Berlin 27/28.1.44 on its 9th Berlin trip.
JB285	PH-G	FTR Berlin 2/3.12.43.
JB287	PH-F	FTR Kassel 22/23.10.43.
JB354	PH-O	Crashed on landing at Wickenby on return from Berlin 27.11.43.
JB357	PH-B/S	FTR Stettin 5/6.1.44.
JB358	PH-J	FTR Berlin 27/28.1.44.
JB359	PH-Q	FTR Berlin 24/25.3.44.
JB405	PH-H	FTR Mailly-le-Camp 3/4.5.44.
JB406	PH-D	FTR Hannover 8/9.10.43.
JB407	PH-A	From 460Sqn. FTR Berlin 29/30.12.43.
JB409	PH-P	To 626Sqn.
JB462	PH-S	FTR Vierzon 30.6/1.7.44.
JB463	PH-R	FTR Berlin 2/3.12.43.
JB464	PH-D	Crashed on approach to Binbrook on return from Berlin 27.11.43.
JB465	PH-V	Crashed on take-off from Wickenby when bound for Berlin 23.11.43.
JB478	PH-C	FTR Berlin 2/3.12.43.
JB536	PH-F	FTR Düsseldorf 3/4.11.43.
JB537	PH-N	FTR Berlin 23/24.11.43.

JB540	PH-L	FTR Schweinfurt 24/25.2.44.
JB542	PH-M	FTR Brunswick 14/15.1.44.
JB544	PH-K	To TFU.
JB559	PH-E/Z	To 626Sqn.
JB561		From 630Sqn. to 300Sqn.
JB609	PH-F	To 626Sqn and back. FTR Leipzig 19/20.2.44.
JB643		From 7Sqn. Became ground instruction machine.
JB650	PH-E	FTR Berlin 27/28.1.44.
JB660	PH-T	To BCIS.
JB683/G		From 97Sqn. to 1668CU.
JB709	PH-O	FTR from mining sortie 9/10.4.44.
JB715	PH-U	Crashed near Wickenby on return from Berlin 16.12.43.
JB716	PH-X	Crashed on landing at Aston Down on return from a mining sortie 10/11.8.44.
JB718	PH-V	To 7Sqn and back. to 101Sqn.
JB748	PH-N/Z	FTR Mailly-le-Camp 3/4.5.44.
LL909	PH-Y	FTR Duisburg 14.10.44.
LL910	PH-A	FTR Siracourt 29.6.44.
LL917	PH-C	Crashed on landing at Wickenby on return from Mimoyecque 22.6.44.
LM106	PH-H	FTR Courtrai 20/21.7.44.
LM107	PH-Z	FTR Stuttgart 28/29.7.44.
LM137		To 626Sqn.
LM213	PH-G	FTR Zeitz 16/17.1.45.
LM224	PH-B	
LM225	PH-C	FTR Kiel 26/27.8.44.
LM230	PH-A	FTR Kiel 26/27.8.44.
LM301	PH-O	To 100Sqn.
LM313	PH-D	FTR from mining sortie 28/29.4.43.
LM321	GZ-H/U- PH-U-	To 460Sqn.
LM328	PH-O-/F²	FTR Turin 12/13.7.43.

LM362	PH-A/F	To 626Sqn.
LM509	PH-M	To 1LFS.
LM514	PH-Q	FTR Mailly-le-Camp 3/4.5.44.
LM516	PH-D	FTR Mailly-le-Camp 3/4.5.44.
LM714	PH-L	FTR Leuna-Merseburg 14/15.1.45.
ME316	PH-V	FTR Bottrop 3/4.2.45.
ME323	PH-P	Shot down by an intruder over Lincolnshire while training 4.3.45.
ME330		
ME526	PH-P/F	FTR Nuremberg 16/17.3.45.
ME632	PH-P	FTR Augsburg 25/26.2.44.
ME642	PH-W	Ditched in Channel on return from Saintes 24.6.44.
ME644	PH-E	To 1651CU.
ME645	PH-V	To 1LFS.
ME742	PH-O	To 626Sqn.
ME758	PH-N	Completed 108 operations.
ME786	PH-L/R	
ME788	PH-Q	Ditched off Skegness on return from Duisburg 14.10.44.
ND324	PH-D/E	FTR Stettin 5/6.1.44.
ND325	PH-C	FTR Berlin 1/2.1.44.
ND342	PH-U	From 156Sqn. FTR Essen 12/13.12.44.
ND404	PH-R	FTR Berlin 15/16.2.44.
ND410	PH-Y	FTR Leipzig 19/20.2.44.
ND424	PH-G/C	FTR Vaires 27/28.6.44.
ND439	PH-K	FTR Berlin 24/25.3.44.
ND441	PH-Z	From 626Sqn. FTR Nuremberg 30/31.3.44.
ND447	PH-C	FTR Stuttgart 15/16.3.44.
ND528	PH-B	FTR Saintes 23/24.6.44.
ND562	PH-D	FTR Nuremberg 30/31.3.44.
ND627	PH-U	FTR Orleans 4/5.7.44.
ND650	PH-Y	FTR Berlin 24/25.3.44.
ND679	PH-F	FTR Aachen 27/28.5.44.

ND699	PH-P	FTR Stuttgart 28/29.7.44.
ND707		From 166Sqn. Returned to 166Sqn.
ND710	PH-L	FTR Berlin 24/25.3.44.
ND715	PH-R	FTR Düsseldorf 22/23.4.44.
ND749	PH-J	To 1668CU Aug 44.
ND799	PH-L	Crashed on landing at Faldingworth on return from Foret du Croc 6.7.44.
ND842	PH-K	FTR Vierzon 30.6/1.7.44.
ND844	PH-M	FTR Aulnoye 10/11.4.44.
ND873	PH-N/H	FTR Essen 26/27.4.44.
NE134	PH-O/D	FTR Dortmund 22/23.5.44.
NF925	PH-P/T	From 300Sqn. FTR Cleves 7/8.2.45.
NF928	PH-S	FTR Duisburg 14.10.44.
NF967	PH-C	FTR Dortmund 29.11.44.
NG116	PH-O	FTR Neuss 23/24.9.44.
NG117	PH-H	
NG282	PH-T	
NG288		To 150Sqn.
NG291		To 150Sqn.
NN712	PH-A	FTR Zeitz 16/17.1.45.
NN718		To 514Sqn.
NN741	PH-O	FTR Dessau 7/8.3.45.
NN800	PH-A	FTR Cologne 2.3.45.
NX564	PH-Y	
NX565	PH-Z	
NX608		
PA190		To 626Sqn.
PA306	PH-W	
PA986	PH-D	FTR Gelsenkirchen 12/13.6.44.
PB194		
PB201		Damaged on operation to Rüsselsheim 25/26.8.44 and SOC.
PB243	PH-D	Crashed in Lincolnshire while training 26.2.45.
PB247	PH-U	FTR Brunswick 12/13.8.44.

PB364		From 35Sqn via 1656CU.
PB476	PH-C/Y	Shot down by an intruder over Lincolnshire while training 4.3.45.
PB739	PH-T	From 626Sqn.
PB748		To 150Sqn.
PB750	PH-Z	
PB846		From 550Sqn. to 300Sqn.
PB849	PH-S	
PB851	PH-S	FTR Munich 7/8.1.45.
PD201	PH-E	Crashed in Lincolnshire on return from Ludwigshafen 15.12.44.
PD207	PH-W	From 300Sqn. FTR Nuremberg 16/17.3.45.
PD270		To 300Sqn.
PD273	PH-K	FTR Stettin 29/30.8.44.
PD275	PH-K	FTR Nuremberg 16/17.3.45.
PD289	PH-J	
PD331	PH-O	FTR Essen 23.10.44.
PD361		To 300Sqn.
PD369	PH-I	
PD390	PH-E	To 626Sqn.
RA574	PH-M	
RA583	PH-G	
RA585	PH-V	
RE122	PH-O	
RE125	PH-B	
RF134		
RF155		
RF161	PH-C	
RF181	PH-G	FTR Nuremberg 16/17.3.45.
RF182	PH-P	FTR Lützkendorf 4/5.4.45.
RF187	PH-L	To 101Sqn.
RF188	PH-U	FTR Nuremberg 16/17.3.45.
SW271		From 626Sqn.

HEAVIEST SINGLE LOSS

12.05.40.	Maastricht.	5 Battles FTR.
11/12.06.43.	Düsseldorf.	5 Lancasters FTR.
16/17.03.45	Nuremberg.	5 Lancasters FTR.

100 SQUADRON

Motto: **Sarang Tebuan Jangan Dijolok**   Code **HW FZ**
      (Never stir up a hornet's nest)

Formed in February 1917 as a night bomber unit, 100 squadron moved to France in March and began operating against bases behind enemy lines. In May 1918 it was re-equipped for strategic bombing, and carried out attacks on industrial targets in Germany until war's end. Thereafter it served in a variety of roles, as an army co-operation, a day bomber, and ultimately torpedo bomber unit. It was in the last-mentioned role that the squadron moved to the Far East in December 1933 to help defend Singapore. By February 1942 the squadron had lost most of its obsolete Vildebeest aircraft in attacks on Japanese landing ships and troop columns, and was amalgamated with 36 Squadron. Reformed at Waltham (Grimsby) under 1 Group Bomber Command in December 1942, the squadron took on Lancasters and joined the burgeoning assault on Germany.

STATIONS

GRIMSBY (WALTHAM)	15.12.42. to 02.04.45.
ELSHAM WOLDS	02.04.45. to 03.12.45.

COMMANDING OFFICERS

Wing Commander	J G W Swain	26.12.42. to 24.04.43.
Wing Commander	R V Mcintyre	24.04.43. to 20.11.43.
Wing Commander	D W Holford	20.11.43. to 17.12.43.
Wing Commander	J F Dilworth	17.12.43. to 25.02.44.
Wing Commander	R V L Pattison	03.03.44. to 20.09.44.
Wing Commander	A F Hamilton	20.09.44. to 07.03.45.
Wing Commander	T B Morton	07.03.45. to 01.07.45.

AIRCRAFT

Lancaster I/III	12.42. to 05.46.

AIRCREW KILLED
593

OPERATIONAL RECORD

Operations	Sorties	Aircraft Losses	% Losses
280	3984	92	2.3%

CATEGORY OF OPERATIONS

Bombing	Mining
267	13

TABLE OF STATISTICS
(Heavy squadrons)

Out of 59 Lancaster squadrons.

18th highest number of Lancaster overall operations in Bomber Command.
12th highest number of Lancaster sorties in Bomber Command.
18th highest number of Lancaster operational losses in Bomber Command.

Out of 20 squadrons in 1 Group.

8th highest number of overall operations in 1 Group.
6th highest number of sorties in 1 Group.
6th highest number of aircraft operational losses in 1 Group.

Out of 14 Lancaster squadrons in 1 Group.

5th highest number of Lancaster overall operations in 1 Group.
5th highest number of Lancaster sorties in 1 Group.
6th highest number of Lancaster operational losses in 1 Group.

AIRCRAFT HISTORIES

LANCASTER.	From January 1943.
L7582	From 106Sqn. to 1667CU.
R5702	From 460Sqn. to 625Sqn.
R5726	From 44Sqn. to 1662CU.
W4154	From 50Sqn. to 1662CU.

W4833		To 101Sqn.
W4836		To 12Sqn.
W4954	HW-D	To 12Sqn.
W4958		To 12Sqn.
W4989	HW-F/F^2	FTR Bochum 12/13.6.43.
W4998	HW-J	FTR Düsseldorf 25/26.5.43.
W4999	HW-G/X	To 625Sqn.
DV159	HW-J/T	FTR Hannover 18/19.10.43.
DV162	HW-J^2	From 1667CU. FTR Kassel 22/23.10.43.
DV176	HW-B	To 550Sqn.
DV189	HW-B^2	From RAE. to 550Sqn.
DV192	HW-P/Z	To 550Sqn and back. FTR Friedrichshafen 27/28.4.44.
DV242	HW-S	To 625Sqn.
DV295	HW-L	From 12Sqn. to 626Sqn.
DV305	HW-D/Y	To 550Sqn.
DV306	HW-N	To 550Sqn.
DV343	HW-X	From 460Sqn. to 550Sqn.
DV345	HW-T	To 550Sqn.
DV364		To 625Sqn.
ED317		From 101Sqn. to 625Sqn.
ED362	HW-E/E^2	FTR Cologne 28/29.6.43.
ED366		To 460Sqn.
ED376		To 15Sqn via 1662CU.
ED389		To 103Sqn.
ED391		To 460Sqn.
ED414		To 1662CU.
ED521		To 460Sqn.
ED525		To 460Sqn.
ED536	HW-O/W	To 550Sqn.
ED540		Crashed on landing at Grimsby while training 15.2.43.
ED544	HW-Q	FTR Essen 12/13.3.43.

ED549	HW-S	Crashed at Langar on return from mining sortie 5.3.43.
ED553	HW-Q/R	FTR Cologne 16/17.6.43.
ED555	HW-A/E	FTR Leipzig 20/21.10.43.
ED556	HW-B	To 9Sqn and back. FTR Krefeld 21/22.6.43.
ED557	HW-Y	FTR Stettin 20/21.4.43.
ED559	HW-D	FTR from mining sortie 4/5.3.43.
ED560		Crashed on take-off from Grimsby while training 16.2.43.
ED561	HW-F	From 467Sqn. FTR Turin 12/13.7.43.
ED562	HW-N/N²	To 576Sqn.
ED563	HW-G	FTR Pilsen 16/17.4.43.
ED564	HW-H	FTR Pilsen 16/17.4.43.
ED568	HW-T	FTR Duisburg 8/9.4.43.
ED583	HW-K/U/X	Exploded over Lincolnshire during altitude test and familiarization 4.10.43.
ED587	HW-V	FTR Munich 9/10.3.43.
ED609	HW-J/O	FTR Cologne 28/29.6.43.
ED647	HW-H/T	FTR Peenemünde 17/18.8.43.
ED652	HW-C	Crashed on take-off at Grimsby bound for Berlin 23.8.43.
ED653	HW-E	FTR Stuttgart 14/15.4.43.
ED658		To 460Sqn.
ED688	HW-A/A²/N	FTR Hamburg 2/3.8.43.
ED705	HW-C/H/P/Y	FTR Hamburg 2/3.8.43.
ED709	HW-S	FTR Stettin 20/21.4.43.
ED710	HW-D	Crash-landed near Coltishall on return from Bochum 14.5.43.
ED732	HW-L/W	Crashed on take-off from Wickenby during training 21.8.43.
ED749	HW-B/J/K/S	To 300Sqn.
ED750	HW-M/V	To 460Sqn.
ED760	HW-L	FTR Frankfurt 10/11.4.43.
ED774	HW-L	From 460Sqn. FTR Berlin 23/24.8.43.
ED786	HW-P	FTR Düsseldorf 11/12.6.43.

ED814		From 97Sqn. to 625Sqn.
ED815	HW-G/M/P	FTR Schweinfurt 24/25.2.44.
ED821	HW-A	From 12Sqn. FTR Essen 27/28.5.43.
ED824	HW-E	From 12Sqn. Crash-landed at Grimsby following early return from mining sortie 21.5.43.
ED883	HW-V	From 156Sqn. FTR Mannheim 23/24.9.43.
ED938		From 97Sqn. to 625Sqn.
ED942		From 460Sqn. to 550Sqn.
ED973	HW-D	From 460Sqn. FTR Oberhausen 14/15.6.43.
ED976	HW-S	From 460Sqn. FTR Düsseldorf 11/12.6.43.
ED988	HW-J	FTR Gelsenkirchen 25/26.6.43.
ED991	HW-H/K	FTR Berlin 18/19.11.43.
EE107	HW-U	From 97Sqn. to 550Sqn.
EE139	HW-A/R	To 550Sqn.
EE140	HW-C	Crash-landed at Grimsby on return from Cologne 16/17.6.43.
	FZ-C	
EE169	HW-D/O/S	FTR Hamburg 27/28.7.43.
EE171	HW-K/Z	FTR Berlin 23/24.8.43.
EE180	HW-D	FTR Berlin 23/24.8.43.
EE181	HW-A²	FTR Mönchengladbach 30/31.8.43.
EE183	HW-P	FTR Turin 12/13.7.43.
HK802		From 195Sqn. No operations.
JA699	HW-S	From 460Sqn. Became ground instruction machine.
JA714		From 156Sqn. to 625Sqn.
JA930	HW-E/Y	FTR Berlin 3/4.9.43.
JA934	HW-F	To 550Sqn.
JA969	HW-N	FTR Berlin 3/4.9.43.
JB122	HW-T	To 625Sqn.
JB141	HW-C	To 626Sqn.
JB148	HW-O	Crashed in Lincolnshire on return from Kassel 22/23.10.43.

JB289	HW-J²/K/T	From 1656CU. to 550Sqn and back. FTR Reims 22/23.6.44.
JB291	HW-A²/D	From 1656CU. FTR Leipzig 3/4.12.43.
JB549	HW-C	FTR Berlin 2/3.1.44.
JB554	HW-K²	Crashed on approach to Grimsby on return from Berlin 27.11.43.
JB557	HW-L/U	To 1667CU.
JB560	HW-N	From 460Sqn. Crashed near Kelstern on return from Berlin 16/17.12.43.
JB563	HW-G	To 550Sqn and back. FTR Frankfurt 22/23.3.44.
JB564	HW-D²	From 460Sqn. FTR Berlin 23/24.11.43.
JB594	HW-O	FTR Berlin 23/24.12.43.
JB596	HW-H	Crashed in Lincolnshire on return from Berlin 16.12.43.
JB602	HW-A	Crash-landed at Grimsby on return from Brunswick 14/15.1.44.
JB603	HW-E	FTR Hannover 5/6.1.45.
JB604	HW-J/S	FTR Schweinfurt 24/25.2.44.
JB605	HW-O	Abandoned over Surrey on return from Berlin 19.11.43.
JB614	HW-D	FTR Essen 26/27.4.44.
JB673	HW-P	To 550Sqn and back. FTR Berlin 30/31.1.44.
JB674	HW-Q	From 550Sqn. Collided with JB678 (100Sqn) near Grimsby on return from Berlin 17.12.43.
JB678	HW-F	From 550Sqn. Collided with JB674 (100Sqn) near Grimsby on return from Berlin 16/17.12.43.
JB740	HW-R	FTR Berlin 1/2.1.44.
LL887	HW-H	FTR Düsseldorf 22/23.4.44.
LL898	HW-L	Crashed in the sea during bombing practice 2.1.45.
LL915	HW-V	FTR Stuttgart 25/26.7.44.
LL941		To 166Sqn.
LL952	HW-W²	From 460Sqn. Ditched in sea during gunnery practice 21.5.45.
LL958	HW-H	FTR Vierzon 30.6/1.7.44.

LL960	HW-D	FTR Duisburg 21/22.5.44.
LM175	HW-D	To 1656CU.
LM301	HW-E/V	From 12Sqn. to 550Sqn.
LM317	HW-D/D²/U	To 625Sqn.
LM319	HW-Q	To 550Sqn.
LM320	HW-C/FZ-C	FTR Düsseldorf 25/26.5.43.
LM321	HW-K	From 550Sqn. FTR Acheres 10/11.6.44.
LM333	HW-V	FTR Berlin 23/24.8.43.
LM379	HW-S	To 550Sqn.
LM542	HW-S	FTR Dortmund 22/23.5.44.
LM569	HW-T	FTR Scholven-Buer 18/19.7.44.
LM584	HW-F²/Q	
LM585	HW-S	FTR Foret de Nieppe 31.7/1.8.44.
LM619		From 460Sqn. to 1668CU.
LM620	HW-K	FTR Buer 18/19.7.44.
LM621	HW-C	FTR Vierzon 30.6/1.7.44.
LM622	HW-P	From 460Sqn. FTR Kiel 26/27.8.44.
LM623	HW-S	From 460Sqn. FTR Chemnitz 14/15.2.45.
LM634	HW-H	Crashed on take-off from Grimsby when bound for Sannerville 18.7.44.
LM644	HW-B²	
LM658	HW-W	FTR Brunswick 12/13.8.44.
LM672	HW-V/Y	
LM688		
LM716	HW-K	Crashed on landing at Carnaby while training 13.4.45.
LM723	HW-H	FTR Cologne 2.3.45.
LM739		
LM741	HW-A²	To 1656CU.
ME296		To 166Sqn.
ME448		
ME497	HW-E/E²	
ME648	HW-R²	To 300Sqn.
ME670	HW-Q	FTR Dortmund 22/23.5.44.

ME677	HW-X	FTR Duisburg 21/22.5.44.
ME828	HW-F	FTR Frankfurt 12/13.9.44.
ND326	HW-F/J	To 550Sqn and back. to 463Sqn.
ND327		Collided with ED730 (550Sqn) over Lincolnshire when bound for Berlin 24.12.43.
ND328	HW-G^2/W	From 156Sqn. to 550Sqn and back. FTR Karlsruhe 24/25.4.44.
ND356	HW-O	From 625Sqn.
ND360	HW-N	FTR Berlin 30/31.1.44.
ND388	HW-G	From 550Sqn. FTR Cologne 24/25.12.44.
ND391	HW-H	FTR Berlin 15/16.2.44.
ND392		To 460Sqn.
ND398	HW-B	FTR Berlin 30/31.1.44.
ND413	HW-R	Crashed in Lincolnshire on return from Courtrai 20/21.7.44.
ND456	HW-C	Crash-landed at Woodbridge following early return from Berneval 2/3.6.44.
ND458	HW-A/A^2	To BCIS.
ND571	HW-N	FTR Leipzig 19/20.2.44.
ND593	HW-B	FTR Schweinfurt 24/25.2.44.
ND594	HW-Q/P	FTR Acheres 10/11.6.44.
ND595	HW-V	FTR Augsburg 25/26.2.44.
ND639		From 625Sqn. to 1656CU.
ND642	HW-N	FTR Berlin 24/25.3.44.
ND644	HW-N	FTR Nuremberg 16/17.3.45 after 115 operations.
ND658		To 460Sqn.
ND675	HW-S	FTR from mining sortie 9/10.4.44.
ND681	HW-B	FTR Stuttgart 15/16.3.44.
ND785	HW-B	FTR Cologne 20/21.4.44.
ND972	HW-W	To 550Sqn.
ND975		To 625Sqn via 1 Group Special Duties Flight.
ND995	HW-K	From 625Sqn. FTR Rüsselsheim 25/26.8.44.
NF978	HW-Q/Q^2	
NG292	HW-V^2	

NG328	HW-G²	
NN784	HW-L²	
NX568		
PA177	HW-J²	
PA189	HW-P	FTR Zeitz 16/17.1.45.
PA221	HW-V/V²	
PA270	HW-H	
PA317		
PA969	HW-N/M	FTR Gelsenkirchen 12/13.6.44.
PB117	HW-D	From 460Sqn. FTR Nuremberg 16/17.3.45.
PB172	HW-W	FTR Stuttgart 28/29.7.44.
PB462	HW-P²	
PB518	HW-P	FTR Nuremberg 2/3.1.45.
PB532	HW-S²	From 550Sqn.
PB569	HW-Y	FTR Bottrop 3/4.2.45.
PB572	HW-F	FTR Ludwigshafen 1/2.2.45.
PB839		To 460Sqn.
PD310		From 166Sqn.
PD420	HW-D	Abandoned over Lancashire on return from Cologne 24.12.44.
RE118	HW-N/N²	
RF191		To 460Sqn.

HEAVIEST SINGLE LOSS.

23/24.08.43.	Berlin	4 Lancasters FTR.
16/17.12.43.	Berlin.	4 Lancasters crashed on return.
24/25.02.44.	Schweinfurt.	4 Lancasters FTR.

101 SQUADRON

Motto: **Mens Agitat Molem**   Code **SR**
    (Mind over matter)

Formed as a night bomber squadron in July 1917, 101 Squadron moved to France and spent the remainder of the Great War operating against enemy airfields, communications and dumps in northern France and Belgium. The squadron was disbanded on the last day of 1919, and remained on the shelf until being reformed in March 1928. Blenheims arrived in 1938, and this was the type operated by the squadron at the outbreak of WWII. Initially a training unit, the squadron began offensive operations with 2 Group in June 1940, carrying out shipping sweeps and attacks on invasion barge concentrations in Channel ports. The squadron converted to Wellingtons in April 1941, and in July transferred to 3 Group for standard night bombing operations. In late September 1942 the squadron joined 1 Group and re-equipped with Lancasters. A year later it added radio counter measures to its bombing role, carrying special equipment known as Mandrel or Airborne Cigar to jam enemy night fighter communications. This role continued to the end of the war, even after the formation of 100 Group as a dedicated RCM force in November 1943. As a result 101 Squadron aircraft were present on almost all major operations, even when 1 Group itself remained on the ground, and this led to a higher than average casualty rate.

STATIONS

HOLME-ON-SPALDING-MOOR	29.09.42. to 15.06.43.
LUDFORD MAGNA	15.06.43. to 01.10.45.

COMMANDING OFFICERS

Wing Commander	E C Eaton	01.06.42. to 26.01.43.
Wing Commander	D A Reddick	26.01.43. to 27.07.43.
Wing Commander	G A Carey-Foster	27.07.43. to 18.01.44.
Wing Commander	R I Alexander	18.01.44. to 31.07.44.
Wing Commander	M H De L Everest	31.07.44. to 21.01.45.
Wing Commander	I M Gundrey-White	21.01.45. to 12.04.46.

AIRCRAFT

Wellington 1C	04.41. to 10.42.
Wellington III	02.42. to 10.42.
Lancaster I/III	10.42. to 08.46.

OPERATIONAL RECORD
1 GROUP

Operations	Sorties	Aircraft Losses	% Losses
316	4932	113	2.5%

CATEGORY OF OPERATIONS

BOMBING	MINING
304	12

Wellington

Operations	Sorties	Aircraft Losses	% Losses
8	37	0	0.0%

CATEGORY OF OPERATIONS

BOMBING	MINING
6	2

Lancaster

Operations	Sorties	Aircraft Losses	% Losses
308	4895	113	2.3%

CATEGORY OF OPERATIONS

BOMBING	MINING
298	10

TABLE OF STATISTICS
(Heavy squadrons)

15th highest number of overall operations in Bomber Command.
4th highest number of sorties in Bomber Command.
10th equal highest number (with 12Sqn) of aircraft operational losses in Bomber Command.

Out of 59 Lancaster squadrons.

11th highest number of Lancaster overall operations in Bomber Command.
2nd highest number of Lancaster sorties in Bomber Command.
7th highest number of Lancaster operational losses in Bomber Command.

Out of 42 Wellington squadrons.

15th highest number of Wellington overall operations in Bomber Command.

9th highest number of Wellington sorties in Bomber Command.

10th equal highest number (with 99Sqn) of Wellington operational losses in Bomber Command.

Out of 20 squadrons in 1 Group.

5th highest number of overall operations in 1 Group.
5th highest number of sorties in 1 Group.
5th highest number of aircraft operational losses in 1 Group.

Out of 13 Wellington squadrons in 1 Group.

Lowest number of Wellington operations, sorties and aircraft operational losses in 1 Group.

Out of 14 Lancaster squadrons in 1 Group.

3rd highest number of Lancaster overall operations in 1 Group.
2nd highest number of Lancaster sorties in 1 Group.
4th highest number of Lancaster operational losses in 1 Group.

AIRCRAFT HISTORIES

WELLINGTON.		From April 1941 to October 1942.
X3455	SR-V	From 156Sqn. to 142Sqn.
X3965	SR-R	To 150Sqn.
Z1625	SR-H	To 150Sqn.
Z1661	SR-F	To 150Sqn.
Z1726	SR-U	To 142Sqn.
Z1748	SR-E	To 12Sqn.
BJ572	SR-U	
BJ581	SR-M	From 57Sqn. to 142Sqn.
BJ659	SR-T	To 23 OTU.
BJ705		From 57Sqn. to 142Sqn.
BJ768	SR-G	To 142Sqn.

BJ961		To 150Sqn.
BJ972		To 150Sqn.
BK298	SR-C	To 142Sqn.
BK299	SR-P	To 142Sqn.
LANCASTER.		**From October 1942. (* = ABC)**
R5482	SR-Q	From 97Sqn. Crashed while landing at Holme-on-Spalding Moor on return from air-test 20.12.42.
R5507		From 1660CU. to 1656CU.
W4231		From 83Sqn via 1662CU and 1667CU. to 1LFS.
W4275	SR-A/C	FTR Cologne 8/9.7.43.
W4276	SR-D	To 207Sqn.
W4309	SR-B	To 1667CU.
W4311	SR-F/O	FTR Wuppertal 24/25.6.43.
W4312	SR-H	Crashed on landing at Holme-on-Spalding-moor on return from air-test 23.12.43.
W4313	SR-G	FTR Wilhelmshaven 11/12.2.43.
W4319	SR-N	Crashed in North Yorkshire after being engaged by friendly AA fire while on return from mining sortie 17.12.42.
W4321	SR-P	From 1656CU. First off on Sqn's first Lancaster operation. FTR Berlin 17/18.1.43.
W4322	SR-O	To 460Sqn and back. FTR Berlin 27/28.3.43.
W4324	SR-M	FTR Hannover 22/23.9.43.
W4326		No operations. Crashed in Wales while training 16.11.42.
W4779		To 1656CU.
W4782	SR-J	FTR from mining sortie 8/9.12.42.
W4784	SR-E	FTR Dortmund 4/5.5.43.
W4796	SR-R	FTR Essen 4/5.1.43.
W4833	SR-C	From 100Sqn. to 625Sqn.
W4851		From 156Sqn. to 1656CU.
W4862	SR-E	FTR Essen 12/13.3.43.
W4863	SR-G	Crashed on approach to Holme-on-Spalding-Moor on return from Dortmund 23/24.5.43.

W4882		From 156Sqn. to 1662CU.
W4888	SR-Z/P	FTR Dortmund 4/5.5.43.
W4889	SR-Z	To 1656CU.
W4919	SR-A	FTR Dortmund 23/24.5.43.
W4923	SR-N/N2/N-	Damaged beyond repair during operation to Mannheim 23/24.9.43.
W4951	SR-O/P	FTR Stuttgart 14/15.4.43.
W4966	SR-F/G²	To 166Sqn.
W4967	SR-P	From 626Sqn. FTR Courtrai 20/21.7.44.
W4993	SR-X	To 625Sqn.
W4995	SR-N	To 625Sqn.
W4996	SR-G/G²	To 166Sqn.
W4997	SR-E	To 5MU May 44.
W5009	SR-Z	To 625Sqn.
DV194	SR-V	To 625Sqn.
DV230	SR-T	From SIU. FTR Hannover 18/19.10.43.
DV231	SR-A	From SIU. FTR Berlin 27/28.1.44.
DV236	SR-G	FTR Berlin 15/16.2.44.
DV245	SR-S	FTR Bremen (119th op) 23.3.45.
DV264	SR-L	FTR Nuremberg, shot down by Halifax 30/31.3.44.
DV265	SR-F	FTR Düsseldorf 3/4.11.43.
DV266	SR-U	FTR Hannover 18/19.10.43.
DV267	SR-K	FTR Leipzig 19/20.2.44.
DV268	SR-O/O²	FTR Berlin 26/27.11.43.
DV269	SR-M	FTR Berlin 2/3.1.44.
DV270	SR-E	Crashed in Lincolnshire while training 5.12.43.
DV275	SR-X²	To 463Sqn and back. FTR Mailly-le-Camp 3/4.5.44
DV276	SR-R	FTR Nuremberg 30/31.3.44.
DV283	SR-P	From 44Sqn. Abandoned over Lincolnshire on return from Berlin 17.12.43.
DV285	SR-Q	FTR Berlin 26/27.11.43.
DV287	SR-N	FTR Brunswick 14/15.1.44.

DV288	SR-D/Q	FTR Aulnoye 10/11.4.44.
DV289	SR-T	FTR Berlin 26/27.11.43.
DV290	SR-X	From SIU. Crashed at USAAF Welford on return from Nuremberg 30/31.3.44.
DV291	SR-V	From SIU via 32MU. Crashed on take-off from Ludford Magna when bound for Berlin 22.11.43.
DV292	SR-Y/E/O	From SIU. FTR Brunswick 12/13.8.44.
DV298	SR-E/I/J	FTR Gelsenkirchen/Dahlbusch 14.3.45.
DV299	SR-K²	FTR Berlin 16/17.12.43.
DV300	SR-W	FTR Berlin 16/17.12.43.
DV301	SR-F/Y	FTR Vierzon 30.6/1.7.44.
DV302	SR-J/H	Completed 121 operations. to 46MU.
DV303	SR-U	FTR Berlin 30/31.1.44.
DV304	SR-X	To 61Sqn.
DV307	SR-Z	FTR Berlin 1/2.1.44.
DV308	SR-V	FTR Berlin 1/2.1.44.
DV389	SR-P/X	FTR Aachen 24/25.5.44.
DV407	SR-R/R²/V²	To 46MU.
ED317	SR-Q	From 1656CU. to 100Sqn.
ED320	SR-R/U	From 57Sqn. Destroyed in landing accident at Ford on return from Milan 13.8.43.
ED321	SR-D/E/K	To 625Sqn.
ED322	SR-T	Crashed off Welsh coast on return from Mannheim 6/7.12.42.
ED327	SR-C/D/O/O²	To 166Sqn.
ED328	SR-S	FTR Berlin 23/24.8.43.
ED370	SR-B/D/J	To 103Sqn.
ED372	SR-E/H/K	From 83Sqn. to 166Sqn.
ED373	SR-T/K	FTR Gelsenkirchen 25/26.6.43.
ED374	SR-Z	Crash-landed at Holme-on-Spalding-Moor on return from Lorient 17.2.43.
ED375	SR-V	FTR St Nazaire 22/23.3.43.
ED377	SR-X/O/Q	FTR from mining sortie 27/28.6.43.
ED379	SR-F/L	FTR Pilsen 16/17.4.43.

ED380		To 103Sqn.
ED382	SR-J/J²	To 625Sqn.
ED410	SR-X-/X²	FTR Berlin 3/4.9.43.
ED422	SR-E/E2/H	To 166Sqn.
ED433	SR-F	To 44Sqn.
ED443	SR-B	FTR Essen 21/22.1.43.
ED446	SR-N	Crashed on beach near Hornsea during air-test 20.3.43.
ED447	SR-Q	FTR Hamburg 30/31.1.43.
ED552	SR-Q	Crashed in Yorkshire while training 29.3.43.
ED608	SR-T	FTR Duisburg 9/10.4.43.
ED618	SR-X/X-	FTR Duisburg 9/10.4.43.
ED623		From 626Sqn. to 1LFS.
ED650	SR-L	FTR Krefeld 21/22.6.43.
ED659	SR-T	FTR Berlin 3/4.9.43.
ED660	SR-U-/V	FTR Düsseldorf 25/26.5.43.
ED697	SR-V	FTR Cologne 8/9.7.43.
ED728	SR-Y	FTR from mining sortie 27/28.4.43.
ED736	SR-W	FTR Essen 3/4.4.43.
ED775	SR-Z	Crash on approach to Coltishall on return from Dortmund 24.5.43.
ED776	SR-U-	Crashed while landing at Holme-on-Spalding-Moor on return from Dortmund 5.5.43.
ED807	SR-X	Crashed while landing at Holme-on-Spalding-Moor following early return from Spezia 13/14.4.43.
ED809	SR-W	To 625Sqn.
ED830	SR-X	Crashed on approach to Holme-on-Spalding-Moor on return from Dortmund 5.5.43.
ED835	SR-T	Crashed on approach to Holme-on-Spalding-Moor on return from Dortmund 5.5.43.
ED841	SR-R	From 156Sqn. to 166Sqn.
ED951	SR-P	To 625Sqn.
ED987	SR-A-	FTR Bochum 12/13.6.43.
EE137	SR-U/A	To 166Sqn.

EE182		To 103Sqn.
EE192	SR-Y	FTR Berlin 23/24.8.43.
JA715	SR-M²/C	From 156Sqn. Collided with ME863 and crashed in France during operation to Ludwigshafen 1/2.2.45.
JA863	SR-U²	FTR Hamburg 27/28.7.43.
JA926	SR-A	FTR Mannheim 5/6.9.43.
JA928		To 83Sqn.
JA965*	SR-K²	From SIU. Shot down by intruder near Wickenby on return from Hannover 28.9.43.
JA977*	SR-J	From SIU. FTR Mannheim 23/24.9.43.
JB128*	SR-U²	FTR Berlin 2/3.12.43.
JB142	SR-Y	To 166Sqn.
JB149	SR-R²	FTR Berlin 3/4.9.43.
JB150	SR-S/P²	FTR Berlin 31.8/1.9.43.
JB151		To 166Sqn.
JB718	SR-Q	From 12Sqn.
LL750	SR-P	FTR Friedrichshafen 27/28.4.44.
LL751	SR-F	FTR Evreux 11/12.6.44.
LL755*	SR-R/R²/U	FTR Bremen 23.3.45.
LL756*	SR-Z/Q	Crashed on landing at Ludford Magna on return from le Havre 6.9.44.
LL757*	SR-W	FTR Stettin 29/30.8.44.
LL758*	SR-A	FTR Saarbrücken 5/6.10.44.
LL771*	SR-L/S/Y	FTR Breskens 11.10.44.
LL772*	SR-R/R²	From 626Sqn.
LL773*	SR-U/D	Crashed at Woodbridge on return from Sterkrade 17.6.44.
LL774*	SR-U	FTR Duisburg 14/15.10.44.
LL779*	SR-V	FTR Homburg 20/21.7.44.
LL829	SR-J/A	From 626Sqn.
LL832*	SR-K²	FTR Nuremberg 30/31.3.44.
LL833	SR-O	Ditched in the Channel during D-Day support operation 6.6.44.

LL849	SR-O	From 626Sqn. Crashed near Lichfield while training 12.8.44.
LL860*	SR-R/I	FTR Schweinfurt 26/27.4.44.
LL861*	SR-H	FTR Nuremberg 30/31.3.44.
LL862*	SR-L/K	FTR Homburg 20/21.7.44.
LL863*	SR-H/M	FTR Vierzon 30.6/1.7.44.
LM161	SR-E/F	
LM312	SR-U	To 166sqn.
LM318	SR-Y	FTR Gelsenkirchen 25/26.6.43.
LM325	SR-J/U-	FTR Mülheim 22/23.6.43.
LM341	SR-L	To 166sqn.
LM363*	SR-P	FTR Berlin 2/3.12.43.
LM364*	SR-N²	FTR Berlin 2/3.12.43.
LM365*	SR-H	From SIU. FTR Düsseldorf 3/4.11.43.
LM367*	SR-C	From SIU. FTR Brunswick 14/15.1.44.
LM368*	SR-B	To 467Sqn.
LM369*	SR-I/W	To 1656CU.
LM370*	SR-K²	FTR Berlin 18/19.11.43.
LM371*	SR-T	FTR Berlin 29/30.12.43.
LM387*	SR-O	FTR Berlin 20/21.1.44.
LM389*	SR-Y	Crashed in Yorkshire on return from Berlin 17.12.43.
LM395*	SR-Q	FTR Dortmund 22/23.5.44.
LM417*	SR-S/A	FTR Mailly-le-Camp 3/4.5.44.
LM457*	SR-A/G/V²	SOC 2.1.45.
LM459	SR-K	FTR Bourg Leopold 27/28.5.44.
LM462*	SR-V²	FTR Stuttgart 28/29.7.44.
LM463*	SR-N²/K	FTR Nuremberg 30/31.3.44.
LM464*	SR-U²/E	Crashed in Suffolk on return from Frankfurt 18/19.3.44.
LM467*	SR-Z/J	FTR Mailly-le-Camp 3/4.5.44.
LM472*	SR-T/V²	From 626Sqn. FTR Brüx 16/17.1.45.
LM474*	SR-N²/X²	FTR Sterkrade 16/17.6.44.
LM479*	SR-C/F	FTR Stettin 29/30.8.44.

LM493*	SR-X	FTR Friedrichshafen 27/28.4.44.
LM508	SR-P	FTR Wesseling 21/22.6.44.
LM596		To 626Sqn.
LM598*	SR-M²	FTR Brunswick 12/13.8.44.
LM755	SR-N	FTR Dortmund 29.11.44.
ME305*	SR-N/N²	
ME310*	SR-Z/X	
ME419*	SR-V²	
ME494*	SR-I	
ME517	SR-M	
ME518	SR-P	
ME558*	SR-Q	FTR Stuttgart 15/16.3.44.
ME564*	SR-J/Z	FTR Mailly-le-Camp 3/4.5.44.
ME565*	SR-W/Q	FTR Foret de Cerisy 7/8.6.44.
ME566*	SR-S/X	FTR Brunswick 14/15.1.44.
ME590*	SR-C	To 1651CU.
ME592*	SR-T/D	FTR Stettin 29/30.8.44.
ME613*	SR-L²/M²	FTR Wesseling 21/22.6.44.
ME616*	SR-B	FTR Vierzon 30.6/1.7.44.
ME617*	SR-N	FTR Rüsselsheim 12/13.8.44.
ME618	SR-J	FTR Nuremberg 30/31.3.44.
ME619	SR-U	FTR Düsseldorf 22/23.4.44.
ME837*	SR-L	
ME847*	SR-D	To 300Sqn.
ME857*	SR-C	FTR Rüsselsheim 25/26.8.44.
ME863*	SR-I/K	Collided with JA715 (101Sqn) and crashed in France during operation to Ludwigshafen 1/2.2.45.
ME865*	SR-X/K	FTR Bochum 4/5.11.44.
ND983*	SR-D/B	Crashed while landing at Ludford Magna on return from le Havre 6.9.44.
NF924	SR-C	Crash-landed at Ludford Magna 4.1.45.
NF933*	SR-L²	
NF936*	SR-F	FTR Bochum 4/5.11.44.

NF954*	SR-W	Crashed at Ludford Magna 21.3.45.
NF982*		FTR Neuss 23/24.9.44.
NF983*	SR-D/B	Collided with another aircraft over the sea while bound for Neuss 23/24.9.44.
NG128*	SR-B	
NG129*	SR-Z	
NG131*	SR-M²/W	FTR Ulm 17/18.12.44.
NG139*	SR-W²	
NG402*	SR-C	
NG405*	SR-L	
NN705*	SR-O	FTR Rüsselsheim 25/26.8.44.
NX569	SR-W	
NX572	SR-S	
NX575	SR-U	
NX579		
NX609	SR-S/A/A²	
NX610	SR-F2	
PA237*	SR-R/V	FTR Pforzheim 23/24.2.45.
PA238*	SR-Z/Z²	
PA281*	SR-J	
PB237*	SR-M	FTR St Vith 26.12.44.
PB256*	SR-P	FTR Ludwigshafen 1/2.2.45.
PB258*	SR-V	FTR Brunswick 12/13.8.44.
PB350*	SR-G	
PB399*	SR-T/J	
PB456*		Crashed in Scotland on exercise 13.9.44.
PB457*	SR-V	Destroyed by fire during maintenance at Ludford Magna 3.2.45.
PB573		From 170Sqn. Returned to 170Sqn.
PB634*	SR-U	FTR Bonn 28/29.12.44.
PB671*	SR-M	FTR Dortmund 20/21.2.45.
PB673	SR-V/Y	From 626Sqn. to BCIS.
PB692	SR-K²	From 626Sqn. FTR Gelsenkirchen 6.11.44.
PB748*	SR-Y	From 150Sqn.

PB788*	SR-E/E²	
PB800*	SR-N	
PD268*	SR-O	FTR Dessau 7/8.3.45.
PD396	SR-O/A	
RA523	SR-I	FTR Pforzheim 23/24.2.45.
RA595	SR-Q	
RA597	SR-V	
RE138	SR-W/D²	
RE154	SR-X²	
RE157	SR-R	
RE161	SR-L²	
RE162		
RE163	SR-T²	
RF125	SR-K	
RF187	SR-S	From 12Sqn.
RF261	SR-B	
RF262	SR-H²	
RF263		
RF264	SR-H	
RF268		

HEAVIEST SINGLE LOSS.

30/31.03.44.	Nuremberg.	7 Lancasters. 6 FTR.
		1 crashed on return.

103 SQUADRON

MOTTO **NOLI ME TANGERE** (No one to touch me)   Code **PM**

Originally formed on the 1st of September 1917, 103 Squadron moved to France in May 1918 to conduct bombing operations against supply bases and communications, a role which it was to repeat twenty-two years to the month later when war came once more to Europe. For most of the intervening period 103 Squadron, like so many others, did not exist, having been disbanded in October 1919, and it was not until 1936 that the squadron was resurrected, again as a light bomber unit. In July 1938 Fairey

Battles began to replace the Hawker Hinds, and as the clouds of war gathered in 1939, 103 Squadron was earmarked to join the Advanced Air Striking Force. Having lost most of its aircraft in the battle for France the squadron remnant returned to the UK in June 1940, and became a founder member of the newly constituted 1 Group Bomber Command.

STATIONS

CHALLERANGE	06.09.39. to 27.09.39.
MONTHOIS	27.09.39. to 28.11.39.
PLIVOT	28.11.39. to 15.02.40.
BETHENIVILLE	15.02.40. to 16.05.40.
RHEGES/ST LUCIEN FERME	16.05.40. to 04.06.40.
OZOUER-le-DOYEN	04.06.40. to 14.06.40.
SOUGE	14.06.40. to 16.06.40.
HONINGTON	16.06.40. to 03.07.40.
NEWTON	03.07.40. to 11.07.41.
ELSHAM WOLDS	11.07.41. to 26.11.45.

COMMANDING OFFICERS

Wing Commander	H J Gemmell	27.01.39. to 12.03.40.
Wing Commander	T C Dickens	12.03.40. to 23.11.40.
Squadron Leader	C E R Tait	23.11.40. to 05.12.40.
Wing Commander	C E Littler	05.12.40. to 04.04.41.
Wing Commander	B E Lowe	04.04.41. to 25.08.41.
Wing Commander	R S Ryan	25.08.41. to 09.03.42.
Wing Commander	J F H Du Boulay	09.03.42. to 09.09.42.
Wing Commander	R A C Carter	09.09.42. to 17.04.43.
Wing Commander	J A Slater	17.04.43. to 18.10.43.
Wing Commander	E D Mck Nelson	18.10.43. to 06.05.44.
Wing Commander	H R Goodman	06.05.44. to 12.05.44.
Wing Commander	J R St John	12.05.44. to 01.12.44.
Wing Commander	D F Macdonald	01.12.44. to 07.08.45.

AIRCRAFT

Battle	08.38. to 10.40.
Wellington	10.40. to 07.42.
Halifax	07.42. to 11.42.
Lancaster	11.42. to 11.45.

AIRCREW KILLED
973

OPERATIONAL RECORD

Operations	Sorties	Aircraft Losses	% Losses
519	5840	179	3.1%

CATEGORY OF OPERATIONS

BOMBING	MINING
486	33

Battles

Operations	Sorties	Aircraft Losses	% Losses
16	51	1	2.0%

Figures do not include operations with the AASF.

Wellingtons

Operations	Sorties	Aircraft Losses	% Losses
144	1116	31	2.8%

CATEGORY OF OPERATIONS

BOMBING	MINING
138	6

Halifax

Operations	Sorties	Aircraft Losses	% Losses
15	137	12	8.8%

Lancaster

Operations	Sorties	Aircraft Losses	% Losses
344	4536	135	3.0%

CATEGORY OF OPERATIONS

BOMBING	MINING
317	27

A further 22 Lancasters were destroyed in crashes.

TABLE OF STATISTICS
(Heavy squadrons)

20th highest number of overall operations in Bomber Command.
14th highest number of sorties in Bomber Command.
6th highest number of aircraft operational losses in Bomber Command.
15th equal (with 78Sqn) highest number of bombing raids in Bomber Command.

Out of 6 Battle squadrons.

Highest equal (with 142 and 150 Sqns) number of Battle operations in Bomber Command.
2nd highest number of Battle sorties in Bomber Command.
2nd equal (with 12Sqn) highest number of Battle losses in Bomber Command.

Out of 42 Wellington squadrons.

16th highest number of overall Wellington operations in Bomber Command.
12th highest number of Wellington sorties in Bomber Command.
15th equal (with 40Sqn) highest number of Wellington operational losses in Bomber Command.

Out of 30 Halifax squadrons.
(Excluding 100 Group)

Lowest number of Halifax overall operations in Bomber Command.
Lowest number of Halifax sorties in Bomber Command.
Lowest number of Halifax operational losses in Bomber Command.
Highest Halifax percentage loss rate in Bomber Command.

Out of 59 Lancaster squadrons.

7th highest number of Lancaster overall operations in Bomber Command.
6th highest number of Lancaster sorties in Bomber Command.
3rd highest number of Lancaster operational losses in Bomber Command.

Out of 20 squadrons in 1 Group.

Highest number of overall operations in 1 Group.
2nd highest number of sorties in 1 Group.

Highest number of operational losses in 1 Group.

Out of 13 Wellington squadrons in 1 Group.

7th highest number of Wellington overall operations in 1 Group.
5th highest number of Wellington sorties in 1 Group.
6th highest number of Wellington operational losses in 1 Group.
The only 1 Group squadron to operate Halifaxes.
The only 1 Group squadron to operate all 4 aircraft types in service with the group.

Out of 14 Lancaster squadrons in 1 Group.

Highest number of Lancaster overall operations in 1 Group.
3rd highest number of Lancaster sorties in 1 Group.
2nd highest number of Lancaster operational losses in 1 Group.

AIRCRAFT HISTORIES

BATTLE.	**To October 1940**.
K9264	FTR from attacks in Luxembourg 10.5.40.
K9265	To 8MU.
K9266	To 1 Salvage Section.
K9268	To 20MU.
K9269	To AASF.
K9270	FTR from attacks in Luxembourg 10.5.40.
K9271	Force-landed in France during reconnaissance operation 27.9.39.
K9295	To 3 Salvage Section.
K9297	To SF Abingdon.
K9298	To 52Sqn.
K9299	To 8MU.
K9372	FTR from attacks in Luxembourg 10.5.40.
K9374	Lost in France June 40. Details uncertain.
K9392	From 150Sqn. to 8MU.
K9404	From 52Sqn. Abandoned in France during withdrawal 16.5.40.
K9408	From 52Sqn. to RCAF.

K9409	From 52Sqn. DBR during operation to Vernon 10.6.40. and SOC.
K9411	From 52Sqn. to 8MU.
K9456	To 8MU.
K9460	From 52Sqn via 12 OUT and 6MU. to 27MU.
K9471	From 35Sqn via 47 and 6MU. to 27MU.
L4941	To 63Sqn.
L4942	To 150Sqn.
L4957	From 52Sqn. to 8MU.
L5010	From 6MU. FTR Calais 9/10.9.40.
L5011	From 3 BGS via 27MU. to 12Sqn.
L5038	To 38MU.
L5125	To 27MU.
L5190	From 16Sqn. FTR Sedan 14.5.40.
L5204	To 22MU.
L5205	To 110 Wg.
L5206	To 6 AACU.
L5207	To RCAF.
L5208	To 110 Wg.
L5209	To 6 AACU.
L5210	To SAAF.
L5211	To 110 Wg. Via 22MU.
L5212	To 22MU.
L5213	To 22MU.
L5214	To 3 Gp TF.
L5234	From 15Sqn. Abandoned in France during withdrawal 16.5.40.
L5236	From 15Sqn. Force-landed in France while training 1/2.3.40.
L5237	From 150Sqn. to 301Sqn.
L5244	From 40Sqn. to RAAF.
L5246	From 40Sqn. FTR from operations against troop columns and communications in France 9/10.6.40.
L5336	From 10MU. to 22MU.

L5358	From 10MU. to 20MU.
L5363	From 10MU. to 27MU.
L5381	From 235Sqn via 10MU. to MU.
L5395	From 27MU. to 20MU.
L5431	From 20MU. to 38MU.
L5432	From 20MU. to 12 OUT via 9MU.
L5433	From 20MU. Crashed on approach to Cottesmore while training 3.8.40.
L5444	From 27MU. to 9MU via Rollason.
L5465	From 8MU. Lost in France June 1940. Details uncertain.
L5469	From 150Sqn. to 18MU after taxying accident at Newton 3.8.40.
L5479	From 6MU. to 9MU via Rollason.
L5508	From 8MU. Lost in France June 40. Details uncertain.
L5509	From 8MU. Lost in France June 40. Details uncertain.
L5511	From 8MU. Lost in France June 40. Details uncertain.
L5512	From 8MU. FTR Bouillon 12.5.40.
L5513	From 8MU. Lost in France June 40. Details uncertain.
L5514	From 218Sqn. FTR Roumont 26.5.40.
L5515	From 8MU. FTR Roumont 26.5.40.
L5516	From 6MU. FTR Sedan 14.5.40..
L5525	From 6MU. to 38MU.
L5532	From 300Sqn. to 12Sqn.
L5792	From 18MU. to 4 Gp TTF.
N2157	From 8MU. to 38MU.
N2163	From 20MU. to 20MU.
N2253	From 6MU. FTR Poix 8.6.40.
N2255	From 6MU. to 9MU via Rollason.
P2163	From 6MU. Lost in France June 40. Details uncertain.

P2191	From 142Sqn. FTR Sedan 14.5.40.
P2193	From 142Sqn. FTR Bouillon 12.5.40.
P2256	From 226Sqn. Crashed in France while training 27.3.40.
P2278	To 4BGS via 22MU.
P2303	To 22MU.
P2304	From 8MU. to 9MU after belly-landing 31.8.40.
P2305	From 8MU. to 20MU.
P2306	From 8MU. to 20MU.
P2307	From 8MU. to 9MU.
P2308	From 8MU. to 12Sqn via 27MU.
P2311	From 8MU. to 12Sqn.
P2312	From 8MU. to 150Sqn.
P2314	From 8MU. Lost in France May 40. Details uncertain.
P2315	From 218Sqn. FTR Poix 8.6.40.
P2328	From 10MU. FTR Vernon 10.6.40.
P2357	From 20MU. Lost in France May 40. Details uncertain.
P5237	From 27MU. to 12Sqn.
WELLINGTON.	**From October 1940 to July 1942.**
L7813	From 150Sqn. Crashed on landing at Newton while training 13.11.40.
L7819	From 301Sqn. to ASRTU.
L7886 PM-X	From 305Sqn. Abandoned over Lincolnshire on return from Frankfurt 21.9.41.
N2770	FTR Brest 24.7.41.
N2849	FTR Duisburg 16/17.6.41.
N2996	From 38Sqn. to CGS and back. to CGS.
N2997	From 38Sqn. to CGS.
R1041	To 15 OTU.
R1043	Force-landed in Somerset during operation to Brest 30/31.3.41.
R1061	From 300Sqn. FTR Lübeck 28/29.3.42.

R1140		From Exeter. to 14 OTU.
R1163		From 75Sqn. to 16 OTU.
R1213		From 305Sqn. FTR Mannheim 29/30.8.41.
R1217		Damaged beyond repair operation to Duisburg 16/17.10.41.
R1234		From 12 OTU. Crashed soon after take-off from Kirmington for transit flight 31.5.42.
R1274		From 301Sqn. to 11 OTU.
R1344		From 300Sqn. to 21 OTU.
R1347		From 300Sqn. to 21 OTU.
R1393		Ditched off Suffolk coast on return from Essen 25/26.3.42.
R1395		FTR Hamburg 15/16.1.42.
R1396		FTR Turin 10/11.9.41.
R1397		FTR Emden 24/25.7.41.
R1445		To 11 OTU.
R1446		To 23 OTU.
R1459		From 301Sqn. to 29 OTU.
R1467		To 20 OTU.
R1494		FTR Hannover 15/16.5.41.
R1538		To 18 OTU.
R1539		Force-landed in Lincolnshire during an operation to Frankfurt 20/21.9.41.
R1588		To 156Sqn.
R1617	PM-T	From 300Sqn. FTR Bremen 2/3.7.42.
R1667		From 301Sqn. to 21 OTU.
R1760		To 20 OTU.
R3215		To 18 OTU.
T2475		To 150Sqn.
T2506		From 305Sqn. Force-landed in Eire on return from Frankfurt and interned 24/25.10.41.
T2610		Ditched in the North Sea during operation to Hannover 10/11.2.41.
T2617		To 11 OTU.
T2621	PM-T	FTR Düsseldorf 25/26.2.41.

T2921		From 301Sqn. FTR from mining sortie 23/24.6.42.
T2965		To 21 OTU.
T2996	PM-C	FTR Osnabrück 12/13.6.41.
T2999	PM-P	Force-landed near Elsham Wolds on return from Emden 26.11.41.
W5612		Force-landed in Nottinghamshire following attack by intruder on return from Brest 31.3.41.
W5656		FTR Frankfurt 5/6.8.41.
W5664	PM-H	FTR Essen 12/13.4.42.
W5690		From 301Sqn. to 20 OTU.
X3204		Ditched in North Sea on return from Hamburg 3.8.41.
X3221		From 57Sqn. to 11 OTU.
X3414		From 115Sqn. to 150Sqn.
X3448		From 115Sqn. to 150Sqn.
X3762		To 150Sqn.
X9609		FTR Berlin 20/21.9.41.
X9665		From 301Sqn. FTR Berlin 20/21.9.41.
X9666		From 301Sqn. to 20 OTU.
X9675		To 26 OTU.
X9792		To 11 OTU.
X9794		FTR Mannheim 7/8.11.41.
X9813		Crashed on approach to Elsham Wolds 1.9.41.
X9816		From 150Sqn. Crashed on landing at Elsham Wolds while training 5.5.42.
Z1108		From 156Sqn. to 11 OTU.
Z1140		To 29 OTU.
Z1141		FTR St Nazaire 19/20.5.42.
Z1142		To 21 OTU.
Z1152		To 21 OTU.
Z1171		To 16 OTU.
Z8714		From 25 OTU. FTR from shipping strike (Channel Dash) 12.2.42.
Z8833	PM-L	From 150Sqn. FTR Nantes 4/5.5.42.

Z8840		From 150Sqn. to 15 OTU.
Z8843		To 16 OTU.
DV452		FTR Cologne 30/31.5.42.
DV578		From 150Sqn. to 29 OTU.
DV579	PM-Z	FTR Rostock 25/26.4.42.
DV596		From 27 OTU. to 11 OTU.
DV611		FTR Bremen 2/3.7.42.
DV612	PM-J	To 11 OTU.
DV697		To 26 OTU.
DV699		FTR Essen 5/6.6.42.
DV704		To 11 OTU.
DV773	PM-J	FTR Essen 8/9.6.42.
DV818		FTR Emden 22/23.6.42.
DV831	PM-R	FTR from mining sortie 23/24.6.42.
DV878		To 11 OTU.
DV882		To 1481Flt.
DV923		From 29 OTU. to 11 OTU.
HD946		To 16 OTU.
HF897		To 1481Flt.
HALIFAX.		From July 1942 to November 1942.
R9379		From 76Sqn. Conversion Flt only. Crashed on approach to Elsham Wolds 1.8.42.
R9380		From 102Sqn. Conversion Flt only. to 1656CU.
R9390		From 102Sqn via 460CF. Conversion Flt only. to 1656CU.
R9422		From 35Sqn. to 1656CU.
V9983		From 35Sqn. to 1656CU.
W1182		To 158Sqn.
W1185		From 460Sqn. to 51Sqn.
W1187		To 1656CU.
W1188	PM-D	FTR Milan 24/25.10.42.
W1189		FTR Osnabrück 6/7.10.42.
W1212		To 51Sqn.

W1213		FTR Cologne 15/16.10.42.
W1216	PM-Q	FTR Aachen 5/6.10.42.
W1217		To 158Sqn.
W1218		Crashed in Lincolnshire while training 28.7.42.
W1219		FTR Duisburg 6/7.9.42.
W1220		FTR Bremen 4/5.9.42.
W1223	PM-U	FTR Milan 24/25.10.42.
W1224		To 51Sqn.
W1225		Crashed in the Humber on return from Duisburg 7.8.42.
W1243		Conversion Flt only. Crashed on landing at Elsham Wolds 22.9.42.
W1251		To 158Sqn.
W1270		FTR Kassel 27/28.8.42.
W7705		To 1656CU.
W7772		To 51Sqn.
W7818		From 460Sqn. to 51Sqn.
W7819		From 103CF. to 1656CU.
W7846		To 1656CU.
W7850	PM-A	FTR Cologne 15/16.10.42.
W7860		To 51Sqn.
W7861		To 51Sqn.
BB202		To 1656CU via 103CF.
BB204		FTR Saarbrücken 28/29.8.42.
BB214		FTR Nuremberg 28/29.8.42.
BB219		To 78Sqn.
BB221		To 76Sqn and back. to 1662CU.
BB223		To 51Sqn.
DG229		To 1656CU via 103CF.
DT482		From 103CF. to 1656CU.
DT483		From 460CF. to 51Sqn.
DT485		To 158Sqn.
DT495		To 1445Flt.
DT505		To 158Sqn.

DT506		To 51Sqn.
DT513		To 51Sqn.
DT523		To 1656CU.

LANCASTER.		From November 1942.
R5674		From 207Sqn. to 1662CU.
W4132		From 1667CU. to 1LFS.
W4318	PM-C	Ditched in the Channel on return from Spezia 13/14.4.43.
W4323	PM-C	Destroyed in ground accident at Elsham Wolds 23.8.43.
W4328		No operations. to 12Sqn.
W4333	PM-B	Crashed in Cambridgeshire during training 4.3.43.
W4334	PM-R	FTR Duisburg 20/21.12.42.
W4335	PM-F	FTR Essen 21/22.1.43.
W4336	PM-U	FTR Cologne 26/27.2.43.
W4337	PM-K	FTR Berlin 2/3.12.43.
W4338	PM-L	FTR Essen 13/14.1.43.
W4339	PM-M	FTR Frankfurt 2/3.12.42.
W4340	PM-A	First off on squadron's first Lancaster operation. FTR Essen 21/22.1.43.
W4361	PM-N	FTR Berlin 1/2.3.43.
W4362	PM-P	FTR Milan 14/15.2.43.
W4363	PM-U	FTR from mining sortie 6/7.7.43.
W4364	PM-D	FTR Nuremberg 27/28.8.43.
W4376		From 57Sqn. to 166Sqn.
W4786		FTR from mining sortie 17/18.12.42.
W4787		FTR Munich 21/22.12.42.
W4788		From 12Sqn. FTR Hamburg 3/4.3.43.
W4820	PM-S	FTR Munich 21/22.12.42.
W4821		To 9Sqn and back. to 300Sqn via 1656CU & 1LFS.
W4827	PM-W	FTR Gelsenkirchen 25/26.6.43.
W4828	PM-G	FTR Spezia 13/14.4.43.

W4845		To 1656CU.
W4848	PM-L	FTR Pilsen 16/17.4.43.
W4852		To 15Sqn via 1654CU.
W4857	PM-V	Crashed near Elsham Wolds during training 27.2.43.
W4860		FTR Munich 9/10.3.43.
W4880	PM-H	FTR Berlin 1/2.3.43.
W4901	PM-W	FTR Cologne 16/17.6.43.
W5012	PM-O	FTR Cologne 3/4.7.43.
DV180		To 166Sqn.
DV193		From 460Sqn via 1LFS. to 1LFS.
DV220	PM-L	To 166Sqn.
DV221	PM-K	FTR Hannover 27/28.9.43.
DV333		From 460Sqn. to 576Sqn.
DV342		To 576Sqn.
ED370		From 101Sqn. to 460Sqn.
ED380	PM-F	From 101Sqn. FTR Lorient 16/17.2.43.
ED384	PM-H	FTR Essen 9/10.1.43.
ED389	PM-J2	From 100Sqn. FTR Hamburg 24/25.7.43.
ED396		FTR Oberhausen 14/15.6.43.
ED417		Collided with Halifax JN966 (428Sqn) over County Durham on return from Berlin 26/27.11.43.
ED419	PM-X	FTR Essen 12/13.3.43.
ED528	PM-Z	FTR Gelsenkirchen 25/26.6.43.
ED612	PM-J	FTR Oberhausen 14/15.6.43.
ED614	PM-G	FTR Stettin 20/21.4.43.
ED626	PM-G	FTR Emmerich 1.4.43.
ED645	PM-W/F	FTR Hamburg 2/3.8.43.
ED646	PM-V/E	FTR Berlin 31.8/1.9.43.
ED701	PM-B2	FTR Leverkusen 22/23.8.43.
ED713	PM-N	To 576Sqn.
ED714	PM-L	To 12Sqn.

ED724	PM-M/R	Crash-landed on approach to Bodney on return from Duisburg 10.4.43.
ED725	PM-P	FTR Peenemünde 17/18.8.43.
ED731		To 166Sqn.
ED733	PM-X	FTR from mining sortie 28/29.4.43.
ED751	PM-S	FTR Mannheim 5/6.9.43.
ED767		To 576Sqn.
ED769	PM-U	FTR Turin 12/13.7.43.
ED773	PM-U	FTR Mülheim 22/23.6.43.
ED878	PM-G/V	FTR Hamburg 24/25.7.43.
ED879	PM-E	Crashed during take-off at Elsham Wolds for night flying test 9.6.43.
ED881	PM-K/S	FTR Leipzig 20/21.10.43.
ED882	PM-A	From 97Sqn. FTR Mannheim 9/10.8.43.
ED884	PM-L	FTR Essen 25/26.7.43.
ED888	PM-M/M2	To 576Sqn and back. Completed 135 operations including 11 to Berlin. to 10MU.
ED904		To 166Sqn.
ED905	PM-X	To 166Sqn.
ED913		To 576Sqn.
ED914	PM-Z	FTR Düsseldorf 11/12.6.43.
ED916	PM-J	FTR Bochum 12/13.6.43.
ED922	PM-C	FTR Hamburg 2/3.8.43.
ED942	PM-B	To 460Sqn.
ED945	PM-R	FTR Cologne 16/17.6.43.
EE182		From 101Sqn. to U.S.A. July 1943.
EE196		To 166Sqn.
JA672	PM-E	FTR Cologne 3/4.7.43.
JA704		To 166Sqn.
JA855	PM-A	FTR Essen 25/26.7.43.
JA857	PM-M	From 576Sqn. FTR Dessau 7/8.3.45.
JA866	PM-E	FTR Hamburg 24/25.7.43.
JA868		To 576Sqn.
JA957		To 576Sqn.

JA962		From 582Sqn. to 1668CU.
JB147	PM-C	FTR Hannover 18/19.10.43.
JB152	PM-H	FTR Mannheim 23/24.9.43.
JB153	PM-D	Crashed soon after take-off from Wymeswold on air-test 8.9.43.
JB276	PM-F	FTR Kassel 22/23.10.43.
JB277	PM-M	FTR Berlin 27/28.1.44.
JB278	PM-L	Ditched in North Sea on return from Karlsruhe 24/25.4.44.
JB279	PM-E	FTR Hannover 18/19.10.43.
JB319		To 5LFS.
JB346		Crashed soon after take-off from Elsham Wolds during air-test 3.10.43.
JB349	PM-G	FTR Hannover 18/19.10.43.
JB350	PM-L	FTR Berlin 26/27.11.43.
JB376	PM-B	FTR Kassel 22/23.10.43.
JB400	PM-K	FTR Berlin 2/3.12.43.
JB401	PM-P	FTR Berlin 2/3.12.43.
JB403	PM-T	FTR Berlin 2/3.12.43.
JB423		From 460Sqn. Damaged beyond repair during an operation to Berlin 26/27.11.43.
JB454		FTR Frankfurt 20/21.12.43.
JB458	PM-C	FTR Berlin 26/27.11.43.
JB460		To 576Sqn.
JB487	PM-G	FTR Berlin 29/30.12.43.
JB527	PM-B	FTR Berlin 26/27.11.43.
JB528	PM-Q	FTR Berlin 23/24.11.43.
JB530		Collided with ND334 (103Sqn) in Elsham circuit on return from Leipzig 19/20.2.44.
JB550		FTR Leipzig 3/4.12.43.
JB551		To 5LFS.
JB555	PM-D	To 576Sqn.
JB655		To 1656CU.
JB658		FTR Berlin 16/17.12.43.
JB670		Crashed in Lincolnshire after collision with

		LM332 (576Sqn) when bound for Berlin 16.12.43.
JB730	PM-P	FTR Berlin 23/24.12.43.
JB732	PM-S	FTR Aulnoye 10/11.4.44.
JB733	PM-K	FTR Hasselt 11/12.5.44.
JB736	PM-N	FTR Nuremberg 30/31.3.44.
JB744		To 576Sqn and back. FTR Frankfurt 18/19.3.44.
JB745	PM-I	FTR Leipzig 19/20.2.44.
JB746	PM-I	FTR le Havre 31.7.44.
JB747	PM-M	FTR Berlin 2/3.1.44.
LL913		Crashed in Yorkshire on return from Düsseldorf 22/23.4.44.
LL941	PM-E	From 166Sqn. FTR Stuttgart 24/25.7.44.
LL946	PM-Z	FTR Dortmund 22/23.5.44.
LL963	PM-D	FTR from mining sortie 15/16.5.44.
LL964	PM-H	From 460Sqn. FTR Cologne 31.10/1.11.44.
LM116	PM-D	FTR Stettin 29/30.8.44.
LM124		To 6LFS.
LM131	PM-V	Abandoned over Lincolnshire on return from Dortmund 12.3.45.
LM132	PM-I	To 57Sqn.
LM173	PM-M	FTR Sterkrade 16/17.6.44.
LM177	PM-Z	FTR from mining sortie 4/5.4.45.
LM243	PM-T	FTR Agenville 31.8.44.
LM272		To 5MU.
LM292		Abandoned over Lincolnshire on return from Fontenay-le-Marmion 7/8.8.44.
LM293		Crashed while landing at Elsham Wolds on return from Ertvelde-Rieme 18.8.44.
LM295	PM-Z	
LM314	PM-J	From 97Sqn. FTR Kassel 22/23.10.43.
LM332		To 576Sqn.
LM335		To 166Sqn.
LM343	PM-F	FTR Mannheim 5/6.9.43.
LM381		From 460Sqn. to 576Sqn.

LM538	PM-H	FTR Stuttgart 28/29.7.44.
LM682	PM-O	FTR Dresden 13/14.2.45.
ME392	PM-Y	FTR Chemnitz 5/6.3.45.
ME449	PM-T	FTR from mining sortie 12/13.3.45.
ME475	PM-L	
ME551	PM-Y	
ME649		From 460Sqn. FTR Essen 12/13.12.44.
ME665	PM-C	FTR Berlin 24/25.3.44.
ME671		To 300Sqn.
ME673	PM-J/I	FTR Mailly-le-Camp 3/4.5.44.
ME674	PM-T	FTR Revigny 12/13.7.44.
ME698	PM-U	From 460Sqn.
ME721	PM-M	FTR Nuremberg 30/31.3.44.
ME722	PM-E	FTR Duisburg 21/22.5.44.
ME736		From 622Sqn. FTR Friedrichshaven 27/28.4.44.
ME738	PM-S	FTR Friedrichshaven 27/28.4.44.
ME741	PM-G	FTR Düsseldorf 22/23.4.44.
ME746		From 166Sqn.
ME773	PM-U	FTR Revigny 14/15.7.44.
ME799	PM-K	FTR Stuttgart 28/29.7.44.
ME847	PM-R	From 15Sqn. to 57Sqn.
ME848	PM-E	From 15Sqn. FTR Nuremberg 16/17.3.45.
ND329	PM-A	FTR Frankfurt 22/23.3.44.
ND334		Collided with JB530 (103Sqn) in Elsham circuit on return from Leipzig 19/20.2.44.
ND362	PM-Q	From 576Sqn. FTR Aachen 27/28.5.44.
ND363	PM-A	FTR Berlin 15/16.2.44.
ND381		To 1LFS.
ND397	PM-R	FTR Stettin 5/6.1.44.
ND402		From 576Sqn. Crashed while landing at Elsham Wolds on return from Essen 27.3.44.
ND408	PM-T	FTR Leipzig 19/20.2.44.
ND411	PM-J	FTR Mailly-le-Camp 3/4.5.44.
ND417	PM-P	FTR Augsburg 25/26.2.44.

ND420	PM-G	FTR from mining sortie 9/10.4.44.
ND572		To 57Sqn.
ND613	PM-R	From 625Sqn. FTR Fontaine-le-Pin 14.8.44.
ND624	PM-F	FTR Aachen 24/25.5.44.
ND629	PM-G	FTR Dortmund 22/23.5.44.
ND632		Crashed while landing at Ford on return from Rüsselsheim 25/26.8.44.
ND638		Damaged beyond repair over Karlsruhe 24/25.4.44.
ND656		From 460Sqn. to 1666CU.
ND700	PM-X	FTR Hasselt 11/12.5.44.
ND847	PM-R	FTR Essen 26/27.4.44.
ND861	PM-H	From 300Sqn. Crashed in Humber Estuary while training 4.1.45.
ND903	PM-G	From 576Sqn. FTR Stuttgart 25/26.7.44.
ND905	PM-B	FTR Mailly-le-Camp 3/4.5.44.
ND925	PM-C	FTR Aachen 27/28.5.44.
ND990		Abandoned over Carnaby on return from Revigny 12/13.7.44.
ND993	PM-I	FTR Revigny 12/13.7.44.
NE117	PM-J	FTR Stuttgart 28/29.7.44.
NE136	PM-L	FTR Revigny 14/15.7.44.
NE173	PM-F	FTR Vire 6/7.6.44.
NF909	PM-J	FTR Pforzheim 23/24.2.45.
NF913	PM-H	FTR Dessau 7/8.3.45.
NF999	PM-T	FTR Munich 7/8.1.45.
NG173		
NG276	PM-E	FTR Leuna 6/7.12.44.
NG360	PM-F	
NG391		To 166Sqn.
NG420	PM-Q	FTR Cologne 24/25.12.44.
NG491	PM-R	FTR Hanau 18/19.3.45.
NG492	PM-D	FTR Nuremberg 16/17.3.45.
NN758	PM-S	FTR Nuremberg 16/17.3.45.

NN766	PM-R	FTR Munich 7/8.1.45.
PA217		
PA278		
PA303	PM-E	
PA319		
PA985		Crash-landed in Buckinghamshire on return from Stuttgart 28/29.7.44.
PA997		To 576Sqn.
PA999	PM-S	FTR Revigny 12/13.7.44.
PB147	PM-C	FTR Stuttgart 28/29.7.44.
PB363	PM-F	FTR La Nieppe 18.8.44.
PB365	PM-B	FTR Stettin 29/30.8.44.
PB465	PM-F	FTR Dortmund 29.11.44.
PB528	PM-D	FTR Hannover 5/6.1.45.
PB563	PM-G	FTR Chemnitz 5/6.3.45.
PB637	PM-L	FTR from mining sortie 6/7.1.45.
PB673		To 626Sqn.
PB786		To 153Sqn.
PB898		To 1660CU.
PD198	PM-W	From 9Sqn.
PD236	PM-X	To 57Sqn.
PD272	PM-K	FTR Mannheim 1.3.45.
PD281	PM-B/S	
PD335		From 166Sqn.
PD365		To 166Sqn.
RA500	PM-B	FTR Dessau 7/8.3.45.
RA515	PM-N	FTR Pforzeim 23/24.2.45.
RA528		
RA566		
RA579		
RE121	PM-I	
RF186		
RF193		To 57Sqn.
RF229		

HEAVIEST SINGLE LOSS

28/29.07.44.   Stuttgart   4 Lancasters FTR.
                                                             1 Crashed on return.

142 SQUADRON

Motto: **Determination**   Code **WT QT**

142 Squadron was formed in the Middle East in February 1918 for reconnaissance duties in Egypt and Palestine. It lost its identity in February 1920, and remained on the shelf until being reformed as a day bomber unit in June 1934. It again found itself overseas in the Western Desert during the Abyssinian crisis, but returned to the UK in November 1936 and re-equipped with the Hawker Hind. Fairey Battles arrived in March 1938, and the squadron was sent to France at the outbreak of WWII to serve with the Advanced Air Striking Force. Withdrawn to the UK in June 1940, the squadron joined the reconstituted 1 Group Bomber Command, and carried out limited operations against invasion barge concentrations in Channel Ports. Conversion to Wellingtons began in November 1940, and the squadron participated in the various campaigns throughout the following two years. In December 1942 the bulk of the squadron was posted to Algeria, leaving a home echelon to rebuild and continue operations. At the end of January 1943 the home echelons of 142 and 150 Squadrons merged to form 166 Squadron. The overseas element was disbanded in Italy in October 1944, and later in the month 142 Squadron was reformed as a Pathfinder Mosquito unit, a role in which it continued for the remainder of the war.

STATIONS

BERRY-AU-BAC	02.09.39. to 12.09.39.
PLIVOT	12.09.39. to 16.05.40.
FAUX-VILLECERF	16.05.40. to 06.06.40.
VILLIERS-FAUX	06.06.40. to 15.06.40.
WADDINGTON	15.06.40. to 03.07.40.
BINBROOK	03.07.40. to 12.08.40.
EASTCHURCH	12.08.40. to 06.09.40.
BINBROOK	06.09.40. to 26.11.41.
GRIMSBY	26.11.41. to 19.12.42.
KIRMINGTON	19.12.42. to 27.01.43.

COMMANDING OFFICERS

Wing Commander	W R Sadler	01.10.40. to 11.07.41.
Wing Commander	R L Kippenberger	11.07.41. to 20.11.41.
Wing Commander	S S Bertram	20.11.41. to 27.04.42.
Wing Commander	D G Simmons	27.04.42. to 11.11.42.
Wing Commander	T W Bamford	11.11.42. to 27.01.43.
Wing Commander	C L Falconer	03.39. to 01.10.40.

AIRCRAFT

Battle	03.38. to	01.41.
Wellington II	11.40. to	10.41.
Wellington IV	10.41. to	10.42.
Wellington III	09.42. to	01.43.

OPERATIONAL RECORD

Operations	Sorties	Aircraft Losses	% Losses
181	1136	51	4.5%

CATEGORY OF OPERATIONS

Bombing	Mining	Leaflet
148	32	1

Battles

Operations	Sorties	Aircraft Losses	% Losses
16	63	4	6.3%

All bombing

Wellingtons

Operations	Sorties	Aircraft Losses	% Losses
165	1073	47	4.4%

CATEGORY OF OPERATIONS

Bombing	Mining	Leaflet
132	32	1

AIRCRAFT HISTORIES

BATTLE.	**To January 1941.**
K7647	From 185Sqn. to 150Sqn.
K7652	From 46Sqn. to RCAF 3.41.
K7696	FTR Laon 19.5.40.
K7697	
K7699	SOC 3.40.
K7700	Abandoned at Berry-au-Bac airfield 17.5.40.
K7701	To RCAF 4.5.41.
K7703	To RCAF 18.10.40.
K9184	To 4BGS.
K9204	From 150Sqn. to RCAF 7.9.41.
K9219	To 98Sqn.
K9259	From 185Sqn. Destroyed on the ground at Berry-au-Bac airfield during air raid 12.5.40.
K9274	From 12Sqn. to RCAF 18.10.40.
K9292	To RCAF 31.8.40.
K9293	Lost in France May 40. Details uncertain.
K9301	From XVSqn. to 5FPP.
K9333	FTR from attack on bridges at Sedan 14.5.40.
K9336	To 207Sqn.
K9337	To 226Sqn.
K9366	From XVSqn. Abandoned at Berry-au-Bac airfield 17.5.40.
K9367	From XVSqn. Lost in France May 40. Details uncertain.
K9406	From 52Sqn. to RCAF 10.3.41.
K9444	From 52Sqn via 12 OTU. to 150Sqn.
L4936	Abandoned in France May 40.
L4937	To RCAF 25.4.41.
L5042	From 150Sqn. to RCAF 5.2.41.
L5052	From 305Sqn. to RCAF 15.7.41.
L5077	To SAAF 16.2.41.
L5080	To RCAF 31.3.41.

L5113	Crashed in Oxfordshire during training 4.8.40.
L5200	From 105Sqn. FTR from operations in the battle area 11.6.40.
L5226	From XVSqn. FTR Laon 19.5.40.
L5227	To 12Sqn.
L5231	From XVSqn. FTR from attacks on troop columns in Luxembourg 10.5.40.
L5235	From XVSqn. to 218Sqn.
L5238	Force-landed in France during operation against troop columns in Luxembourg 10.5.40.
L5240	From 40Sqn. to 12Sqn.
L5242	From 40Sqn. Damaged during operation against troop columns in Luxembourg 10.5.40 and abandoned.
L5259	From 9BGS. to RCAF 6.41.
L5285	To 88Sqn.
L5327	Lost in France May 40. Details uncertain.
L5367	To SAAF 11.5.41.
L5368	From 304Sqn. Crashed on landing at Llandow while training 16.12.40. (Last Battle to be lost by active bomber squadron).
L5391	From 12Sqn. Force-landed near Binbrook while training 22.10.40.
L5397	Battle-damaged and abandoned in France 14.6.40.
L5428	From 226Sqn. Abandoned over Lincolnshire on return from Calais 13/14.10.40.
L5436	Lost in France May 40. Details uncertain.
L5440	Abandoned at Berry-au-Bac airfield 17.5.40.
L5443	Destroyed by fire on the ground at Faux-Villecerf 20.5.40.
L5453	To RCAF 11.3.41.
L5456	To RCAF 11.9.41.
L5457	Lost in France June 40. Details uncertain.
L5464	To SAAF 9.3.41.
L5501	To RCAF 31.8.41.

L5502	FTR Brussels aerodrome 28/29.7.40.
L5503	FTR Boulogne 22/23.8.40.
L5507	Crashed at Eastleigh airfield during night flying training 26.8.40.
L5517	FTR from attack on bridges at Sedan 14.5.40.
L5533	To RAAF 3.4.41.
L5543	To 150Sqn.
L5546	To 12Sqn.
L5560	To SAAF 5.2.41.
L5566	SOC 9.2.41.
L5569	To RCAF 21.5.41.
L5578	From 150Sqn. FTR from attacks on troop columns in Luxembourg 10.5.40.
L5582	From 88Sqn. FTR Boulogne 22/23.8.40.
L5584	FTR Brussels aerodrome 28/29.7.40.
L5586	To RCAF 3.4.41.
L5589	To RCAF 7.3.41.
L5592	To RCAF 21.2.41.
N2025	From RAE. SOC 12.9.40.
N2083	From 1 AAS. to RCAF 11.3.41.
N2087	To SD Flt.
N2088	Crashed in France while training 7.4.40.
N2099	From 152Sqn. to RCAF 27.10.40.
N2103	From 266Sqn. to RCAF 5.2.41.
N2189	To 301Sqn.
N2248	To RCAF 7.3.41.
P2177	From 105Sqn. to SAAF 29.3.41.
P2188	To 63Sqn.
P2189	To 218Sqn.
P2190	To 105Sqn.
P2191	To 103Sqn.
P2192	To 218Sqn.
P2193	To 103Sqn.

P2194	Lost in France with the AASF June 1940. Details uncertain.
P2195	FTR from attack on bridges at Sedan 14.5.40.
P2199	To 1 FTS.
P2200	To 226Sqn.
P2201	To 218Sqn.
P2246	From 226Sqn. FTR from attack on bridges at Sedan 14.5.40.
P2249	From 218Sqn. FTR from attack on bridges at Maastricht 12.5.40.
P2302	To RCAF 13.3.41.
P2310	SOC 4.9.40.
P2321	To SAAF 11.7.41.
P2325	To RCAF 2.3.41.
P2327	From 150Sqn. Crashed near Binbrook while training 22.10.40.
P2329	To RCAF 7.4.41.
P2333	FTR from attack on bridges at Sedan 14.5.40.
P5238	Force-landed with battle damage and abandoned 19.5.40.
P5240	From 245Sqn. to RAAF 2.3.41.
P6568	From 150Sqn. to RCAF 13.3.41.
P6572	To 15 EFTS.
P6600	SOC 26.9.40.
P6602	From 150Sqn. to RAAF 3.4.41.
P6603	To India 16.9.40.
WELLINGTON.	**From November 1940 to January 1943.**
R1490	From 301Sqn. to 18 OTU.
R1655	From 460Sqn. to 18 OTU.
W5355	To 12Sqn.
W5356	To 12Sqn.
W5359	To 305Sqn.
W5363	To 12Sqn.

W5364	QT-H	Crashed in Sussex following early return from Cologne 31.7.41.
W5368		To 405Sqn.
W5370		To 305Sqn.
W5373		From 12Sqn. Crashed almost immediately after take-off from Binbrook during training 12.1.41.
W5374		To 305Sqn.
W5377		To 12Sqn.
W5378	QT-A	FTR Stettin 29/30.9.41.
W5383		To 12Sqn.
W5384		Ditched in North Sea on return from Stettin 19/20.9.41.
W5386		FTR Bremen 27/28.6.41.
W5387		To 12Sqn.
W5393		To 12Sqn.
W5395		To 12Sqn.
W5423		To 305Sqn.
W5433		FTR Berlin 12/13.8.41.
W5440		To 12Sqn.
W5446		To 1446Flt.
W5455		To 305Sqn.
W5462		To 1443Flt.
W5494		From 99Sqn. to 1443Flt.
W5499		Lost 10.9.41. Details uncertain.
W5514		To 12Sqn.
W5585		To 12Sqn.
X3334		To 166Sqn.
X3455	QT-D	From 101Sqn. FTR Milan 24/25.10.42.
X3812		From 101Sqn. to 12Sqn.
X3960	QT-Q	From 101Sqn. Crashed in Lincolnshire on return from Cologne 15/16.10.42.
X3987		From 12Sqn. to 22 OTU.
Z1202		FTR Hamburg 30.11/1.12.41.
Z1203	QT-O	FTR Lübeck 28/29.3.42.

Z1205	QT-W	From 458Sqn. FTR Essen 6/7.4.42.
Z1206		To 10 OTU.
Z1207	QT-U	FTR Emden 20/21.1.42.
Z1208	QT-S	FTR Cologne 30/31.5.42.
Z1209	QT-Z	FTR Cologne 30/31.5.42.
Z1210	QT-M	FTR Bremen 21/22.10.42.
Z1211		FTR Mannheim 7/8.11.41.
Z1214	QT-C	From 458Sqn. FTR Bremen 4/5.9.42.
Z1216		To 301Sqn.
Z1219	QT-V	From 301Sqn. FTR from mining sortie 23/24.9.42.
Z1220		From 301Sqn. to 19 OTU.
Z1221		To 104 OTU.
Z1243		Crashed soon after take-off from Grimsby while training 25.11.42.
Z1245		To 300Sqn.
Z1247	QT-K	FTR Brest 6/7.2.42.
Z1261		From 458Sqn. Crashed immediately after take-off from Middle Wallop during training 10.6.42.
Z1266	QT-M	From 300Sqn. FTR Kassel 27/28.8.42.
Z1274	QT-P	From 458Sqn. FTR Lübeck 28/29.3.42.
Z1281		To 305Sqn.
Z1283	QT-N	FTR Essen 26/27.3.42.
Z1286		From 458Sqn. to 300Sqn.
Z1287	QT-Q	FTR Duisburg 25/26.7.42.
Z1289		To 104 OTU.
Z1292		FTR Hamburg 30.11/1.12.41.
Z1311		To 460Sqn.
Z1315		To 104 OTU.
Z1316	QT-H	FTR Saarbrücken 29/30.7.42.
Z1318		To 18 OTU.
Z1319	QT-W	FTR Hamburg 26/27.7.42.
Z1321	QT-V	FTR Essen 26.3.42.

Z1324	QT-A	From 458Sqn. FTR from mining sortie 9/10.7.42.
Z1325		From 460Sqn. to 18 OTU.
Z1330	QT-B	FTR Bremen 17/18.1.42.
Z1338	QT-D	From 458Sqn. FTR Kassel 27/28.8.42.
Z1340		To 301Sqn.
Z1341	QT-L	Force-landed in Norfolk when bound for Duisburg 14.7.42.
Z1342	QT-T	Ditched in the Channel on return from Frankfurt 8/9.9.42.
Z1376	QT-M	FTR Hamburg 26/27.7.42.
Z1380	QT-A	FTR Essen 16/17.9.42.
Z1390		From 301Sqn. to 18 OTU.
Z1392		From 460Sqn. to 305Sqn.
Z1393		To 305Sqn.
Z1396	QT-B	FTR Kassel 27/28.8.42.
Z1408	QT-P	FTR Duisburg 21/22.7.42.
Z1410	QT-Z	Crashed at Thoresby Bridge following early return from Essen 1/2.6.42.
Z1411	QT-Z	FTR Kassel 27/28.8.42.
Z1414		To 18 OTU.
Z1416		To 18 OTU.
Z1419		To 300Sqn.
Z1420		To 18 OTU.
Z1424	QT-F	FTR Kassel 27/28.8.42.
Z1459		To 305Sqn.
Z1461	QT-F	FTR Hamburg 26/27.7.42.
Z1466	QT-L	FTR Karlsruhe 2/3.9.42.
Z1469		To 18 OTU.
Z1477	QT-Z	FTR Düsseldorf 10/11.9.42.
Z1478	QT-B	Crashed in Wattisham circuit on return from Saarbrücken 2.9.42.
Z1480	QT-I	FTR Essen 16/17.9.42.
Z1482		From 460Sqn. to 18 OTU.
Z1487	QT-Z	FTR from mining sortie 5.8.42.

Z1494		From 460Sqn. to 18 OTU.
Z1686		To 166Sqn.
Z1726		From 101Sqn. to 166Sqn.
Z8339		To 305Sqn.
Z8343		To 305Sqn.
BJ581		From 101Sqn. to 300Sqn.
BJ705		From 101Sqn. to 166Sqn.
BJ711	QT-Z	From 101Sqn. FTR Hamburg 9/10.11.42.
BJ768	QT-Q	From 101Sqn. FTR from mining sortie 8/9.11.42.
BJ780		To 12Sqn.
BJ819		To 12Sqn.
BJ821		From 12Sqn. to 30 OTU.
BJ913		To 166Sqn.
BJ914		To 29 OTU.
BJ916		To 199Sqn.
BK159		To 166Sqn.
BK198	QT-P	From 12Sqn. FTR from mining sortie 7/8.11.42.
BK236		To 300Sqn.
BK277		To 166Sqn.
BK278	QT-C	FTR from mining sortie 16/17.11.42.
BK279		To 17 OTU.
BK280	QT-F	Crashed on take-off from Davidstowe Moor for transit flight 13.11.42.
BK281	QT-M	Crashed on Dartmoor on return from Aachen 5/6.10.42.
BK298	QT-L	From 101Sqn. Crashed on take-off from Manston for transit flight 26.10.42.
BK299		From 101Sqn. to 166Sqn.
BK303		To 300Sqn.
BK304		To 166Sqn.
BK305		To 300Sqn.
BK368		To 166Sqn.
BK385	QT-N	FTR from mining sortie 24/25.10.42.

BK459		To 166Sqn.
BK460		To 12Sqn.
BK515		To 166Sqn.
BK516		To 300Sqn.
BK536	QT-C	FTR Turin 20/21.11.42.
BK537		To 15 OTU.
DF550	QT-N	FTR Essen 16/17.9.42.
DF551		To 311 FTU.
DF552		To North Africa.
DF642	QT-J	Crashed on landing at Manston on return from Cologne 16.10.42.
DF666		FTR Düsseldorf 15/16.8.42.
DF667		FTR Kassel 27/28.8.42.
DF668		To 428Sqn.
DF690		To North Africa.
DF691		To North Africa.
DF693		To North Africa.
DF694		To Middle East.
DF699		
DF702		To North Africa.
DF704		To North Africa.
DF708		Damaged beyond repair in accident 18.12.42.
DF734		To North Africa.

150 SQUADRON

Motto: **Always Ahead**   Codes **JN IQ**
    (Greek text)

Formed in Macedonia in the Balkans in April 1918, 150 Squadron was originally a fighter unit. It remained overseas until being disbanded in September 1919. Reformation took place at Boscombe Down in August 1938, and the squadron moved to France on the outbreak of WWII as a member of the Advanced Air Striking Force. Having suffered heavy losses during the battle for France, the squadron was withdrawn to the UK in June 1940, and became a founder member of the new 1 Group Bomber Command. Wellingtons arrived in October, and the squadron performed a standard night bomber role for the next two years. In December 1942 the bulk of the squadron was posted to Algeria, and the home echelon merged with the remnant of 142 Squadron at the end of January 1943 to form 166 Squadron. The overseas element was disbanded in early October 1944, and a new 150 Squadron was formed later in the month from C Flight of 550 Squadron. Equipped with Lancasters the Squadron took part in operations against Germany until war's end.

STATIONS

CHALLERANGE	02.09.39. to 11.09.39.
ECURY-SUR-COOLE	11.09.39. to 15.05.40.
POUAN	15.05.40. to 03.06.40.
HOUSSAY	03.06.40. to 15.06.40.
ABINGDON	15.06.40. to 19.06.40.
STRADISHALL	19.06.40. to 03.07.40.
NEWTON	03.07.40. to 10.07.41.
SNAITH	10.07.41. to 26.10.42.
KIRMINGTON	26.10.42. to 27.01.43.
FISKERTON	01.11.44. to 22.11.44.
HEMSWELL	22.11.44. to 07.11.45.

COMMANDING OFFICERS

Wing Commander	A Hesketh	03.03.39. to 03.12.40.
Wing Commander	G J C Paul	03.12.40. to 17.06.41.
Wing Commander	R A C Carter	17.06.41. to 06.12.41.
Wing Commander	K J Mellor	06.12.41. to 29.06.42.
Wing Commander	E J Carter	29.06.42. to 28.11.42.
Wing Commander	R A C Barclay	01.12.42. to 27.01.43.
Wing Commander	G G Avis	01.11.44. to 19.04.45.
Wing Commander	P A Rippon	19.04.45. to 07.11.45.

AIRCRAFT

Battle	08.38. to 10.40.
Wellington IC/III	10.40. to 01.43.
Lancaster I/III	11.44. to 11.45.

OPERATIONAL RECORD

Operations	Sorties	Aircraft Losses	% Losses
289	2557	56	2.2%

CATEGORY OF OPERATIONS

Bombing	Mining
264	25

Battles
(Excluding AASF)

Operations	Sorties	Aircraft Losses	% Losses
16	50	0	0.0%

Wellingtons

Operations	Sorties	Aircraft Losses	% Losses
200	1667	50	3.0%

CATEGORY OF OPERATIONS

Bombing	Mining
175	25

Lancaster

Operations	Sorties	Aircraft Losses	% Losses
73	840	6	2.2%

TABLE OF STATISTICS

Out of 42 Wellington squadrons.

9th highest number of Wellington overall operations in Bomber Command.
6th highest number of Wellington sorties in Bomber Command.
6th highest number of Wellington operational losses in Bomber Command.

Out of 59 Lancaster squadrons.

47th highest number of Lancaster overall operations in Bomber Command.
48th highest number of Lancaster sorties in Bomber Command.
52nd highest number of Lancaster operational losses in Bomber Command.

Out of 20 squadrons in 1 Group.

7th highest number of overall operations in 1 Group.
12th highest number of sorties in 1 Group.
11th highest number of aircraft operational losses in 1 Group.

Out of 6 Battle squadrons in 1 Group.

Highest equal (with 103 and 142Sqns) number of Battle overall operations in 1 Group.
3rd highest number of Battle sorties in 1 Group.
Lowest equal (with 300 and 301Sqns) number of Battle operational losses in 1 Group.

Out of 13 Wellington squadrons in 1 Group.

4th highest number of Wellington overall operations in 1 Group.
2nd highest number of Wellington sorties in 1 Group.
2nd highest number of Wellington operational losses in 1 Group.

Out of 14 Lancaster squadrons in 1 Group.

2nd lowest number of Lancaster overall operations in 1 Group.
Lowest number of Lancaster sorties in 1 Group.Lowest number of Lancaster operational losses in 1 Group.

AIRCRAFT HISTORIES

BATTLE	To October 1940.
K7647	From 142Sqn. to 27MU.
K9204	From XVSqn. to 142Sqn.
K9272	To 52Sqn.
K9282	To XVSqn.
K9283	Crashed on landing at Ecury-sur-Coole on return from reconnaissance sortie 30.9.39.
K9369	From XVSqn. Damaged beyond repair during operation to Luxembourg 10.5.40.
K9379	To 20MU.
K9380	To 6MU.
K9387	FTR from reconnaissance sortie 30.9.39.
K9388	To CGS via Abingdon.

K9389		To 22MU.
K9390	JN-I	FTR from operation to Luxembourg 10.5.40.
K9392		To 103Sqn.
K9417		From 12Sqn. to 6 ASP.
K9444		From 142Sqn. to 27MU.
K9483		FTR Sedan 14.5.40.
K9484		FTR from reconnaissance sortie 30.9.39.
L4938		From XVSqn. to 22MU.
L4942		From 103Sqn. to 22MU.
L4945		To 22MU.
L4946		FTR Sedan 14.5.40.
L4947		To 22MU.
L4948		Lost in France. Details uncertain.
L4953		From 52Sqn. to Abingdon.
L5042		To 142Sqn.
L5057		To 27MU.
L5058		To 9MU.
L5103		To 9MU.
L5106		To 38MU.
L5112		FTR from attacks on communications and troop columns 8.6.40.
L5215		To 110 Wing via 22MU.
L5216		To 88Sqn via 22MU.
L5217		To 110 Wing via 22MU.
L5218		To 22MU.
L5219		To 22MU.
L5220		To 22MU.
L5221		To 22MU.
L5222		To 22MU.
L5223		To 8BGS via 22MU.
L5224		To 22MU.
L5225		Crashed on approach to Ecury-sur-Coole while training 20.9.39.
L5237		From 218Sqn. to 103Sqn.

L5288		FTR Abbeville 7.6.40.
L5421		From 6MU. to 12 OTU.
L5434		To 18 OTU.
L5437		FTR Vernon-Poix 13.6.40.
L5447		To 12 OUT via 9MU.
L5459		FTR Roumont 26.5.40.
L5469		To 103Sqn.
L5510		To 38MU.
L5512		From 103Sqn. Returned to 103Sqn.
L5524		FTR Vernon-Poix 13.6.40.
L5528		Destroyed in explosion at Newton 27.7.40.
L5539		FTR from operation to Luxembourg 10.5.40.
L5540	JN-C	FTR from operation to Luxembourg 10.5.40.
L5541		FTR from French battle area 15.6.40.
L5543		From 142Sqn. to Rollason.
L5545		To 20MU.
L5548		To 38MU.
L5563		From Andover. to Rollason.
L5578		To 142Sqn.
L5579		From 218Sqn. to 27MU.
L5583		FTR from the French battle area 19.5.40.
L5591		FTR Foret de Gault 13.6.40.
L5593		To Fairey.
L5630		From 98Sqn. to 12Sqn.
N2028		FTR from reconnaissance sortie 30.9.39.
N2093		FTR from reconnaissance sortie 30.9.39.
N2169		To 9MU.
P2179		From 12Sqn. to 9MU.
P2182		From 12Sqn. FTR Sedan 14.5.40.
P2183		From 12Sqn. to 218Sqn via 1 Salvage Section.
P2184		From 12Sqn. Lost in France May/June 1940.
P2244		From 226Sqn. Crashed in France while training 31.3.40.
P2266		To 4BGS via 22MU.

P2276		To 4BGS via 22MU.
P2312		From 103Sqn. to 18 OTU.
P2327		To 142Sqn.
P2334		Destroyed in air raid at Ecury-sur-Coole 11.5.40.
P2336		FTR Neufchateau 12.5.40.
P5232		FTR Sedan 14.5.40.
P5235		FTR from battle area 19.5.40.
P5236		To 12Sqn.
P6568		To 142Sqn.
P6602		To 142Sqn.
WELLINGTON		**From October 1940 to January 1943.**
L7813		To 103Sqn.
L7870		To ATA.
N2758		To 20 OTU.
N2952		From 38Sqn. Became ground instruction machine.
N2998		From 38Sqn. Crash-landed at Newton while training 13.11.40.
R1016	JN-A	From 305Sqn. FTR Hannover 14/15.8.41.
R1042		To 29 OTU.
R1044	JN-Y	Crashed in Leicestershire on return from Boulogne 28.5.41.
R1216		To 23 OTU.
R1374	JN-G	FTR St Nazaire 7/8.5.41.
R1375		To 25 OTU.
R1394	JN-V	FTR Hannover 14/15.8.41.
R1412		To 21 OTU.
R1414		To 23 OTU.
R1435	JN-H	FTR Hamburg 10/11.5.41.
R1444		To 26 OTU.
R1463		Crashed in Yorkshire on return from intruder sortie 21/22.2.42.
R1469		From 149Sqn. to 7 OTU.
R1491		To 15 OTU.

R1495	JN-B	FTR Hamburg 16/17.7.41.
R1592		From 301Sqn. to 57Sqn.
R1606	JN-G	FTR Mannheim 7/8.11.41.
R1644	JN-L	FTR Düsseldorf26/27.6.41.
R1716		To 304Sqn.
R3288	JN-B	Crashed in Wales on return from Lorient 21.3.41.
T2475		From 103Sqn. to 12 OTU.
T2510		To 29 OTU.
T2574		From 300Sqn. to 21 OTU.
T2618		Force-landed in Yorkshire on return from Emden 16.11.41.
T2622	JN-D	Crash-landed at Snaith during training 22.8.41.
T2960		From 305Sqn. Damaged beyond repair during operation to Frankfurt 24/25.10.41.
T2967	JN-J	FTR Mannheim 22/23.10.41.
W5667		To 18 OTU.
W5719	JN-S	Crashed in Derbyshire following early return from Cologne 31.7.41.
W5721	JN-Z	From 305Sqn. FTR Frankfurt 6/7.8.41.
W5722		From 305Sqn. Force-landed in Suffolk on return from Mannheim 28.8.41.
X3175		From 300Sqn. to 21 OTU.
X3279	JN-M	FTR Emden 6/7.6.42.
X3283		From 9Sqn. to 300Sqn.
X3288	JN-H	From 9Sqn. FTR Cologne 27/28.4.42.
X3304		FTR Frankfurt 8/9.9.42.
X3305	JN-X	From 57Sqn. Crashed almost immediately after take-off from Snaith when bound for Rostock 23/24.4.42.
X3309	JN-N	FTR Bremen 27/28.6.42.
X3310	JN-A	FTR Hamburg 9/10.11.42.
X3313		FTR Karlsruhe 2/3.9.42.
X3349		To 23 OTU.
X3407	JN-A	From 101Sqn. FTR Stuttgart 5/6.5.42.

X3413		From 115Sqn. to 199Sqn.
X3414		From 103Sqn. FTR Frankfurt 24/25.8.42.
X3418		FTR Kassel 27/28.8.42.
X3448	JN-N	From 103Sqn. Crashed in Lincolnshire on return from Cologne 31.5.42.
X3450		From 115Sqn. to 26 OTU.
X3451		From 75Sqn. to 419Sqn and back via 75Sqn. Crashed in Yorkshire following early return from Stuttgart 6.5.42.
X3459		From 75Sqn. to 300Sqn.
X3463		From 9Sqn. to 12 OTU.
X3465		To 27 OTU.
X3544		To 166Sqn.
X3548		To 300Sqn.
X3552		FTR Cologne 15/16.10.42.
X3590	JN-L	FTR Duisburg21/22.7.42.
X3673		Crashed on landing at Blyton on return from Stuttgart 6.5.42.
X3674	JN-H	FTR Essen 5/6.6.42.
X3698		Crashed almost immediately after take-off from Snaith when bound for Duisburg 7.8.42.
X3700	JN-R	FTR Cologne 27/28.4.42.
X3725	JN-N	FTR Essen 8/9.6.42.
X3743	JN-D	To 82 OTU.
X3744		Crashed on landing at Coltishall on return from Mainz 11/12.8.42.
X3745		To 57Sqn and back. FTR Frankfurt 8/9.9.42.
X3755		To 57Sqn and back via 75Sqn. FTR Essen 19.7.42.
X3762		From 103Sqn. FTR Saarbrücken 19/20.9.42.
X3795		FTR Duisburg 25/26.7.42.
X3797	JN-A	Crashed in Suffolk on return from Duisburg14.7.42.
X3805		To 15 OTU.
X3807		To 166Sqn.

X3870		To 199Sqn.
X3888		To 166Sqn.
X3939		To 166Sqn.
X3957		FTR from mining sortie 28/29.10.42.
X3965		From 101Sqn. to 166Sqn.
X9638		From 22 OTU. Returned to 22 OTU.
X9683		From 305Sqn. to 18 OTU.
X9811		From 25 OTU. Crash-landed on the Yorkshire coast on return from Frankfurt 21.9.41.
X9812		To 1481Flt.
X9814	JN-O	FTR Poissy2/3.4.42.
X9815		From 300Sqn. to 1481Flt.
X9816		To 103Sqn.
X9830	JN-H	FTR from intruder sortie 21/22.2.42.
X9832		From 149Sqn. to 23 OTU.
X9871		From 40Sqn. to 311Sqn.
Z1072		To 304Sqn.
Z1076		FTR Brest 11/12.2.42.
Z1078		Crashed in the Cheviots on return from Hamburg 15.1.42.
Z1092		To 22 OTU.
Z1150		To 1481Flt.
Z1593		FTR Osnabrück 9/10.8.42.
Z1608	JN-M	FTR Essen 16/17.6.42.
Z1610	JN-K	FTR Bremen 27/28.6.42.
Z1625		From 101Sqn. FTR Emden 31.10.42.
Z1651		
Z1661		From 101Sqn. to 300Sqn.
Z1671	JN-D	Force-landed in Yorkshire on return from Bremen 4/5.9.42.
Z8833		From 300Sqn. to 103Sqn.
Z8840		From 101Sqn. to 103Sqn.
Z8849		Crash-landed at Snaith during air-test 14.12.41.

Z8851		Crash-landed in Surrey on return from Frankfurt 3.9.41.
BJ588		Crashed during emergency landing in Lincolnshire following early return from Mainz 12/13.8.42.
BJ591		Crashed on approach to Lympne on return from Frankfurt 8/9.9.42.
BJ608		FTR Osnabrück 9/10.8.42.
BJ618		To 166Sqn.
BJ645		To 166Sqn.
BJ649		Crash-landed at Middle Wallop on return from Saarbrücken 28/29.8.42.
BJ651	JN-M	FTR Frankfurt 24/25.8.42.
BJ666	JN-S	FTR Bremen 27/28.6.42.
BJ754		To 26 OTU.
BJ766		From 75Sqn. to 156Sqn.
BJ776		To 12Sqn.
BJ777		To 12Sqn.
BJ827		To 27 OTU.
BJ829	JN-G	Abandoned over Kent on return from Aachen 5/6.10.42.
BJ831		FTR Frankfurt 24/25.8.42.
BJ877		FTR Essen 16/17.9.42.
BJ881		FTR Saarbrücken 29/30.7.42.
BJ961		From 101Sqn. to 166Sqn.
BJ972		From 101Sqn. to 300Sqn.
BJ973		To 166Sqn.
BK139		To 166Sqn.
BK180		Crashed while landing at Kirmington during training 20.12.42.
BK194	JN-B	FTR from mining sortie 28/29.11.42.
BK196		To 300Sqn.
BK266		To 17 OTU.
BK267		To 300Sqn.
BK300		To 199Sqn.

BK301	JN-Q	FTR from mining sortie 15/16.11.42.
BK309	JN-N	From 101Sqn. FTR from mining sortie 23/24.10.42.
BK310		From 101Sqn. Crashed in Somerset during a mining sortie 28/29.10.42.
BK311		From 101Sqn. Crashed on approach to Elsham Wolds during training 10.10.42.
BK360		
BK361		To 166Sqn.
BK511		To 300Sqn.
BK538	JN-U	Crashed at Manston following early return from Turin 21.11.42.
DV447		FTR Essen 9/10.3.42.
DV556		To 215Sqn.
DV558		To 304Sqn.
DV578		To 103Sqn.
DV593		FTR Dortmund 14/15.4.42.
DV594		To 304Sqn.
LANCASTER		**From November 1944.**
JB613	IQ-Y	From 625Sqn.
LM721	IQ-W	From 149Sqn.
ME328	IQ-J/Z	
ME451	IQ-D	FTR Hildesheim 22.3.45.
ME486	IQ-H	
NG163	IQ-C	
NG164	IQ-D	From 625Sqn. FTR Osterfeld 31.12/1.1.45.
NG263	IQ-A	Abandoned over Oxfordshire on return from Dahlbusch (Gelsenkirchen) 13.3.45.
NG264	IQ-B	
NG268	IQ-G	
NG273		To 576Sqn.
NG288	IQ-H	From 12Sqn.
NG291	IQ-K	From 12Sqn.
NG295	IQ-D	

NG333	IQ-S	
NG359	IQ-L	
NG421	IQ-M	Collided with PB515 (153Sqn) and crashed near Lincoln on return from Nuremberg 2.1.45.
NN742	IQ-U	
NN743	IQ-Z	FTR Essen 12/13.12.44.
NN752	IQ-R	
NX557	IQ-F	
NX582		
NX583		
PB254		From 460Sqn.
PB738	IQ-O	
PB746		
PB747	IQ-E	
PB748		From 12Sqn.
PB780	IQ-T	FTR Pforzheim 23/24.2.45.
PB781	IQ-V	
PB817	IQ-Q	
PB853	IQ-P	FTR Harpenerweg Benzol plant at Dortmund 24.3.45.
PD421	IQ-F	FTR Dortmund 20/21.2.45.
RA544		To 153Sqn.
RA584		
RA586	IQ-L	
RF243	IQ-N	
RF245		

HEAVIEST SINGLE LOSS.

30.09.39.	Saarbrücken.	4 Battles FTR, 1 crashed on return.

153 SQUADRON

Motto: **Noctividus**
    (Seeing by night).

Code **P4**

This squadron was formed in November 1918 as a night fighter unit, but the Great War ended before it had time to assemble. Disbanded in June 1919 it was reformed in Northern Ireland in October 1941, and operated successively Defiants, Beaufighters, Spitfires and Hurricanes. The squadron moved to Algeria in December 1942, and a detachment was sent to Sardinia in July 1944 for intruder sorties over southern France and northern Italy. The squadron was disbanded in early September 1944, and reformed a month later at Kirmington as a Lancaster unit in 1 Group Bomber Command. It carried out standard bomber operations until the end of hostilities.

STATIONS

KIRMINGTON   07.10.44. to 15.10.44.
SCAMPTON   15.10.44. to 28.09.45.

COMMANDING OFFICERS

Wing Commander F S Powley   07.10.44. to 05.04.45.
Squadron Leader T W Rippingale (Temp) 05.04.45. to 09.04.45.
Wing Commander G F Rodney   09.04.45. to 28.09.45.

AIRCRAFT

Lancaster I/III   07.10.44. to 28.09.45.

OPERATIONAL RECORD

Operations	Sorties	Aircraft Losses	% Losses
75	1041	22	2.1%

CATEGORY OF OPERATIONS

Bombing	Mining
70	5

TABLE OF STATISTICS

Out of 20 squadrons in 1 Group.

17th highest number of overall operations in 1 Group.

16th highest number of sorties in 1 Group.
16th highest number of aircraft operational losses in 1 Group.

Out of 14 Lancaster squadrons in 1 Group.

12th highest number of overall Lancaster operations in 1 Group.
12th highest number of Lancaster sorties in 1 Group.
12th highest number of Lancaster operational losses in 1 Group.

AIRCRAFT HISTORIES

LANCASTER.		**From October 1944.**
JB297	P4-B	From 166Sqn. FTR Duisburg 14.10.44.
LM550	P4-C	From 166Sqn.
LM750	P4-R	From 166Sqn. FTR from mining sortie 3/4.3.45.
LM752	P4-S	From 166Sqn. Damaged by flak during operation to Cologne 2.3.45. and SOC.
LM754	P4-E	From 166Sqn.
ME384	P4-P	
ME424	P4-N	FTR Bremen 22.4.45.
ME485	P4-D	
ME541	P4-A	Damaged by flak during operation against oil target 24.3.45. and SOC following emergency landing at Eindhoven.
ME544	P4-T	
ME812	P4-F	From 166Sqn.
ND757	P4-V	To 1656CU.
NE113	P4-H	From 166Sqn.
NG167	P4-Y	
NG184	P4-U	From 166Sqn. FTR Mannheim 1.3.45.
NG185	P4-A	From 166Sqn. FTR Duisburg 22/23.1.45.
NG189	P4-P	From 166Sqn. Force-landed at Melsbroek (Belgium) during an operation to the Urft Dam 3.12.44 and subsequently destroyed during the Luftwaffe's Operation Bodenplatte 1.1.45.
NG190	P4-T	From 166Sqn. FTR Duisburg 14.10.44.
NG201	P4-T	FTR Essen 11.3.45.

NG218	P4-K/B	From 166Sqn.
NG335	P4-V	FTR Zeitz 16/17.1.45.
NG488	P4-A	FTR Misburg 15/16.3.45.
NG500	P4-V	
NN785	P4-D	FTR Dortmund 20/21.2.45.
NN803	P4-O	FTR Chemnitz 14/15.2.45.
NX556	P4-J	
NX563	P4-R	From 576Sqn. FTR from mining sortie 4/5.4.45.
NX573	P4-A	
PA168	P4-G	From 166Sqn.
PA264	P4-O	
PA313	P4-R	
PB472	P4-K	From 576Sqn.
PB515	P4-N	Collided with NG421 (150Sqn) over Lincolnshire when bound for Nuremberg 2.1.45.
PB633	P4-J	From 166Sqn. FTR Ulm 17.12.44.
PB636	P4-D	From 166Sqn. FTR Duisburg 22/23.1.45.
PB638	P4-O	From 166Sqn. FTR Stuttgart 28/29.1.45.
PB639	P4-I	FTR Düsseldorf 2/3.11.44.
PB642	P4-W	From 166Sqn. FTR Nuremberg 16/17.3.45.
PB783	P4-I	
PB786	P4-Q	From 103Sqn. Damaged by flak during mining sortie 12.3.45 and SOC.
PB872	P4-X	FTR Chemnitz 5/6.3.45.
PD343	P4-Q	From 166Sqn. Damaged on approach to land at Scampton after training flight 30.11.44. to 550Sqn.
PD378	P4-L	Abandoned over Allied territory while returning from Bottrop 3.2.45.
PD380	P4-X	FTR Dortmund 24.11.44.
RA526	P4-J	FTR from mining sortie 12/13.3.45.
RA544	P4-U	From 150Sqn. FTR from mining sortie 4/5.4.45.
RA545	P4-X	From 170Sqn.
RA582	P4-L	
RF205	P4-W	

HEAVIEST SINGLE LOSS.

14.10.44.	Duisburg.	2 Lancasters FTR.
22.01.45.	Duisburg.	2 Lancasters FTR.
04.04.45.	Mining.	2 Lancasters FTR.

166 SQUADRON

Motto **Tenacity**   Code **AS**

166 Squadron was formed in June 1918 to operate heavy bombers against targets in Germany, but the Armistice came before operations began. Disbandment took place at the end of May 1919, and the squadron remained on the shelf until reforming in November 1936. It became a training unit in June 1938, and continued in this role until merging with 97 Squadron to form 10 O.T.U in April 1940. It reformed once more when the home echelons of 142 and 150 Squadrons merged in late January 1943 to operate Wellingtons in 1 Group Bomber Command. The squadron took on Lancasters in September 1943, and performed a standard bomber role for the remainder of the war.

STATIONS

KIRMINGTON   26.01.43. to 18.11.45.

COMMANDING OFFICERS

Wing Commander	R A C Barclay	26.01.43. to 03.07.43.
Wing Commander	R J Twamley	03.07.43. to 15.12.43.
Wing Commander	C Scragg	15.12.43. to 15.01.44.
Wing Commander	F S Powley	15.01.44. to 30.04.44.
Wing Commander	D A Garner	30.04.44. to 14.12.44.
Wing Commander	R L Vivian	14.12.44. to 17.08.45.

AIRCRAFT

Wellington III	27.01.43. to	04.43.
Wellington X	02.43. to	09.43.
Lancaster I/III	09.43. to	18.11.45.

OPERATIONAL RECORD

Operations	Sorties	Aircraft Losses	% Losses
291	5068	153	3.0%

CATEGORY OF OPERATIONS

Bombing	Mining
245	46

Wellingtons

Operations	Sorties	Aircraft Losses	% Losses
76	789	39	4.9%

CATEGORY OF OPERATIONS

Bombing	Mining
43	33

Lancasters

Operations	Sorties	Aircraft Losses	% Losses
215	4279	114	2.7%

CATEGORY OF OPERATIONS

Bombing	Mining
202	13

TABLE OF STATISTICS

Out of 59 Lancaster squadrons.

25th highest number of Lancaster overall operations in Bomber Command.
9th highest number of Lancaster sorties in Bomber Command.
6th highest number of Lancaster operational losses in Bomber Command.

Out of 20 squadrons in 1 Group.

6th highest number of overall operations in 1 Group.
4th highest number of sorties in 1 Group.
4th highest number of aircraft operational losses in 1 Group.

Out of 13 Wellington squadrons in 1 Group.

9th highest number of Wellington overall operations in 1 Group.
8th highest number of Wellington sorties in 1 Group.
5th highest number of Wellington operational losses in 1 Group.

Out of 14 Lancaster squadrons in 1 Group.

6th highest number of Lancaster overall operations in 1 Group.
4th highest number of Lancaster sorties in 1 Group.
3rd highest number of Lancaster operational losses in 1 Group.

AIRCRAFT HISTORIES

WELLINGTON		Jan 1943 to Sept 1943.
X3334	AS-P/W	From 142Sqn. FTR Frankfurt 10/11.4.43.
X3367		From 9Sqn. to 156Sqn.
X3544	AS-H	From 150Sqn. FTR Lorient 7/8.2.43.
X3807	AS-Z	From 150Sqn. to 23.O.T.U.
X3888		From 150Sqn. to 23 O.T.U.
X3939	AS-B	From 150Sqn. to 305Sqn.
X3965	AS-W/L	From 150Sqn. FTR Bochum 29/30.3.43.
Z1686	AS-R	From 142Sqn. to 23 O.T.U.
Z1726	AS-S	From 142Sqn. to 23 O.T.U.
BJ618	AS-A	From 150Sqn. to 30 O.T.U.
BJ645	AS-C	From 150Sqn. to 18 O.T.U.
BJ705	AS-U	From 142Sqn. to 305Sqn.
BJ913		From 142Sqn. to 1481 B&G Flt.
BJ961	AS-M	From 150Sqn. FTR Cologne 26/27.2.43.
BJ973	AS-J	From 150Sqn. FTR Wilhelmshaven 19/20.2.43.
BK139	AS-G	From 150Sqn. to 30 O.T.U.
BK159		From 142Sqn. Crashed while trying to land at Colerne on return from Lorient 29.1.43.
BK277	AS-T	From 142Sqn. to CGS via 48MU.
BK299	AS-Q	From 142Sqn. FTR from mining sortie 6/7.4.43.
BK304	AS-X	From 142Sqn. to 30 O.T.U.
BK361	AS-F	From 150Sqn. FTR Duisburg 8/9.4.43.
BK368	AS-P	From 142Sqn. FTR from mining sortie 9/10.3.43.
BK459	AS-T	From 142Sqn. FTR Frankfurt 10/11.4.43.
BK460	AS-V	From 12Sqn. Crash-landed in Somerset

following mid-air collision with Halifax W1182 of 158Sqn on return from Lorient 13.2.43.

BK464	AS-X	From 150Sqn. FTR Frankfurt 10/11.4.43.
BK515	AS-P	From 142Sqn. FTR Lorient 29/30.1.43.
HE234	AS-X	From 30 O.T.U. to 20 O.T.U.
HE235	AS-H	From 30 O.T.U. FTR Düsseldorf 25/26.5.43.
HE244	AS-D	From 23MU. FTR Dortmund 4/5.5.43.
HE290	AS-J	From 23MU. FTR Dortmund 23/24.5.43.
HE328	AS-T	To 18 O.T.U. via 48MU.
HE346	AS-M	FTR Gelsenkirchen 25/26.6.43.
HE349	AS-K	From 199Sqn. Damaged beyond repair during landing at Kirmington on return from a mining sortie 25.8.43. and SoC.
HE361	AS-V	FTR from mining sortie 3/4.4.43.
HE415	AS-A	From 30 O.T.U. to 20 O.T.U.
HE427	AS-O	From 30 O.T.U. to 17 O.T.U.
HE464	AS-W	From 300Sqn. FTR Hamburg 2/3.8.43.
HE479	AS-X	From 26.O.T.U. to 26 O.T.U.
HE486	AS-L	From 30 O.T.U. FTR Dortmund 23/24.5.43.
HE544	AS-K	From 51MU. Crashed on Essex coast on return from Mönchengladbach 31.8.43.
HE545	AS-H	From 51MU. FTR Bochum 29/30.3.43.
HE578	AS-G	From 48MU. FTR from mining sortie 2/3.8.43.
HE614	AS-B	From 48MU. to 17 O.T.U.
HE631	AS-V	FTR from mining sortie 3/4.3.43.
HE633	AS-J	To 23MU.
HE655	AS-D	From 425Sqn. FTR Dortmund 23/24.5.43.
HE658	AS-S	FTR Duisburg 8/9.4.43.
HE699	AS-M	From 23MU. FTR Düsseldorf 25/26.5.43.
HE742	AS-F	From 23MU. to 1481 B&G Flt.
HE752	AS-W	From 23MU. FTR Essen 27/28.5.43.
HE806	AS-T	To 84 O.T.U.
HE810	AS-Y	FTR Hamburg 29/30.7.43.
HE862	AS-L	FTR Mannheim16/17.4.43.

HE901	AS-Q	From 196Sqn. FTR from a mining sortie 27/28.8.43.
HE922	AS-S	Abandoned over Lincolnshire when bound for Cologne 28.6.43.
HE923	AS-R	FTR Dortmund 4/5.5.43.
HE924	AS-C	FTR Krefeld 21/22.6.43.
HE925	AS-T	To 1481 B&G Flt.
HE988	AS-U	From 196Sqn. FTR Mönchengladbach 30/31.8.43.
HE994	AS-D	From 48MU. to 84 O.T.U.
HF453	AS-X	From 199Sqn. FTR from mining sortie 8/9.7.43.
HF455	AS-V	From 48MU. Crashed on take-off from Kirmington 2.8.43.
HF483	AS-S	From 48MU. FTR from mining sortie 12/13.8.43.
HF486	AS-L	FTR Dortmund 23/24.5.43.
HF489		From 199Sqn. Force-landed near Kirmington during training 9.7.43.
HF588	AS-L	To 84 O.T.U.
HF589	AS-W	FTR Gelsenkirchen 25/26.6.43.
HF592	AS-H	To 84 O.T.U.
HF593	AS-N	To 84 O.T.U.
HF594	AS-Q	FTR Wuppertal 24/25.6.43.
HF595	AS-Y	FTR Cologne 3/4.7.43.
HF596	AS-A	From 199Sqn. FTR from mining sortie 15/16.8.43.
HF603	AS-C	From 431Sqn. to 84 O.T.U.
HZ278	AS-N	From 23MU. FTR from mining sortie 28/29.4.43.
HZ280	AS-Q	From 23MU. FTR Bochum 13/14.5.43.
HZ314	AS-P	From 23MU. FTR Hamburg 24/25.7.43.
HZ410	AS-V	From 18MU. Destroyed by fire at Kirmington 13.5.43.
HZ581	AS-R	To 84 O.T.U.
JA120	AS-M	To 84 O.T.U.

JA129	AS-W	To 300Sqn.
LN396	AS-X	To 84 O.T.U.
LN397	AS-P	FTR Mönchengladbach 30/31.8.43.
LN446	AS-B	To 84 O.T.U.
LN455	AS-D	To 84 O.T.U.
LN552	AS-Y	To 1481 B&G Flt.
LN553		To 300Sqn via 1481 B&G Flt.
MS493		From 425Sqn. to 20 O.T.U.

LANCASTER.		**From September 1943.**
R5552	AS-P^2	From 97Sqn via 20MU. FTR Frankfurt 20/21.12.43.
R5862	AS-N^2	From 1660CU. FTR Berlin 20/21.1.44.
W4376	AS-S^2	From 103Sqn. to 300Sqn.
W4780	AS-H^2	From 460Sqn via 1656CU. FTR Berlin 2/3.1.44.
W4966	AS-C^2	From 101Sqn. Crash-landed in Essex on return from Berlin 23.11.43.
W4994	AS-S/Z	From 12Sqn. to 1656CU.
W4996	AS-R	From 101Sqn. FTR Berlin 27/28.1.44.
DV180	AS-W	From 103Sqn. FTR Berlin 28/29.1.44.
DV220	AS-J	From 103Sqn. Flew 12 Berlin operations. FTR Leipzig 19/20.2.44.
DV247	AS-F	From 460Sqn. FTR Berlin 26/27.11.43.
DV309	AS-Y	To 550Sqn.
DV310	AS-R	To 189Sqn via 5LFS.
DV365	AS-Z^2	Damaged in landing at Ford on return from Berlin 26.11.43. to 576Sqn.
DV367	AS-K/T	Flew 14 Berlin operations. FTR Versailles 7/8.6.44.
DV386	AS-A^2	To 576Sqn.
DV387	AS-W	FTR Berlin 26/27.11.43.
DV404	AS-S/Z	FTR Brunswick 14/15.1.44.
DV406	AS-Y	FTR Berlin 30/31.1.44.
ED327	AS-B^2	From 101Sqn. to 300Sqn.
ED366	AS-C	From 460Sqn. FTR Kassel 22/23.10.43.

ED372	AS-S	From 101Sqn. FTR Hannover 27/28.9.43.
ED411	AS-H²	From 57Sqn. FTR Berlin 16/17.12.43.
ED422		Crashed after colliding with trees on approach to Kirmington following air-test 17.11.43.
ED716		From 550Sqn. to 1667CU.
ED731	AS-T²/Q	From 103Sqn. FTR Berlin 24/25.3.44 on 12th operation to Berlin.
ED841	AS-L	From 101Sqn. FTR Berlin 15/16.2.44.
ED875	AS-J	From 97Sqn. Crashed in Lincolnshire following early return from Hannover 28.9.43.
ED904	AS-Y	From 103Sqn. FTR Bochum 29/30.9.43.
ED905	AS-X	From 103Sqn. Completed 100 sorties. to 550Sqn.
ED993	AS-C	From 12Sqn. Crashed on approach to Kirmington following early return from Hannover 9.10.43.
EE137	AS-B/C²	From 101Sqn. FTR Brunswick 14/15.1.44.
EE193		From 57Sqn. to 550Sqn.
EE196	AS-Z	From 103Sqn. FTR Kassel 22/23.10.43.
EE200	AS-F	From 7Sqn. Crashed on take-off from Kirmington when bound for Aulnoye and burned out 10.4.44.
JA704	AS-A	From 103Sqn. FTR Hannover 27/28. 9.43.
JA712	AS-G	From 83Sqn. to 550Sqn.
JA865	AS-A	From 12Sqn. FTR Berlin 23/24.11.43.
JB142	AS-P	From 101Sqn. Crash-landed in Lincolnshire during air-test 22.5.44.
JB145	AS-D	From 12Sqn. FTR Berlin 2/3.12.43.
JB151	AS-H/O	From 101Sqn. FTR Frankfurt 22/23.3.44.
JB297	AS-B²	From 405Sqn. to 153Sqn.
JB639	AS-S	From 626Sqn. Crashed in Lincolnshire on return from Berlin 16.12.43.
JB644	AS-A²	From 405Sqn. FTR Revigny 12/13.7.44.
JB649	AS-O/Z	From 626Sqn. FTR Stuttgart 25/26.7.44.
LL743	AS-L/U	FTR Mailly-le-Camp 3/4.5.44.

LL749	AS-J^2	FTR Essen 26/27.3.44.
LL896	AS-R	FTR Revigny 12/13.7.44.
LL903	AS-B	FTR Friedrichshafen 27/28.4.44.
LL916	AS-X	FTR Aachen 27/28.5.44.
LL941		From 100Sqn. to 103Sqn.
LL954	AS-E	FTR Dortmund 22/23.5.44.
LM126	AS-A^2	FTR Versailles 7/8.6.44.
LM135	AS-N	FTR Acheres 10/11.6.44.
LM176	AS-X	Crashed on approach to Kirmington on return from Karlsruhe 4.12.44.
LM289	AS-Y	Crashed in Lincolnshire on return from Lutzkendorf 5.4.45.
LM312	AS-K	From 101Sqn. FTR Leipzig 20/21.10.43.
LM335	AS-O	From 103Sqn. Crashed on take-off from Kirmington when bound for Schweinfurt 24.2.44.
LM341	AS-B	From 101Sqn. FTR Leipzig 20/21.10.43.
LM382	AS-Q	Crash-landed at Manston following early return with battle damage from Leipzig 19/20.2.44. Participated in 10 operations to Berlin.
LM385	AS-N	Crashed in Lincolnshire on return from Berlin 16.12.43.
LM386	AS-M/V	FTR Stuttgart 25/26.7.44.
LM388	AS-W	FTR Revigny 12/13.7.44.
LM390	AS-F	FTR Magdeburg 21/22.1.44.
LM392	AS-A	To 550Sqn.
LM521	AS-F	Force-landed at Woodbridge with battle damage on return from Aachen 28.5.44.
LM529	AS-I	FTR Karlsruhe 24/25.4.44.
LM550	AS-B	To 153Sqn.
LM581	AS-X	FTR Gelsenkirchen 12/13.6.44.
LM586	AS-E	FTR Chateau Bernapre 27/28.6.44.
LM651		From 427Sqn. to 22MU.
LM652	AS-R	FTR from mining sortie 26/27.8.44.

LM687	AS-N	Abandoned over France on return from Nuremberg 2.1.45.
LM689	AS-H	From 626Sqn. to 22MU.
LM694	AS-M²	FTR from mining sortie 26/27.8.44.
LM722	AS-D	FTR Neuss 23/24.9.44.
LM750		To 153Sqn.
LM752		To 153Sqn.
LM754		To 153Sqn.
ME296	AS-V	From 100Sqn. FTR Zeitz 16/17.1.45.
ME297	AS-Q	
ME318	AS-E	From 32MU. FTR Karlsruhe 4/5.12.44.
ME428		From 32MU. to 550Sqn.
ME446	AS-T	
ME447	AS-B²/E	FTR Mannheim 1.3.45.
ME499	AS-D	
ME500	AS-P	
ME521	AS-A	FTR Hannover 25.3.45.
ME624	AS-X	FTR Nuremberg 30/31.3.44.
ME627	AS-Z	FTR Leipzig 19/20.2.44.
ME635	AS-C	FTR Berlin 24/25.3.44.
ME636	AS-E	FTR Berlin 15/16.2.44.
ME637	AS-F	FTR Leipzig 19/20.2.44.
ME638	AS-B	FTR Nuremberg 30/31.3.44.
ME639	AS-A	FTR Augsburg 25/26.2.44.
ME641	AS-B	Collided in the air with JB547 of 460Sqn near Binbrook when bound for Schweinfurt and crashed in Lincolnshire 24.2.44.
ME643	AS-E	FTR Mailly-le-Camp 3/4.5.44.
ME647	AS-J	FTR Osterfeld 31.12/1.1.45.
ME648	AS-J²	From 300Sqn. FTR Ludwigshafen 1.2.45.
ME686	AS-V	FTR Nuremberg 30/31.3.44.
ME720	AS-X	FTR Friedrichshafen 27/28.4.44.
ME746	AS-C/R²	Completed 125 sorties. to 103Sqn.
ME748	AS-Q	FTR Duisburg 14/15.10.44.

ME749	AS-Z	FTR Mailly-le-Camp 3/4.5.44.
ME754	AS-S²	From 75Sqn. to 100Sqn.
ME775	AS-N	FTR Orleans 19/20.5.44.
ME777	AS-K²	FTR Gelsenkirchen 12/13.6.44.
ME779	AS-S	FTR Hasselt 11/12.5.44.
ME806	AS-J²	Collided with PD227 also of 166Sqn and crashed into the Sea on return from Paulliac 5.8.44.
ME812	AS-F	To 153Sqn.
ME829	AS-G	FTR Neuss 23/24.9.44.
ME835	AS-T	FTR Bochum 4/5.11.44.
ME839	AS-N	FTR Trossy-St-Maximin 3.8.44.
ND366		To 460Sqn.
ND382	AS-Z	From 32MU. FTR Berlin 28/29.1.44.
ND399	AS-R	FTR Gelsenkirchen 12/13.6.44.
ND401	AS-D	FTR Berlin 24/25.3.44.
ND405	AS-C	From 550Sqn.
ND506	AS-L²	From 57Sqn. FTR Pforzheim 23/24.2.45.
ND579	AS-M	FTR Duisburg 21/22.5.44.
ND614	AS-A	Crashed on landing at Kirmington on return from Kiel 24.7.44.
ND620	AS-I	FTR Berlin 24/25.3.44.
ND621	AS-U	FTR Revigny 14/15.7.44.
ND623	AS-G/F	From 32MU. to Flight Refuelling Ltd.
ND625	AS-S	FTR from mining sortie 9/10.4.44.
ND626	AS-O	FTR from mining sortie 26/27.10.44.
ND628	AS-T	FTR Stuttgart 24/25.7.44.
ND634	AS-U	From 460Sqn. FTR Stuttgart 24/25.7.44.
ND635	AS-M	FTR Nuremberg 2.1.45.
ND651	AS-G	FTR Calais 2/3.6.44.
ND678	AS-Q	FTR Caen 7.7.44.
ND705	AS-F	FTR Frankfurt 18/19.3.44.
ND707	AS-D/E	FTR Lutzkendorf 5.4.45.
ND757	AS-L	To 153Sqn.

ND798	AS-C	FTR Nuremberg 30/31.3.44.
ND806	AS-S	FTR Düsseldorf 22/23.4.44.
ND825	AS-J²	FTR Friedrichshafen 27/28.4.44.
ND857	AS-K/G	
ND956	AS-I	FTR Duisburg 21/22.5.44.
ND996	AS-N	FTR Aachen 27/28.5.44.
NE112	AS-M	FTR Agenville 31.8.44.
NE113	AS-H	To 153Sqn.
NE114	AS-S	FTR Dortmund 22/23.5.44.
NE170	AS-I	FTR Agenville 31.8.44.
NE180		From 218Sqn. Became ground instruction machine.
NF974	AS-R	FTR Frankfurt 12/13.9.44.
NF986	AS-P	Crashed near Kirmington on return from Bochum 4.11.44.
NG114	AS-S	FTR Harpenerweg Benzol plant at Dortmund 24.3.45.
NG115	AS-U	
NG136	AS-Z	To 153Sqn.
NG140		From 90Sqn.
NG165	AS-J	From 550Sqn.
NG183	AS-D	From 576Sqn. FTR Dortmund 20/21.2.45.
NG185		To 153Sqn.
NG200	AS-V	FTR Freiburg 27/28.11.44.
NG254	AS-A²	
NG255	AS-I	
NG290	AS-B	From 550Sqn. FTR Munich 7/8.1.45.
NG297	AS-K²	FTR Cologne 24/25.12.44.
NG303	AS-P	Crash-landed at Leeming following early return from Coblenz 22.12.44.
NG304	AS-A/T	
NG391	AS-M	From 103 or 550Sqn. FTR Ludwigshafen 1.2.45.
NG393		
NN707	AS-K²	

NN713		
NN763	AS-F	
NN770	AS-B	
PA179	AS-A	FTR Dortmund 20/21.2.45.
PA231	AS-O	
PA234	AS-M	FTR Nuremberg 16/17.3.45.
PA236	AS-B²/W	
PA305	AS-X	
PA308	AS-W	
PA320	AS-Y	
PA321	AS-R	
PB153	AS-O/J²	FTR Nuremberg 16/17.3.45.
PB242	AS-E	Crash-landed at Manston on return from Neuss 23.9.44.
PB515	AS-I	To 153Sqn.
PB632	AS-L	To 38MU.
PB635	AS-G	From 576Sqn. FTR Nuremberg 2.1.45.
PB636		To 153Sqn.
PB638		To 153Sqn.
PB639		To 153Sqn.
PB642		To 153Sqn.
PB648	AS-B	From 625Sqn. FTR Düren 16.11.44.
PB896		From 186Sqn.
PB926		To 156Sqn.
PD202	AS-R²	FTR Revigny 12/13.7.44.
PD224	AS-A²/K²	FTR Duisburg 14.10.44.
PD226	AS-U	FTR from mining sortie 29/30.8.44.
PD227	AS-V	Collided with a Hurricane over Lincolnshire during fighter affiliation exercise, and crashed killing all ten occupants 12.10.44.
PD239	AS-Z	FTR Emmerich 7.10.44.
PD260	AS-N	FTR Brunswick 12/13.8.44.
PD261	AS-S	FTR Stettin 29/30.8.44.
PD310	AS-R	To 100Sqn.
PD335	AS-K	To 103Sqn.

PD343		To 550Sqn.
PD365	AS-X	From 103Sqn. FTR Hildesheim 22.3.45.
PD384	AS-H	
PD385	AS-W	FTR Ludwigshafen 1.2.45.
PD394	AS-P	FTR Chemnitz 14/15.2.45.
PD397	AS-V	FTR Cologne 24/25.12.44.
RA501	AS-N	Crash-landed at Manston with battle damage on return from Dortmund 21.2.45 and declared beyond economical repair.
RA589	AS-S	
RF154	AS-B	FTR Nuremberg 16/17.3.45.
RF158	AS-N	
RF211	AS-M	
RF244	AS-J²	
RF278	AS-V	

170 SQUADRON

Motto: **Videre Non Videri**   Code **TC**
(To see and not to be seen)

Formed in June 1942 as a tactical reconnaissance unit equipped with Mustangs, 170 squadron later added low level defensive patrols over the south coast and intruder raids on communications targets in France. In July 1943 the squadron joined the 2TAF, but was disbanded in January 1944. The squadron reformed at Kelstern from C Flight of 625 Squadron in October 1944, and operated Lancasters as a standard 1 Group unit until war's end.

STATIONS

KELSTERN	15.10.44. to 22.10.44.
DUNHOLME LODGE	22.10.44. to 29.11.44.
HEMSWELL	29.11.44. to 14.11.45.

COMMANDING OFFICERS

Wing Commander	P D W Hackforth	15.10.44. to 25.02.45.
Wing Commander	Templeman-Rooke	25.02.45.

AIRCRAFT

Lancaster I/III   15.10.44. to 11.45.

OPERATIONAL RECORD

Operations	Sorties	Aircraft Losses	% Losses
63	980	13	1.3%

All bombing

TABLE OF STATISTICS

Out of 20 Squadrons in 1 Group.

18th highest number of overall operations in 1 Group.
17th highest number of sorties in 1 Group.
18th highest number of aircraft operational losses in 1 Group.

Out of 14 Lancaster squadrons in 1 Group.

Lowest number of Lancaster overall operations in 1 Group.
13th highest number of Lancaster sorties in 1 Group.
13th highest number of Lancaster operational losses in 1 Group.

AIRCRAFT HISTORIES

LANCASTER.		From October 1944.
LM732	TC-B/C	From 625Sqn.
LM749	TC-Y	From 625Sqn. FTR Nuremberg 16/17.3.45.
ME302	TC-U	Crashed on take-off from Hemswell when bound for Ludwigshafen 1.2.45.
ME306	TC-S	
ME307	TC-O	FTR Nuremberg 16/17.3.45.
ME320	TC-L	FTR Chemnitz 5/6.3.45.
ME388	TC-H	From 153Sqn. FTR Dessau 7/8.3.45.
ME418	TC-V	From 153Sqn. FTR Dessau 7/8.3.45.
ME437	TC-B	
ME496	TC-K	FTR Nuremberg 16/17.3.45.
ND385	TC-F	From 576Sqn.
ND452	TC-D/N	From 625Sqn.

ND658	TC-P	From 460Sqn.
ND863	TC-E	From 625Sqn.
ND992	TC-A	From 625Sqn. to 227Sqn.
NG202	TC-T	
NG349	TC-A/A²	
NG403	TC-Q	
NN739	TC-Q	FTR Bottrop 3/4.2.45.
NN744	TC-V	FTR Duisburg 21/22.2.45.
NX577	TC-K	
PA311	TC-V	
PA312	TC-N	
PB397	TC-X	FTR Munich 7/8.1.45.
PB480	TC-G/G²	From 625Sqn.
PB573	TC-H	To 101Sqn and back. FTR Duisburg 21/22.2.45.
PB581		From 625Sqn.
PB595	TC-J	From 625Sqn. FTR Pforzheim 23/24.2.45.
PB693	TC-N/W	
PB704	TC-R	FTR Kiel 9/10.4.45.
PB728	TC-W	
PB752	TC-M	
PB753		To 576Sqn.
PD206	TC-B	From 625Sqn. FTR Scholven-Buer 29/30.12.44.
RA529	TC-U	
RA540	TC-L	
RA545		To 153Sqn.
RA575	TC-H	
RE126	TC-Y	
RF199	TC-J/J²	
SW276		To 576Sqn.

199 SQUADRON

Motto: **Let Tyrants Tremble**   Code **EX**

First formed in June 1917 as a training unit for pilots destined for a night bombing role, 199 Squadron was disbanded in June 1919. It remained on the shelf until November 1942, when it was resurrected in 1 Group Bomber Command as a standard bomber squadron operating Wellingtons. In June 1943 the squadron was transferred to 3 Group and converted to Wellingtons. In May 1944 it would take on RCM duties with 100 Group.

STATIONS

BLYTON	07.11.42. to 03.02.43.
INGHAM	03.02.43. to 20.06.43.

COMMANDING OFFICERS

Wing Commander	C R Hattersley	07.11.42. to 11.12.42.
Wing Commander	A S B Blomfield	11.12.42. to 20.03.43.
Wing Commander	L W Howard	20.03.43. to 06.10.43.

AIRCRAFT

Wellington III	11.42. to 05.43.
Wellington X	03.43. to 07.43.

OPERATIONAL RECORD

Wellington

Operations	Sorties	Aircraft Losses	% Losses
58	475	12	2.5%

CATEGORY OF OPERATIONS

Bombing	Mining
35	23

TABLE OF STATISTICS

Out of 20 squadrons in 1 Group.

19th number of overall operations in 1 Group.
18th highest number of sorties in 1 Group.
19th highest number of aircraft operational losses in 1 Group.

Out of 13 Wellington squadrons in 1 Group.

11th highest number of Wellington overall operations in 1 Group.
10th highest number of Wellington sorties in 1 Group.
11th highest number of Wellington operational losses in 1 Group.

AIRCRAFT HISTORIES

WELLINGTON.		**From November 1942 to July 1943.**
X3413		From 150Sqn. to 82 OTU.
X3812		From 101Sqn. to 29 OTU.
X3819		To 30 OTU.
X3870	EX-S	From 150Sqn. FTR Lorient 13/14.2.43.
Z1600	EX-C	Crashed on take-off from Ingham when bound for Cologne 26.2.43.
Z1602		To 1481Flt.
Z1748		From 12Sqn. FTR Lorient 13/14.2.43.
BJ582		From 57Sqn via 11 OTU. to 1481Flt.
BJ609		From 12Sqn. to 300Sqn.
BJ647		To 26 OTU.
BJ819		From 12Sqn. to 1481Flt.
BJ889		From 12Sqn. Crash-landed in Lincolnshire while training 28.1.43.
BJ916		From 142Sqn. to 1481Flt.
BJ960		From 12Sqn. to 29 OTU.
BJ991		From 101Sqn. to 30 OTU.
BK158	EX-G	Crashed in Lincolnshire during air-test 13.3.43.
BK300		From 150Sqn. to 18 OTU.
BK354		From 300Sqn. to CGS.
BK366		From 12Sqn. to 30 OTU.
BK367	EX-U	From 12Sqn. FTR from mining sortie 6/7.2.43.
BK507	EX-E	FTR Lorient 7/8.2.43.
BK509		To 30 OTU.
BK514	EX-T	FTR Turin 9/10.12.42.
BK541		To 1481Flt.
HE277	EX-Q	FTR Düsseldorf 11/12.6.43.

HE331		To 20 OTU.
HE345		To 305Sqn.
HE349		To 166Sqn.
HE424		To 82 OTU.
HE428		From 30 OTU. to 82 OTU.
HE462		From 30 OTU. to 20 OTU.
HE467		From 30 OTU. to 20 OTU.
HE470		From 196Sqn. to 20 OTU.
HE490		To 20 OTU.
HE495	EX-L	FTR from mining sortie 8/9.4.43.
HE519		FTR Essen 12/13.3.43.
HE634	EX-S	FTR Essen 27/28.5.43.
HE702	EX-Y	FTR Duisburg 12/13.5.43.
HE741		To 82 OTU.
HE787		To 82 OTU.
HE919		To 82 OTU.
HE920		Crashed on landing at Ingham while training 2.6.43.
HE921		To 18 OTU.
HE989		From 196Sqn. to 466Sqn.
HF452		To 305Sqn.
HF453		To 116Sqn.
HF487		To 300Sqn.
HF488	EX-U	FTR Düsseldorf 25/26.5.43.
HF489		To 166Sqn.
HF490		To 305Sqn.
HF590		To 300Sqn.
HF591		To 300Sqn.
HF596		To 166Sqn.
HF597	EX-Y	FTR from mining sortie 13/14.6.43.
HF598		To 300Sqn.
HZ259		From 300Sqn. to 17 OTU.
HZ262		To 20 OTU.
HZ263	EX-E	FTR Essen 12/13.3.43.

HZ277	From 425Sqn. FTR Düsseldorf 11/12.6.43.
HZ281	To 20 OTU.
HZ358	Crashed on landing at Ingham while training 28.5.43.
HZ582	FTR Dortmund 23/24.5.43.
LN406	From 30 OTU. to 20 OTU.

300 (MAZOWIECKI) SQUADRON

No motto: Code **BH**

Formed at Bramcote in Warwickshire on the 1st of July 1940, 300 Squadron was initially equipped with Battles, and, on joining 1 Group Bomber Command, carried out night operations against barge concentrations in Channel ports. Conversion to Wellingtons took place in October, and operations with the type continued until March 1944, when Lancasters arrived. By this time, the other Polish squadrons had been either disbanded or transferred to other commands, and it was left to 300 Squadron to carry the Polish flag in Bomber Command through to the end of hostilities.

STATIONS

BRAMCOTE	01.07.40. to 22.08.40.
SWINDERBY	22.08.40. to 18.07.41.
HEMSWELL	18.07.41. to 18.05.42.
INGHAM	18.05.42. to 31.01.43.
HEMSWELL	31.01.43. to 22.06.43.
INGHAM	22.06.43. to 01.03.44.
FALDINGWORTH	01.03.44. to 28.12.46.

COMMANDING OFFICERS

Wing Commander	K P Lewis (British Adviser)	
Wing Commander	W Makowski	01.07.40. to 18.07.41.
Wing Commander	S Cwynar Dfc	19.07.41. to 27.01.42.
Wing Commander	R Sulinski	27.01.42. to 09.07.42.
Wing Commander	W Dukszto	09.07.42. to 31.10.42.
Wing Commander	A Kropinski	31.10.42. to 04.05.43.
Wing Commander	M Kucharski	04.05.43. to 18.11.43.

Wing Commander	K Kuzian Dfc	18.11.43. to 18.01.44.
Wing Commander	A Kowalczyk	18.01.44. to 01.04.44.
Wing Commander	T Pozyczka	01.04.44. to 02.02.45.
Wing Commander	B Jarkowski	02.02.45. to 17.09.45.

AIRCRAFT

Battle	01.07.40. to 11.40.
Wellington IC	11.40. to 09.41.
Wellington IV	09.41. to 01.43.
Wellington III	01.43. to 04.43.
Wellington X	04.43. to 03.44.
Lancaster I/III	03.04.44. to 10.46.

OPERATIONAL RECORD

Operations	Sorties	Aircraft Losses	% Losses
468	3684	77	2.1%

CATEGORY OF OPERATIONS

Bombing	Mining
363	105

Battles

Operations	Sorties	Aircraft Losses	% Losses
7	47	0	0.0%

All bombing

Wellingtons

Operations	Sorties	Aircraft Losses	% Losses
323	2421	47	1.9%

CATEGORY OF OPERATIONS

Bombing	Mining
218	105

LANCASTERS

Operations	Sorties	Aircraft Losses	% Losses
138	1216	30	2.5%

All bombing

TABLE OF STATISTICS

Out of 59 Lancaster squadrons in Bomber Command.

37th highest number of Lancaster overall operations in Bomber Command.
44th highest number of Lancaster sorties in Bomber Command.
37th highest number of Lancaster operational losses in Bomber Command.

Out of 20 squadrons in 1 Group.

3rd highest number of overall operations in 1 Group.
7th highest number of sorties in 1 Group.
7th highest number of aircraft operational losses in 1 Group.

Out of 6 Battle squadrons in 1 Group.

Lowest number of Battle overall operations in 1 Group.
4th highest number of Battle sorties in 1 Group.
Lowest (equal with 150 and 301Sqns) number of Battle operational losses in 1 Group.

Out of 13 Wellington squadrons in 1 Group.

Highest number of Wellington overall operations in 1 Group.
Highest number of Wellington sorties in 1 Group.
4th highest number of Wellington operational losses in 1 Group.

Out of 14 Lancaster squadrons in 1 Group.

11th highest number of Lancaster overall operations in 1 Group.
11th highest number of Lancaster sorties in 1 Group.
11th highest number of Lancaster operational losses in 1 Group.

AIRCRAFT HISTORIES

BATTLE.		From July 1940 to October 1940.
L5317	BH-T	To RCAF 18.12.40.
L5318	BH-L	To RCAF 16.12.40.
L5353	BH-O/V	To RCAF 26.2.41.
L5356	BH-R	Crashed in Nottinghamshire while training 29.10.40.
L5365		From 234Sqn. to RCAF 18.12.40.

L5425	BH-B	To RAAF 15.1.41.
L5426	BH-L/W	To RCAF 5.2.41.
L5427	BH-K	To RCAF 13.5.41.
L5429	BH-V	To 304Sqn.
L5490	BH-F	To RCAF 28.11.40.
L5492	BH-M	To RCAF 18.12.40.
L5499	BH-M/Y	Crashed in Nottinghamshire on return from Calais 13.10.40.
L5529	BH-N/V	To RAAF 15.1.41.
L5530	BH-A	To RCAF 13.5.41.
L5532	BH-K/T	To 103Sqn.
L5537		To RCAF 26.2.41.
L5567	BH-S	To RCAF 5.2.41.
N2127	BH-H	To RCAF 16.12.40.
N2147	BH-Q	To RCAF 11.12.40.
N2241	BH-G	To RCAF 11.12.40.
P2309	BH-J	To RCAF 5.2.41.

WELLINGTON.		**From October 1940 to April 1944.**
L7789	BH-G	From 9Sqn. to 18 OTU and back. to 305Sqn.
L7817	BH-P	To 149Sqn.
L7873	BH-R/F	To 99Sqn.
P9228	BH-Y	From 9Sqn via RAE. to 22 OTU and back. to 5GpTF
R1035	BH-A	Crashed on approach to Swinderby on return from Antwerp 28.12.40.
R1061	BH-J	To 103Sqn.
R1178	BH-L	Ditched off Norfolk coast on return from Hamburg 26.7.41.
R1184	BH-B	FTR Cologne 10/11.7.41.
R1211	BH-T	To 21 OTU.
R1273	BH-H	Crashed almost immediately after take-off from Langham when bound for Berlin 23.3.41.
R1327	BH-W	To 18 OTU.
R1344	BH-L	To 103Sqn.

R1347	BH-D	To 103Sqn.
R1510	BH-H	Crashed at Hemswell while training 24.9.41.
R1610	BH-O	Crashed almost immediately after take-off from Hemswell while training 7.5.42.
R1617	BH-S	To 103Sqn.
R1620	BH-M	To 104 OTU.
R1640	BH-A	Ditched in North Sea on return from Bremen 29/30.6.41.
R1641	BH-Z	Crashed almost immediately after take-off from Hemswell when bound for Duisburg 18.8.41.
R1642	BH-X	FTR Bremen 3/4.7.41.
R1705	BH-U	FTR Mannheim 7/8.11.41.
R1715	BH-S/P	To 104 OTU.
R1725	BH-Q	FTR Essen 8/9.6.42.
R1795	BH-X/K	From 458Sqn. to 104 OTU.
R3212	BH-V	From 149Sqn. to 18 OTU.
T2574	BH-F/R	To 150Sqn.
T2608	BH-Q	To 21 OTU.
T2623	BH-K	To 21 OTU.
T2719	BH-M	Crashed on take-off from Langham when bound for Berlin 23.3.41.
T2886	BH-U	To 18 OTU.
W5665	BH-M	FTR Bremen 18/19.6.41.
W5666	BH-H	FTR Düsseldorf 11/12.6.41.
X3175	BH-L	To 150Sqn.
X3283	BH-M	From 150Sqn. to 1481Flt.
X3459	BH-B	From 150Sqn. to 1481Flt.
X3548	BH-N	From 150Sqn. to 83 OTU.
X9639	BH-E	FTR Hamburg 25/26.7.41.
X9676	BH-M	FTR Frankfurt 6/7.8.41.
X9815		To 150Sqn.
X9829		To 304Sqn.
Z1183	BH-J	From 458Sqn. FTR Hamburg 3/4.5.42.
Z1204	BH-V	From 301Sqn. FTR Bremen (301Sqn crew) 2/3.7.42.

Z1213	BH-H	FTR Essen 12/13.4.42.
Z1215	BH-E	To 301Sqn and back via 458Sqn. FTR Emden 19/20.6.42.
Z1220	BH-X/U	To 301Sqn.
Z1244	BH-R/E/B	SOC 14.7.44.
Z1245	BH-P	From 142Sqn. to 305Sqn.
Z1250	BH-N/K	FTR Kiel 13/14.10.42.
Z1255		From 301Sqn. Returned to 301Sqn.
Z1256	BH-Z/A	FTR Emden 19/20.6.42.
Z1258	BH-N	From 301Sqn. FTR Düsseldorf 10/11.9.42.
Z1264	BH-D	To A&AEE and back.
Z1265	BH-K	Crashed in Nottinghamshire on return from Hamburg 15/16.1.42.
Z1266	BH-J	To 142Sqn.
Z1267	BH-P	FTR Hamburg 17/18.4.42.
Z1268	BH-Q/T/N	To 18 OTU.
Z1269	BH-L	FTR Essen 26/27.3.42.
Z1270	BH-T	FTR Hamburg 26/27.7.42.
Z1271	BH-A	FTR Mannheim 7/8.11.41.
Z1275	BH-W	To 104 OTU.
Z1276	BH-Z/W	FTR Cologne 27/28.4.42.
Z1278		From 460Sqn. to 305Sqn.
Z1279	BH-Z/X	From 458Sqn. to 305Sqn.
Z1282	BH-F	Crashed while trying to land at Exeter on return from Brest 7.2.42.
Z1286	BH-P	From 142Sqn. to 301Sqn.
Z1288	BH-N	From 460Sqn. to 305Sqn.
Z1291	BH-F	From 458Sqn. Ditched in North Sea on return from Bremen 4.6.42.
Z1318	BH-L	From 18 OTU. to 301Sqn.
Z1320	BH-K	From 458Sqn. FTR Bremen 4/5.9.42.
Z1326	BH-B	Ditched in North Sea on return from Bremen 3.7.42.
Z1332	BH-D	To 104 OTU.

Z1343	BH-L	From 460Sqn. FTR from mining sortie 8/9.11.42.
Z1382	BH-V	To 104 OTU.
Z1387	BH-Q	FTR Lorient 14/15.1.43.
Z1398	BH-L/B/J	To 301Sqn.
Z1400	BH-K	From 460Sqn. to 104 OTU.
Z1401	BH-O	From 460Sqn. FTR Mannheim 6/7.12.42.
Z1407	BH-Z	To 104 OTU.
Z1409	BH-A	FTR Osnabrück 17/18.8.42.
Z1415	BH-X/E	To 305Sqn.
Z1419	BH-V	From 142Sqn. to 305Sqn.
Z1421	BH-V	FTR from mining sortie 3/4.11.42.
Z1465	BH-S	To 104 OTU.
Z1475	BH-X	FTR Cologne 15/16.10.42.
Z1488	BH-W	FTR Frankfurt 24/25.8.42.
Z1489	BH-J	Ditched in North Sea on return from Wilhelmshaven 9.7.42.
Z1490	BH-C	From 301Sqn. to 305Sqn.
Z1495	BH-J	From 460Sqn. FTR from intruder sortie to Essen 25.11.42.
Z1661	BH-Z	From 150Sqn. to 82 OTU.
Z8833	BH-B	To 150Sqn.
BJ581		From 142Sqn. to 23 OTU.
BJ609		From 199Sqn. Crash-landed in Lincolnshire while training 8.4.43.
BJ972	BH-S	From 150Sqn. to CGS.
BK150	BH-Q	From 199Sqn. FTR Essen 5/6.3.43.
BK196	BH-D	From 150Sqn. to 15 OTU.
BK236	BH-P	From 142Sqn. to CGS.
BK267	BH-O	From 150Sqn. to 148Sqn.
BK303	BH-Q	From 142Sqn. FTR from mining sortie 3/4.2.43.
BK305	BH-E	From 142Sqn. Crashed in Lincolnshire during air test 20.2.43.
BK354		To 199Sqn.
BK356	BH-G	To 30 OTU.

BK443	BH-V	To 30 OTU.
BK511	BH-X	From 150Sqn. FTR Hamburg 3/4.2.43.
BK516	BH-K	From 142Sqn. FTR from mining sortie 13/14.3.43.
HE147	BH-C	To 18 OTU.
HE148	BH-T	FTR Duisburg 8/9.4.43.
HE289	BH-A	To 18 OTU.
HE291	BH-V	FTR from mining sortie 22/23.4.43.
HE295	BH-P	FTR Duisburg 12/13.5.43.
HE327	BH-S	FTR Krefeld 21/22.6.43.
HE373	BH-E	From 16 OTU. to 11 OTU.
HE381	BH-X	From 30 OTU. to 23 OTU.
HE420	BH-T	To 18 OTU.
HE447	BH-ZY	To 18 OTU.
HE464	BH-J/F	From 30 OTU. to 166Sqn.
HE701	BH-U	To 23 OTU.
HE749	BH-O	To 166Sqn.
HE768	BH-B/N	FTR from mining sortie 15/16.8.43.
HE769	BH-B	To 12 OTU.
HE805	BH-C/W	To 1481Flt.
HE807	BH-O	Force-landed in Nottinghamshire when bound for Hamburg 3.8.43.
HE813	BH-E/L	From 305Sqn. to 12 OTU.
HE869	BH-D	To 11 OTU.
HE985	BH-C/W	FTR Krefeld 21/22.6.43.
HF480	BH-V	To 11 OTU.
HF487	BH-S	From 199Sqn. to 11 OTU.
HF490	BH-O	From 305Sqn. FTR from mining sortie 7/8.10.43.
HF590	BH-X	From 199Sqn. Crashed on landing at Ingham on return from mining sortie 8.10.43.
HF591	BH-B	From 199Sqn. Crashed in Lincolnshire during air-test 21.6.43.
HF598	BH-E/M	From 199Sqn. Crashed in Lincolnshire during an air test 19.12.43.

HF605	BH-P	FTR Hamburg 2/3.8.43.
HF606	BH-C	FTR Wuppertal 24/25.6.43.
HZ259		To 199Sqn.
HZ373	BH-A	To 11 OTU.
HZ374	BH-K	FTR Dortmund 23/24.5.43.
HZ375	BH-Q/N	To 11 OTU.
HZ376	BH-G	FTR Wuppertal 24/25.6.43.
HZ438	BH-J	FTR Cologne 28/29.6.43.
HZ439	BH-V	To 18 OTU.
HZ484		From 466Sqn. to 432Sqn.
HZ486	BH-Z	From 466Sqn. FTR Essen 25/26.7.43.
JA116	BH-Q	FTR Mönchengladbach 30/31.8.43.
JA117	BH-F	FTR from mining sortie 20/21.2.44.
JA129	BH-T	From 166Sqn. to 1481Flt.
JA451	BH-J	From 432Sqn. to 16 OTU.
LN242	BH-L/D	To 12 OTU.
LN297	BH-T/P	To 11 OTU.
LN298	BH-B	To 11 OTU.
LN299	BH-G	To 11 OTU.
LN390	BH-C	From 305Sqn. to 18 OTU.
LN391	BH-P	From 305Sqn. to 16 OTU.
LN393	BH-A	FTR from mining sortie 11/12.11.43.
LN507	BH-K	To 16 OTU.
LN508	BH-U	Crash-landed in Warwickshire when bound for mining sortie 7.11.43.
LN544	BH-O	To 26 OTU.
LN552	BH-D	From 166Sqn via 1481Flt. to 82 OTU.
LN553	BH-W	From 166Sqn via 1481Flt. to 16 OTU.
LN555	BH-Z	To 14 OTU.
LN600	BH-L/E	To 14 OTU.
LN697	BH-U	To 14 OTU.
LN707	BH-R	Crashed on landing at Ingham on return from mining sortie 15.1.44.
LP230		To 16 OTU.

LANCASTER.		**From April 1944.**
L7541		From 550Sqn. to 1LFS.
R5866		From 1LFS. to 1LFS.
W4241		From 1LFS. No operations. to 1LFS.
W4376	BH-A/O	From 166Sqn. to 1LFS.
W4821		From 103Sqn via 1656CU & 1LFS. to 1LFS.
DV165		From 1667CU. Training only. to 1LFS.
DV278	BH-A	From 625Sqn. FTR Falaise 14.8.44.
DV282	BH-I/P	FTR Aachen 27/28.5.44.
DV286	BH-C	From 44Sqn. FTR Gelsenkirchen 12/13.6.44.
ED327	BH-H/R	From 166Sqn. FTR Stettin 29/30.8.44.
ED382	BH-H	From 625Sqn. to 1LFS.
ED749	BH-S	From 100Sqn. to 1LFS.
ED779	BH-L	From 57Sqn. to 1LFS.
ED814	BH-N	From 625Sqn. FTR Vierzon 30.6/1.7.44.
EE124	BH-M	From 50Sqn. Crashed in Faldingworth circuit on return from a flying bomb site at les Hayons 24.6.44.
HK541		To 75Sqn.
JA683	BH-S	From 460Sqn. FTR Gelsenkirchen 12/13.6.44.
JA922	BH-J	From 626Sqn. to 1LFS.
JB559		From 626Sqn. to 1LFS.
JB561	BH-B	From 12Sqn. FTR Rüsselsheim 25/26.8.44.
JB646	BH-T	From 626Sqn. to 1656CU.
JB661		From 7Sqn. to 626Sqn.
LL798	BH-V	From 626Sqn. to 1LFS.
LL804	BH-F	From 115Sqn. to 1660CU.
LL807	BH-N/K	FTR Gelsenkirchen 12/13.6.44.
LL855	BH-G	FTR Karlsruhe 24/25.4.44.
LL856	BH-E/O/E	To 6LFS.
LL857	BH-B	Crashed while landing at Faldingworth following early return from Dortmund 23.5.44.
LL947	BH-W	FTR Stettin 29/30.8.44.
LL959		To 625Sqn.

LM141	BH-D	From 460Sqn. FTR Gelsenkirchen 6.11.44.
LM160		From 186Sqn. to 626Sqn.
LM172	BH-Q	FTR Rüsselsheim 25/26.8.44.
LM178	BH-U	FTR Stuttgart 24/25.7.44.
LM486	BH-C	FTR Karlsruhe 24/25.4.44.
LM487	BH-J	FTR Dortmund 22/23.5.44.
LM488	BH-D	FTR Kiel 23/24.7.44.
LM632	BH-O	From 626Sqn. FTR Kiel 9/10.4.45.
ME470	BH-F	
ME546	BH-I	
ME549	BH-M	
ME594	BH-B	From 625Sqn. Crashed while landing Faldingworth during training 23.7.44.
ME648	BH-A	From 100Sqn. to 166Sqn.
ME671	BH-B	From 103Sqn. to 576Sqn.
ME744	BH-P/V/P	From 460Sqn. FTR Wiesbaden 2/3.2.45.
ME780		To 625Sqn.
ME847	BH-Z	From 101Sqn. to 15Sqn.
ND861		From 460Sqn. to 103Sqn.
ND863		From 460Sqn. to 625Sqn.
ND984	BH-P	FTR Stuttgart 24/25.7.44.
NF925		To 12Sqn.
NF959	BH-R	FTR Duisburg 14.10.44.
NG265	BH-V	
NG266	BH-L	FTR Pforzheim 23/24.2.45.
NG269	BH-G/K	
NG283	BH-W	
NG501	BH-U	FTR Cologne 2.3.45.
NN718	BH-A	From 514Sqn. Force-landed at Brussels-Melsbroek airfield in Belgium during Operation Exodus.
NN746	BH-N	
NN748	BH-G	

PA160	BH-E	Crashed on approach to Faldingworth on return from Leuna 15.1.45.
PA161	BH-X	FTR Pforzheim 23/24.2.45.
PA163	BH-M	FTR Stettin 29/30.8.44.
PA185	BH-W	Collided with NF932 (550Sqn) when bound for Dresden 13.2.45.
PA220	BH-P	
PA233	BH-J	
PA261	BH-L	
PA262	BH-X	
PA269	BH-U	
PB171	BH-K	FTR Scholven-Buer 18/19.7.44.
PB252	BH-M	FTR Stuttgart 25/26.7.44.
PB705	BH-B	
PB722	BH-B/J	FTR Dortmund 20/21.2.45.
PB730	BH-R	
PB823	BH-T	FTR Nuremberg 2/3.1.45.
PB846	BH-K	From 12Sqn. FTR Stuttgart 28/29.1.45.
PB854	BH-I	FTR Cologne 2.3.45.
PD204		From 625Sqn. Returned to 625Sqn.
PD207		To 12Sqn.
PD257	BH-O	FTR Zeitz 16/17.1.45.
PD270		From 12Sqn.
PD361	BH-H	From 12Sqn.
PD379	BH-S	
PD383	BH-Z	
PD387	BH-D	
RF242	BH-T	
RF262	BH-R	
SW279	BH-E	From 626Sqn.

301 (POMORSKI) SQUADRON

No motto: Code **GR**

Formed on the 26th of July 1940, 301 Squadron was the second Polish unit to form in Bomber Command. Equipped with Battles the squadron began operations against barge concentrations in Channel ports in September. In October conversion took place to Wellingtons, and operations with the type continued until the end of March 1943, when a shortage of Polish recruits led to its disbandment, and the transfer of most of its personnel to 300 Squadron.

STATIONS

BRAMCOTE	26.07.40. to 28.08.40.
SWINDERBY	28.08.40. to 18.07.41.
HEMSWELL	18.07.41. to 07.04.43.

COMMANDING OFFICERS

Squadron Leader	C G Skinner (British Adviser)	
Wing Commander	R Rudkowski	22.07.40. to 27.07.41.
Wing Commander	W J Piotrowski	27.07.41. to 01.04.42.
Wing Commander	S Krzystyniak	01.04.42. to 26.06.42.
Wing Commander	M Brzozowski	26.06.42. to 03.07.42.
Wing Commander	H Kolodziejek	04.07.42. to 25.09.42.
Wing Commander	A Dabrowa	25.09.42. to 07.04.43.

AIRCRAFT

Battle	24.07.40. to 11.40.
Wellington IC	10.40. to 08.41.
Wellington IV	08.41. to 04.43.

OPERATIONAL RECORD

Operations	Sorties	Aircraft Losses	% Losses
250	1260	29	2.3%

CATEGORY OF OPERATIONS

Bombing	Mining	Leaflet
198	51	1

Battles

Operations	Sorties	Aircraft Losses	% Losses
8	40	0	0.0%

All bombing

Wellingtons

Operations	Sorties	Aircraft Losses	% Losses
242	1220	29	2.4%

CATEGORY OF OPERATIONS

Bombing	Mining	Leaflet
190	51	1

TABLE OF STATISTICS

Out of 20 squadrons in 1 Group.

9th highest number of overall operations in 1 Group.
13th highest number of sorties in 1 Group.
15th highest number of aircraft operational losses in 1 Group.

Out of 6 Battle squadrons in 1 Group.

4th (equal with 12Sqn) highest number of overall Battle operations in 1 Group.
5th highest number of Battle sorties in 1 Group.
Lowest (equal with 150 and 300Sqns) number of Battle operational losses.

Out of 13 Wellington squadrons in 1 Group.

2nd highest number of Wellington overall operations in 1 Group.
4th highest number of Wellington sorties in 1 Group.
8th highest number of Wellington operational losses in 1 Group.

AIRCRAFT HISTORIES

BATTLE.		From July 1940 to November 1940.
K9247		From 88Sqn. to 103Sqn.
L5048	GR-F	From 304Sqn. to RCAF 4.5.41 via 9MU.
L5075		To 18 OTU.
L5193		From 218Sqn. to RCAF 16.12.40.
L5237		From 103Sqn. to RCAF 7.3.41.
L5316	GR-L	To RCAF 16.12.40 via 47MU.

L5351	GR-N	Crashed in Norfolk when bound for Boulogne 24/25.9.40.
L5392	GR-M	To RCAF 11.6.41 via 47MU.
L5445	GR-R	To RCAF 28.5.41 via 27MU.
L5448	GR-K	To RCAF 28.5.41 via 47MU.
L5449	GR-P	To RCAF 18.12.40 via 47MU.
L5535	GR-Q	To Farnborough.
L5536	GR-S	To RCAF 16.12.40 via 47MU.
L5549	GR-J	To SAAF 16.2.41via 27MU.
L5551	GR-B	To RAAF 18.2.41 via 27MU.
L5555	GR-H	To RCAF 16.12.40 via 47MU.
L5556	GR-G	To RCAF 17.3.41 via 27MU.
L5557		To RCAF 16.12.40.
L5575	GR-A	To RCAF 26.2.41 via 27MU.
L5597	GR-C	Crashed near Bramcote while training 8.8.40.
N2189		From 142Sqn. to RCAF 16.12.40.
P6567	GR-E	To RCAF via 27MU.
P6569	GR-D	To RCAF 16.12.40 via 47MU.

WELLINGTON.		**From October 1940 to March 1943.**
L7819	GR-P	To 103Sqn.
L7874	GR-S	Crashed on landing at Swinderby while training 21.3.41.
N3013	GR-Z	From 99Sqn. to 25 OTU.
P9214	GR-X	From 214Sqn via 15 OTU. to CCDU.
R1006	GR-H	To 21 OTU.
R1026	GR-R	Crashed in Nottinghamshire on return from Bremen 23.6.41.
R1047	GR-J	To 17 OTU.
R1064	GR-A	To 304Sqn.
R1065		To 11 OTU.
R1227	GR-M	FTR Bremen 8/9.5.41.
R1235		To 18 OTU.
R1236		To 18 OTU.

R1274	GR-F	To 103Sqn.
R1340	GR-C	
R1348	GR-O	Crashed at Swinderby on return from Osnabrück 13.6.41, and collided on the ground with GR-K.
R1349	GR-N	To 12 OTU.
R1365	GR-D	FTR Bremen 18/19.6.41.
R1366	GR-L	To 27 OTU.
R1373	GR-L	FTR Bremen 29/30.6.41.
R1390	GR-K/R/E	FTR Emden 6/7.6.42.
R1459	GR-J	To 103Sqn.
R1490	GR-F/T	From 458Sqn. to 142Sqn and back via 18 OTU. to 305Sqn.
R1492	GR-M	FTR Bremen 3/4.7.41.
R1520	GR-L/W/O	To 305Sqn and back. to 305Sqn.
R1525	GR-E	To 305Sqn.
R1535	GR-A/C/J/G	Crashed in Northumberland on return from mining sortie 9.1.43.
R1585	GR-M/F	FTR from mining sortie 11/12.10.42.
R1590	GR-H	FTR Essen 26/27.3.42.
R1592		From 305Sqn. to 150Sqn.
R1615	GR-G	FTR Essen 2/3.6.42.
R1616	GR-G	To 27 OTU.
R1619	GR-U	Crashed on landing at Swinderby while training 26.4.41.
R1650	GR-C/G	To 460Sqn.
R1667	GR-D	From 305Sqn. to 103Sqn.
R1796	GR-U	To 17 OTU and back. to 18 OTU.
T2517	GR-A	Shot down by intruder near Digby on return from Bremen 1.1.41.
T2518	GR-K	Shot down by intruder at Wellingore on return from Bremen 2.1.41.
T2576	GR-G/D	Crashed immediately after take-off from Hemswell while training 25.7.41.
T2625	GR-B	FTR Hamburg 8/9.8.41.
T2850	GR-E	To 99Sqn.

T2921	GR-H	To 103Sqn.
W5613	GR-S	To 18 OTU.
W5690	GR-W	To 103Sqn.
W5714		To 15 OTU.
W5715		From 101Sqn. Returned to 101Sqn.
X3163	GR-K	To RAE.
X9616	GR-T	To 115Sqn.
X9661	GR-N	To 15 OTU.
X9665	GR-K	To 103Sqn.
X9666	GR-H	To 103Sqn.
X9679	GR-L	To 149Sqn.
Z1204	GR-V	From 458Sqn. to 300Sqn.
Z1215		From 300Sqn. to 458Sqn.
Z1216		From 142Sqn. to 460CF.
Z1217	GR-W	FTR Bremen 21/22.10.41.
Z1219	GR-G	From 458Sqn. to 142Sqn.
Z1220		From 300Sqn. to 142Sqn.
Z1252	GR-T	Force-landed in Norfolk on return from Essen 12/13.4.42.
Z1253	GR-B	To 18 OTU.
Z1255	GR-D/Z	To 300Sqn and back. FTR from mining sortie 8/9.10.42.
Z1257	GR-J	FTR Kiel 12/13.3.42.
Z1258	GR-F	To 300Sqn.
Z1259	GR-O	To 460Sqn.
Z1260	GR-N/T	To A&AEE and back. to 305Sqn.
Z1262	GR-R	FTR Essen 26/27.3.42.
Z1263	GR-P	To 305Sqn.
Z1272		From 458Sqn. to 305Sqn.
Z1273	GR-T	From 458Sqn. to 305Sqn.
Z1277	GR-Z	FTR Mannheim 7/8.11.41.
Z1280		From 458Sqn. to 18 OTU.
Z1284	GR-K	From 460Sqn. to 305Sqn.

Z1285	GR-S	Shot down by intruder off Lincolnshire coast on return from Münster 22/23.1.42.
Z1286	GR-G	From 300Sqn. to 305Sqn.
Z1314	GR-M	FTR Bremen 2/3.7.42.
Z1317	GR-U	FTR Rostock 26/27.4.42.
Z1318	GR-L	From 300Sqn. Crash-landed at Langar on return from Lorient 26.1.43.
Z1322	GR-U	From TFU. to 305Sqn.
Z1329	GR-Z	SOC 1.11.44.
Z1331	GR-C	FTR Essen 5/6.6.42.
Z1333	GR-L	From 458Sqn. FTR Essen 10/11.4.42.
Z1336	GR-A/T/J	To 104 OTU.
Z1337	GR-O	Abandoned over Devon on return from Mannheim 6/7.12.42.
Z1340	GR-C	From 142Sqn. to 305Sqn.
Z1345	GR-D	FTR Emden 22/23.6.42.
Z1375	GR-R	To 104 OTU.
Z1377	GR-F	From 458Sqn. FTR Kiel 25/26.2.42.
Z1379	GR-J	FTR Dortmund 14/15.4.42.
Z1384	GR-D	From 460Sqn. to 305Sqn.
Z1385	GR-F	To 460Sqn.
Z1386	GR-P	FTR from mining sortie 5/6.8.42.
Z1389	GR-C	To 305Sqn.
Z1390	GR-J	To 142Sqn.
Z1397	GR-A	Crashed on landing at Hibaldstow, Lincolnshire on return from Hamburg 15.1.42.
Z1398	GR-J	From 300Sqn. to 305Sqn.
Z1402	GR-O	To 18 OTU.
Z1403	GR-A	To 305Sqn.
Z1405	GR-T	FTR Duisburg 21/22.7.42.
Z1406	GR-G	FTR Duisburg 21/22.7.42.
Z1423	GR-M	To 305Sqn.
Z1460	GR-I	To 305Sqn.
Z1464		From 460Sqn. to 305Sqn.

Z1467	GR-L	FTR Essen 5/6.6.42.
Z1468	GR-I	Crash-landed in Lincolnshire on return from Dortmund 15.4.42.
Z1471	GR-O	To 305Sqn.
Z1472	GR-H	FTR from air-sea rescue sortie 22.7.42.
Z1474	GR-B/D/R	To 305Sqn.
Z1479	GR-A	FTR Bremen 25/26.6.42.
Z1490		To 300Sqn and back via 305Sqn & 18 OTU. to 104 OTU.
Z1491	GR-Z	FTR Saarbrücken 28/29.8.42.
Z1492	GR-G	To 104 OTU.
Z1493	GR-H	To 104 OTU.

304 (SLASKI) SQUADRON

No motto: Code **NZ**

Formed at Bramcote in August 1940, 301 Squadron was initially equipped with Fairy Battles, but no operations were carried out before re-equipment took place with Wellingtons in November. In the event it was April 1941 before operations began, and these continued until May 1942, at which time the squadron was transferred to Coastal Command.

STATIONS

BRAMCOTE	22.08.40. to 02.12.40.
SYERSTON	02.12.40. to 19.07.41.
LINDHOLME	19.07.41. to 10.05.42.

COMMANDING OFFICERS

Wing Commander	W M Graham (British Adviser)	
Wing Commander	J Bialy	22.08.40. to 20.12.40.
Wing Commander	P Dudzinski	20.12.40. to 12.11.41.
Wing Commander	S Poziomek	12.11.41. to 16.08.42.

AIRCRAFT

Battle	22.08.40. to 11.40.

Wellington IC   11.40. to 07.43.

OPERATIONAL RECORD

Operations	Sorties	Aircraft Losses	% Losses
100	464	18	3.9%

CATEGORY OF OPERATIONS

Bombing	Leaflet
99	1

TABLE OF STATISTICS

Out of 20 squadrons in 1 Group.

16th highest number of overall operations in 1 Group.
19th highest number of sorties in 1 Group.
17th highest number of aircraft operational losses in 1 Group.

Out of 13 Wellington squadrons in 1 Group.

8th highest number of overall Wellington operations in 1 Group.
11th highest number of Wellington sorties in 1 Group.
10th highest number of Wellington operational losses in 1 Group.

AIRCRAFT HISTORIES

WELLINGTON.		**From November 1940 to May 1942.**
L7789		From 305Sqn. to 1481Flt.
N2840		Shot down by intruder near Newark on return from Rotterdam 18.7.41.
N2852	NZ-D	FTR Emden 20/21.10.41.
N2989		Crashed on landing at Docking 13.5.43.
N2899		From 115Sqn. Crashed 7.5.42.
P9289		From 15 OTU. to 20 OTU.
R1002		Crash-landed on approach to Langham, Norfolk on return from Bremen 15.7.41.
R1003		To 27 OTU.

R1014		Crashed immediately after take-off from Syerston during training 6.2.41.
R1064		From 301Sqn. FTR Ostend 16/17.12.41.
R1212		Crashed while landing at Syerston during training 15.4.41.
R1215	NZ-M	FTR Mannheim 7/8.11.41.
R1230	NZ-E	FTR Essen 10/11.4.42.
R1232		To 18 OTU.
R1245	NZ-Q	From RAE. to 105 OTU.
R1268	NZ-T	Crashed in Co Durham while training 14.12.40.
R1392	NZ-N	Crashed in Sussex on return from Boulogne 28.5.41.
R1413	NZ-J	Posted with squadron to Coastal Command 7.5.42.
R1443		FTR le Havre 6/7.5.41.
R1473		FTR Bremen 8/9.5.41.
R1504		From 25 OTU. to 7 OTU.
R1602		Damaged beyond repair 10.3.42.
R1657	NZ-H	From 23 OTU. Became ground instruction machine.
R1660	NZ-A	To 15 OTU.
R1697	NZ-S	From 305Sqn. to 30 OTU.
R1704	NZ-P	Posted with squadron to Coastal Command 7.5.42.
R1761		Crashed while landing at Madley during training 19.8.41.
R3215		From 18 OTU. to Warwick Training Unit.
T5631		To 248Sqn.
W5627	NZ-B	From 214Sqn. FTR Cologne 27/28.4.42.
W5668		To 311Sqn.
W5688	NZ-G	To 18 OTU.
W5718		From 40Sqn. to 3 OTU.
W5720	NZ-Q	Ditched in North Sea on return from Hamburg 27.10.41.
X3164		Ditched off Cromer on return from Hamburg

		30.11.41.
X9620		FTR Emden 24/25.7.41.
X9664	NZ-L	From 305Sqn. to 311Sqn.
X9680	NZ-J	From 305Sqn. to 14 OTU.
X9687		From 15 OTU. FTR Essen 12/13.4.42.
X9764		From 75Sqn. FTR Cologne 5/6.4.42.
X9827		To 311Sqn.
X9829	NZ-O	From 300Sqn. FTR Rostock 23/24.4.42.
X9831		From 1505BAT Flt.
Z1072	NZ-G	From 150Sqn. Posted with squadron to Coastal Command 7.5.42.
Z1082		FTR Wilhelmshaven 10/11.1.42.
Z1088	NZ-D	FTR Cologne 27/28.4.42.
Z1112	NZ-M	To 3 OTU.
Z1172	NZ-V	Posted with Squadron to Coastal Command 7.5.42.
DV423		FTR Wilhelmshaven 10/11.1.42.
DV437	NZ-H	Crash-landed in Cambridgeshire on return from Essen 13.4.42.
DV441	NZ-Q	Posted with squadron to Coastal Command 7.5.42.
DV558		From 150Sqn. to 105 OTU.
DV594	NZ-D	From 150Sqn. to 3 OTU.
DV597	NZ-T	To 7 OTU.
DV735		From 214Sqn via 16 OTU. to 3 OTU.
DV759		From 57Sqn via 18 OTU. to 3 OTU.
DV820		To 3 OTU.
DV920		To 3 OTU.
HF836	NZ-E	To 7 OTU.

305 (WIELKOPOLSKA) SQUADRON

No motto: Code **SM**

Formed at Bramcote late in August 1940 305 Squadron was initially equipped with Battles, but carried out no operations before trading them in for Wellingtons in November. Operations began in April 1941 under the banner of 1 Group Bomber Command, and these continued until August 1943, at which point the Squadron was transferred to the 2TAF for daylight bombing.

STATIONS

BRAMCOTE	29.08.40. to 04.12.40.
SYERSTON	04.12.40. to 20.07.41.
LINDHOLME	20.07.41. to 23.07.42.
HEMSWELL	23.07.42. to 22.06.43.
INGHAM	22.06.43. to 05.09.43.

COMMANDING OFFICERS

Wing Commander	J K M Drysdale (British Adviser)	
Wing Commander	J Jankowski	29.08.40. to 29.03.41.
Wing Commander	B Kleczynski	29.03.41. to 08.08.41.
Wing Commander	R Beill	08.08.41. to 21.06.42.
Wing Commander	K Sniegula	21.06.42. to 17.01.43.
Wing Commander	T Czolowski	17.01.43. to 28.07.43.
Wing Commander	K Konopasek	28.07.43. to 01.08.44.

AIRCRAFT

Battle	29.08.40. to 11.40.
Wellington IC	11.40. to 07.41.
Wellington II	07.41. to 08.42.
Wellington IV	08.42. to 05.43.
Wellington X	05.43. to 09.43.

OPERATIONAL RECORD

Operations	Sorties	Aircraft Losses	% Losses
211	1063	30	2.8%

CATEGORY OF OPERATIONS

Bombing	Mining
160	51

TABLE OF STATISTICS

Out of 20 squadrons in 1 Group.

10th highest number of overall operations in 1 Group.
15th highest number of sorties in 1 Group.
14th highest number of aircraft operational losses in 1 Group.

Out of 13 Wellington squadrons in 1 Group.

3rd highest number of overall Wellington operations in 1 Group.
7th highest number of Wellington sorties in 1 Group.
7th highest number of Wellington operational losses in 1 Group.

AIRCRAFT HISTORIES

WELLINGTON.		From November 1940 to September 1943.
L4262		From 9Sqn via 11 OTU. to 15 OTU.
L7789		From 300Sqn. to 304Sqn.
L7869		To 214Sqn.
L7886	SM-B	To 103Sqn.
N2875		From 115Sqn. to 11 OTU.
P2519		From 214Sqn via 15 OTU. to 27 OTU.
P2531		From 214Sqn. to CGS.
P9216		From 37Sqn via 11 OTU. to 27 OTU.
R1016	SM-A	To 150Sqn.
R1017	SM-K	Crashed in Nottinghamshire following mid-air collision while training 12.6.41.
R1019	SM-L	To 12 OTU.
R1213	SM-D	To 103Sqn.
R1214	SM-N	FTR Emden 2/3.5.41.
R1228	SM-E	To 311Sqn.
R1322	SM-F	FTR Bremen 8/9.5.41.
R1332		To TFU.
R1409		To 15 OTU.
R1490	SM-M	From 301Sqn. to 104 OTU.

R1520		From 301Sqn. Returned to 301Sqn and back. to 104 OTU.
R1525	SM-S	From 301Sqn. to 104 OTU.
R1530	SM-A	From 460Sqn. to 104 OTU.
R1592	SM-R	To 301Sqn.
R1667	SM-E	To 301Sqn.
R1696	SM-F	FTR Bremen 18/19.6.41.
R1697	SM-J	To 304Sqn.
R1762	SM-G	FTR Osnabrück 9/10.7.41.
T2506	SM-M	To 103Sqn.
T2960	SM-O	To 150Sqn.
W5359	SM-P	From 142Sqn. to 1443Flt.
W5370	SM-V	From 142Sqn. to OAPU.
W5374	SM-J	From 142Sqn. Crashed in Northamptonshire on return from Cologne 23.12.41
W5420	SM-D	To 1446Flt.
W5423	SM-R	From 142Sqn. FTR Kiel 26/27.2.42.
W5428		From 12Sqn. to 1446Flt.
W5447	SM-H	From 218Sqn. to 12Sqn and back. to 1446Flt.
W5453	SM-E	From 104Sqn. to 1443Flt.
W5455	SM-L	From 142Sqn. to 1446Flt.
W5463	SM-E	FTR Cologne 16/17.8.41.
W5478		To 1443Flt.
W5515		From 405Sqn. to 1446Flt.
W5519	SM-U	Ditched off Cromer on return from Essen 11.4.42.
W5526	SM-J	From 218Sqn. FTR le Havre 15/16.9.41.
W5529	SM-W	From 99Sqn. Crashed while landing at Lindholme following air-test 3.10.41.
W5533	SM-T	To 1446Flt.
W5550	SM-C	From 405Sqn. to 1443Flt.
W5557	SM-G	Crashed on approach to Lindholme on return from Cologne 27.9.41.
W5563	SM-Q	Ditched off Kent coast following early return from Frankfurt 2/3.9.41.

W5566	SM-H	From 115Sqn. Crashed while trying to land at Lindholme on return from Hamburg 18.4.42.
W5567	SM-M	From 149Sqn. FTR Lübeck 28/29.3.42.
W5573	SM-O	From 149Sqn. Crashed near Blyton on return from Stuttgart 6.5.42.
W5579	SM-L	FTR Dunkerque 16/17.10.41.
W5590	SM-A	Ditched in North Sea on return from Hamburg 4.5.42.
W5591	SM-B	Crashed while trying to land at Lindholme whilst in transit 16.10.41.
W5592	SM-N	To 1446Flt.
W5593	SM-P	FTR Frankfurt 5/6.8.41.
W5721	SM-H	To 150Sqn.
W5722	SM-N	To 150Sqn.
W5723	SM-F	Abandoned off Essex coast on return from Boulogne 24/25.6.41.
W5726	SM-Q	FTR Bremen 14/15.7.41.
X3939		From 166Sqn. to 30 OTU.
X9664	SM-K	To 304Sqn.
X9680		To 304Sqn.
X9683	SM-P	To 150Sqn.
Z1245	SM-D	From 300Sqn. FTR Kassel 27/28.8.42.
Z1248	SM-K	From A&AEE.
Z1260	SM-B	From 301Sqn. to 104 OTU.
Z1263		From 301Sqn. to 104 OTU.
Z1264	SM-D	From 300Sqn. to 104 OTU.
Z1272	SM-N	From 301Sqn. Crashed in Lincolnshire during mining sortie to Brest 13.1.43.
Z1273	SM-P	From 301Sqn. to 104 OTU.
Z1278	SM-F	From 300Sqn. Ditched off Sussex coast on return from Mannheim 6/7.12.42.
Z1279	SM-O	From 300Sqn. FTR from mining sortie 31.10/1.11.42.
Z1281	SM-K	From 142Sqn. FTR Saarbrücken 28/29.8.42.
Z1284		From 301Sqn. to 104 OTU.

Z1286	SM-G	From 301Sqn. SOC 23.1.44.
Z1288	SM-L	From 300Sqn. Ditched in North Sea during early return from Wilhelmshaven 19.2.43.
Z1322		From 301Sqn. to 104 OTU.
Z1340	SM-L	From 301Sqn. to Leconfield.
Z1378	SM-G	To 104 OTU.
Z1384		From 301Sqn. to 104 OTU.
Z1389		From 301Sqn. SOC 1.11.44.
Z1392	SM-O	From 142Sqn. FTR Hamburg 3/4.2.43.
Z1393	SM-W	From 142Sqn. Crashed on take-off from Hemswell for air test 19.12.42.
Z1395		From 460Sqn. to 104 OTU.
Z1398	SM-C	From 301Sqn. Became ground instruction machine.
Z1403	SM-A/O	From 301Sqn. to 104 OTU.
Z1415	SM-N	From 300Sqn. FTR from mining sortie 29/30.1.43.
Z1419	SM-X	From 300Sqn. to 104 OTU.
Z1423		From 301Sqn. SOC 24.3.44.
Z1459		From 142Sqn. SOC 1.7.44.
Z1460	SM-N	From 301Sqn. to 104 OTU.
Z1464		From 301Sqn. to 104 OTU.
Z1471	SM-O	From 301Sqn. FTR from mining sortie 20/21.8.42.
Z1473	SM-O	From 460Sqn. to 104 OTU.
Z1474		From 301Sqn. to 104 OTU.
Z1476	SM-F	From 460Sqn. FTR from mining sortie 23/24.9.42.
Z1481	SM-D	To 104 OTU.
Z1490	SM-M	From 300Sqn. to 18 OTU.
Z1496	SM-S	FTR from mining sortie 19/20.11.42.
Z8339	SM-N	From 142Sqn. FTR Emden 19/20.6.42.
Z8343	SM-S	From 142Sqn. to 311 FTU.
Z8372	SM-Q	Destroyed by fire after landing at Stradishall on return from Hannover 26.1.42.

Z8399	SM-N	From 218Sqn. SOC 20.4.44.
Z8406	SM-G	FTR Hamburg 3/4.5.42.
Z8416	SM-E	To Manufacturers.
Z8422	SM-V	From 15 OTU. to 1446Flt.
Z8425	SM-K	To 1446Flt.
Z8427	SM-W	Crashed near Lindholme on return from Ostend 16.12.41.
Z8435	SM-F	To 12Sqn.
Z8438	SM-B	Crashed on landing at Lindholme on return from Cologne 14.3.42.
Z8495		From 75Sqn. to 12Sqn.
Z8513		To 1443Flt.
Z8519	SM-M	To Christchurch.
Z8523	SM-N	From 158Sqn. to 12Sqn.
Z8528	SM-R	From 158Sqn. Ditched in North Sea on return from Bremen 25/26.6.42.
Z8537	SM-Y	Ditched off Yorkshire coast on return from Emden 20/21.6.42.
Z8581	SM-W	To TFU.
Z8583	SM-Z	Crashed in Norfolk on return from Essen 2.6.42.
Z8586	SM-W	Crash-landed near Lindholme on return from Dortmund 15.4.42.
Z8587	SM-G	To 12Sqn.
Z8595	SM-W	From 158Sqn. to 12Sqn.
Z8596	SM-A	From 405Sqn. to 1443Flt.
Z8597	SM-C	From 158Sqn. to 1443Flt.
Z8599	SM-R	FTR Stuttgart 5/6.5.42.
Z8601	SM-M	Ditched off Suffolk coast on return from Essen 6.6.42.
Z8645	SM-Q	Crashed in Yorkshire during air-test 2.5.42.
BJ705	SM-G	From 166Sqn. to 18 OTU.
LN390	SM-U	To 300Sqn.
LN391	SM-P	To 300Sqn.
HE345	SM-P	From 199Sqn. Crash-landed near Ingham while training 11.7.43.

HE347	SM-F	FTR Krefeld 21/22.6.43.
HE594	SM-J	From 424Sqn. Crashed on approach to Hemswell while training 10.6.43.
HE689	SM-H	From 424Sqn. to 22 OTU.
HE691	SM-K	From 424Sqn. to 83 OTU.
HE705	SM-A	From 424Sqn. to 17 OTU.
HE813		From 166Sqn. to 300Sqn.
HE986	SM-D	To 1481Flt.
HF452	SM-J	From 199Sqn. to 1481Flt.
HF463	SM-A	To 1481Flt.
HF472	SM-S	Crash-landed in Lincolnshire on return from Hamburg 25.7.43.
HF490	SM-O	From 199Sqn. to 300Sqn.
HF491	SM-L	To 1481Flt.
HF492	SM-M	Crashed in Lincolnshire while training 25.5.43.
HF570		To 84 OTU.
HZ372	SM-E	From 420Sqn. to 27 OTU.
HZ467	SM-C	FTR Hamburg 2/3.8.43.
MS495	SM-B	To 17 OTU.

458 SQUADRON

Motto: **We Find And Destroy**   Code **FU**

Formed in New South Wales Australia in July 1941, 458 Squadron was the second Australian unit to arrive in Bomber Command. It eventually found its way to 1 Group, where it began to operate on Wellingtons in October of that year. Its time with Bomber Command was cut short by a posting to the Middle East in February 1942.

STATIONS

Holme-On-Spalding Moor   25.08.41. to 22.02.42.

COMMANDING OFFICERS

Wing Commander   N G Mulholland   25.08.41. to 22.02.42.

AIRCRAFT

Wellington   25.08.41. to 06.45.

OPERATIONAL RECORD

Operations	Sorties	Aircraft Losses	% Losses
10	65	3	4.6%

All bombing

TABLE OF STATISTICS

Out of 20 squadrons in 1 Group.

Lowest number of overall operations in 1 Group.
Lowest number of sorties in 1 Group.
Lowest number of aircraft operational losses in 1 Group.

Out of 13 Wellington squadrons in 1 Group.

12th highest number of overall Wellington operations in 1 Group.
12th highest number of Wellington sorties in 1 Group.
12th highest number of Wellington operational losses in 1 Group

AIRCRAFT HISTORIES

WELLINGTON.		From October 1941 to February 1942.
R1490		To 301Sqn.
R1695		To 460Sqn.
R1765		Abandoned over Hampshire on return from le Havre 22/23.10.41.
R1775		FTR Emden 15/16.11.41.
R1785		FTR Cherbourg 9.1.42.
R1795		To 300Sqn.
Z1161		From 99Sqn. to 21 OTU.
Z1174		To 1446Flt.
Z1182	FU-G	Crashed soon after take-off from Holme-on-Spalding-Moor when bound for Brest 6.1.42.
Z1183		To 300Sqn.
Z1204		To 301Sqn.

Z1205		To 142Sqn.
Z1212		To 460Sqn.
Z1214		To 142Sqn.
Z1215		From 301Sqn. to 300Sqn.
Z1218	FU-D	FTR Antwerp 20/21.10.41.
Z1219		To 301Sqn.
Z1246		Destroyed by fire on the ground at Holme-on-Spalding-Moor 24.11.41.
Z1254		To 460Sqn.
Z1261		From De Havilland. to 142Sqn.
Z1272		To 301Sqn.
Z1273		To 301Sqn.
Z1274		To 142Sqn.
Z1279		To 300Sqn.
Z1280		To 301Sqn.
Z1286		To 142Sqn.
Z1290		To 460Sqn.
Z1291		To 300Sqn.
Z1312		Crashed in Dorset following early return from Cherbourg 9.1.42.
Z1320		To 300Sqn.
Z1324		To 142Sqn.
Z1333		To 301Sqn.
Z1338		To 142Sqn.
Z1377		To 301Sqn.
DV501		To 26 OTU.
DV502		To Middle East.
DV521		To Middle East.
DV522		To 1443Flt.
DV539		To Middle East.
DV541		To Middle East.
DV550		To 15 OTU.
DV555		To Middle East.

460 SQUADRON RAAF

Motto: **Strike And Return**   Codes **UV AR**

Formed on the 15th of November 1941, 460 Squadron was the second Australian unit to form in 1 Group Bomber Command, following in the footsteps of 458 Squadron. Initially equipped with Wellingtons the squadron went to war for the first time in March 1942, and took part in operations until October, when conversion took place to Lancasters. Thereafter, the squadron remained at the forefront of operations until war's end, setting performance records for Lancaster sorties and bomb tonnage along the way.

STATIONS

MOLESWORTH	15.11.41. to 04.01.42.
BREIGHTON	04.01.42. to 14.05.43.
BINBROOK	14.05.43. to 27.07.45.

COMMANDING OFFICERS

Wing Commander	A L G Hubbard	21.11.41. to 02.09.42.
Wing Commander	K W Kaufman	02.09.42. to 14.12.42.
Wing Commander	J F Dilworth	14.12.42. to 16.02.43.
Wing Commander	C E Martin	16.02.43. to 01.10.43.
Wing Commander	R A Norman	01.10.43. to 09.10.43.
Wing Commander	F A Arthur	09.10.43. to 11.01.44.
Wing Commander	H D Marsh	11.01.44. to 15.05.44.
Wing Commander	J K Douglas	15.05.44. to 12.10.44.
Wing Commander	K R J Parsons	12.10.44. to 11.44.
Squadron Leader	J Clark	11.44. to 12.12.44.
Wing Commander	J Roberts	13.12.44. to 01.45.
Wing Commander	M G Cowan	01.45. to 07.45.

AIRCRAFT

Wellington	30.11.41. to	10.42.
Halifax II (Training only)	08.42. to	10.42.
Lancaster I/III	06.10.42. to	08.46.

OPERATIONAL RECORD

Operations	Sorties	Aircraft Losses	% Losses
368	6238	169	2.7%

CATEGORY OF OPERATIONS

Bombing	Mining	Leaflet
330	36	2

Wellingtons

Operations	Sorties	Aircraft Losses	% Losses
61	538	29	5.4%

CATEGORY OF OPERATIONS

Bombing	Mining	Leaflet
50	9	2

Lancasters

Operations	Sorties	Aircraft Losses	% Losses
307	5700	140	2.5%

CATEGORY OF OPERATIONS

Bombing	Mining
280	27

TABLE OF STATISTICS

7th highest number of sorties in Bomber Command.
Equal 12th (with 106Sqn) highest number of aircraft operational losses in Bomber Command.

Out of 42 Wellington squadrons.

31st highest number of Wellington overall operations in Bomber Command.
26th highest number of Wellington sorties in Bomber Command.
18th highest number of Wellington operational losses in Bomber Command.

Out of 59 Lancaster squadrons.

Equal 12th (with 83Sqn) highest number of Lancaster overall operations in Bomber Command.
Highest number of Lancaster sorties in Bomber Command.
2nd highest number of Lancaster operational losses in Bomber Command.

Out of 20 squadrons in 1 Group.

4th highest number of overall operations in 1 Group.
Highest number of sorties in 1 Group.
3rd highest number of aircraft operational losses in 1 Group.

Out of 13 Wellington squadrons in 1 Group.

10th highest number of Wellington overall operations in 1 Group.
9th highest number of Wellington sorties in 1 Group.
8th equal (with 301Sqn) highest number of Wellington operational losses in 1 Group.

Out of 14 Lancaster squadrons in 1 Group.

4th highest number of Lancaster overall operations in 1 Group.
Highest number of Lancaster sorties in 1 Group.
Highest number of Lancaster operational losses in 1 Group.

AIRCRAFT HISTORIES

WELLINGTON.		From November 1941 to October 1942.
R1530		From ATA. to 305Sqn.
R1650		From 301Sqn. Became ground instruction machine 4.43.
R1655		From TFU. to 142Sqn.
R1695	UV-Y	From 458Sqn. FTR Düsseldorf 10/11.9.42.
Z1212	UV-V	From 458Sqn. FTR Kassel 27/28.8.42.
Z1214		From 142Sqn. FTR Bremen 4/5.9.42.
Z1216	UV-S	From 301Sqn. FTR Düsseldorf 10/11.9.42.
Z1249	UV-K	FTR Essen 2/3.6.42.
Z1251	UV-X	FTR Dunkerque 13/14.3.42.
Z1254	UV-L	From 458Sqn. FTR Stuttgart 6/7.5.42.
Z1259	UV-W	From 301Sqn. FTR Kassel 27/28.8.42.
Z1278		To 300Sqn.
Z1284		To 301Sqn.
Z1288		To 300Sqn.
Z1290	UV-T	From 458Sqn. FTR Kiel 28/29.4 42.
Z1311	UV-Z	From 142Sqn. FTR Essen 1/2.6.42.

Z1323		Force-landed at Ford on return from Duisburg 6/7.9.42.
Z1325		To 142Sqn.
Z1327		Crashed in Yorkshire while training 17.2.42.
Z1328	UV-U	FTR from mining sortie 12/13.7.42.
Z1334		To 18 OTU.
Z1335	UV-C	FTR Hamburg 26/27.7.42.
Z1343		To 300Sqn.
Z1344	UV-W	FTR Essen 1/2.6.42.
Z1381	UV-H	FTR Bremen 2/3.7.42.
Z1383	UV-D	FTR from mining sortie 21/22.6.42.
Z1384		To 301Sqn.
Z1385	UV-Z	From 301Sqn. FTR Bremen 13/14.9.42.
Z1388	UV-J	FTR Gennevilliers 29/30.5.42.
Z1391	UV-R	FTR Gennevilliers 29/30.5.42.
Z1392		To 142Sqn.
Z1394	UV-Q	FTR Essen 2/3.6.42.
Z1395		To 305Sqn.
Z1399	UV-P	FTR Duisburg 25/26.7.42.
Z1400		To 300Sqn.
Z1401		To 300Sqn.
Z1404	UV-J	FTR Mainz 12/13.8.42.
Z1412	UV-W	FTR Essen 8/9.6.42.
Z1413	UV-X	FTR Stuttgart 6/7.5.42.
Z1422	UV-W	FTR from mining sortie 4/5.8.42.
Z1462	UV-R	FTR Duisburg 25/26.7.42.
Z1463	UV-L	FTR Osnabrück 9/10.8.42.
Z1464		To 301Sqn.
Z1470	UV-R	FTR Bremen 2/3.7.42.
Z1473		To 305Sqn.
Z1476		To 305Sqn.
Z1482		To 142Sqn.
Z1483	UV-D	FTR Hamburg 26/27.7.42.
Z1484		To 18 OTU.

Z1485	UV-B	FTR Saarbrücken 28/29.8.42.
Z1486	UV-H	FTR Emden 19/20.6.42.
Z1494		To 142Sqn.
Z1495		To 300Sqn.

HALIFAX.	**From August 1942 to October 1942. Training only**.
R9390	From 102Sqn. Conversion Flight only. to 103Sqn CF.
R9429	From 102Sqn CF. to 1658 HCU.
W1004	From 102Sqn via 460Sqn CF. to 1652 HCU.
W1011	From 102Sqn. Conversion Flight only. to 1656 HCU.
W1185	To 103Sqn.
W1227	To 460Sqn CF and back. to 1658 HCU.
W1234	To 35Sqn.
W1235	To 419Sqn.
W1236	To 76Sqn.
W1272	Conversion Flight only. Crashed in Yorkshire while training 22.9.42.
W7781	To 76Sqn.
W7817	To 419Sqn.
W7818	To 103Sqn.
DG219	Conversion Flight only. to 1656 HCU.
DG304	To 518Sqn.
DT481 UV-B	Crashed in Lincolnshire while training 19.9.42.
DT483	Conversion Flight only. to 103Sqn.
DT484	From 460Sqn CF. to 1656 HCU.
DT524	To 158Sqn.

LANCASTER.	**From October 1942.**
R5500	From 207Sqn. to 1656CU.
R5685	From 50Sqn. to 1667CU.
R5702	From 106Sqn. to 100Sqn.
R5745 UV-C	From 207Sqn. Blew up on the ground at

		Binbrook in incident involving DV172 on 3.7.43.
W4162	AR-J²	From 83Sqn via NTU. FTR Berlin 23/24.11.43.
W4248		From 9Sqn. to 622Sqn via 1667CU.
W4263	AR-L/B/U	From 1656CU. to 625Sqn.
W4273	UV-A	FTR Stuttgart 22/23.11.42.
W4274	UV-B	FTR Essen 4/5.1.43.
W4301	AR-H	From 61Sqn. FTR Munich 2/3.10.43.
W4308	UV-C	FTR Düsseldorf 23/24.1.43.
W4310	UV-F/C-	FTR Kiel 4/5.4.43.
W4316	AR-Q	FTR Bochum 12/13.6.43.
W4320	AR-F/D	FTR Wuppertal 24/25.6.43.
W4322		From 101Sqn. No operations. Returned to 101Sqn.
W4325	UV-O	FTR Stettin 20/21.4.43.
W4327	UV-Y/S	FTR Berlin 29/30.3.43.
W4329	AR-T/K	FTR Bochum 12/13.6.43.
W4330	UV-H	FTR Stettin 20/21.4.43.
W4331	UV-R	FTR Pilsen 16/17.4.43.
W4332	AR-V/M	FTR Cologne 16/17.6.43.
W4780		To 166Sqn via 1656CU.
W4783	AR-G	To Australia as veteran of 90 operations.
W4785	UV-J	First off on Squadron's first Lancaster operation. FTR Duisburg 8/9.4.43.
W4816	UV-K	Abandoned over Yorkshire coast on return from Berlin 17/18.1.43.
W4817	UV-K	FTR Düsseldorf 27/28.1.43.
W4818	UV-A/K/B	FTR Dortmund 4/5.5.43.
W4837	UV-M	FTR Lorient 26/27.1.43.
W4844	AR-Z/D	FTR Cologne 3/4.7.43.
W4864		Crashed in bad weather in Shropshire while training 3.3.43.
W4879	UV-M/D	Crash-landed at South Cerney on return from St Nazaire 23.3.43.
W4881	AR-K	From 12Sqn. FTR Berlin 2/3.12.43.

W4927	AR-C	Damaged beyond repair during an operation to Kassel 22/23.10.43.
W4939	AR-L	FTR Krefeld 21/22.6.43.
W4941		To 5LFS.
W4942	UV-F	FTR Pilsen 16/17.4.43.
W4956	UV-J	FTR Stettin 20/21.4.43.
W4960	AR-R	FTR Düsseldorf 11/12.6.43.
W4967	AR-H	To 626Sqn.
W4984	AR-J	FTR Dortmund 23/24.5.43.
W4985	AR-O	FTR Wuppertal 29/30.5.43.
W4986	AR-F	FTR Dortmund 23/24.5.43.
W4987		FTR Hamburg 24/25.7.43.
W4988	AR-Q	Force-landed in Sweden during an operation to Berlin 3/4.9.43.
W5005	AR-L/E/E²	To 550Sqn.
W5007	AR-O	From 1656CU. Crashed while trying to land at Elsham Wolds on return from Cologne 17.6.43.
DV160		FTR Oberhausen 14/15.6.43.
DV161		From 1667CU. to 57Sqn.
DV172		Blew up at Binbrook 3.7.43.
DV173		Crashed in Lincolnshire on return from Berlin 17.12.43.
DV174		FTR Mannheim 23/24.9.43.
DV175	AR-E	To 5LFS.
DV193		To 103Sqn via 1LFS.
DV219		From 12Sqn. FTR Hannover 22/23.9.43.
DV247		To 166Sqn.
DV296	AR-E²	FTR Berlin 2/3.12.43.
DV333		To 103Sqn.
DV340		To 9Sqn.
DV341	AR-C²	FTR Berlin 18/19.11.43.
DV342		To 103Sqn.
DV343		To 100Sqn.
DV359		Force-landed in Co.Durham while training 1.4.44.

ED315	AR-D/P/W	From 44Sqn. Crashed on landing at Binbrook during training 28.6.43.
ED354	UV-/WO	FTR Duisburg 26/27.3.43.
ED366		From 100Sqn. to 166Sqn.
ED369	AR-L/A	Crash-landed at Hawkinge on return from Cologne 9.7.43.
ED370	AR-B²	From 103Sqn. FTR Berlin 26/27.11.43.
ED391	UV-E	From 100Sqn. FTR Berlin 29/30.3.43.
ED421		FTR Berlin 23/24.8.43.
ED521	UV-B	From 100Sqn. FTR Duisburg 9/10.4.43.
ED525	AR-N	From 100Sqn. to 467Sqn.
ED535		From 467Sqn. FTR Hamburg 29/30.7.43.
ED658	AR-O	From 100Sqn. FTR Hannover 8/9.10.43.
ED664	AR-A²	FTR Berlin 23/24.11.43.
ED711	UV-U	FTR Pilsen 16/17.4.43.
ED730		To 550Sqn.
ED750	AR-E²	From 100Sqn. FTR Nuremberg 30/31.3.44.
ED759	AR-X	FTR Wuppertal 29/30.5.43.
ED774	AR-S	FTR Berlin 23/24.8.43.
ED804	AR-Z	FTR Essen 27/28.5.43.
ED942		From 103Sqn. to 100Sqn.
ED973		To 100Sqn.
ED976		To 100Sqn.
ED985	AR-Y/C²	FTR Hannover 18/19.10.43.
ED986	AR-B/B-/J/J²	FTR Berlin 31.8/1.9.43.
EE132		FTR Berlin 3/4.9.43.
EE138		FTR Berlin 3/4.9.43.
EE166		FTR Mülheim 22/23.6.43.
EE167		FTR Oberhausen 14/15.6.43.
JA680		Force-landed in Yorkshire on return from Hannover 28.9.43.
JA683	AR-D²	To 300Sqn.
JA687		Destroyed at Binbrook when ME646 blew up 7.3.44.

JA688	AR-G²	Crashed on approach to Binbrook on return from Essen 26.7.43.
JA689		FTR Hamburg 29/30.7.43.
JA699		To 100Sqn.
JA856	AR-C	FTR Munich 2/3.10.43.
JA859		FTR Hannover 22/23.9.43.
JA860	AR-C²	FTR Berlin 27/28.1.44.
JA861		FTR Hannover 27/28.9.43.
JA862		To 625Sqn.
JB296	AR-K	From 1656CU. FTR Berlin 27/28.1.44.
JB298	AR-Q	From 1656CU. FTR Berlin 29/30.12.43.
JB407		To 12Sqn.
JB423		To 103Sqn.
JB547	AR-D²/N	Collided with ME641 (166Sqn) near Binbrook while training 24.2.44.
JB560		To 100Sqn.
JB564		To 100Sqn.
JB598	AR-C	FTR Essen 26/27.3.44.
JB600	AR-O	FTR from mining Sortie 9/10.4.44.
JB606	AR-H	FTR Berlin 1/2.1.44.
JB607	AR-N	FTR Berlin 29/30.12.43.
JB608	AR-J	FTR Berlin 2/3.12.43.
JB610	AR-H	FTR Leipzig 19/20.2.44.
JB611	AR-R	FTR Berlin 2/3.12.43.
JB613		To 625Sqn.
JB637	AR-B	FTR Berlin 27/28.1.44.
JB647		Crashed in Lincolnshire while training 24.11.43.
JB657		Crashed in Lincolnshire on return from Berlin 16/17.12.43.
JB662		Crashed on take-off from Binbrook when bound for Rouen 18.4.44.
JB700	AR-L/J	FTR Vire 6/7.6.44.
JB702	AR-M	FTR Magdeburg 21/22.1.44.
JB704		Crashed while trying to land at Binbrook on return from Berlin 16.12.43.

JB734	AR-R²	FTR from mining sortie 9/10.4.44.
JB738	AR-T	To 106Sqn and back. Crashed soon after take-off from Binbrook when bound for Berlin 2.1.44.
JB739	AR-E	FTR Berlin 20/21.1.44.
JB741	AR-J	FTR Mailly-le-Camp 3/4.5.44.
JB742	AR-D	FTR Augsburg 25/26.2.44.
JB743		To 625Sqn.
LL906	AR-B	FTR Friedrichshafen 27/28.4.44.
LL907	AR-A	To 1653CU.
LL918	AR-S	From 625Sqn. to 61Sqn.
LL951	AR-C	FTR Duisburg 21/22.5.44.
LL952		To 100Sqn.
LL957	AR-E²	FTR Scholven-Buer 18/19.7.44.
LL964	AR-D²	To 103Sqn.
LM141		To 300Sqn.
LM315	AR-A-/K²	FTR Schweinfurt 24/25.2.44.
LM316	AR-Y/H²	FTR Berlin 2/3.12.43.
LM321		From 12Sqn. to 550Sqn.
LM324		FTR Oberhausen 14/15.6.43.
LM331		Crashed 12.6.43 and SOC.
LM375		To 106Sqn.
LM380		To 626Sqn.
LM381		To 103Sqn.
LM523	AR-L²	FTR Friedrichshafen 27/28.4.44.
LM525	AR-T	FTR Düsseldorf 22/23.4.44.
LM530		To 626Sqn.
LM531	AR-R	FTR Mailly-le-Camp 3/4.5.44.
LM545	AR-J	FTR Merville 27/28.5.44.
LM547	AR-F²	FTR Reims 22/23.6.44.
LM619		To 100Sqn.
LM622		To 100Sqn.
LM623	AR-A²	To 100Sqn.
ME326	AR-P	Collided with PD286 (626Sqn) over Belgium on return from Wiesbaden 2/3.2.45.

ME357		To 49Sqn.
ME640	AR-M	FTR Berlin 24/25.3.44.
ME646		No operations. Blew up at Binbrook 7.3.44.
ME649	AR-J²	To 103Sqn.
ME663	AR-M	FTR from mining sortie 9/10.4.44.
ME676		To 625Sqn.
ME696	AR-B²	FTR Acheres 10/11.6.44.
ME698		From A&AEE. to 103Sqn.
ME727	AR-X²	Crashed soon after take-off from Binbrook when bound for Villeneuve-St-George 9.4.44.
ME728	AR-Z²/F²	FTR Mailly-le-Camp 3/4.5.44.
ME740	AR-E	FTR Mailly-le-Camp 3/4.5.44.
ME744		To 300Sqn.
ME755	AR-Z	FTR Revigny 14/15.7.44.
ME776		To 550Sqn.
ME781		To 1651CU.
ME784		Crash-landed at Manston on return from Siracourt 29.6.44.
ME785	AR-H²	FTR Gelsenkirchen 12/13.6.44.
ME793	AR-G²	FTR Vaires 27/28.6.44.
ND361	AR-R	FTR Nuremberg 30/31.3.44.
ND364	AR-F	FTR Friedrichshafen 27/28.4.44.
ND366		From 166Sqn. Crashed in Lincolnshire on return from Magdeburg 22.1.44.
ND392		From 100Sqn. to 1656CU.
ND393	AR-E	FTR Stuttgart 15/16.3.44.
ND394	AR-J²	FTR Schweinfurt 24/25.2.44.
ND419		Crashed in Lincolnshire on return from Stuttgart 21.2.44.
ND463	AR-S	FTR Berlin 24/25.3.44.
ND521	AR-F²	From 207Sqn. to 576Sqn.
ND553		From SIU. Crashed during training flight 30.4.44, killing F/O Brian Jagger of F/L Shannon's Dams crew.
ND569	AR-E	FTR Leipzig 19/20.2.44.

ND584		From SIU. to BDU.
ND586	AR-B	FTR Aulnoye 10/11.4.44.
ND615		To 1656CU.
ND630	AR-G	FTR Mailly-le-Camp 3/4.5.44.
ND634	AR-G	To 166Sqn.
ND652	AR-C	FTR Essen 26/27.4.44.
ND654	AR-R	From SIU. FTR Courtrai 20/21.7.44.
ND656		To 103Sqn.
ND658		From 100Sqn. to 170Sqn.
ND674	AR-C^2	FTR Hasselt 11/12.5.44.
ND677/G		To 49Sqn.
ND713		From SIU. to 1LFS and back. to 49Sqn.
ND738	AR-E	FTR Nuremberg 30/31.3.44.
ND791		From SIU. to 49Sqn.
ND822		From SIU. Crashed at Ludford Magna following early return from Leuna 14.1.45.
ND860	AR-J	From 7Sqn. Loaned to 1 Group SDF Binbrook, and FTR from Mailly-le-Camp 3/4.5.44.
ND861		From 635Sqn. to 300Sqn.
ND863		From 35Sqn. to 300Sqn.
ND864	AR-A^2	To 626Sqn.
ND959		To 1661CU.
ND967		To 429Sqn 4.45.
ND968		
ND970	AR-S	FTR Stuttgart 28/29.7.44.
ND971	AR-K^2	FTR Leuna 6/7.11.44.
NE116	AR-G	FTR Reims 22/23.6.44.
NE139		Crashed on take-off from Binbrook while training 4.7.44.
NE141	AR-P	FTR Aschaffenburg 21/22.11.44.
NE142		To 49Sqn.
NE144	AR-F^2	From R.A.E. FTR Stettin 29/30.8.44.
NE163		To 626Sqn.
NE164		To 550Sqn.

NE174	AR-M	FTR Orleans 4/5.7.44.
NE176		To 49Sqn via 1LFS.
NG404		
NG466	AR-Y-	FTR Bruchstrasse 21/22.3.45.
NG468	AR-J²	FTR Duisburg 21/22.2.45.
NG502	AR-J	Shot down by intruder while training 4.3.45.
NN799	AR-K/M	
NX560	AR-J²	
NX570	AR-P	
NX585	AR-K/M	FTR Berchtesgaden 25.4.45.
NX588	AR-C	
NX589	AR-T	
NX603		
NX604	AR-D	
NX605	AR-B	
NX606	AR-C	
NX607	AR-N	
PA230		
PA257		
PA304	AR-K	
PB116		To 1661CU.
PB117		To 100Sqn.
PB125	AR-L	FTR Trossy-St-Maximin 3.8.44.
PB152	AR-Z	FTR Stuttgart 19/20.10.44.
PB155	AR-K	Crashed on approach to Kelstern on return from Hanau 19.3.45.
PB175	AR-A	FTR Stuttgart 19/20.10.44.
PB176	AR-M	FTR Raimbert 31.8.44.
PB187	AR-E	FTR Dortmund 12.3.45.
PB213		To 1661CU.
PB226	AR-G	To 49Sqn.
PB227		To 1661CU.
PB254	AR-K	Damaged during operation to Emmerich 7.10.44. to 150Sqn after repair.

PB255	AR-X/E	FTR Cologne 24/25.12.44.
PB285		To 1661CU.
PB301	AR-J	FTR Bottrop 3/4.2.45.
PB351	AR-H²	Crashed in Norfolk on return from Essen 23.10.44.
PB352		To 218Sqn.
PB379	AR-E/E²	Crash-landed in Sweden on the way home from Stettin 29/30.8.44.
PB383		To 49Sqn.
PB406		To 49Sqn.
PB407	AR-U	FTR Emmerich 7.10.44.
PB459	AR-V	FTR Dortmund 29.11.44.
PB463		To 49Sqn.
PB469	AR-H	FTR Aschaffenburg 21/22.11.44.
PB471	AR-F²	FTR Dortmund 20/21.2.45.
PB479		To 49Sqn.
PB522	AR-G²	To 49Sqn.
PB541	AR-E²	FTR Wanne-Eickel 18/19.11.44.
PB542	AR-D²	FTR Essen 12/13.12.44.
PB557	AR-A²/B²/R²	FTR Chemnitz 5/6.3.45.
PB559	To 49Sqn.	
PB567	AR-U	From 1LFS. FTR Cologne 31.10/1.11.44.
PB807	AR-H	FTR Wiesbaden 2/3.2.45.
PB812		Crashed in Lincolnshire while training 10.2.45.
PB816	AR-E²	FTR Nuremberg 16/17.3.45.
PB839		From 100Sqn.
PB873		To 49Sqn.
PB875		To 49Sqn.
PB878		From 207Sqn.
RA524	AR-V	FTR Cologne 2.3.45.
RA525		
RA572		
RA598		
RE124		

| RF191 | AR-J | From 100Sqn. |
| RF196 | AR-E | Crashed in Lincolnshire on return from Lützkendorf 5.4.45. |

RF212

RF232

RF233

RF246

RF247

RF248

RF250

RF251

RF254

HEAVIEST SINGLE LOSS.

| 02/03.12.43. | Berlin. | 5 Lancasters. |
| 03/04.05.44. | Mailly-le-Camp. | 5 Lancasters. |

550 SQUADRON

Motto: **Per Ignum Vincimus**   Code **BQ**
(Through fire we conquer)

550 Squadron was formed in November 1943 as the second unit, after 625 Squadron, to be sporned in 1 Group from a C Flight of 100 Squadron. It began operations immediately, and remained an important part of the strategic bombing campaign until war's end.

STATIONS
GRIMSBY   25.11.43. to 03.01.44.
NORTH KILLINGHOLME   03.01.44. to 31.10.45.

COMMANDING OFFICERS

Wing Commander	J J Bennett	25.11.43. to 15.05.44.
Wing Commander	P E G Connolly	15.05.44. to 15.07.44.
Wing Commander	A F M Sisley	15.07.44. to 31.08.44.
Squadron Leader	B J Ramond	01.09.44. to 18.09.44.
Wing Commander	B Bell	18.09.44. to 22.02.45.
Wing Commander	J C McWatters	25.02.45.

AIRCRAFT

Lancaster I/III   25.11.43. to 10.45.

OPERATIONAL RECORD

Operations	Sorties	Aircraft Losses	% Losses
192	3582	59	1.6%

All bombing

TABLE OF STATISTICS

Out of 59 Lancaster squadrons.

31st highest number of overall Lancaster operations in Bomber Command.
20th highest number of Lancaster sorties in Bomber Command.
26th equal (with 630Sqn) number of Lancaster operational losses in Bomber Command.

Out of 20 squadrons in 1 Group.

13th highest number of overall operations in 1 Group.
8th highest number of sorties in 1 Group.
10th highest number of aircraft operational losses in 1 Group.

Out of 14 Lancaster squadrons in 1 Group.

9th highest number of Lancaster overall operations in 1 Group.
7th highest number of Lancaster sorties in 1 Group.
9th highest number of Lancaster operational losses in 1 Group.

AIRCRAFT HISTORIES

L7541		From 1660CU. to 300Sqn.
W5005	BQ-N	From 460Sqn. Flew 94 operations in total. Ditched in Humber on return from Kiel 27.8.44.
DV176		From 100Sqn. to storage.
DV189	BQ-T/T²	From 100Sqn. FTR Berlin 1/2.1.44.
DV192		From 100Sqn. Returned to 100Sqn.
DV200	BQ-M	From 12Sqn via 1LFS. to 1LFS.
DV279	BQ-M	Abandoned over Norfolk on return from Scholven-Buer 19.7.44.

DV305	BQ-Q	From 100Sqn. Crash-landed at Woodbridge on return from its 10th Berlin operation 31.1.44. and declared damaged beyond repair.
DV306	BQ-E	FTR Brunswick 14/15.1.44.
DV309	BQ-S	From 166Sqn. FTR Duisburg 21/22.5.44.
DV343	BQ-X²	From 100Sqn. FTR Berlin 23/24.12.43.
DV345		From 100Sqn. Crashed in Lincolnshire on return from Berlin 2.1.44.
ED536		From 100Sqn. to 1LFS.
ED562	BQ-G	From 576Sqn. Abandoned over Lincolnshire on return from Revigny 18.7.44.
ED716		From 44Sqn. to 166Sqn.
ED730	BQ-G²	From 460Sqn. Crashed in Lincolnshire following collision with ND327 of 100Sqn when bound for Berlin 24.12.43.
ED905	BQ-F/Q	From 166Sqn. to 1LFS.
ED942	BQ-Q	From 100Sqn. FTR Augsburg 25/26.2.44.
EE107	BQ-O	From 100Sqn. FTR Magdeburg 21/22.1.44.
EE139	BQ-B	From 100Sqn. Flew 11 Berlin operations. to 1656CU.
EE193	BQ-D/C	From 166Sqn. FTR Stettin 29/30.8.44.
HK796		From 195Sqn. No operations.
HK800	BQ-O	From 195Sqn. No operations.
HK801		From 186Sqn. No operations.
JA712	BQ-O/H	From 166Sqn. FTR Aachen 27/28.5.44.
JA918	BQ-W	From A&AEE. FTR Mardyck 9/10.5.44.
JA934	BQ-H	From 100Sqn. FTR Berlin 15/16.2.44.
JB289		From 100Sqn. Returned to 100Sqn.
JB345	BQ-C	From 582Sqn.
JB563		From 100Sqn. Returned to 100Sqn.
JB673	BQ-A	From 100Sqn. Returned to 100Sqn.
JB674		To 100Sqn.
JB678		To 100Sqn.
LL747	BQ-P	FTR Sterkrade 16/17.6.44.
LL748	BQ-D	From 576Sqn. to 1LFS.

LL796	BQ-O	From 576Sqn. FTR Revigny 12/13.7.44.
LL800	BQ-A	From 576Sqn. to 1660CU.
LL810	BQ-R/K	FTR Aachen 27/28.5.44.
LL811	BQ-J	To 1LFS.
LL826	BQ-H	FTR Mailly-le-Camp 3/4,.5.44.
LL831	BQ-U	To 1LFS.
LL834	BQ-K	Ditched in the North Sea while training 22.4.44.
LL836	BQ-E	FTR Aulnoye 10/11.4.44.
LL837	BQ-Q	FTR Revigny 14/15.7.44.
LL838	BQ-S	From 576Sqn. Abandoned over Kent on return from Mimoyecques 22.6.44.
LL850	BQ-L	Crash-landed at Manston on return from Caen 7.7.44.
LL851	BQ-V	FTR Duisburg 21/22.5.44.
LL852	BQ-X	FTR Stuttgart 15/16.3.44.
LM134	BQ-H	FTR Sterkrade 16/17.6.44.
LM182		
LM228	BQ-G²	
LM229	BQ-S	Crashed on take-off from Killingholme when bound for Orleans 4.7.44.
LM273	BQ-D/O	FTR Pforzheim 23/24.2.45.
LM301	BQ-V⁻	From 100Sqn. FTR Berlin 2/3.12.43.
LM319	BQ-A	From 100Sqn. FTR Duisburg 21/22.5.44.
LM321		From 460Sqn. to 100Sqn.
LM379	BQ-S	From 100Sqn. FTR Berlin 26/27.11.43.
LM392	BQ-J	From 166Sqn. FTR Stuttgart 15/16.3.44.
LM425	BQ-N	FTR Nuremberg 30/31.3.44.
LM455	BQ-F/T	FTR Stuttgart 28/29.7.44.
LM460	BQ-R	To 1666CU.
LM461	BQ-U	FTR Leipzig 19/20.2.44.
LM647	BQ-S	FTR Revigny 12/13.7.44.
ME301	BQ-R/X/K	FTR Lützkendorf 4/5.4.45.
ME390	BQ-A	
ME428	BQ-O	From 166Sqn. FTR Dessau 7/8.3.45.

ME503	BQ-R	FTR Dessau 7/8.3.45.
ME519	BQ-U	
ME542		
ME548	BQ-Q	FTR Hanau 18/19.3.45.
ME556	BQ-F	FTR Acheres 6/7.6.44.
ME581	BQ-D	FTR Düsseldorf 22/23.4.44.
ME582	BQ-E	FTR Augsburg 25/26.2.44.
ME583	BQ-P	From 576Sqn. to 1LFS.
ME687	BQ-X	To 576Sqn.
ME776		From 460Sqn.
ME840	BQ-V	FTR Sterkrade 16/17.6.44.
ND328		From 100Sqn. Returned to 100Sqn.
ND388		To 100Sqn.
ND396	BQ-D	FTR Berlin 30/31.1.44.
ND403	BQ-G	From 625Sqn. to 576Sqn.
ND405		From 576Sqn. to 166Sqn.
ND425	BQ-C	FTR Nuremberg 30/31.3.44.
ND531	BQ-A^2	To 630Sqn.
ND733	BQ-J	To 9Sqn.
ND972	BQ-W	From 100Sqn.
NE164	BQ-O	From 460Sqn FTR Stuttgart 28/29.7.44.
NF931	BQ-A^2	
NF932	BQ-B^2	Collided with PA185 of 300Sqn over Lincolnshire when bound for Dresden 13.2.45.
NF962	BQ-A/V	FTR Agenville 31.8.44.
NF963	BQ-A	Broke up over Yorkshire while training 4.10.44.
NF998	BQ-D	Crashed on landing at Manston on return from Pforzheim 24.2.45.
NG120		
NG132	BQ-E^2/F^2	Shot down by intruder over Yorkshire while training 17.2.45.
NG133	BQ-F^2	FTR Duisburg 14.10.44.
NG134		
NG135		

NG165

NG192   BQ-L   FTR Stuttgart 19/20.10.44.

NG221   BQ-F/F²

NG243   BQ-M²

NG246

NG250   BQ-F

NG251   BQ-J   FTR Leuna 6/7.12.44.

NG287   BQ-Q   FTR Misburg 15/16.3.45.

NG289

NG290

NG331   BQ-M   FTR Hannover 5/6.1.45.

NG336   BQ-B   FTR Nuremberg 16/17.3.45.

NG363   BQ-P   FTR Munich 7/8.1.45.

NG390   BQ-X

NN715   BQ-A   FTR Duisburg 21/22.2.45.

PA268   BQ-F²

PA288   BQ-R

PA309   BQ-V

PA325

PA991   BQ-E   FTR Wemars Cappel 28.8.44.

PA995   BQ-K/V   FTR Dessau 7/8.3.45.

PB514

PB532   To 100Sqn.

PB562   BQ-M   FTR Gelsenkirchen 6.11.44.

PB707   BQ-L²

PB843

PB846   To 12Sqn.

PB864   To 1660CU.

PD208   BQ-V   Crashed in Northamptonshire on return from
                        Fontaine-le-Pin 14.8.44.

PD221   BQ-R   FTR Bottrop 3/4.2.45.

PD255   BQ-T   FTR Düsseldorf 2/3.11.44.

PD313

PD319   BQ-G   FTR Duisburg 14.10.44.

PD320	BQ-H	FTR Dortmund 24.3.45.
PD321		
PD343	BQ-S	From 166Sqn.
PD382		
RA502	BQ-Z	Abandoned over France following collision with NG202 of 170Sqn on return from Ludwigshafen 1.2.45.
RA503	BQ-C	
RA547		
RF135		
RF136	BQ-B²	
RF214		
RF237	BQ-H	

576 SQUADRON

Motto: **Carpe Diem**   Code **UL**
            (Seize the day)

Part of 1 Group's expansion program in November 1943, 576 Squadron was formed from C Flight of 103 Squadron, and began operations a week later. It remained a frontline Lancaster bomber squadron until the end of hostilities.

STATIONS

| **ELSHAM WOLDS** | 25.11.43. to 31.10.44. |
| **FISKERTON** | 31.10.44. to 13.09.45. |

COMMANDING OFFICERS

Wing Commander	G T B Clayton	25.11.43. to 23.06.44.
Wing Commander	B D Sellick	24.06.44. to 28.02.45.
Wing Commander	MacAllister	01.03.45. to 06.45.

AIRCRAFT

| **Lancaster I/III** | 25.11.43. to 13.09.45. |

OPERATIONAL RECORD

Operations	Sorties	Aircraft Losses	% Losses
191	2788	66	2.4%

CATEGORY OF OPERATIONS

Bombing	Mining
189	2

TABLE OF STATISTICS

Out of 59 Lancaster squadrons.

32nd highest number of Lancaster overall operations in Bomber Command.
28th highest number of Lancaster sorties in Bomber Command.
23rd equal (with 514 and 625Sqns) highest number of Lancaster operational losses in Bomber Command.

Out of 20 squadrons in 1 Group.

14th highest number of aircraft overall operations in 1 Group.
10th highest number of sorties in 1 Group.
8th equal (with 625Sqn) highest aircraft operational losses in 1 Group.

Out of 14 Lancaster squadrons in 1 Group.

7th highest number of overall Lancaster operations in 1 Group.
10th highest number of Lancaster sorties in 1 Group.
7th equal (with 625Sqn) highest number of Lancaster operational losses in 1 Group.

AIRCRAFT HISTORIES

R5853		From 1660CU. to 1LFS.
W4123		From 83Sqn via NTU. FTR Berlin 2/3.12.43.
W4245	UL-S^2	From 156Sqn via NTU. FTR Berlin 30/31.1.44.
DV333	UL-C^2/K^2	From 103Sqn. FTR Stettin 5/6.1.44.
DV342		From 103Sqn. FTR Berlin 16/17.12.43.
DV365		From 166Sqn. FTR Duisburg 21/22.5.44.
DV386	UL-E^2	From 166Sqn. FTR Leipzig 19/20.2.44.

ED562		From 100Sqn. to 550Sqn.
ED713	UL-W^2	From 103Sqn. FTR Berlin 23/24.12.43.
ED767	UL-A^2	From 103Sqn. to 1651CU.
ED888	UL-M^2/V^2	From 103Sqn. Returned to 103Sqn. Completed a total of 135 operations, 11 to Berlin.
ED913	UL-U^2	From 103Sqn. FTR Berlin 23/24.12.43.
ED994		From 57Sqn. to 467Sqn.
JA715	UL-W^2	From 97Sqn. to 101Sqn.
JA857		From 635Sqn. to 103Sqn.
JA868		From 103Sqn. to 1656CU.
JA957	UL-X^2	From 103Sqn. to 9Sqn.
JA968	UL-Y^2	From 7Sqn. FTR Montdidier 4.5.44.
JB410		From 405Sqn.
JB460	UL-V^2	From 103Sqn. FTR Flers 24/25.6.44.
JB555		From 103Sqn. to 1668CU.
JB744		From 103Sqn. Returned to 103Sqn.
HK759	UL-G^2	
LL748		To 550Sqn.
LL794		To 1651CU.
LL796		To 550Sqn.
LL799	UL-N^2	FTR Stuttgart 28/29.7.44.
LL800	UL-S^2	To 550Sqn.
LL830		FTR Aulnoye 10/11.4.44.
LL838		To 550Sqn.
LL905	UL-H^2	FTR Stuttgart 28/29.7.44.
LM120		To 405Sqn.
LM122	UL-X^2	FTR Düsseldorf 2/3.11.44.
LM133		FTR Stettin 16/17.8.44.
LM227	UL-I	
LM294	UL-G^2	
LM332		From 103Sqn. Collided with JB670 (103Sqn) over Lincolnshire when bound for Berlin 16/17.12.43.
LM381		From 103Sqn. FTR Brunswick 14/15.1.44.

LM438		To 3LFS.
LM439	UL-T^2	FTR Aachen 24/25.5.44.
LM469		FTR Berlin 24/25.3.44.
LM470	UL-U^2	FTR Nuremberg 30/31.3.44.
LM471	UL-J^2	FTR Berlin 24/25.3.44.
LM492	UL-J	
LM527		Damaged on take-off and abandoned 30.4.44.
LM532	UL-A^2	FTR Orleans 4/5.7.44.
LM594	UL-A	
LM651		
LM679		
ME317		FTR Nuremberg 16/17.3.45.
ME492		
ME583		To 550Sqn.
ME585	UL-H^2	FTR Brunswick 14/15.1.44.
ME586	UL-B^2	FTR Mailly-le-Camp 3/4.5.44.
ME593		FTR Berlin 27/28.1.44.
ME671	UL-V^2	From 300Sqn. FTR Lützkendorf 4/5.4.45.
ME687		From 550Sqn. FTR Dortmund 22/23.5.44.
ME703		Damaged beyond repair Mailly-le-Camp 3/4.5.44.
ME726	UL-X^2	FTR from mining sortie 15/16.5.44.
ME735		FTR Duisburg 21/22.2.45.
ME792		FTR from mining sortie 26/27.8.44.
ME800	UL-W^2	FTR Stettin 29/30.8.44.
ME801	UL-W^2	
ME810	UL-K^2	FTR Sterkrade 16/17.6.44.
ME811		FTR Vire 6/7.6.44.
ME854		FTR Frankfurt 12/13.9.44.
ME862		From 625Sqn.
ND362		To 103Sqn.
ND385	UL-N^2/W^2	To 170Sqn.
ND386	UL-P^2	FTR Berlin 28/29.1.44.
ND402		To 103Sqn.

ND403		From 550Sqn. Damaged beyond repair 12.5.44.
ND405		From 550Sqn.
ND416		FTR Stettin 5/6.1.44.
ND521		From 460Sqn.
ND783		FTR Aubigne Racan 6/7.5.44.
ND859	UL-L²	FTR Revigny 12/13.7.44.
ND903		To 103Sqn.
ND994		FTR Revigny 14/15.7.44.
NE115	UL-B²	FTR Düsseldorf 1/2.11.44.
NE171	UL-Y²	FTR Aachen 24/25.5.44.
NF975	UL-J²	FTR Dortmund 20/21.2.45.
NF976	UL-Q²	
NG119	UL-D²	FTR Wiesbaden 2/3.2.45.
NG183		To 166Sqn.
NG273		From 150Sqn.
NG464		FTR. Abandoned near Reims 22.2.45.
NN711	UL-L²	FTR Neuss 23/24.9.44.
NN749		
NN750	UL-M²	Crashed at Manston on return from Bonn 27/28.12.44.
NN806	UL-M	Crashed on take off from Fiskerton when bound for Rotterdam during Operation Manna 8.5.45.
NX562	UL-F	
NX563		To 153Sqn.
NX576		
PA173		FTR Munich 7/8.1.45.
PA175	UL-K/K²	From 625Sqn.
PA176		From 625Sqn.
PA265		FTR Nuremberg 16/17.3.45.
PA282	UL-C	
PA307	UL-W	
PA318	UL-E	
PA997		From 103Sqn. FTR Sterkrade 16/17.6.44.
PB128	UL-S²	FTR Stuttgart 28/29.7.44.

PB253	UL-A²	FTR Stuttgart 28/29.7.44.
PB265	UL-V²/W²	FTR Stuttgart 24/25.7.44.
PB400	UL-J²	FTR Kiel 26/27.8.44.
PB472		To 153Sqn.
PB574		From 625Sqn.
PB635		To 166Sqn.
PB753	UL-X	From 170Sqn.
PB785		FTR Nuremberg 16/17.3.45.
PD232		FTR Dresden 13/14.2.45.
PD235	UL-N²	FTR Calais 24.9.44.
PD271	UL-T	
PD309	UL-W²	FTR Zeitz 16/17.2.45.
PD312		FTR Wiesbaden 2/3.2.45.
PD363		FTR Dessau 7/8.3.45.
PD376	UL-C²	From 625Sqn.
PD403		FTR Chemnitz 5/6.3.45.
RA514		
RA516		FTR Duisburg 21/22.2.45.
RA562	UL-B	
RA563		
RA587		
RA594	UL-V	
RE127	UL-L	
RF120		FTR Dessau 7/8.3.45.
RF197		From 630Sqn.
RF200	UL-D	
RF213		From 625Sqn.
SW270	UL-K	
SW276	UL-G/G²	From 170Sqn.

625 SQUADRON

Motto: **We Avenge**   Code **CF**

The first of two units to be formed from 100 Squadron in late 1943, 625

Squadron first saw the light of day on the 1st of October, and began operations almost three weeks later at Hannover. The squadron remained at the forefront of bomber operations until war's end.

STATIONS

WALTHAM (GRIMSBY)	01.10.43. to 13.10.43.
KELSTERN	13.10.43. to 06.04.45.
SCAMPTON	06.04.45. to 07.10.45.

COMMANDING OFFICERS

Wing Commander	T Preston	01.10.43. to 26.03.44.
Wing Commander	D D Haig	26.03.44. to 16.09.44.
Wing Commander	Mackay	16.09.44. to 18.11.44.
Wing Commander	J L Barker	18.11.44.

AIRCRAFT

Lancaster I/III	13.10.43. to 07.10.45.

OPERATIONAL RECORD

Operations	Sorties	Aircraft Losses	% Losses
193	3385	66	1.9%

CATEGORY OF OPERATIONS

Bombing	Mining
191	2

TABLE OF STATISTICS

Out of 59 Lancaster squadrons.

30th highest number of Lancaster overall operations in Bomber Command.
22nd highest number of Lancaster sorties in Bomber Command.
23rd equal (with 514 and 576Sqns) highest number of Lancaster operational losses in Bomber Command.

Out of 20 squadrons in 1 Group.

12th highest number of overall operations in 1 Group.
9th highest number of sorties in 1 Group.
8th equal (with 576Sqn) highest aircraft operational losses in 1 Group.

Out of 14 Lancaster squadrons in 1 Group.

8th highest number of overall Lancaster operations in 1 Group.
8th highest number of Lancaster sorties in 1 Group.
7th equal (with 576Sqn) highest number of Lancaster operational losses in 1 Group.

AIRCRAFT HISTORIES

R5702	CF-B/Y	From 100Sqn. FTR Berlin 15/16.2.44.
W4263	CF-M	From 460Sqn. to 1LFS.
W4833	CF-J	From 101Sqn. FTR Stuttgart 15/16.3.44.
W4993	CF-J	From 101Sqn. to BDU.
W4995	CF-L	From 101Sqn. to 1LFS.
W4999	CF-G	From 100Sqn. Wrecked on landing at Kelstern on return from Berlin 2.12.43.
W5009	CF-Z	From 101Sqn. FTR Nuremberg 30/31.3.44.
DV194	CF-F	From 101Sqn. FTR Stuttgart 15/16.3.44.
DV242		From 100Sqn. to 3 LFS.
DV278	CF-V	To 300Sqn.
DV362	CF-B	To 5LFS.
DV364	CF-D	From 100Sqn. FTR Berlin on its 12th Berlin operation 28/29.1.44.
DV392	CF-Q	FTR Leipzig 3/4.12.43.
ED317	CF-W	From 100Sqn. FTR Berlin 24/25.3.44.
ED321	CF-U/V	From 101Sqn. Düsseldorf 3/4.11.43.
ED382		From 101Sqn. to 300Sqn.
ED809	CF-T	From 101Sqn. FTR Berlin 26/27.11.43.
ED814	CF-K	From 100Sqn. to 300Sqn.
ED398	CF-C	From 100Sqn. Completed 13 Berlin operations. FTR Gelsenkirchen 12/13.6.44.
ED940	CF-P	From 97Sqn. to 5LFS.

ED951	CF-A	From 101Sqn. Crashed in Lincolnshire on return from Berlin 16.12.43.
HK797		From 195Sqn. No operations.
JA714	CF-R	From 100Sqn. FTR Leipzig 20/21.10.43.
JA862	CF-T	From 460Sqn. Completed 11 Berlin operations. FTR Leipzig 19/20.2.44.
JB122	CF-H	From 100Sqn. FTR Berlin 30/31.1.44.
JB613		From 460Sqn. to 150Sqn.
JB743	CF-C	From 460Sqn. FTR Vierzon 30.6/1.7.44.
LL894	CF-T	FTR from mining sortie 15/16.5.44.
LL897	CF-P	FTR Acheres 10/11.6.44.
LL918		From 626Sqn. to 460Sqn.
LL956	CF-Q/S	Crashed soon after take-off from Kelstern when bound for Duisburg 14.10.44.
LL962	CF-U	FTR Stuttgart 28/29.7.44.
LM103	CF-N	FTR Frankfurt 12/13.9.44.
LM139	CF-G	FTR Acheres 10/11.6.44.
LM163	CF-J	FTR Trossy-St-Maximin 3.8.44.
LM168	CF-K/R	FTR Kiel 26/27.8.44.
LM174	CF-P	FTR Kiel 23/24.7.44.
LM317	CF-U	From 100Sqn. FTR Mailly-le-Camp 3/4.5.44.
LM384	CF-X	FTR Leipzig 19/20.2.44.
LM421	CF-Q	FTR Berlin 23/24.12.43.
LM424	CF-B	FTR Berlin 16/17.12.43.
LM427	CF-G	FTR Tergnier 31.5/1.6.44.
LM512	CF-H/M	Collided with Lancaster NF965 of 622Sqn over Belgium on return from Frankfurt 12/13.9.44.
LM513	CF-Y	FTR Duisburg 21/22.5.44.
LM515	CF-W	From 626Sqn. FTR Mailly-le-Camp 3/4.5.44.
LM546	CF-O	FTR Stuttgart 28/29.7.44.
LM674	CF-U	FTR Stettin 16/17.8.44.
LM691	CF-O	Collided with Halifax LL599 of 462Sqn over France on return from Essen 23.10.44.
LM714	CF-P	From 12Sqn. FTR Kiel 23/24.7.44.
LM731	CF-G²/N	FTR Wanne-Eickel 9.11.44.

LM732		To 170Sqn.
LM747	CF-L	To GH Flight at Methwold and back.
LM749	CF-K²	To 170Sqn.
ME332		
ME502		
ME524		
ME588	CF-A	FTR Leipzig 19/20.2.44.
ME594	CF-B	To 300Sqn.
ME676	CF-F	From 460Sqn. Abandoned over Sussex on return from Raimbert 31.8.44.
ME682	CF-E	To 75(NZ)Sqn.
ME684	CF-V	FTR Berlin 24/25.3.44.
ME697	CF-A	FTR Mailly-le-Camp 3/4.5.44.
ME731	CF-S	FTR Cologne 20/21.4.44.
ME733	CF-Z	FTR Brunswick 12/13.8.44.
ME734	CF-J	Shot down by intruder near Kelstern on return from Rouen 19.4.44.
ME780	CF-A	From 300Sqn.
ME862		From 90Sqn. to 576Sqn.
ND356		To 100Sqn.
ND403		To 550Sqn.
ND407		Crashed while landing at Kelstern during training 10.4.44.
ND452		From 97Sqn. to 170Sqn.
ND459	CF-M	FTR Vierzon 30.6/1.7.44.
ND461	CF-W	FTR Berlin 27/28.1.44.
ND596	CF-K/H	FTR Frankfurt 18/19.3.44.
ND613	CF-R	To 103Sqn.
ND619	CF-D/E²	To 1662CU.
ND636	CF-B²/O	FTE Aulnoye 10/11.4.44.
ND637	CF-L	Collided with ED606 of 463Sqn over Lincolnshire on return from Stuttgart 15/16.3.44.
ND639	CF-X	To 100Sqn.
ND641	CF-T	FTR Berlin 24/25.3.44.

ND742	CF-F	FTR Acheres 10/11.6.44.
ND863	CF-L/O²	From 300Sqn. to 170Sqn.
ND975		On loan from 100Sqn via Special Duties Flight. FTR Vierzon 30.6/1.7.44.
ND992	CF-A	To 170Sqn.
ND995	CF-W	To 100Sqn.
NE137	CF-L/B²	To 1667CU.
NF993	CF-T	From 626Sqn.
NF996	CF-J²	FTR Chemnitz 14/15.2.45.
NG164		To 153Sqn.
NG169	CF-B²	FTR Nuremberg 16/17.3.45.
NG237	CF-S	FTR Nordhausen 3.4.45.
NG238	CF-E²	FTR Düren 16.11.44.
NG239	CF-A	FTR Wanne-Eickel 9.11.44.
NG240	CF-F²	FTR Chemnitz 5/6.3.45.
NG253		
NG267	CF-Y	FTR Dortmund 20/21.2.45.
NG294	CF-H	FTR Ludwigshafen 15/16.12.44.
NG324	CF-L²	FTR Dessau 7/8.3.45.
NG334		
NG337		
NG411		
NG412		
NG418		
NN699	CF-C	Crashed on landing at Kelstern on return from attacking the Urft Dam at Heimbach 3.12.44.
NN748	CF-P/P²	From 300Sqn.
NN757	CF-C²	
NN798	CF-K²	
PA174	CF-G	From 626Sqn. Crashed in Essex on return from Essen 23.10.44.
PA175	CF-K²	To 576Sqn.
PA176	CF-H²	To 576Sqn.
PA229		

PB126	CF-T	FTR Vierzon 30.6/1.7.44.
PB150	CF-G/V/V²	Completed 100 operations, including Operation Manna.
PB154	CF-Y	FTR Bochum 4/5.11.44.
PB158	CF-G/G²	FTR Cologne 2.3.45.
PB464	CF-U/W	
PB480	CF-J	To 170Sqn.
PB531	CF-H	FTR Essen 23.10.44.
PB536	CF-F	
PB556		FTR from training flight 8/9.11.44.
PB574	CF-A²	To 576Sqn.
PB580	CF-U	
PB581	CF-A	To 170Sqn.
PB595		To 170Sqn.
PB648		To 166Sqn.
PB703		To 195Sqn.
PB708	CF-K	To 1660CU.
PB735	CF-D	To 1660CU.
PB736	CF-C/G	To 1660CU.
PB815	CF-O	FTR Pforzheim 23/24.2.45.
PB850		To 1660CU.
PD200	CF-B	To 97Sqn.
PD204	CF-P²	To 300Sqn and back. FTR Plauen 10/11.4.45.
PD206	CF-M/B²	To 170Sqn.
PD375	CF-R	FTR Chemnitz 5/6.3.45.
PD376	CF-C²	To 576Sqn.
PD388	CF-Z	FTR Merseburg (Leuna) 14/15.1.45.
RF145	CF-Z	FTR Nuremberg 16/17.3.45.
RF146	CF-G²	
RF189		
RF197		To 576Sqn.
RF213		To 576Sqn.

HEAVIEST SINGLE LOSS

30.6/1.7.44.	Vierzon.	4 Lancasters FTR.

626 SQUADRON

Motto: **To Srive And Not to Yield**   Code **UM**

Formed from C Flight of 12 Squadron in November 1943, 626 Squadron was part of 1 Group's expansion program during the final quarter of the year. Operating Lancasters, the squadron remained at the forefront of operations until the end of hostilities.

STATIONS

WICKENBY   07.11.43. to 14.10.45.

COMMANDING OFFICERS

Wing Commander	P Haynes	07.11.43. to 08.02.44.
Wing Commander	Q W A Ross	08.02.44. to 25.03.44.
Wing Commander	G F Rodney	25.03.44. to 11.10.44.
Wing Commander	J H N Molesworth	11.10.44. to 16.04.45.
Wing Commander	D F Dixon	16.04.45. to 26.10.45.

AIRCRAFT

Lancaster I/III   07.11.43. to 26.10.45.

OPERATIONAL RECORD

Operations	Sorties	Aircraft Losses	% Losses
205	2628	59	2.3%

CATEGORY OF OPERATIONS

Bombing	Mining
187	18

TABLE OF STATISTICS

Out of 59 Lancaster squadrons.

27th highest number of Lancaster overall operations in Bomber Command.
29th highest number of Lancaster sorties in Bomber Command.
26th equal (with 550 and 630Sqns) highest number of Lancaster operational losses in Bomber Command.

Out of 20 squadrons in 1 Group.

11th highest number of overall operations in 1 Group.
11th highest number of sorties in 1 Group.
10th equal (with 550Sqn) highest aircraft operational losses in 1 Group.

Out of 14 Lancaster squadrons in 1 Group.

7th highest number of overall Lancaster operations in 1 Group.
10th highest number of Lancaster sorties in 1 Group.
9th equal (with 550Sqn) highest number of Lancaster operational losses in 1 Group.

Aircraft Histories

LANCASTER.		From November 1943.
W4967	UM-G²	From 460Sqn. to 101Sqn.
W4990	UM-V²	From 12Sqn. to 1LFS.
DV171	UM-F²	From 12Sqn. to 463Sqn.
DV177	UM-K²	From 12Sqn. Shot down by intruder near Boxted on return from Karlsruhe 25.4.44.
DV190	UM-B²	From 12Sqn. FTR Berlin 1/2.1.44.
DV244	UM-L²	From 12Sqn. FTR Karlsruhe 24/25.4.44.
DV281	UM-D²	FTR Mailly-le-Camp 3/4.5.44.
DV295	UM-M²	From 100Sqn. Crashed on approach to Marham on return from Berlin 27.11.43.
DV388	UM-S²	FTR Berlin 26/27.11.43.
DV390		Crashed while landing at Coltishall during training 29.11.43.
ED424	UM-E²	From 12Sqn. FTR Karlsruhe 24/25.4.44.

ED623	UM-M^2	From 207Sqn. to 101Sqn.
EE133	UM-C^2	From 12Sqn. to 1LFS.
EE148	UM-S^2	From 617Sqn. FTR Mailly-le-Camp 3/4.5.44.
HK539	UM-A^2	FTR Berlin 24/25.3.44.
HK544	UM-W^2	To 75Sqn.
JA864	UM-D^2	From 12Sqn. FTR Berlin 2/3.12.43.
JA922	UM-J^2	From 12Sqn. to 300Sqn.
JB141	UM-N^2	From 100Sqn. FTR Brunswick 14/15.1.44.
JB409	UM-P^2	From 12Sqn. FTR Hasselt 11/12.5.44.
JB559	UM-H^2	From 12Sqn. to 300Sqn.
JB595	UM-O^2/B^2	FTR Berlin 15/16.2.44.
JB599	UM-Q^2	FTR Frankfurt 22/23.3.44.
JB609		From 12Sqn. Returned to 12Sqn.
JB639		To 166Sqn.
JB646	UM-R^2	To 300Sqn.
JB649		To 166Sqn.
JB661	UM-C^2	From 300Sqn. FTR Munich 7/8.1.45.
LL753	UM-Z^2	FTR Mailly-le-Camp 3/4.5.44.
LL772	UM-F^2	To 101Sqn.
LL797	UM-B^2	FTR Schweinfurt 24/25.2.44.
LL798	UM-N^2	To 300Sqn.
LL829	UM-T^2	To 101Sqn.
LL835	UM-C^2	To 38MU.
LL839	UM-X^2	FTR Essen 26/27.3.44.
LL849	UM-B^2	To 101Sqn.
LL895	UM-Y^2	FTR Stuttgart 28/29.7.44.
LL918	UM-C^2	To 615Sqn.
LL959	UM-A^2	FTR Leuna 14/15.1.45.
LL961	UM-S^2	FTR Munich 7/8.1.45.
LM102	UM-Z^2	FTR Reims 22/23.6.44.
LM105	UM-T^2	FTR Duisburg 21/22.2.45.
LM112	UM-A^2	FTR Caen 7.7.44.
LM113	UM-B^2	To 15Sqn.
LM136	UM-D^2	FTR Courtrai 20/21.7.44.

LM137	UM-G²	From 12Sqn. FTR Frankfurt 12/13.9.44.
LM140	UM-O²	FTR Rüsselsheim 25/26.8.44.
LM160	UM-F²	From 300Sqn. to 15Sqn.
LM270	UM-D²	Crashed in Lincolnshire while training 9.9.44.
LM290	UM-W²	FTR Bochum 4/5.11.44.
LM362	UM-A²	From 12Sqn. Crashed on approach to Wickenby on return from Berlin 27.11.43.
LM380	UM-S²	From 460Sqn. FTR Berlin 27/28.1.44.
LM391	UM-T²	To 1664CU.
LM393	UM-W²	FTR Berlin 24/25.3.44.
LM472	UM-U²	To 101Sqn.
LM515		To 625Sqn.
LM530	UM-J²	From 460Sqn.
LM596	UM-V²	From 101Sqn. FTR Duisburg 14/15.10.44.
LM599	UM-W²	FTR Brunswick 12/13.8.44.
LM632	UM-Q²	To 300Sqn.
LM633	UM-T²	FTR Courtrai 20/21.7.44.
LM635	UM-I²	
LM689	UM-N²	To 166Sqn.
LM726	UM-P²	FTR Dortmund 20/21.2.45.
ME576	UM-A²	FTR Brunswick 14/15.1.44.
ME577	UM-T²	Ditched in the North Sea on return from Stettin 5/6.1.44.
ME584	UM-Y²	
ME587	UM-X²	FTR Berlin 30/31.1.44.
ME589	UM-D²	FTR Leipzig 19/20.2.44.
ME742	UM-B²	From 12Sqn. FTR Stettin 29/30.8.44.
ME750	UM-G²	To 1666CU 11.44.
ME774	UM-L²	FTR Vierzon 30.6/1.7.44.
ME830	UM-K²	To A&AEE 2.45.
ND324	UM-D²	From 12Sqn. FTR Stettin (12Sqn crew) 5/6.1.44.
ND441		To 12Sqn.
ND864	UM-N²	From 460Sqn.

ND952	UM-E²	FTR Vierzon 30.6/1.7.44.
ND964	UM-K²	FTR Duisburg 21/22.5.44.
ND983	UM-Q²	To 101Sqn.
ND984	UM-H²	To 300Sqn.
ND985	UM-W²	FTR Aachen 27/28.5.44.
NE118	UM-U²	FTR Dortmund 22/23.5.44.
NE163	UM-T²	From 460Sqn. FTR Duisburg 14.10.44.
NF907	UM-K²	FTR from mining sortie 18/19.2.45.
NF993		To 625Sqn.
NG244	UM-E²	Crashed near Wickenby soon after take-off for Koblenz 22.12.44.
NG247	UM-D²	From 300Sqn. to 39MU.
NG248	UM-H²	To 138Sqn.
NG285	UM-O²	
NG354		
PA190	UM-G²	From 12Sqn. FTR Nordhausen 3.4.45.
PA216	UM-C²	FTR from mining sortie 18/19.2.45.
PA989	UM-U²	FTR Rüsselsheim 27/28.8.44.
PA990	UM-R²	
PA993	UM-H²	Crashed while on approach to Wickenby on return from Stuttgart 20.10.44.
PB260	UM-Z²	To 463Sqn.
PB411	UM-Y²	FTR Lützkendorf 4/5.4.45.
PB412	UM-Z²	FTR from mining sortie 4/5.10.44.
PB561	UM-X²	Crash-landed at Manston on return from Osterfeld 31.12.44.
PB687	UM-Q²	FTR Osterfeld 31.12.44.
PD286	UM-O²	FTR following collision with ME326 (460Sqn) over France on return from Wiesbaden 2/3.2.45.
PD287	UM-U²	
PD295	UM-B²	FTR Lützkendorf 4/5.4.45.
PD314	UM-J²	Crashed while landing at Wragby on return from Dortmund 11/12.11.44.
PD315	UM-D²	
PD390		From 12Sqn.

PD391	UM-W²	
PD393	UM-N²	FTR Nuremberg 16/17.3.45.
PD404	UM-Q²	
PD432	UM-E²	
RA535	UM-X²	
RA543	UM-A²	
RF156	UM-P²	
RF159	UM-C²	
RF241	UM-S²	
RF255	UM-G²	
RF256	UM-T²	
SW271	UM-L²	To 12Sqn.
SW279		To 300Sqn.

HEAVIEST SINGLE LOSS

26/27.11.43.	Berlin	1 Lancaster FTR
		2 crashed on return.
03/04.05.44	Mailly-le-Camp	. 3 Lancasters FTR.

BIBLIOGRAPHY

Alexander. Richard, *101 Squadron. Special Operations.*

Bowyer. Chaz, *Bomber Group at War.* Book Club Associates.

Bowyer. Chaz, *The Wellington Bomber.* William Kimber.

Bowman. Martin, *Wellington. The Geodetic Giant.* Airlife.

Brookes. Andrew, *Bomber Squadron at War.* Ian Allan.

Brunswig. Hans, *Feuersturm über Hamburg.* Motor Buch Verlag.

Charlwood. Don, *No Moon Tonight.* Goodall Publications.

Chorley. W R, *Royal Air Force Bomber Command Losses. Vols 1,2,3,4,5,6.* Midland Counties Publications.

Clutton-Brock. Oliver, *Massacre over the Marne.* Patrick Stephens Ltd.

Cooper. Alan W, *Bombers over Berlin.* Patrick Stephens Ltd.

Currie. Jack, *Battle Under the Moon.* Air Data.

Finn. Sid, *Black Swan.* Newton.

Franks. Norman, *Valiant Wings.* Crecy.

Garbett. Mike, /Goulding. Brian, *Lancaster at War. Vols 1,2,3.* Ian Allan.

Girbig. Werner, *Start im Morgengrauen.* Motor Buch Verlag.

Holmes. Harry, *Avro Lancaster. The definitive record.* Airlife.

Halley. J J, *The Lancaster File.* Air-Britain.

Halley. James J, *The Squadrons of the Royal Air Force.* Air-Britain.

Jackson. Robert, *Air War over France.* Ian Allan.

Mason. Francis K, *The Avro Lancaster.* Aston Publications.

Messenger. Charles, *Bomber Harris.* Arms and Armour Press.

Middlebrook. Martin, *The Berlin Raids.* Viking Press.

Middlebrook. Martin, / Everett. Chris, *Bomber Command War Diaries.* Viking.

Musgrove. Gordon, *Pathfinder Force.* MacDonald and Janes.

Robertson. Bruce, *Lancaster. The Story of a Famous Bomber.* Harleyford Publications Ltd.

Saward. Dudley, *Bomber Harris.* Cassel.

Thompson DFC*. Walter, *Lancaster to Berlin.* Goodall Publications

Wadsworth. Michael P, *They Led the Way.* Highgate.

Ward. John, *Beware of the Dog at War.*

White. Arthur, *The Hornets' Nest. History of 100 Squadron RAF 1917-1994.* Square One Publications.

Wright. Jim, *On Wings of War. A history of 166 Squadron.*

Royal Air Force Aircraft Serial Numbers. All Volumes. Air-Britain.

Most of the figures used in the statistics section of this work, have been drawn from The Bomber Command War Diaries by Martin Middlebrook and Chris Everitt, and I am indebted to Martin Middlebrook for allowing me to use them. The statistics for the four Polish units taken from the above publication differ markedly from those published by Polish historian J Cynk.

KEY TO ABBREVIATIONS

A&AEE	Aeroplane and Armaments Experimental Establishment.
AA	Anti-Aircraft fire.
AACU	Anti-Aircraft Cooperation Unit.
AAS	Air Armament School.
AASF	Advance Air Striking Force.
AAU	Aircraft Assembly Unit.
ACM	Air Chief Marshal.
ACSEA	Air Command South-East Asia.
AFDU	Air Fighting Development Unit.
AFEE	Airborne Forces Experimental Unit.
AFTDU	Airborne Forces Tactical Development Unit.
AGS	Air Gunners School.
AMDP	Air Members for Development and Production.
AOC	Air Officer Commanding.
AOS	Air Observers School.
ASRTU	Air-Sea Rescue Training Unit.
ATTDU	Air Transport Tactical Development Unit.
AVM	Air Vice-Marshal.
BAT	Beam Approach Training.
BCBS	Bomber Command Bombing School.
BCDU	Bomber Command Development Unit.
BCFU	Bomber Command Film Unit.

BCIS	Bomber Command Instructors School.
BDU	Bombing Development Unit.
BSTU	Bomber Support Training Unit.
CF	Conversion Flight.
CFS	Central Flying School.
CGS	Central Gunnery School.
C-in-C	Commander in Chief.
CNS	Central Navigation School.
CO	Commanding Officer.
CRD	Controller of Research and Development.
CU	Conversion Unit.
DGRD	Director General for Research and Development.
EAAS	Empire Air Armament School.
EANS	Empire Air Navigation School.
ECDU	Electronic Countermeasures Development Unit.
ECFS	Empire Central Flying School.
ETPS	Empire Test Pilots School.
F/L	Flight Lieutenant.
Flt	Flight.
F/O	Flying Officer.
FPP	Ferry Pilots School.
F/S	Flight Sergeant.
FTR	Failed to Return.
FTU	Ferry Training Unit.
G/C	Group Captain.
Gp	Group.
HCU	Heavy Conversion Unit.
HGCU	Heavy Glider Conversion Unit.
LFS	Lancaster Finishing School.
MAC	Mediterranean Air Command.
MTU	Mosquito Training Unit.
MU	Maintenance Unit.
NTU	Navigation Training Unit.
OADU	Overseas Aircraft Delivery Unit.

OAPU	Overseas Aircraft Preparation Unit.
OTU	Operational Training Unit.
P/O	Pilot Officer.
PTS	Parachute Training School.
RAE	Royal Aircraft Establishment.
SGR	Scool of General Reconnaissance.
Sgt	Sergeant.
SHAEF	Supreme Headquarters Allied Expeditionary Force.
SIU	Signals Intelligence Unit.
S/L	Squadron Leader.
SOC	Struck off Charge.
SOE	Special Operations Executive.
Sqn	Squadron.
TF	Training Flight.
TFU	Telecommunications Flying Unit.
W/C	Wing Commander.
Wg	Wing.
WIDU	Wireless Intelligence Development Unit.
W/O	Warrant Officer.